STYLE AND THE SINGLE GIRL

S·T·Y·L·E
and the
SINGLE GIRL

How Modern Women
Re-Dressed the Novel, 1922–1977

Hope Howell Hodgkins

THE OHIO STATE UNIVERSITY PRESS | COLUMBUS

Copyright © 2016 by The Ohio State University.
All rights reserved.

Library of Congress Cataloging-in-Publication Data

Names: Hodgkins, Hope Howell, 1960– author.
Title: Style and the single girl : how modern women re-dressed
   the novel, 1922–1977 / Hope Howell Hodgkins.
Description: Columbus : The Ohio State University Press, [2016] |
   "2016" | Includes bibliographical references and index.
Identifiers: LCCN 2016002600 | ISBN 9780814213018 (cloth ;
   alk. paper) | ISBN 0814213014 (cloth ; alk. paper)
Subjects: LCSH: Clothing and dress in literature. | Fashion in
   literature. | Single women in literature. | Fashion—Social aspects—
   Great Britain—History—20th century. | English fiction—20th
   century—History and criticism. | Modernism (Literature)
Classification: LCC PR830.C59 H63 2016 | DDC 823.009/3559—dc23
LC record available at http://lccn.loc.gov/2016002600

Cover design by Regina Starace
Text design by Juliet Williams
Type set in Goudy Old Style and Bauer Bodoni
Printed by Thomson-Shore, Inc.

Cover image: Mary Cassatt, *The Fitting*, 1890–91. Color aquatint with
drypoint from three plates, on buff laid paper, 376 × 256 mm (image/
plate); 471 × 309 mm (sheet), John H. Wrenn Memorial Collection,
1942.351, Image No. 00085064-01, The Art Institute of Chicago.

∞ The paper used in this publication meets the minimum requirements
of the American National Standard for Information Sciences—
Permanence of Paper for Printed Library Materials. ANSI Z39.48-1992.

9 8 7 6 5 4 3 2 1

CONTENTS

List of Illustrations		vii
Acknowledgments		ix
Preface: The Subject of Dress		xiii
CHAPTER 1	Introducing Modernism, à la Mode	1
PART I	The Singular Modern Woman	43
CHAPTER 2	The Self-Fashioned Dorothy L. Sayers	57
CHAPTER 3	Jean Rhys and Modeling for Men	90
PART II	The Homefront Style: The War in *Vogue* and Literature	123
CHAPTER 4	How *Vogue* Changed Clothes in War	127
CHAPTER 5	Literature in Wartime	157
PART III	Stylish Spinsters in a Postwar World	189
CHAPTER 6	Pym, Spark, and the Postwar Comedy of the Object	199
CHAPTER 7	Spark, Pym, and the Glamorous Ends of Style	231
CODA	Lasting Modes	258
Works Cited		261
Index		277

ILLUSTRATIONS

FIGURE 1   Suit (unknown maker), 1740–60. Brooklyn Museum Costume Collection at the Metropolitan Museum of Art. Image © The Metropolitan Museum of Art.   22

FIGURE 2   Beau Brummell (John Cook). © National Portrait Gallery, London.   25

FIGURE 3   Dorothy Leigh Sayers by Sir William Hutchison. © National Portrait Gallery, London.   63

FIGURE 4   Gertie Millar as Mary Gibbs in "Our Miss Gibbs" by Rita Martin. © National Portrait Gallery, London.   97

FIGURE 5   Ella Gwendolen Rees Williams, aka Jean Rhys (1890–1979), c. 1921. Photo by Pearl Freeman / Bridgeman Images.   101

FIGURE 6   World War II Utility dress. © Imperial War Museum (D 14844).   142

FIGURE 7   Miller in Hitler's Bath [David E. Scherman] / [The LIFE Picture Collection] / Getty Images.   146

FIGURE 8   Dior "Bar" Suit, 1947. © The Metropolitan Museum of Art.   154

FIGURE 9   Barbara Pym with Henry Harvey ("Lorenzo"), early 1930s (Barbara Pym Estate).   203

FIGURE 10   Muriel Spark, circa 1963. (Popperfoto/Getty Images).   242

ACKNOWLEDGMENTS

MY DEEPEST THANKS go to my family. Christopher Hodgkins, best of husbands, patiently read and reread drafts, offered wise advice when asked, and provided precious support. My son George carefully proofread the manuscript and gave sharp-eyed commentary on the contents as well. During the long writing process my daughters, lovely Mary and elegant Alice, themselves grew into stylish young single women. My parents, Dr. B. D. and Georgeanna Howell, taught me to read early and to love the Word. Sadly they cannot read this book now, but the good is never lost.

I am grateful to friends, especially the über-stylish Deborah Bell, professor of costume design at the University of North Carolina at Greensboro, who received hundreds of pages of this manuscript and returned both expert commentary and enthusiastic encouragement. My dear longtime friend Dr. Ruth Williams and her husband, Dr. Stephen Gieser, cheerfully housed and fed me during my researches at the Wade Center. Ever since, they have provided salutary nudges ("What, your book isn't done yet?"). Both my sister and brother-in-law, Amy and Dan McLellan, and my brother, Jonathan Howell, proved generous hosts (in Nashville and New York, respectively) as I researched and presented papers on style and the single girl. Closer to home, Dr. Pamela McRae provided tea and far-ranging book discussions.

Like many academic books, this study was born in a class, my Contemporary British Literature and Culture at the University of North Carolina at Greensboro. It first appeared in embryo at a 2008 Modern Language Association session on narrative, whereupon Sandy Crooms, then senior editor at the Ohio State University Press, prompted me to nurse it into a book. Subsequently, David Herman praised and encouraged my initial sortie into Muriel Spark, publishing it both in *Modern Fiction Studies* and in his critical collection, *Muriel Spark: Twenty-First-Century Perspectives* (Johns Hopkins). Kathleen Joslin and Daneen Wardrop proved warm and insightful editors as I revised my essay on the young Jean Rhys for their *Crossings on Text and Textile*. Most recently Lindsay Martin, my editor at Ohio State University Press, has been cheerful and hard-working throughout, while two anonymous readers offered valuable responses.

I also have benefited from public opportunities to present and discuss these stylish single girls and their novels, often learning more than I taught. Through presenting a paper in a Modernist Studies Association seminar on authorial biography, I learned to delineate the tightropes we walk between style and content, art and life. My lecture to the Barbara Pym Society in Cambridge, Massachusetts, prompted audience members to share striking first-person anecdotes about wartime dress. And my presentation on Muriel Spark at Hunter College's Artist's Institute of New York, in conjunction with the Lucy McKenzie exhibit, highlighted for me Spark's multimedial and postmodern fascinations.

Throughout my researches I have been impressed by the generosity of librarians and archivists. Thank you to Colin Harris of Special Collections in Oxford University's Bodleian Library; to Sally Harrower of the National Library of Scotland; to Laura Schmidt of Wheaton College's Marion E. Wade Center; and to the cheerful staff at London's Westminster Reference Library, where I read copies of wartime British *Vogue* unavailable in the United States. The staff of London's National Portrait Gallery repeatedly helped me navigate their website when it stymied my efforts to request images for this book. Tom Sopko, president of the North American Barbara Pym Society, not only put me in touch with Laura Morris and Hazel Holt of the Pym Estate but also kindly provided images from the Pym website.

In addition, I am grateful for permission to quote from the following sources:

> *Simmel on Culture: Selected Writings.* Ed. David Frisby and Mike Featherstone. © 1997 Sage Publications (London). Used by permission.
> Translations of Stéphane Mallarmé's *La Dernière Mode.* Copyright A. M. Cain and P. N. Furbank, 2004, *Mallarmé on Fashion: A Translation*

of the Fashion Magazine La Dernière Mode, with Commentary. Berg Publishers, used by permission of Bloomsbury Publishing Plc.

"The Importance of Being Vulgar" by Dorothy L. Sayers, 12 February 1936. 5–6; 16, 17. [Unpublished ms of speech.] Dorothy L. Sayers Manuscript Collection MS-118, The Marion E. Wade Center, Wheaton College, Wheaton, IL. Used courtesy of David Higham Associates and the Wade Center.

"Ars Poetica" from COLLECTED POEMS 1917–1982 by Archibald MacLeish. Copyright © 1985 by The Estate of Archibald MacLeish. Reprinted by permission of Houghton Mifflin.

Papers of Barbara Mary Crampton Pym (1913–80) (Bodleian Libraries, University of Oxford. Shelfmarks MSS. Pym 1–178). Used by kind permission of the Bodleian Libraries and The Barbara Pym Estate.

"Air-Raid." POEMS © The Estate of Stephen Spender, 2004. Reprinted by kind permission of the Estate of Stephen Spender.

An earlier version of part III and chapter 6 appeared as "Stylish Spinsters: Spark, Pym, and the Comedy of the Object." Copyright © 2008 Purdue Research Foundation. This article was first published in *MFS* 54:3 (2008), 523–43. Reprinted with permission by Johns Hopkins University Press.

A shorter version of chapter 3 was published as "Modeling for Men: The Early Jean Rhys," in *Crossings in Text and Textile*. Ed. Katherine Joslin and Daneen Wardrop. © 2015 University of New Hampshire Press.

PREFACE

The Subject of Dress

"ON THE SUBJECT of dress," wrote novelist Elizabeth Bowen, "almost no one, for one or another reason, feels truly indifferent: if their own clothes do not concern them, somebody else's do" ("Dress" 111). Dress, she added, "is the one art the unqualified must practice." Recently Sean Latham put it more academically: "When subjected to the rules of fashion, art loses its claim to an autonomous sphere of creative activity" ("Am I" 7). Whether in practice or in theory, the subject of dress breaches the boundaries of modernist aesthetics.

This book examines writers who breached those boundaries. I did not set out to study modern women's dress; I planned only to write about the ways novelists presented single girls. Yet I could not help noticing that these writers' clever and effective uses of dress often reflected their styles of prose—and that the clothing details made it harder to separate each author from her fictional characters. The boundaries between writer and text were breached by the subject of dress. Furthermore, my own scholarly boundaries were breached. At conferences, my presentations on fictional dress and style evoked not only scholarly discussion but comments on my clothing. At home in my study, I grew self-conscious about working in jeans and T-shirt: what would the editors of *Vogue* say? And I confronted existential questions: If no one sees what I wear, all day long, can I be said to have dressed at all? Only gradually did I realize that my subjects, and the women they wrote about, struggled with the same issues.

If the above questions sound silly, it is because we think of clothing styles as trivial, and as feminine: two assumptions that are both deeply true and ultimately false. Many scholars easily presume that the subject of dress is shallow, precisely because it engages everyone, not merely an aesthetically educated elite. Moreover, since in our culture fashion especially interests women, some men—and women—find it a field unworthy of analysis. Yet dress details *are* profound, because the personal is profound. This study takes seriously the boundary-breaching nature of "the subject of dress," including the significance of biography in the literary uses of dress. And neither dress style nor writing style is separable from content, as my analyses aim to demonstrate: *pace* some high modernists, art never is an autonomous space.

Moreover, clothing—especially artfully styled clothing—is about seeing and being seen. Anne Hollander put it well: "The most important aspect of clothing is the way it looks.... The way clothes look depends not on how they are designed or made but on how they are perceived" (*Seeing through Clothes* 311). Dress is about subject-object relations. And while the perceiving subject and the observed object are old bogies in feminism, the art of fashion complicates that dichotomy. As certain feminists have bemoaned, fashion makes the object willingly complicit with the viewer's gaze: a fashionable dresser wants to be observed.[1] Yet nearly all women and men are willing objects of the sartorial gaze. We know that certain styles become certain roles. The man who pulls on old sweats for running, or mindlessly ties a single Windsor for his five hundredth day of business, is preparing to be seen in a certain role just as surely as (although perhaps less consciously than) the woman who tries several outfits before stepping out the door. Both are objects of the other's gaze, and

---

1. From America's Amelia Bloomer and Susan B. Anthony to the Victorian Rational Dress Society, original feminists tended to decry fashionable dressing as constrictive, humiliating, and pandering to male desires; their continuing perspective was vividly voiced by Germaine Greer in *The Female Eunuch* (1971). But other influential twentieth-century women, from Coco Chanel to Gloria Steinem, implicitly contradicted those assumptions through their own stylized public images. For a summary of the ongoing feminist debates, see Fred Davis, "Antifashion," 93–94.

not necessarily reluctant objects. If you dress in the morning, you play the game. If you dress stylishly, you aim to be a contender.

So it should not be a tremendous leap from dress style to literary style, for clothing is a rhetoric, a communicative activity. Like language, clothing is ubiquitous; wildly varied; individual to its user, yet holding elements of a common culture; frequently read sexually; often used to charm, to persuade, to mask hidden feelings, or to project a longed-for self; and perennially misinterpreted. Yet fashion like fiction is an art, not a discourse, because both clothing and writing are colored by seemingly infinite variations of style. And just as literary art complicates simple words, so stylish dress may be seen as an artistic sharpening of clothing's natural rhetoric.

Let me explain. To say that dress is rhetorical is not to claim that it makes clear discursive statements; rather, it is to acknowledge our persistent itch to read the so-called language of clothes. For even though cultural critics and fashion theorists recognize that dress is not a language— it is only *like* a language—they still struggle to interpret it. Fred Davis has carefully delineated what clothing styles are not: not a language, and not a code if that means a "conventional sign code"; rather, he writes, dress evokes "an aesthetic code" without reliable interpretative rules (*Fashion, Culture, and Identity* 5, 10). There exists no authoritative dictionary for the reading of dress. Accordingly, Malcolm Barnard offers a wealth of references to theories of what fashionable clothing says, to such an extent that what fashion communicates seems to be simultaneously arbitrary and indeterminate (*Fashion as Communication* 145). Still, as we dress, and as we live among more-or-less clothed creatures, we sense a daily barrage of clothing statements, even in everyday dress, and even if we fail to grasp what's being said. As Davis reminds us, "ambiguity falls well short of meaninglessness . . . [Rather, it] recognizes the possibility of alternative, contradictory, or obscure interpretations" (*Fashion, Culture* 22).

In fact, everyday watchers and wearers of clothing know that its mixture of mores and mystery increases the appeal of interpretation. To say, as Alison Lurie did in *The Language of Clothes*, that bright red traditionally is associated with aggression, desire, and sexuality (194, 197) does not explain why someone wears that color. When the aptly-named Scarlett, in the MGM film *Gone with the Wind* (1938), dons a low-cut red gown for a party hosted by her rival, we know that both her husband's jealousy and Scarlett's own nature fit the color stereotypes. But saintly Melanie insists on reading the dress charitably: "What a lovely dress, Scarlett darling! . . .

I do need you to help me receive my guests" (Howard 228).[2] Red is not defused of its passionate associations but mystified, when individual wearer meets individual observer.

Even conventionally prescribed clothing does not speak unequivocally. Queen Victoria wore black for decades after Prince Albert's death, but late in life she began to sport fashionable white bonnets. A message that she had recovered from grief? Or simply, as James Joyce's character Bloom speculates, characteristic of female vanity? "Victoria and Albert.... But in the end she put a few violets in her bonnet. Vain in her heart of hearts" (*Ulysses* 6: 550, 551). Conversely in the mid-twentieth century, with heavy mourning garb no longer *de rigueur*, Jacqueline Kennedy wore unadulterated black to the funeral of her assassinated husband, President John F. Kennedy. Draped in a waist-length black veil, the famous fashionista suddenly looked like a pious Italian peasant woman. Using her clothing to make a statement of grief (as she had done a few days previously, by refusing to remove her blood-spattered outfit on the day her husband died), Kennedy showed a strong consciousness of her dressed body as an observed object: she had been urged to change her stained suit; she need not have worn such a huge black-lace mantilla. Ironically, her anxiety about being misinterpreted led to a wealth of deconstructive readings, most famously embodied in the Andy Warhol pop artworks *Jackie (The Week That Was)* (1963) and *Jackie Triptych* (1964). The sartorial choices of Victoria and Jackie—both prominent historical women—were elaborately interpreted in the art of their eras. Evidently, the more straightforward the dress style, the more ambiguous the statement, particularly when linked to a high-fashion icon such as Kennedy. As with high-art literature, high fashion makes us expect complexity.

This book does not itself theorize high fashion—and in fact there is no monological explanation of fashion or dress. Likewise, I do not use one literary methodology: I employ the texts to suggest their own critical approaches, which is the heart of rhetorical readings of fiction. Literary themes always intertwine with my stylistic discussions: for instance, Lord Peter Wimsey's dandyism is reflected in both his dress and his speech, and his style forms a continuum with Dorothy Sayers's flashy yet conventional writing style. Similarly, in Barbara Pym's *Excellent Women*, her

---

2. In Margaret Mitchell's 1936 novel, Scarlett wears a green dress. The filmmakers, reveling in the new Technicolor, understandably turned Scarlett's "scarlet woman" gown red.

drably dressed protagonist embodies the author's understated narration. So, in discussing the complex links between literary styles and dress styles, this book forefronts the individual fictions and their authors, rather than fashion history or previous theoretical readings of dress. Tellingly, in *The Fashion System* Roland Barthes concludes that fashion in itself signifies nothing: since in fashion writing the presumptive focus of desire is the clothing displayed, Barthes interprets fashion in terms of falsely prompted desires (303). It is a tautology familiar to consumers: fashionable clothes prompt desires for the latest fashion, which merely exists to fulfill the desires it creates.

Consumption, however, is not the only desire related to dress. In fact language *about* clothes is less profound than the clothing's own rhetoric, which, like all rhetoric, depends upon desire. Rhetoric, the classical art of persuasion, is, as Richard Weaver wrote, "an art of emphasis embodying an order of desire" (211). Since all rhetoric entails a communicative endeavor between two or more people, all rhetoric partakes of a desire to persuade, even if it is only the fundamental "Listen to me!" Thus it has been understood that literature is rhetorical, at least since the publication of Wayne C. Booth's classic *Rhetoric of Fiction* (1961). The ensuing flood of poststructuralist theory pointed out all the impossible complications of literary rhetoric: the potentials for artistic failure, for audience misreadings, for cultural illiteracies, and simply for messages lost in transit. The originator's desires may be unclear to the receiver, or rejected, or willfully misread. For that matter, who can say that an author's purported desires are genuine? But there is nothing truly new in these critiques. Since ancient times, philosophers have bemoaned and celebrated rhetoric's sophistic potential, which becomes especially likely in the elaborate and covert rhetorics of art, such as literature.

Likewise fashion, as high-art dress, intensifies the rhetoric of clothing. Even simple dress may raise issues of masquerade and of seduction. Striking fashions, however, seem blatantly to project the wearer's longings: "Look at me!" "Admire me!" "Envy me!" "Desire me!" "I want to be [fill in the blank]." On receiving these rhetorics we must ask, *Whose* desires are embodied in any particular wearing of a certain outfit? One might guess that a winning dress style includes the viewers' desires, such that their response to the above imperatives is, "Yes!" Even that assumption, however, eliminates certain dandy and carnival fashions, including early punk, for whom "Look at me!" may mean "Be outraged by me!" Still, a successful outfit in some sort comprehends viewers' desires, for—again—fashion always is about seeing and being seen.

As a rhetorical study, this book presumes the reader's willingness to take an interdisciplinary interest in fields not his or her own, along with the consequent need for background explanations and set parameters. My introductory chapter provides an overview, which delineates certain aspects of modernism and the modern; describes historical backgrounds for analyzing and explaining style, in words and in dress; gives a context for the field of fashion studies; and briefly looks at high modernist uses of dress in literature. This introduction does none of these things exhaustively, and I trust that the expert will forgive my recital of truisms, while also discovering some new and intriguing juxtapositions. Although books on fashion and fiction are increasing, in studies of later modernism and women writers there is surprisingly little discussion of dress. Most examinations of dress and modern literature have been theoretical, such as Ulrich Lehmann's *Tigersprung: Fashion in Modernity* (2000), which described the fashion theories of Charles Baudelaire and Stéphane Mallarmé, and Elizabeth Wilson's influential *Adorned in Dreams: Fashion and Modernity* (1985; updated 2003). A few are limited to one significant writer, as in R. S. Koppen's excellent *Virginia Woolf, Fashion, and Literary Modernity* (2009). In contrast my book, while not ignoring its predecessors, chronicles the uses of dress and literary style in several modern women writers. And since the modernist canon, with its artificial boundaries, disintegrates under scrutiny, this approach enables a new but coherent account outside of conventional categories.

Throughout this book, my four very different subjects—Dorothy L. Sayers, Jean Rhys, Barbara Pym, and Muriel Spark—are set against a background of normative male writers, of swiftly changing modes (in everything from gender roles to dress), and of historical upheaval, most significantly the Second World War. It is not the only way to study novels, and these are not the only women who might be studied in this way. But each of these writers overtly recognized dress as a double-edged weapon, to be turned upon those who demeaned single women. And because the subject of dress is so personal—and so, I argue, wrapped up with a consciousness of others' perceptions—these women, known for their personal concerns with dress and with singleness, tellingly demonstrate the nexus between dress style and writing style. Happily, they form a sequence, beginning with the Victorian and Edwardian upbringings of Sayers and

Rhys, through their flourishing careers in the 1920s and 1930s, to the abrupt watershed of World War II. When the next generation, Pym and Spark, began to publish fiction in the postwar years, vast changes had occurred, but issues of style and single girls, like the novelistic marriage plot, remained surprisingly vital.

I should note that full marriage-plot readings, beginning with Rachel Blau DuPlessis's *Writing beyond the Ending* (1985) and Joseph Allen Boone's *Tradition Counter Tradition* (1987), demonstrate in detail how traditional English-language novels, for all their variations, follow patterns that impose "a 'center' of meaning, of coherence, in the name of romantic wedlock" (Boone 46). For this study I assume the marriage plot as previous to modernism, in two senses: it was socially antiquated by modernity, and its vestiges nevertheless remained hugely important for women. My interest lies in marriage plot as eschatological expectation, in which a satisfying conclusion means, according to the old joke, that her wedding must be the happiest day of a girl's life—thus ending the book, the story, and evidently the characters' existences. My four subjects, strongly aware of the post-Victorian state of their society and their art no less than their clothing, consistently resist, avoid, or overturn that traditional conclusion, but in no consistent way. Their protagonists respond to marriage-plot clichés as societal assumptions and, whether right or wrong, often part of their own psyches. Rather than condemning the longings as retrograde, or celebrating only transgressive impulses, these writers simply unravel, with sly wit and sympathy, the tangled desires of various single girls, illustrating them through the willing complicity of dress style.

This book makes no claim to be a complete survey of modern women writers, nor is it a recovery project for obscure novelists. I have deliberately chosen novelists whose work is available in contemporary editions, readable, and even enticing for the nonspecialist. Each of my subjects has both a respectable body of criticism and many devoted readers. Rhys may hover on the borders of high modernism, but her novels are not hard to read; and although Spark has been variously classed as "late modern" and "postmodernist," she is reasonably accessible. Sayers and Pym are frankly popular, which to me is no denigration. Just as these women do not write only of high fashion but also of everyday dress, so this book examines popular attitudes toward women, dress, and novels. While laying a foundation for my discussion in high modernist approaches to literary style, I also trace the divergent literary paths taken by these writers who—all well-read in modernism—like most modern women did not feel impelled to follow one aesthetic doctrine. Like my brief survey of fashion theory, which examines not merely haute couture but everyday dress style, this eclectic project considers avant-garde literature but lands in popular fiction.

Nor does every chapter in my book aim to do the same thing, since the topics of modernism and modernity, women writers, and the literary uses of dress bristle with unexpected points. Accordingly, this account opens with high modernist literary styles and the foundations of dress analysis and then proceeds to closely read the fiction and dress styles of two very different modern women writers, Sayers and Rhys. I then turn to the dress and literary cruces of World War II—and finally examine the culmination of all these influences, as shown in the postwar writers Pym and Spark. Since the latter novelists serve to demonstrate the aftermath of modern and modernist stylistics, I read their fiction and styles under thematic headings that offer less closure than my holistic interpretations of the earlier writers. The still-open questions of postmodernism haunt the final chapters.

In order to lay a foundation for how these modern women re-dressed the novel, chapter 1 describes modernism's associations with fashion since the time of Baudelaire and the nineteenth-century aesthetes, who celebrated both clothing and literary style. This vaunted convergence of the modern and *la mode* often remained theoretical on the part of male writers, although a significant minority of male dandies refused to concede the sartorial field. Thus it was women novelists, like nineteenth-century women in general, who became the practical users of stylish dress, with intriguing reverberations in high modernist writers including James Joyce, D. H. Lawrence, and Virginia Woolf.

Following the introductory chapter, Part I presents "The Singular Modern Woman." For Victorians the spinster had been a pathetic or saintly figure, and any other sort of single woman beyond the pale. But modern women writers strove to break those stereotypes. In the twenties and thirties, dress style became a potent literary weapon in the struggle to dissociate female identity from marriage. This section's two chapters discuss very different modes of modern interwar fiction, Dorothy Sayers's detective novels and Jean Rhys's literary impressionism. Chapter 2 follows Sayers's personal trajectory, from questing single girl to married (but not conventionally happy) author. In her popular fiction and essays, the independent-minded spinster is glorified, sartorial concerns are played with, and the question of "who wears the trousers" shown to be an issue that mingles power with fashion. Sayers's enticing but impersonal writing style served as a masquerade, ironically modeled upon similar defenses in her dandy Lord Peter Wimsey. In striking contrast, chapter 3 shows how Jean Rhys used a highbrow but intimate writing style to present a grim view of women, their dress, and their relations to men. Her protagonists are single girls but definitely not traditional spinsters. Like the young Rhys, they live by their looks, coveting clothes as a means of attracting the men who will support and possibly love them. Thus Rhys's high-modern fictions suggest that style is an enthrallment for both sexes. By the time of *Good Morning, Midnight* (1939), however, her desperate single girl offers a clear-eyed understanding of dying modernism and the tragedy of objectification. For Sayers to use dandy-style in her popular novels was both to critique and to modernize Victorian dress concepts; likewise Rhys's Edwardian roots, as a chorus girl dressing for men, colored her literary impressionist fiction. Thus both women, in their prewar fictions, used dress to comment wittily and bitterly on marital ambitions and gender relations.

World War II killed modernist styles, as Part II shows in chapters on homefront dress and homefront fiction. War casts a cold, clarifying light on the self-conscious arts of both fashion and high literature: war, waged by objectifying one race or nation for the sake of favoring another, is the supreme objectification project. Chapter 4 tells how wartime British *Vogue* made the homefront dress style a hallmark of minimized simplicity for Englishwomen. By war's end, the fashion magazine was publishing serious articles about the liberation of Europe, illustrated by photos of naked concentration camp victims—and uneasily observing the frivolous styles sported by women in occupied France. Yet postwar British women would embrace Christian Dior's luxuriant, feminine New Look. Chapter 5 describes how, like dress styles, British literature in wartime veered between nostalgia for high-modern aestheticism and stark realism, emerging with a new eclecticism. Cyril Connolly, through his wartime journal *Horizon*, strove to preserve high art. Against his initial aims, and strikingly like British *Vogue*, Connolly began to publish starkly realistic fiction and poetry as he pragmatically acknowledged the changes wrought by war. Meanwhile, many writers juggled past norms with an uncertain future: Evelyn Waugh satirized and dissected his own romantic nostalgia, while other novelists foreshadowed postwar literatures politically or through minimized style. Most trenchantly, Elizabeth Bowen's wartime ghost stories used subject-object play with dress to show that, despite the exigencies of war, there remained an abiding gulf between male and female perspectives.

Part III delineates how the postwar single girl was more than ever disrespected, as marriage remained the approved conclusion to a woman's story. Yet these two final chapters, while showing two ways that modern women finished off the traditional marriage plot, also suggest how women's stylistic anxieties persist in the postmodern world. Chapter 6 finds Muriel Spark and Barbara Pym resurrecting the seemingly outmoded spinster together with the traditionally feminine, trivial topic of dress. Each writer used a diminished literary style to enact the minimalizing of British prospects following World War II—a common theme in postwar fiction. Furthermore, Spark's sexually confident single girls and Pym's shy spinsters modeled corresponding dress styles, as both writers employed a comedy of the object, teaching women to laugh at their own desires as well as at men's. And finally, with modernity aging, chapter 7 shows Pym and Spark moving beyond comedy to examine the plight of the single woman through the figure of the femme fatale. Spark's *The Driver's Seat* unites sex, dress, and death in a glorification of style alone, while Pym's *The Sweet Dove Died* portrays glamour as a response to aging and loss. Whether comic diminishment or aestheticized death, these approaches brilliantly satirize traditional expectations for the single girl's relation to style, while still groping to resolve continuing questions of style and the single girl.

From Sayers's formulaic conventionalism (despite showy touches, à la Wimsey) to the gritty modernist unveiling of Rhys's skulls beneath the skin, and from Pym's humble, spinsterish understatement to Spark's flamboyant stylistics—which nearly overwhelm her presumed meanings—the modern subject of dress puts paid to the traditional marriage plot. But it also demonstrates the tensions that underlay women's styles throughout the twentieth century. Although modernity had unsettled traditional mores, including intransigent gender roles and class divisions, certain assumptions remained deeply entrenched in Western culture: while high-styled language—literature—traditionally was dominated by men, fashionable clothing was seen as the province of women. These stylistic domains first converged and clashed on modernism's literary battlefields, and that is where this book starts.

CHAPTER 1

Introducing Modernism, à la Mode

> It is most true, *stilus virum arguit*, our style betrays us.
> —Robert Burton, *The Anatomy of Melancholy*

WE ARE NO LONGER MODERN, and so we struggle to comprehend modernist modes. Those modes include a fascination with style, elaborate contradictions, and a self-assurance that most timid postmoderns can only dream of attaining: the intellectual complex termed "modernism" claimed entire hemispheres. Yet modernism marginalized females as well as fashion, little dreaming that women novelists would use the new styles—both literary and sartorial—to dissect modernist modes. Thus did modern style betray its users.

Modernity led to modernism, which in turn formed our certitude that our forebears could never comprehend our clever, complex selves. And now, a century past the birth of modernism, modern styles force us to acknowledge that we cannot fully grasp them, either: the modernists are not our peers but our ancestors, as close as our grandparents and as remote. We believe we understand the modernist rebellions, the jubilations, the anxiety-ridden tugs-of-war between past and present—but then we are flummoxed by modern modes, whether artistic or personal. In James Joyce's *Ulysses*, the rebellious young artist Stephen Dedalus insists upon black mourning attire. "Etiquette is etiquette," Buck Mulligan observes mockingly. "He kills his mother but he can't wear grey trousers" (1: 121–22). The contradiction is precisely imaged: moderns often long to kill their mothers, not to mention their fathers. Nevertheless, modernism frequently insisted upon dressing itself, both figuratively and literally, in traditional modes.

We simply cannot assume that we share modernist perspectives on dress. At an early performance of Igor Stravinsky's famously controversial *Sacre du printemps*, the notoriously nontraditional couple Gertrude Stein and Alice Toklas admired the elegant eveningwear of poet Guillaume Apollinaire, and also of writer-photographer Carl Van Vechten. Then riots broke out, to become fixed in the two women's memories by the image of one man in a nearby box using his cane to smash another's opera hat (Stein 167–68). After all, in 1913 both conservative and revolutionary moderns wore evening dress, including top hats, to the ballet.

In any case modernism, like all human movements, was fraught with paradox and must be distinguished from modernity. *Modernity* was an inevitable condition of Western experience, technology-driven, in which the world shrank, life sped up, and humans found themselves impelled into the "shattering stress and disorientation," induced by "too much change in too short a time," that Alvin Toffler called "future shock" (4). *Modernism* was a chosen response to this shock, at least at first: philosophers and artists endeavored to create a theory, a manner of living, or a faith in something—be it art, tradition, or revolution—that might shore up the ruins of European civilization.[1] In pursuit of this recuperative project, literary modernists advocated experimentalism, while they harked back to classic masters; they preached anarchy, but they longed for traditional hierarchies; they claimed that the solipsistic self was one's only truth, while also observing that the self was radically fragmented and indeterminate. As Raymond Williams has noted, literary modernism was both a "distinctive movement" and "strongly characterized by its internal diversity of methods and emphases" (7). Modernists simultaneously were obsessed with Western heritage and fascinated by non-Western religions and art forms. Modernists advocated sexual freedom yet frequently denigrated

---

1. Susan Stanford Friedman defines modernism more broadly, as "the expressive dimension of modernity" encompassing "a range of creative meaning-making forms and cultural practices that engage in substantial and different ways with the historical conditions of a particular modernity" ("Periodizing Modernism" 433). However, Friedman aims to include possible non-Western modernisms while I describe the historical Anglo-European phenomenon.

women. Modernists' poems and novels celebrated irony while earnestly condemning their opponents. Some modernists became Communists, while others embraced Fascism. Any workable definition of modernism must encompass both its contradictions and its passionate assumption of meaning, including its attempts to stylize the experience of modernity.

To "stylize" is to shape and to sharpen. In the beginning, a style (from the Latin *stilus*) was a writing tool, which metonymically came to refer to a manner of speaking or writing. The ancients played with its originating meaning, "to prick," in order to tell stories of unfortunate politicians stabbed to death with a stilus (Plutarchus 545), or unsatisfactory teachers whose students took a sharp revenge. Renaissance writers joked about attacking readers through their sharp stiles.[2] Gradually *style* took on a broader significance, applied to manners, appearance, and behavior. But only slowly did the word become a term of dress, and our initial evidence appears in the late eighteenth century, with the first major woman novelist. In Jane Austen's *Mansfield Park*, Mary Crawford assures her brother that Fanny Price's newfound attractions "may all be resolved into a better stile of dress" (199). "Stile" had been associated with clothing before, but only when the clothing stood as metaphor for writing. With Austen the metaphor dissolved, mingling verbal and sartorial modes. Thus it was a woman, and a fine stylist of writing herself, who first applied the verbal descriptor "style" to dress.

The historical backgrounds matter because modernism was not born ex nihilo, and because this book claims that certain historical parallels existed, and persist, between clothing and literary styles. Accordingly, this chapter begins by summarizing a centuries-long drift, from Protestant moral idealism to modernist literary impressionism, regarding the relation of style to substance. Next, I examine how the early nineteenth century marked several significant moments for the history of style: Victorian thinkers began to objectify fashion by analyzing the meanings of dress, initiating what would become the field of fashion theory. Meanwhile, on the literary front, avant-garde writers such as Charles Baudelaire and

---

2. "Methinks every point I direct my pen to should be the Sharp Execution of a stile at their hearts" (*Addr. Hopeful Yng. Gentry Eng.* 67): 1669; 1770. For this line and for the murderous students, see Lingard under the *Oxford English Dictionary* entry for "style." Some accounts of Julius Caesar's assassination claim that he grabbed at a stilus in a futile effort to ward off his attackers: see C. Suetonius Tranquillus, *The Lives of the Twelve Caesars* (Oxford: Loeb Classical Library, 1913), 113.

Stéphane Mallarmé celebrated dress and fashion while largely ignoring it in their high-art poetry.

The latter part of this chapter interrogates the evident links between modernism, fashion, and gender. Baudelaire famously had proposed that fashion is intrinsic to modernity or, as Ulrich Lehmann puts it, "*La mode et la modernité* are inextricably linked" (9). What does it mean, then, that simultaneously with the new male theorizing, the nineteenth century witnessed a growing feminization of fashion, ironically shadowed by the rise of the male dandy? "Modernism à la Mode" accordingly concludes by briefly surveying high modernist literary uses of dress, revealing striking contrasts between the abbreviated, corralled clothing details in male-authored fiction and Virginia Woolf's deeply personal, multifarious approaches to dress. Women writers, after uneasily avoiding the subject of dress, learned in modernity to wield clothing style as a weapon against those who had used it to demean them.

Clearly, when it comes to dress, "modernity" and "modernism" bleed into one another. And if fashion ("la mode") is peculiarly the province of the modern, then we must study fashion in order to understand modernism. However, given the history we shall survey, and literary modernism's fraught relations to style, that is a big "if." I prefer to begin with the claim, suggested by writers from Baudelaire on, that modern modes of writing are foreshadowed and echoed in modern modes of dress. Certainly, in ways both shallow and profound, our styles betray us all.

STYLE AND SUBSTANCE

To trace historical attitudes toward style is to discover very high aesthetic and ethical stakes. Jessica Burstein captures the radical collapse of earlier beliefs about style in her description of a "cold modernism" that finds "no difference between style and substance . . . between form and content. . . . 'Style' here means both the form of a sentence and the fact of fashion" (12). I suggest that this frequently is true of "hot modernism" (subjectivist impressionism) as well, and that perhaps this collapse signals an eventual breach of the walls dividing high and low culture. Even more, the modernist apotheosis of style began to overwhelm the artificial barriers between men and women. In multitudinous ways, then, as the following examples show, the issue of style demonstrates how modernism undermined previous certainties.

Until the nineteenth century, "style versus substance" was not a dilemma but a moral judgment, and it was assumed that substance mattered more. Literary style was merely, as Restoration poet and clergyman Samuel Wesley stipulated in a 1700 poem, "the Dress of Thought, a modest Dress" (l. 138). This commonplace image popped up a few decades later in Lord Chesterfield's mid-eighteenth-century letters to his son: "Style is the dress of thoughts, and a well-dressed thought, like a well-dressed man, appears to great advantage" (287). Both men employed the sartorial metaphor with little attention to its literal meaning. Words as the "dress" of thought suggested that language was a simple, changeable covering for significant ideas.

Perhaps it is no wonder, then, that later writers with grand artistic aspirations would seek a higher role for style. Certainly style as a mere holder of content remained a familiar concept: in 1899, two centuries after Wesley's poem, the narrator of *Heart of Darkness* describes a traditional seaman's yarn as one in which "the whole meaning . . . lies within the shell of a cracked nut" (20). Joseph Conrad's novella, however, swiftly rejects that traditional view by turning to the proto-modernist sailor Marlow, for whom "the meaning of an episode was not inside like a kernel but outside, enveloping the tale which brought it out only as a glow brings out a haze, in the likeness of one of these misty halos that sometimes are made visible by the spectral illumination of moonshine" (20). Traditionally, style was nothing without content. But in Conrad's literary impressionism, revelatory light and occluding mist mingle inextricably. Two decades later, Virginia Woolf used similar light and mist images, arguing that the life that the novelist should capture is "the semi-transparent envelope, or luminous halo, surrounding us" ("Modern Novels" 33). For these modernists, style was not a simple covering dress but part of the substance.

How did modernism reach this point? Eighteenth-century writers had been certain that style was merely decorative; nineteenth-century Aesthetes reacted against that certitude by valuing style alone. Each attitude was in its way as totalizing as the other. Consider Samuel Johnson's surprising remark that "words are the daughters of earth," while "things are the sons of heaven." Johnson meant merely to affirm the philosophical realism of his lexicographical project, and to be modest about his own genius:

"Words," he continued, "are but the signs of ideas" (238). But such a stolid thesis inevitably provokes its antithesis. Certain nineteenth-century writers began to *épater* their Johnsonian predecessors on the subject of style by affirming words alone as the heavenly entities. As Gustave Flaubert boasted that he would write "un livre sur rien" [a book about nothing], he also spoke of his longing to kick free of Earth's constraints and affirm style as the only artistic value: "En se posant au point de vue de l'Art pur, qu'il n'y en à aucun, le style étant à lui tout seul une manière absolue de voir les choses" (*Correspondance* 2: 345; 16 January 1852) [From the perspective of pure Art . . . style alone might be an absolute manner of seeing things]. More moderately, Aesthetic teacher Walter Pater proposed that the greatest artworks unite surface and content:

> If music be the ideal of all art whatever, precisely because in music it is impossible to distinguish the form from the substance or matter, the subject from the expression, then, literature, by finding its specific excellence in the absolute correspondence of the term to its import, will be but fulfilling the condition of . . . all good art. ("Style" 37)

For Pater, style is no mere "dress" of thought (so easy to remove or change), but neither does he see a metaphysical dichotomy between words and things. Indeed, he optimistically assumes that terms may "absolute[ly]" correspond to their meanings. It is not a conclusion that was much heeded by his followers, for whom beauty meant style and surface decoration—or who simply recognized that style might serve as a decisive rhetorical factor. Near the century's end, Oscar Wilde would put into the mouth of his critic Vivian a celebration of pure style: "It is style that makes us believe in a thing—nothing but style" ("Decay" 83). In fact, Wilde's fin-de-siècle epigrams themselves exemplify the power of style: we admire Wilde's *mots*, and perhaps believe in them, because of their wit and elegant brashness—that is to say, their absolute style. The pious Samuel Wesley would be horrified.

Despite variations, the views of Flaubert, Pater, and Wilde all differ greatly from the dismissive references to style in previous centuries, and their ideas paved the way for modernists such as Conrad and Woolf. Earlier thinkers had referred to limited physical beauties: clothing, flowers, daughters. These later writers used absolutist, nearly religious terminology (Flaubert's "absolute manner," Pater's "ideal of all art"), taking style very seriously indeed. Moreover, the subtle connotations were as important as the overt denotations. Wesley's and Chesterfield's clothing imagery foreshadows later associations of style with fashionable dress. And both the dress metaphors and Dr. Johnson's gendered imagery—where the earthly words are female but heavenly things are male—unself-consciously suggest that style is trivial: neither clothing, to the Puritan-influenced Wesley, nor women, to Samuel Johnson, were of the first importance. No wonder, then, that a thoughtful late eighteenth-century woman such as Mary Wollstonecraft strove to earn respect by scorning style:

> I shall disdain to cull my phrases or polish my style . . . wishing rather to persuade by the force of my arguments, than dazzle by the elegance of my language, I shall not waste my time in rounding periods, or in fabricating the turgid bombast of artificial feelings, which, coming from the head, never reach the heart.—I shall be employed about things, not words! (77)

Wollstonecraft, like Johnson, firmly isolates "things" from "words," privileging the former over the latter. Moreover, she separates dazzling "elegance" and "fabricat[ed]" feelings (clothing terms) from usefulness and sincerity. We cannot, it seems, avoid implicit parallels between writing style and dress style—or the links between dress and women.

This connotative background helps explain our current understanding of the terms *fashion* and *dress*, as well as *style*. *Fashion* the verb was and remains a male-identified action, used for intellectual and artistic making. *Fashion* the noun is a feminine object (*la mode*), a goddess, or a goal. Fashion is a communal phenomenon: you cannot have a fashion with only one person. Dress fashion is socially constructed, dependent upon class divisions and often linked to privileges of money and travel; in addition, it is characterized by change. *Dress* itself is a material enactment, sometimes of fashion, sometimes of necessary coverage or convention. *Style*, however, endeavors to mediate between the intangible desires of fashion and the materiality of dress. In current usage, its definition slides between a near-synonym for fashion—we speak of "stylish dress" or being "in style"—to an acknowledgment of the individual element in dress: "her personal style." This slippage carries over to literature: every writer has his or her individual style, but we also, like Pater, recognize style as a criterion of value. Everyone has a clothing style, but everyone is not stylishly dressed or in style. Similarly, everyone writes in his or her own style, but everyone does not write "with style." When associated with dress, the term *style* always has suggested ambition and upward mobility: Jane Austen refers in *Northanger Abbey* to "the resolute stilishness" of the social-climbing Miss Thorpe (51). In pursuing style, one strives to appropriate fashion for one's own person.

In sum, our stylistic definitions, whether in literature or in dress, tend to contrast the individual to the communal. "Fashion," wrote Georg Simmel, satisfies both our need for "social adaptation," to be like others, and our need for "differentiation, change, and individual contrast" ("The Philosophy of Fashion" 189). However, the increased modern value placed on style may signal future trends both for literature and for fashionable dress. In our own day, the fashion industry sells the sartorial avant-garde an aesthetic of shared nonconformity, and one might argue for a similar paradox in the contemporary-literature marketplace. Seen in this light, *style* is a version of the fashionable that longs to break away from group judgment, and perhaps in modernism style received its manumission.

OBJECTIFYING FASHION

The liberation of style started when nineteenth-century writers began to take fashion seriously. An odd, one-sided interest in dress appears especially in certain avant-garde French writers. Poet Charles Baudelaire wrote essays about fashion as a philosophical and aesthetic topic. In his 1856 novel of "pure style," Flaubert spent many words on Madame Bovary's clothing, even as he satirized her desperate confusion of love and dress. Later in the century, Stéphane Mallarmé founded a woman's magazine and composed minute descriptions of women's fashions for it, although not for his poetry. Simultaneously, in England, serious thinkers such as Thomas Carlyle (1795–1881) and Herbert Spencer (1820–1903) began to propound their views on the meanings of clothing and fashion, with obvious efforts at scholarly distance. All of these new analyses of dress were coolly objectified. For even though male Aesthetes celebrated the principle of style, and often dressed as dandies, *fashion* in the nineteenth century would become a term associated with women—thereby raising the status of neither fashion nor females.

The contributions of Victorian British thinkers lay in their earnest analyses of clothing and fashion. Indeed, these writers found it difficult to separate the one from the other, agreeing almost unanimously that, as Carlyle's Professor put it in *Sartor Resartus* (1833–34), the "first purpose of Clothes . . . was not warmth or decency, but ornament" (29): in all times and cultures people have dressed for the sake of being viewed. Nevertheless, in his philosophical novel Carlyle would, with counterintuitive brilliance, suggest that dress by its very materiality betokened the unseen: "Man is a Spirit, and bound by invisible bonds to *All Men . . . he wears clothes* which are visible emblems of that fact" (47). *Sartor* explains the rise of the dandy as an effort to compensate for loss of religious faith through the "new sect" of painstaking dress. The novel's layered symbols suggest that fashion has unseen depths; it is, in the zestful summary of Carlyle's contemporary William Hazlitt, "haughty, trifling, affected, servile, despotic, mean, and ambitious, precise and fantastical, all in a breath—tied to no rule, and bound to conform to every whim of the moment" ("On Fashion" 52). Dress fashion's lability reflects anarchic, frivolous human nature—and therein lay a fascinating puzzle for serious men.

Certain theorists found the frivolous chaos of fashion almost perfectly explicable in terms of the individual trying to distinguish herself from the group. For instance, the social philosopher Spencer regarded fashion as a bid for power: "Civilized usages obscure the truth that men were not originally prompted to clothe themselves by either the desire for warmth or the thought of decency . . . the dress, like the badge, is at first worn from the wish for admiration" (*The Principles of Sociology* 2: 180). In his view, fashionable dress is employed by the upper classes, in order to inspire envy, and mimicked by the social-climbing middle classes. Following Spencer, American economist Thorstein Veblen (1857–1929) would explain fashion as a symptom of economic impetuses, especially conspicuous consumption: fashionable dress not only shows, he wrote, that "the wearer is able to consume a relatively large value, but it argues at the same time that he consumes without producing" (171). And even though Veblen acknowledges the possibility of dress as an aesthetic act, every attempt at sartorial beauty is, he noted, subordinate to "the norm of conspicuous waste": it must "come up to the accepted standard of expensiveness" (174). This interpretation segues naturally into the uselessness of fashion, particularly as associated with women. Woman's dress differs from man's, Veblen argues, because it "goes even farther than that of men in the way of demonstrating the wearer's abstinence from productive employment" (171). His examples are the skirt, the high heel, and the corset—the latter two items especially cherished in Veblen's day by bourgeois and upper-class women. In truth these privileged females are, in his view, also "servants to whom, in the differentiation of economic functions, has been delegated the office of putting in evidence their master's ability to pay" (182). They dress for the success of their fathers or husbands.

In closely linking feminine fashion to socioeconomic roles, Veblen both excuses and demeans stylish women. Indeed, Veblen and Spencer share with Carlyle a moralizing tendency regarding fashion: they believe that human dress habits reveal spiritual vacuity, greed, pride, envy, and the will to power. Perhaps understandably, then, these gentlemen write as though they do not actually wear clothes themselves. As magisterial commentators on fashion, they distance themselves from what they see as a coercive and irrational force. Human beings who dress fashionably are objects of study for them, and often contemptible objects: "life *à la mode*, instead of being conducted in the most rational manner, is life regulated by spendthrifts and idlers, milliners and tailors, dandies and silly women" (Spencer, "Manners and Fashion" 29–30).

On the other hand, German philosopher Georg Simmel (1858–1918), while acknowledging elements of competition and self-delusion in fashion, regarded it as an art in which aesthetic taste and personal fulfillment are major motives, along with a universal longing for community. Where Carlyle, Spencer, and Veblen are Victorian thinkers, Simmel reads fashion as a modernist. "Style," he writes, "is the aesthetic attempt to solve the great problem of life: an individual work or behaviour, which is closed, a whole, can simultaneously belong to something higher, a unifying encompassing context" ("The Problem" 217). While recognizing both the social snobbery and the contradictions implicit in modish dress, he also sees the attractions of fashion and regards all humanity as implicated in it. Writing in the first decade of the twentieth century, Simmel comments dispassionately upon motives with an objectivity that is more insightful, because more sympathetic, than the willed categories of his predecessors in fashion analysis. Most notably, he presents fashionable Woman not as the contemptible or pathetic Other but as a part of humanity that behaves like a part of humanity. In recognizing "the weakness of the social position to which women were condemned throughout the greatest part of history" ("The Philosophy of Fashion" 196), Simmel theorizes that fashion particularly has offered women the freedom to individualize as well as socialize—twin advantages that he believes constitute the basic appeal of fashion to people in general: through dress you may express yourself, yet also (perhaps even through the same garment) identify and fit in with a group. Thus Simmel suggests that not only is stylish dress benign, it may be liberating.

In two ways, Simmel's interpretations of dress are modernist rather than Victorian. First, he moves toward reading fashion as a language, rather than associating it with inarticulate, primitive societies. Simmel's own interpretations may be simplistic but remain provocative. For example, he does differentiate between the natures of women and men, in essentialist terms that foreshadow Virginia Woolf's discussions of specifically feminine concerns. In "Female Culture," Simmel surmises that "the distinctive psychic quality of woman's nature can be expressed symbolically [in] this: Its periphery is more closely connected with its centre and its aspects are more completely integrated into the whole than holds true for the male nature" (52). This generalization implies that women's dress may serve as literalized metonymy—a significant aid to understanding how women write about dress style. And it also suggests, as Michael Carter has pointed out, that "clothing for men is not a vehicle for the totality of their being but is an element taken from, and appropriate to, their participation in the objective formations of the social order" (73). If men are more objective than women about how they dress, then in Simmel's view women, possessing holistic natures, nonetheless hold an advantage in self-knowledge. Second, Simmel is modernist in his philosophical appreciation for dress style as "the aesthetic attempt to solve the great problem of life" ("The Problem" 217). If that proposal sounds ludicrous, we can recall the similar grandiose claims made for both Victorian and modern poetry. Nobody laughed when Matthew Arnold surmised, in 1880, that "we have to turn to poetry to interpret life for us, to console us, to sustain us" (161). Two decades later, Arthur Symons grandly proclaimed that Symbolist poetry offers "a theory of life" that may help us escape from our miserable knowledge of inevitable death (327). Such exaltations of literature, which until recently had been seen—like fashion—as decorative rather than essential, were common to avant-garde poets and novelists in the nineteenth and early twentieth centuries.

Beneath affinities of modern dress with modern thought lies the implication that modernism and fashion are themselves intricately related.

In *Tigersprung*, Ulrich Lehmann argues that fashion reflects the modern condition in its conscious obsession with a self in flux (108, 129, 158). *La mode* therefore is cousin to *modernité*. (The French *modernité* encompasses both "modernity" and "modernism.") In support, Lehmann copiously quotes from writers including Baudelaire, Mallarmé, and Simmel, as well as Balzac, Flaubert, and Proust. The poets especially provide abundant material for this topic: Baudelaire, the "Father of Symbolism," proves the chief source of theory for Lehmann's thesis, while in the next generation Mallarmé, the premier *Symboliste* poet, offers an example of practice—in his women's fashion magazine. These brilliant poets, known for their esoteric art, spent abundant time writing about clothing, and especially women's clothing; it is instructive to attend to the motives and the limits of their fashion interests.

For Baudelaire, dress was an immediate manifestation of the modern as well as a solution to personal quandaries. In "The Painter of Modern Life" (1859–61), he praised Constantin Guys as an artist in quest of "la modernitè," who "s'agit, pour lui, de dégager de la mode ce qu'elle peut contenir de poétique dans l'historique, de tirer l'éternel du transitoire" ("Le peintre" 68) [concerns himself with extracting from fashion whatever it may contain of the poetic in the historical, by distilling the eternal from the transitory]. Here Baudelaire presents two new, startling concepts: first, that fashion is a worthy subject for an artist; second, that fashion may be linked to the most serious topics: history, eternity. The frivolous, Baudelaire claims, *is* the modern, because it involves the immediate: modernity is "le transitoire, le fugitif, le contingent, la moitié de l'art, dont l'autre moitié est l'éternel et l'immuable" (69) [the transitory, the fugitive, the contingent half of art—of which the other half is the eternal and the immutable]. And we cannot do without this transitory, fugitive element, he argues; successful and beautiful art must join temporality to eternity. "En le supprimant, vous tombez forcément dans le vide d'une beauté abstraite et indéfinissable, comme celle de l'unique femme avant le premier péché" (69) [In suppressing the temporal, you necessarily fall into the void of an abstract and indefinable beauty, like that of the first woman before the first sin]. This aesthetic employs fashion as an example of transience yet leaves space for finding the eternal within it. But observe the theological simile, which introduces concepts of the female and of original sin. Significantly, those of Baudelaire's poems that were most censored, because of erotic, blasphemous, or scatological references, reveal a neoplatonic and religious horror of the body, pictured as "la charogne" [the carcass]. Sartorial finery, then, is for Baudelaire not merely exemplary of the problem of modern-*ity*—its swift pace and ever-fading details—but also of the modern-*ist* effort at resolution of age-old concerns:

> Le mode doit donc être considérée comme un symptôme du goût de l'idéal surnageant dans le cerveau humain au-dessus de tout ce que la vie naturelle y accumule de grossier, de terrestre et d'immonde, comme une déformation sublime de la nature, ou plutôt comme un essai permanent et successif de réformation de la nature . . . toutes les modes sont charmantes, c'est-à-dire relativement charmantes, chacune étant un effort nouveau, plus ou moins heureux, vers le beau, un approximation quelconque d'un idéal. (101–2)

> Fashion must then be considered as a symptom of the taste for the ideal which floats on the human brain, above all that the natural life accumulates there (the gross, the earthly, and the foul), as a sublime deformation of nature, or rather as a permanent and continuing effort at reforming nature . . . all modes are charming, that is to say relatively charming, each fashion being a new effort, more or less successful, at beauty, at approximating an ideal.

Dress, after all, covers the loathsome body, which is a traditional belief. Yet Baudelaire's accompanying concept, that fashion aims at a reformation of the self, toward an ideal beauty, is a new, modernist insight.

However, despite his theorizing about beauty and dress, Baudelaire's poetry makes remarkably little description of clothing. The poems in *Les fleurs du mal* reveal, as do his prose writings, a fascination with death, prostitutes, and opium. They mention perfumes, jewels, and hair, feminine adornments that usually are described in very general terms. Typically, "La Beauté" is an allegorical figure of alternating temptation and aspiration, but she wears no specially defined clothing, commenting, "Je hais le mouvement qui déplace les lignes" (l. 7) [I hate any movement which displaces lines]. As such, this poet's Beauty is not far from that "abstract and indefinable" void that he had urged artists to avoid.

In sum, Baudelaire's fashion theories remain limited; perhaps because of his disgust with the body, he does not describe clothing in his art. He also persists in seeing men and women as absolutely divided, united only in being equally repulsive: "La femme, esclave vile, orgueilleuse et stupide... L'homme, tyran goulu paillard, dur et cupide" ("Le Voyage" ll. 89–92) [Woman, a vile slave, proud and stupid... Man, a greedy tyrant, lustful, hard and covetous]. The bitter language echoes Thorstein Veblen's description of the social roles of the sexes. And the view of woman reflects yet another description of the feminine in "The Painter of Modern Life":

> C'est une espèce d'idole, stupide peut-être, mais éblouissante, enchantresse... non-seulement dans son allure et le mouvement de ses membres, mais aussi dans le mousselines, les gazes, les vastes et chatoyantes nuées d'étoffes dont elle s'enveloppe, et qui sont comme les attributs et le piédestal de sa divinité. (97–98)

> She's a sort of idol, perhaps stupid but dazzling, enchanting... not only in her moving members but also in the muslins, the gauzes, the vast and shimmering clouds of material in which she envelops herself, and which are like the attributes and the pedestal of her divinity.

Here, woman embodies both stupidity and divinity. Her gauzy attire provides a willed obfuscation for both the dressed woman and the observing man—neither of whom, the poet implies, can contemplate the reality of flesh without disgust. For Charles Baudelaire, then, the specific details of clothing may be too close to the body itself: stylistic cloudiness is preferable.

In contrast, poet Stéphane Mallarmé loved enumerating the details of women's clothing. When he founded *La Dernière Mode* in 1874, Mallarmé was enacting a business plan to edit, design, and author a fashion magazine for women. To friends he also mentioned his enthusiasm for publishing "a glorification of beauty" (Lehmann 59). And for eight fortnightly issues, the poet wrote most of the articles himself, seeming to delight in describing the proper jewels for a young girl to wear (Furbank and Cain 5),[3] or Frederick Worth's newly designed "blue-of-dreams" gown (124), or the ideal wedding dress, which included

> a white satin underskirt covered with a Tarleton skirt.... Tunic pleated crosswise and attached to the skirt; on the bottom of the tunic, a fringe

---

3. These references and the following quotations from *La Dernière Mode* are taken from the translated collection by Furbank and Cain.

decorated with white pearl. A broad satin sash to one side, falling on to the tunic and attached to the train with a bow: this bow was itself attached to the skirt with a crown of orange blossom with a train. The bodice was high and had basques.... Everything at once worldly and virginal, and giving no hint of a ball gown, which would have been a grave fault of taste. (96–97)

The wordy details typify Mallarmé's fashion writing, and the fashion writing of his time. The lofty tone proclaims the writer's expertise; nor were the seemingly tedious details tiresome for female readers, who made or ordered the making of their own clothes before the era of fashion photography and off-the-peg styles.

Still, might we not expect this feminine trivia to bore a man? Mallarmé's delight in penning such descriptions seems all the odder in light of his conventional bourgeois lifestyle, on the one hand, and his radically esoteric poetry on the other. What does it mean to veer from perfect glorification of style, in high-art poems, to detailed descriptions of a black-velvet skirt (Furbank and Cain 54)? Mallarmé's fashion writing has led irresistibly to transgender theories, according to which the journal's pseudonyms serve as masks for the quiet teacher's wild desires. But the articles in *La Dernière Mode* did not breach any proprieties of their day, nor was it a deeply kept secret that the manager and editor wrote most of his own material. As Jennifer M. Jones has pointed out, it was not unusual for an eighteenth- or nineteenth-century French fashion magazine to be male-edited and authored, under a female pseudonym (190–91). The puzzle lies simply in the poet's enjoyment of this pretense. Lehmann believes that Mallarmé used the magazine "to indulge in all things futile, facile, and domestic, without having to fear any social, or artistic, sanctions for his less than sublime—that is, non-masculine—behavior" (76–77). As to nonmasculine, however, we should note that a magisterial tone, such as that in the wedding-dress description above, enabled Mallarmé to literally skirt the erotic while demonstrating his mastery over it. Indeed, it was permitted and even expected that men would dictate women's fashions.

Moreover Mallarmé, like Baudelaire, does not describe women's dress styles in his poetry. Far more than the earlier poet, in fact, Mallarmé tended to wax lyrical about classical figures wearing vaguely defined robes very unlike the super-detailed toilettes in *La Dernière Mode*. He certainly did not think that his fashion prose was poetry, though he wittily affirmed its value: "To have the permanence of tulle illusion, or of artificial roses imitating roses and clematis: that is one's dream for every sentence one writes, not for a short story or a sonnet, but about the news of the day" (Furbank and Cain 126). With these words, the writer both celebrates his sartorial journalism and acknowledges its distance from literary art. Fashion writing, he admits, is a pretty illusion, as artificial as silk flowers and not even as permanent as this year's styles. And there is a rhetorical allure in the ephemeral, for which the filmy *tulle illusion*—also fascinating to Baudelaire—offers a fine metaphor. Like Woolf's reality, a "semitransparent halo surrounding us," tulle left a mystery as to where the clothing stopped and the woman's body began. So would moderns find a mystery in discerning where the reference ended and its referent began.

Although these poets persisted in separating their art from their dress interests, they also foreshadowed the uses of style and clothing in modern fiction. In particular, Baudelaire and Mallarmé help point us toward issues of the eternal versus the ephemeral, and of prose as the proper medium for fashion details. And Mallarmé's fashion writing also flirts with a filmy division between the sexes:

> All women love verse, as they do perfumes or jewels. . . . They say there are no real readers any longer, and perhaps this is true; but there are women readers. Only a woman, in her freedom from politics and gloomy cares, has leisure, once her dressing is done, to feel the need to dress her soul as well. (Furbank and Cain 30)

He playfully imagines a novel or book of verse lying face-down for days among the perfumes and jewels, becoming part of the glamorous detritus of the boudoir. The imagery seems first degrading, to literature and to women: poems are equated with dress ornaments, and "there are no real readers . . . but there are women readers." Evidently literature is reduced to slumming in the female world. But Mallarmé's concluding metaphor implies that *only* women now recognize the need of dressing their souls through books: literature, like fashion, is appreciated largely by women in the new modern world. He was mistaken about reading becoming only a female activity. And yet the combination of women, fashion, and literature would become a potent mix in the twentieth century, in part for reasons shown by Mallarmé and Baudelaire.

THE MODERNISM OF FASHION

Is "fashion," then, truly a modernist concept? To understand modernism's special claims on fashion, we must—paradoxically—recall that fashion has existed in some sort from ancient times. The marriage of modernism and *la mode* is vastly complicated when we recall that fashionable clothing has been recorded as long as written documents, and with similar associations. In Aristophanes' *The Clouds* (c. 423–417 BC), a weak father blames his wife for encouraging their son to dress in an upwardly mobile fashion:

> This boy she took, and used to spoil him, saying
> *Oh! When you are driving to the Acropolis, clad*
> *Like Megacles, in your purple*; whilst I said
> *Oh! When the goats you are driving from the fells*
> *Clad like your father, in your sheepskin coat.*
> (271: ll. 70–74; translator's emphases)

Needless to say, the classical Greek teenager prefers purple to sheepskin, recognizing the lifestyle accompanying each clothing style. Lifestyle is also the issue in biblical injunctions against elaborate dress: Isaiah's "daughters of Zion" move like early-day fashion models, "with stretched forth necks and wanton eyes, walking and mincing as they go, and making a tinkling with their feet" (3:16, Authorized Version). However, it is because of their haughtiness and scorn for the poor, says the prophet, that they will be punished and deprived of their "tinkling leg ornaments" and chains, bracelets, bonnets, earrings, headbands, veils, mantles, and "changeable suits of apparel" (3:18–23). Isaiah catalogs the ornaments and parts of female dress in nearly as much detail as would Mallarmé two millennia later—but with negative implications. Hundreds of years later, Paul advocated "modest apparel" for Christian women, suggesting that they adorn themselves "not with braided hair, or gold, or pearls, or costly array; but . . . with good works" (I Timothy 2:9–10). The association of material decoration with specified actions tells us that, like Isaiah and Aristophanes, early Christian teachers saw dress style as an ethical code. Ancient stylish dress communicated high status and contempt for the underprivileged, not unlike some messages sent by dress fashions today. These texts also remind us that, given prosperity, people always have dressed to be viewed, admired, and envied. Victorian theories, that dress is strongly rooted in desire for ornament rather than for coverage, begin to sound plausible indeed. The dress styles described in these ancient documents are those of the privileged: just as the winners write the histories, so the rich wear the fashions.

Nevertheless, theorizing dress style seems to be an ever more elaborate activity of the last two centuries. Modern fashion theories have focused upon psychology, or history, or consumerism, or gender, but a monological approach will not serve. We may adorn our bodies, but we cannot master how others perceive us, or what each of us inadvertently may reveal through clothing. "When we dress," Elizabeth Wilson concludes, "we wear inscribed upon our bodies the often obscure relationship of art, personal psychology, and the social order" (*Adorned* 247). This is, she claims, because fashion is urban, artificial, and an aestheticizing of unnatural human social arrangements (9). In these ways, fashion does peculiarly portray the modern fragmentation of identity. But artificial social roles are not an invention of modern times. And was the human self ever unitary? While clothing, city-dwellers, and artifice have existed since before written history, modernists use style to self-consciously explicate their era's neuroses. And certainly fashion's social transience matters. The constant flux of styles—what was fashionable last month cannot be in style today, as Chanel legendarily said—is intrinsic to modern fashion and the anxiety-creating, fast-paced modern world. So if modernism is specially related to fashion, it may be less originatory than diagnostic.

Might fashion, then, actually resolve the cruxes of modernity? In the sixties, sociologist Herbert Blumer surmised that fashion's first role is to introduce "*order in a potentially anarchic and moving present*" (emphasis in original). "Second," he continued, "fashion serves to detach the grip of the past in a moving world" (289). That is, fashion organizes our present lives and frees us from the tyranny of history. Certainly these claims constitute a modernist reading of fashion's powers: like Simmel and like Baudelaire, Blumer suggests that fashionable style is part of the solution rather than part of the problem. However, the suggestion that fashion may ameliorate modernist angst is itself subject to critique. As Joanne Finkelstein sums up, "fashion succeeds by promising to annul the fragmented condition of modernity with the imposition of a coherent subjectivity" (47)—but the promise may be illusory. If fashion works in this way, why is prosperous Western woman not the happiest of beings? Finkelstein refers to Leslie W. Rabine's study of the "two codes of fashion," according to which women aim at attaining the "frozen perfection" of fashion photos but instead end up "reproducing a self as alienated . . . founded in lack" (Rabine 62, 64). Undeniably, modern fashion photography increased the challenge for stylish women: in the past they could more easily imagine themselves in the clothes so meticulously detailed via words. Now it is hard to see resemblances between their own bodies and the sleek angularity of contemporary models. Additionally many moderns, both women and men, have endeavored to use dress to impose their self-visions upon their viewers and so to control their bodies as perceived objects. But again, such self-staging is not exclusively modern.

Ultimately, the differences between early fashion and modern fashion lie in three characteristics: material availability, the speed of change, and a fresh gendering of fashion.[4] First, material availability has made fashionable dress, in more prosperous nations, available to most people rather than to a tiny court-centered ruling class. But if a fashion cannot be a fashion of one, neither can it be a uniform: when we all dress fashionably, then fashion becomes meaningless. The multiple ironies of widespread fashion may be attributed to the cheaper cloth provided, first through commercial imports in the eighteenth century and then by the machines and factories of the Industrial Revolution. Increased material availability also stemmed from the rise of the bourgeoisie, with more money and leisure to expend on fashion. And Western democracy has made forcible class exclusions from fashion unthinkable, so that medieval sumptuary laws—where commoners could be fined for wearing long points on their shoes, for instance, or peasants were forbidden to wear red (Lauer 71–72, 85)—are unfathomable now. Once the competition is opened to the public, however, the pool of competitors fills quickly and it becomes all the harder to break away from the crowd. Accordingly, material availability means that in the last two hundred years the distinctions necessary to maintain the exclusivity of fashion have not faded away but proliferated.

Second, the speed of change has multiplied exponentially, to a rate unimaginable in earlier centuries and cultures. If fashion indeed is made

---

4. I have not discussed the common generalization that fashion began in medieval Europe (Davis, *Fashion, Culture* 17, 28). One also might say that lyric poetry began then, or that music began in sixteenth-century Europe, because the Petrarchan sonnet or Western polyphonic harmonies were unknown before those eras. But to overgeneralize is to ignore not only ancient history but later vast changes in Western fashion itself, such as the shifts in male attitudes toward dress or the now indispensable fashion prop of photography.

to become unfashionable, then the winning times (to revive the athletic metaphor) are constantly being shortened. Methods for broadcasting the latest fashions have progressed, from word of mouth and public display; to fashion prints, dolls, and journals; to the rise of live models and fashion photography in the modern era; to the use of television and then the Internet to disseminate images. And each technological innovation has increased the speed with which fashions change. In the twentieth and twenty-first centuries it is not, as in medieval Europe, the last century's or last decade's fashions that we must avoid, but last month's.

Nevertheless, in all this change, the third peculiarity of fashion in the modern era burgeoned and grew throughout the nineteenth and twentieth centuries: the challenge of gendered fashion. By gendered fashion I do not mean the details of how women's clothing differs from men's, but how fashion itself has become and remains heavily identified with the female, an identification that became highly significant for modern women and their novels.

FEMALE FASHION AND THE RISE OF THE DANDY

The putative nineteenth-century feminization of fashion is ironically intertwined with the rise of the male fashion designer, and of the dandy. The dandy constituted the dress-obsessed male exception that proved the rule, that regular men no longer concerned themselves with dress; oddly, this masculine nonchalance was initiated by the ur-dandy George Brummell. And eventually that connoisseur of dandyism, Oscar Wilde, at the century's end and on the cusp of modernism, would suggest—through both dress and writing styles—the necessary directions of modernism and style.

In the 1800s fashionable dress—hitherto the mark of the leisure class, whether nobleman or lady—came to be regarded as almost exclusively the province of women. In earlier eras, prosperous European males had sported showy costumes, including bright colors, high heels, and elaborate lace. In Phillip Stubbes's *Anatomie of Abuses* (1583), the pamphleteer spends ten pages ridiculing Elizabethan men's fashions, starting with the "Hattes of England" and advancing through "Great Ruffes," "Costly Shirtes," "English Doublets," "Costly Hosen," and "Costly Nether Stockings," down to "Costly Shoes" and "Coates and Jerkins" (25, 26, 27,

29, 30). Only then does he turn to a more cursory criticism of female fripperies. Clearly for Stubbes men were the fashion leaders. In a later instance of fashionable manliness, seventeenth-century diarist Samuel Pepys recorded with equal care the details of his sexual prowess and the decorations upon his clothes. Even the eighteenth-century Samuel Johnson, no fashion plate, remarked that Greek learning was "like lace; every man gets as much of it as he can" (Boswell 349). Men with the means to dress elaborately did so. Yet men largely ceased to covet lace by the early 1800s. It was just the time when many more men could begin to afford to conspicuously consume—but Victorian bourgeois gentlemen left it to their wives to conspicuously costume. Notably, men began to emphasize style in literature while relinquishing it in dress. The causes of this feminization of Western fashion remain debatable, but fashion's sharp gendering became a significant characteristic of modernity.

Certainly the identification of fashion as female had historical foreshadowing, in biblical writers and in the change of *le mode* to *la mode* in sixteenth-century France, indicating that even then fashion seemed more feminine than masculine. Similar hints appear in eighteenth-century anti-fashion poems. In *Fashion: An Epistolary Satire to a Friend* (1742), Joseph Warton mocks both men and women who order their lives according to Fashion's "Fool-o'erwhelming Flood" (1). For this error Warton, in a trend that would persist into the twentieth century, indicts France: "Strange! that pert Grasshoppers should Lions lead" (4). Blaming the French, and associating fashion with rapid, irrational change, occurs frequently in these poems. Ralph Schomberg's *Fashion: A Poem. Addressed to the ladies of Great-Britain* (1775), despite its title, also critiques men of fashion who make the Grand Tour of Europe and gain nothing but imported dress and vices. Schomberg's term *fashion* encompasses dress and an entire way of life characterized by inconstancy: "*Manners* and *Modes* (nor is it strange) / with every trifling whim will change, / The *fashion* of to-day will vary, / And be to-morrow quite contrary" (17; emphasis in original). The formulation sounds little different from Chanel's, except that it is harshly critical. Lady Fashion is irrational, and her feather-headed fickleness provides sufficient reason for all sensible men to scorn her. Did the Age of Reason, then, triumph over male interest in fashionable dress? Human beings often are admonished to follow more rational courses, and on the whole they rarely do. "The Peer, Prince, Peasant, Soldier, Squire, Divine," Warton laments, "Goddess of Change! bend low before your Shrine" (9).

FIGURE 1. "Greek, sir, is like lace...." Suit (unknown maker), 1740–60. Brooklyn Museum Costume Collection at the Metropolitan Museum of Art, gift of the Brooklyn Museum, 2009; gift of the International Business Machine Corporation; photographed by Lolly Koon. Image © The Metropolitan Museum of Art. Reproduction of any kind is prohibited without express written permission in advance from The Metropolitan Museum of Art.

He advocates reason, but it does not sound as if the fashionable males are listening.

Nevertheless, around the start of the nineteenth century the clothes-wearing habits of the European male changed. Middle- and upper-class men started to opt for gentlemanly conformity rather than self-display. They began wearing simple dark suits with white shirts and cravats, recognizable precursors to the twenty-first-century's business or dress suit. This rise of the dark suit has been amply debated by fashion historians, who agree only that for two centuries it has remained a remarkably constant uniform—and that its corollary, that fashion is largely a feminine concern, also persists to our own day. Although certain fashion theorists recently have challenged this claim, it is hard to refute both the evidence of two hundred years and the common response of the man on the street. The exceptions seem to prove the rule: as we shall see, dandyism is a pushback, from a minority of men, against the feminine appropriation of fashion.[5]

The gender migration in fashionable dress would have astonished a medieval ruler and amused a Renaissance courtier; the reasons remain complex. As noted above, Thorstein Veblen found it unsurprising that the woman should "consume vicariously for the head of the household" (179). In an influential psychoanalytic development of this theory, J. C. Flügel argued that "the Great Masculine Renunciation" of decorative dress stemmed from the leveling influences of the French Revolution and the increased respectability of work, hence "the projection of the [male] exhibitionistic desire onto a person of the opposite sex" (118). Thus bourgeois wives became, in their increasingly elaborate corsets, petticoats, and frills, vicarious symbols of their husbands' successes. Flügel has been critiqued; for instance, to refer to this shift as a "process of democratization in clothing" (113) is to exaggerate by about 50 percent, since many women were and are heavily invested in status fashion. Yet Flügel clearly is right about certain correlations: just as fashion became widely accessible to the larger population, approximately half that population rather abruptly disclaimed interest in it. That disclaimer was accompanied, however, by certain paradoxical features.

Even as men renounced fashion for themselves, they came to rule the fashion world. Certainly, when Mallarmé produced *La Dernière Mode* or

---

5. For a thorough discussion of the male renunciation of fashion, see Tim Edwards's *Fashion in Focus* (chapters 3 and 4).

Oscar Wilde edited *Woman's World*, they were seen as providing needed leadership for women. And when designer Charles Frederick Worth (1825–1895) revolutionized the fashion industry, he also reinforced the gender status quo. As Worth's biographer reminds us, he rose to fame in an era when women sewed their own dresses or hired other women to make them (de Marly 34–35). By the time he opened his Parisian establishment in 1858, Worth was a celebrity dressmaker, the first fashion designer of the modern stripe, whose very name gave a *cachet* to his creations. He not only dressed Empress Eugénie, Sarah Bernhardt, and other privileged ladies but he created a minor sensation by requiring that the wealthy women who wanted his dresses must come to his dressmaking establishment by appointment. Worth was rumored to reject any customer who treated him as a servant. In other words, he made the occupation of dressmaker into a respected profession. In our day, it is easy to recognize the snobbish and monetary value of a designer dress, and hard to comprehend how new Worth's approach was or what a change he wrought in fashion's gender dynamics. Previously the occasional talented woman, such as Marie Antoinette's milliner Rose Bertin, had gained a reputation through dressing royalty. But fame did not raise Bertin's status above that of a valued, clever servant. In fact, Anne Hollander observes that the female identities of *modistes*, the French seamstresses of previous centuries, probably abetted a longstanding disrespect for women's fashions (*Sex and Suits* 76–78). What is certain is that when, in the later 1800s, men following Worth's example began designing women's clothing, fashion design as occupation gained prestige and began to be considered art. Worth himself, as de Marly notes, in his later years posed as an artist in velvet beret, flowing coat, and "a floppy silk scarf knotted at his throat instead of a cravat" (110–11). Men made fashion—women's fashion, that is—into both big business and creative art, once they became its arbiters.

There was, in any case, little room for creativity in men's clothes by the mid-nineteenth century, although men also led the standardization of male fashion. Most famously, George "Beau" Brummell (1778–1840) is considered the originator of the modern dress suit for men. A gentleman of modest birth, Brummell achieved immense influence over wealthy English society in the early 1800s through his close friendship with, and immense influence over, the Prince Regent. Brummell modeled the wearing of simple dark suits with white shirts and scrupulously tied plain cravats, a new sartorial ideal for the Western male. Accordingly, the province

FIGURE 2. Beau Brummell (John Cook). © National Portrait Gallery, London. "Fine linen, plenty of it, and country washing."

of the best men's dress clothes became not Paris couturiers but London's Savile Row tailors, and variations on Brummell's suit have ruled male dress ever since. Brummell's connection to this persistent male convention, and to the simultaneous rise of the dandy, is obvious and yet obscure.

Brummell's innovation was to place an extreme emphasis on conventionality and negation. He popularized a golden mean of proper dress rather than gorgeous display, famously announcing that all a man needed was "fine linen, plenty of it, and country washing" in order to be "correct" (Moers 21). In fact, contrary to later popular images of Beau Brummell as a flowery dandy, the real man fascinated and terrorized society through understatement and negation: at the height of Brummell's influence, a slight frown or shake of the head could send a gentleman back to his dressing room to try again. Brummell's own dressing room became a morning meeting place for his friends, partly because he took so long each day to wash and clothe himself. "Indeed," Ellen Moers comments, "Brummell's major contribution to history was his highly original advocacy of cleanliness. It was a matter of pride with him that he did not need perfume: he did not smell" (32). This description implies Brummell's rejection of French fashion rule (perfume was French) in favor of honest English simplicity—just as those eighteenth-century satirists had advocated. In essence, Brummell's style stressed negation: no dirt, no impropriety, no extreme frills. Even his verbal style thrived on negation: in a society where brilliant conversation was valued and nearly expected, very few of his acquaintances succeeded in recording his bons-mots, if such they were. William Hazlitt described Brummell as "the greatest of small wits," whose clever sayings involved "the exaggerating of the merest trifles into matters of importance." His jests, Hazlitt explains, "hover on the very brink of vacancy, and are in their shadowy composition next of kin to nonentities" ("Brummelliana" 152). This emphasis on Brummell's use of "the merest trifles" suggests the triviality so often attributed to fashion, and to women's thinking. But Hazlitt and others saw George Brummell as employing masculine irony in his nonchalant approach to fashion and to life. He endeavored to negate male frippery and all extremes but the blank slate of the pure, clean self. In so doing, Brummell created a new version of the Renaissance courtier's *sprezzatura* and a new, self-contained model for manliness, prefiguring the twentieth-century concept of "cool."

Can Brummell's influence, however, sufficiently explain the great sea-change in Western male dress? It is more plausible to say that Brummell recognized and appropriated a rising style for men that heralded a new vision of masculinity. The dark suit was a serendipitous fashion step for Western males: it fit a growing interest in middle-class propriety and conformity, providing a semidemocratic uniform for the office. Moreover, it implicitly rebuked foolishly fashion-concerned females—as Brummell himself had implicitly and explicitly rebuked the less-correct fashionable men of his time. Anne Hollander theorizes that the male suit was a happy fashion discovery because it so well reflected the current intellectual and cultural trends. From the sixteenth and seventeenth centuries on, somber, plain clothes had been associated with Puritanism and anti-popery in England: Puritan dress was an extreme, in the eyes of most Britons, but a patriotic extreme.[6] To this perception was added, in the early nineteenth century, a growing Romantic naturalism stemming from neoclassical ideals, so that simple, understated clothing was regarded as manifesting an "antique and natural virtue" (*Sex and Suits* 97). However, Hollander points out, the suit also promoted a modern masculine solidarity. Its general uniformity emphasized the wearer's sex: "All indices of social class and function were contained by the sexual mode, so that men's clothes were always noticeably masculine first" (30). Above all, Hollander finds that the style has persisted because it works. Its sleek shape is attractive on most men, and ironically its uniformity means that, in any given group of men, each individual stands out rather than his clothing (98).

Christopher Breward has questioned claims that men lost interest in fashion in the later Victorian era, finding generalizations about "the Great Masculine Renunciation" exaggerated. But Breward's strongest print evidence for the continuance of male fashions comes from tailors and clothiers, whose professional journals and advertising flyers urged men to care about their clothes (41). Not surprisingly, men appreciated fashion as a profitable business and were willing to don certain styles conducive to business. Breward does convincingly describe the persistence of dandyism in the 1830s, 1840s, and 1850s, not merely in the clothing of wealthy fops but in hard-working males such as Benjamin Disraeli and Charles Dickens. As ambitious young writers, these men were determined to draw attention, and so instead of dark suits they sometimes sported light checked trousers, colorful waistcoats, or dramatic velvet jackets (29). Indeed, the rise of

---

6. Soon France and other Catholic European countries also adopted the dark suit; nevertheless, British and Americans persisted in associating foppery with Continental influence.

the dandy ameliorates assumptions that no nineteenth-century men were interested in sartorial display—although the novelists and the brash young politicians certainly employed dress in order to advance their careers.

The true dandy is deliberately exceptional. It is no accident that his self-conscious figure appears just when the majority of men who could dress elaborately decided to leave that to their womenfolk. Moreover, there were various kinds of dandies, some types nearly opposed to others. Brummell's cold correctness is inimical to the flamboyant decoration and color displayed by Albert D'Orsay and his followers in the following decades. These later, flowery dandies were more akin to the effeminate macaronis of eighteenth-century style, although they did not go to the extremes of flowing curls or four-inch heels. Yet a third kind of dandy sported a Romantic, artistic dress. Artistic dandyism was manifested in a relaxed style, in self-indulgent use of color and luxurious materials—never in uncomfortably precise clothes, extreme cleanliness, or effeminacy. Artistic dress, related to the attention-getting costumes of Disraeli and Dickens, proclaimed a man's independent and creative spirit. Such aesthetic dandyism was frequent by the later 1800s, but it was a bohemian costume far from Brummell's meticulous suits.

Still, the precise gentleman and the colorful bohemian were not completely disconnected. The links between the male dandy and the artistic rebel were latent in dandyism as "a product of the revolutionary upheavals of the late eighteenth century," Moers writes. "When such solid values as wealth and birth are upset, ephemera such as style and pose are called upon to justify the stratification of society" (12). Moers's interpretation echoes Baudelaire's writings about the Parisian dandies who "n'ont pas d'autre état que de cultiver l'idée du beau dans leur personne" ("Le peintre" 92) [have no other reason for existence than to cultivate the idea of beauty in their persons]. Where influential leaders of society were backed by wealth and birth, the dandy's claim to fame lay in his appearance. The Brummellian dandy set a standard for "the gentleman," a title that would become a description of behavior as much as birth. Thus, paralleling the rise of nineteenth-century Aestheticism, the dandy enacted the new rise of style over substance, in literature as well as in society—and an incipient democratization.

But dandyism was also a male personality style, often of cold self-containment. Baudelaire announced that the dandy follows "une espèce de culte de soi-même" [a kind of cult of himself], rather than seeking happiness "dans autrui, dans la femme, par exemple" ("Le peintre" 93) [in another—in woman, for example]. The dandy's dress was an effort both at manliness and at masking, at manliness through masking: "Le caractère de beauté du dandy consiste surtout dans l'air froid qui vient de l'inébranlable résolution de ne pas être ému; on dirait un feu latent qui se fait deviner, qui pourrait mais qui ne veut pas rayonner" ("Le peintre" 96) [A dandy's beauty is characterized above all by an air of coldness, which comes from an unshakeable resolution of not being moved; one might say it is a latent fire, which teases and which could, but does not wish to, blaze up]. Where Baudelaire saw fashionable woman as a dazzling object on a pedestal, he regarded the dandy as an acting subject, a role to be played. Where women dressed (it was assumed) to attract others, especially men, the dandy dressed to demonstrate his indifference to others—especially women. Furthermore, in his masking of a "latent fire" within, Baudelaire's dandy demonstrated the ideal self-objectification of the modern artist.

Of course the dandy was susceptible to parody. *Punch* printed cartoons mocking dandyism, while Gilbert and Sullivan found a hit with *Patience* (1881), their comic opera satirizing the Aesthetic cult, including its followers' pretentious dress. And no dandy was so mocked, and so self-mocking, as Oscar Wilde (1854–1900), in whom we find woven all the strands of the nineteenth-century gendering of fashion: Aesthetic art, dandyism, and *Woman's World*. Unfortunately for Wilde, this delicate fabric tore irreparably with his criminal conviction for gross indecency in 1895, which seemed to confirm publically a growing suspicion that style-conscious males were sexually transgressive. But Wilde not only demonstrates the fall of the Victorian Aesthete, he prefigures the modernist writer, publicizing the links between writerly and dress styles as an inextricable mingling of style and substance.

Wilde invariably presented himself as a self-indulgent lover of beauty, albeit capable of self-mockery, and both his early extravagant dress and his generous, sentimental wit were far from Brummellian negation. But his dandyism evolved. The American lecture tour (1882–83) that made him famous was planned in conjunction with performances of *Patience*—and Wilde dressed the part, as "Professor of Aesthetics" in velvet coat, green cravat, and knee-breeches. However, by the early 1890s, Wilde's dress style was coolly precise with only a single dash of bright color or one jewel, as recommended by Baudelaire. In fact, by the time of his downfall, Wilde carefully staged his concern for outward proprieties to reveal just a glimpse of that Baudelairean "latent fire." Insofar as his career crowned the history of nineteenth-century dandyism, he lived out its range of possibilities; insofar as his end initiated new directions for modernism, he also demonstrated what modernist style would mean.

Therefore, to associate Wilde's dandyism only with the feminization of fashion misses the point. Wilde publicized the links between literary and dress styles, as no one else had; then his fall overtly sexualized those links. The covert assumptions already existed and remain to this day. Certainly Wilde's conviction for homosexual acts may have capped a long-standing popular suspicion about the sexuality of men who concern themselves with dress. As Peter McNeil has shown, even many eighteenth-century macaronis were accused of "a lack of interest in heterosexual desire" ("That Doubtful Gender" 412). Earlier in the nineteenth century, people had exchanged whispered rumors of Albert d'Orsay's odd sexual proclivities. The gender-labeling of dress concerns increased in the twentieth century, when an occupation such as Worth's, or the editing of women's fashion magazines by men, came to be viewed as evidence of gender transgression. Typically, one of Barbara Pym's mid-twentieth-century characters knows immediately that a new acquaintance is homosexual when his gaze moves over her figure in order to appraise, not her body, but the cut and price of her clothing (*The Sweet Dove* 144–45). "Real men," it is believed, do not care about dress, whether their women's or their own.[7]

As Catherine Ksinan has shown, Wilde was not very interested in women's dress though sympathetic to women's rights. In taking editorship of *Lady's World*, he changed the title to *Woman's World* and lessened

---

7. Still, the modern and postmodern commercial realities of fashionable male dressing go beyond simple stereotypes. The postmodern coinage "metrosexual" denotes, as Mark Simpson explains, a fashion-conscious cosmopolitan man with disposable income. He may be of any sexuality, "but this is utterly immaterial because he has clearly taken himself as his own love interest" (1). Nevertheless, as Simpson's description unfolds, it becomes clear that sexuality is indeed material, since the metrosexual is a man who, at the least, aims to stylishly display his body. And for those who know the theories of "the Great Masculine Renunciation," Simpson's analysis sounds familiar: "The stoic, self-denying, modest straight male didn't shop enough (his role was to earn money for his wife to spend), and so he had to be replaced by a new kind of man, one less certain of his identity and much more interested in his image—that's to say, one who was much more interested in being looked at (because that's the only way you can be certain you actually exist)" (2). Who is this twenty-first-century narcissist, this existentialist dresser, but the dandy, reborn on the contemporary pavements of London and New York? As dandy, the metrosexual is concerned with admiration and display rather than physical or emotional contact. Yet the very label reiterates persistent anxieties over the sexuality of men who shop and show. In the fin-de-siècle, those worries were just surfacing.

the emphasis on fashion while including more literature and discussion of ideas (Ksinan 411–23). He hoped to make it an "organ of women of intellect, culture, and position" (Wilde, *Letters* 203). He supported the Rational Dress Society, a favorite cause of his wife, Constance. Unlike Mallarmé, Wilde's journalism does not emphasize women's styles, but like Mallarmé, he largely ignores clothing details in his creative writings. In Wilde's fairy tales and in *Dorian Gray*, if young men's sartorial styles are mentioned, they partake of the same glittering but indeterminate silks and jewels as those that adorn Baudelaire's muses.

The situation with Wilde's dramas is more complex. He wrote and spoke against sartorial originality on stage (Kaplan and Stowell 12), and we find generalized references to dress in *Lady Windermere's Fan*, in which Mrs. Erlynne "enters very beautifully dressed," and *A Woman of No Importance*, where Mrs. Arbuthnot is "the lady in black velvet" (*Complete Plays* 58, 337). The latter's pious mourning attire might have achieved a severe eroticism onstage, as Kaplan and Stowell suggest (26). But only when Wilde revised *An Ideal Husband* for publication, shortly before his death, did he specify "lengthy stage directions ensuring that thematic points would be made by stylistic and sartorial means" (Kaplan and Stowell 27). In this final play, he takes time to liken various women to artworks (*Plays* 109, 110–11, 112). And, strikingly, the adventuress Mrs. Cheveley is introduced by her ball gown of "heliotrope, with diamonds" (*Plays* 112): heliotrope was a known poisonous flower, and the diamonds include a much-discussed serpent brooch.[8] When she visits Lord Goring, she is dressed "Lamia-like . . . in green and silver," with a black cloak "lined with dead rose-leaf silk" (175). Thus her deadly allure is overtly spelled out, as part of the author's literary legacy. Clearly Wilde began to realize he might use dress to characterize morally questionable female characters; still, his dandy males inevitably appear in less individualized costumes (see Kaplan and Stowell 27). "All art is at once surface and symbol," Wilde had announced in his preface to *Dorian Gray* (41). His late dress-style specifications suggest that he was discovering the potential complexity of seemingly surface clothing details—a symbolism soon to be further exploited by certain modern women writers.

---

8. Evidently the ball gown was emerald green in the 1895 production (Kaplan and Stowell 32), but Wilde preferred that his shady lady look "rather like an orchid," a hothouse flower (*Plays* 112).

Most important, all of Wilde's plays demonstrate an aesthetic synesthesia, marrying clothing with concept: "a heart . . . doesn't go with modern dress," Mrs. Erlynne concludes (97). And this feat is performed especially upon ladies of questionable virtue: "There is a fashion in pasts just as there is a fashion in frocks," Lord Goring opines. "Perhaps Mrs. Cheveley's past is merely a slight décolleté one" (149). Mrs. Cheveley herself denies carrying a blackmailing letter with the simple sartorial observation that "a well-made dress has no pockets" (184). Such witticisms go beyond amusement, because the dress images touch the personal, perhaps scandalous selves of their subjects. But they go no deeper, because of their author's aesthetic commitment to beautiful surfaces: to the appearance of conventional morality, softened by sentiment; to happy endings, at least for the characters remaining on stage; and to the dandy's profound belief that style actually makes the man.

Yet Wilde's last writings suggest the limits of Aestheticism. In the rambling prison epistle *De Profundis* (1897), he acknowledges the failure of his self-styling. The man who had celebrated appearances asserts that "the supreme vice is shallowness" (98). The man who dressed and spoke as if all the world was a stage now blames himself for "being a *flâneur*, a dandy, a man of fashion" (151). The man who concluded his American lectures by dramatically whispering, "The secret of life is art" (R. Ellmann, *Oscar Wilde* 166) now miserably announces that "the secret of life is suffering" ("De Profundis" 161). But Wilde does not know what to make of these new insights. He does understand that his situation is modern, and "the dreadful thing about modernity was that it put tragedy into the raiment of comedy, so that the great realities seemed commonplace or grotesque or lacking in style" (183). Thus he remains preoccupied with symbolic style, describing his financial, social, and physical ruin through dress. He cannot aesthetically appreciate his own fall, he mourns, since he is not clothed in purple; rather, "Everything about my tragedy has been hideous, mean, repellant, lacking in style; our very [prison] dress makes us grotesque" (181). He conflates his prison garb with his new suffering, which he terms "prison style." Wilde feels deeply the contrast between a life of "beautiful untrue things" and real life, which lacks style. But from this disjunction he does not proceed as a modernist: finally, he cannot confront modernity.

Wilde's collapse concluded fin-de-siècle Aestheticism. His efforts suggest that a stylish male does confront a steep mountain of stereotypes, that modern fashion indeed is feminized. Nevertheless, Wilde's sartorial evolution, from flamboyance to cold precision, also prefigured the stylistic range of literary modernism. And just as he endeavored to make his life into art, so modernists worked to erase distinctions between style and substance—but with a difference: in embracing the natural world that Wilde consistently rejected, the new writers opened up their art to the small, significant details of life, including details of dress style.

DRESS STYLE IN MODERNIST FICTION

Despite recent efforts to define modernist literature by experimental form and radical politics, rips regularly occur in the theoretical fabric. The customary chronology (1900–1945) for Anglo-American modernism is arbitrary, and the more tightly we squeeze literary modernism, the more it escapes our grasp. An important instance lies in modernists' relations to nineteenth-century realism, which constitutes a key difference between Wildean Aestheticism and modernism. While it has become common to oppose a modernist radical experimentalism to an exhausted, bourgeois nineteenth-century realism, these narrowed definitions cannot withstand a range of critics who point out that modernism frequently co-opted and incorporated realism into itself.[9] Above all the texts themselves suggest that, as Susan Andrade writes, "much of what we call modernism was indeed realism in a new manner" (226): any effort at consistently dividing modernist sheep from realist goats ends in disarray. Astradur Eysteinsson catalogs texts that synthesize modernism and realism, including canonical fictions by Joseph Conrad, Ford Madox Ford, Ernest Hemingway, D. H. Lawrence, and especially James Joyce (117–18). Most important for this study, many modernists, in using mundane details—as realists did—to connect their art to actual history, diverged strikingly from Wilde's celebration of artifice.

Also notable is that the narrowed descriptions of modernism do not serve the quotidian, material subject of dress. Likewise, much modern literature by women is problematized by stringent modernist definitions: as Nancy Paxton notes, until recently even the very high-modernist

---

9. See, for example, thinkers ranging from Frederic Jameson on "cognitive mapping" (277–79, 286–87) to Erich Auerbach on Woolf (463–78). Astradur Eysteinsson critically investigates the generic dichotomizing of realism and modernism (182–90).

Woolf was frequently, because of her "socialist feminism," assigned a place outside modernism (8). For that matter, although modernism's boundaries are indistinct, high modernism is easier to identify. High modernists, who created their most famous texts between 1910 and 1930, were sometimes politically radical and sometimes conservative, while often stylistically avant-garde. What they shared was an abiding belief in the huge importance of their art for modern society. Yet again, neither fashion nor females fit comfortably into the master narrative of high modernism.

This chapter began with modern modes of dress: Joyce's Stephen Dedalus, despite being a rebellious young artist, wears black because his mother has died. The modern cultural elites of Paris, whether conservative or progressive, wore opera hats to ballet performances. It should be evident by now that these styles indicate the Western male's concern to be properly attired, not his enthusiasm for fashion. For most modern men, fashion was a feminine concern; likewise for most high-modernist male writers, dress style was not of great artistic use. Ezra Pound may have sported gaudy bohemian trousers, and T. S. Eliot was rumored to powder his face upon occasion—but such details of personal style were not sufficiently significant for these poets to include in their literature, despite the new penchant for the "image" and quotidian details.[10]

Male high modernists, even when they included details of clothing style, typically boxed them into certain gender stereotypes. For instance, Joyce's *Ulysses* has been called "a book obsessed with fashion," containing "more on-the-money descriptions of fashions in clothes, shoes, ties, hats and underwear than any ten realist novels" (Wicke 30). In fact the six-hundred-plus pages of *Ulysses* also outdo any ten conventional novels in their extraordinarily concrete details of Irish history, of Dublin's geography, of English literature, and of popular music in 1904—to list just a few elements of Joyce's carefully researched cornucopia. And clothing references, for Joyce, encompass familiar clichés. Male dress usually relates to status or money. Thus, when Buck Mulligan urges Stephen to accept the loan of "a lovely pair [of trousers] with a hair stripe, grey" (1: 117–18), it is one more sign of Stephen's unhappy dependence upon a friend's charity. On the other hand, women's dress is about sex, or romance at least.

---

10. In demurral, it is only fair to mention Prufrock's self-consciously detailed morning coat, necktie, and pin; but Eliot's insecure *doppelganger* seems concerned with propriety rather than fashion ("The Love Song of J. Alfred Prufrock" ll. 42–43).

Molly Bloom's frequent dress-thoughts are mostly of intimate garments and all sexualized—"[he] beseeched of me to lift the orange petticoat I had on with the sunray pleats" (18: 308–9)—though she, like the shop-girl, is struck by Blazes Boylan's "stylish tie and socks with the skyblue silk things on them" (18: 421).[11] Likewise, Gerty MacDowell's underclothes are extensively described, from both her perspective and Leopold Bloom's. Even when women's dress is not about sexual enticement in Joyce's fiction, it still is inescapably gendered, associated by Molly herself with menstruation: "whoever suggested that business for women what between clothes and cooking and children" (18: 1129–30). As for small fashion details, they serve to illustrate women's small minds, in particular Gerty's: "She wore a coquettish little love of a hat of wideleaved nigger straw contrast trimmed with an underbrim of eggblue chenille and at the side a butterfly bow of silk to tone" (13: 155–58). Gerty's self-admiring, vulgar terminology mocks trivial female minds; overall, Joyce's judicious use of fashion details carries a whiff of the author's deliberate dabbling in pettiness.

Of the famous high-modernist men, only D. H. Lawrence, in line with his personal interests in design and sexuality, endeavored to take dress beyond gender stereotypes. Lawrence describes female dress in *Women in Love* (1920) with detailed interest. Yet he also interprets these descriptions summarily, telling us that the rich clothing of the New Woman Hermione demonstrates something "macabre" about her, "something repellant" or "bizarre" (9, 150). And Lawrence famously used the sisters' stockings, variously emerald-green or grass-green (2, 6), dark green (75), canary-yellow and bright rose (106), pink-silk (147), pale-yellow (229), silver grey (376), scarlet (388), or royal blue (410) to signify their sexual attractions. In an odd little scene near the novel's end, perhaps truly macabre because it is on the cusp of Gerald's breakdown and consequent death, Gudrun and Ursula gloat over their hoard of Parisian silk stockings. They call them "the jewels," remarking, "One gets the greatest joy of all out of really lovely stockings" (427, 428). The sisters' joy in stockings may reflect their male creator's fetish. But their hyperbolic delight in accessories also appears as an infantile return, as narrow-minded as Gerty's "little love of

---

11. Ann Martin notes that Blazes's spiffy style may—like Mulligan's "primrose waistcoat" and desire for "puce gloves and green boots" (*Ulysses* 1: 550, 516)—be intended to align them with covert homosexuality (Martin 59–60). Clearly *Ulysses* appreciates the modern stereotypes of dandy-style. Neither Stephen nor Bloom is interested in male dress, except (sporadically for Stephen, automatically for Bloom) as a matter of appearing proper.

a hat." Thus Lawrence breaks with most male writers, by creatively using fashion details. But his well-dressed women, despite their intellectual mutterings, ultimately recall Baudelaire's paradox: woman is an enchanting idol—but rather stupid.

Meanwhile, modern women writers struggled both to resist and to transform the traditional stereotypes. Nineteenth- and twentieth-century male writers might safely ignore the topic of dress. But women were forced into self-consciousness, because of their traditional propinquity: should they acknowledge that vulgar old friend, Fashion—or cut him dead in the street? Progressive women had long debated the issue of fashion and their relations to it; its associations with stereotypical female fickleness and shallowness led some early feminists to disclaim any interest in dress. In Mary Wollstonecraft's view, "the fondness for dress, so extravagant in females, arises from ... want of cultivation of mind" (285). Half a century later, George Eliot would mock the *"mind-and-millinery"* species of "Silly Novels by Lady Novelists" (178). Indeed, Frances Burney, the Brontës, and Eliot herself typically mentioned clothing merely in passing. Of the pioneering female novelists, only Jane Austen, in the serene security of her small ivory worlds, took time to depict women shopping for materials, planning hats and gowns, making them, and self-consciously wearing them. Many women who wanted their ideas to be taken seriously were cagey about, if not downright hostile to, fashionable dress, and a feminist backlash against fashion stretched across most of the twentieth century as well (Rabine 59). Following World War II, Simone de Beauvoir sardonically commented on modern men's dream-use of women's clothing: "Les hommes ont supplié longtemps les femmes de ne pas abandonner les robes longues, les jupons, les voilettes, les gants montants, les hautes bottines: tout ce qui accentue en l'Autre le différence le rend plus désirable" (314) [For a long time men have begged women not to abandon long dresses, petticoats, veils, long gloves, high-heeled shoes: all that accentuates the difference of the Other renders her more desirable]. And in 1970 Germaine Greer would mock the lady of leisure who "totters about the smartest streets and plushiest hotels with [her mate's] fortune upon her back and bosom" (52). These classic feminists sought a high, serious moral purpose for their campaigns, one that seemed at odds with personal style.

Yet twentieth-century female novelists retained a desire to show what women's lives truly were like, including the petty details. And some women, such as Virginia Woolf, exercised their new freedoms through writing about dress. In *The Gender of Modernity*, Rita Felski justly warns against equating high modernism with modernity in women's lives and writings: "The works of Woolf or Stein, for example, may reveal much more about the specific context of the aristocratic-bohemian female subcultures of Bloomsbury and the Left Bank in the 1920s" (27–28). And indeed they may, but even Woolf's writings do not reveal any one consistent view on women's lives. Regarding dress style and fashion in particular, Woolf employed a multitude of perspectives and literary uses, far beyond those of her male counterparts. Modernity itself was "often staged as a crisis of sartorial representation in her fiction" (Garrity, "Virginia Woolf and Fashion" 195), and Woolf variously used fashion as a class indicator, a test for male chauvinism, a marker of history, and occasionally indeed as a sign of trivial female minds. Clothing also appears in her fiction as a consumerist prize, as a costume for performance, and—most intimately—as metonymy for the secret self.

Woolf's usages evolved and migrated. In *The Voyage Out* (1915), an early version of Clarissa Dalloway impresses the colonial British in South America with a white evening dress that makes the other women "look coarse and slovenly." In private, Clarissa critiques the other women's styles ("she dresses, of course, in a potatosack"), adding complacently, "They . . . think us such poops for dressing in the evening. However, I can't help that; I'd rather die than come in to dinner without changing—wouldn't you? It matters ever so much more than the soup" (43, 46). Clarissa demonstrates the imperial stereotype of evening dress as a mixture of feminine competition and Anglo-snobbery. But sixteen years later in *The Waves* (1931), pretty Jinny, characterized from childhood by her longing for shining, "fiery" silk costumes (21, 34), describes a mystery beneath formal dress:

> I feel myself shining in the dark. Silk is on my knee. . . .
>   I am ready now to join men and women on the stairs, my peers. I pass them, exposed to their gaze, as they are to mine. Like lightning we look but do not soften or show signs of recognition. Our bodies communicate. [. . .]
>   Among the lustrous green, pink, pearl-grey women stand upright the bodies of men. They are black and white; they are grooved beneath their clothes with deep rills. (101–2)

Woolf's later novel does not critique social dress so much as X-ray it: Jinny's attraction to silk is both frivolous and glamorous, exhibiting a prerational understanding that it is the communication of bodies that excites, bodies that actually are tinted and marked by their clothing.[12] The women themselves acquire the lustrous colors of their gowns; the men's bodies are comically "grooved," as if branded by their evening wear. And the idea of beautiful clothing that physically marks the wearer goes far deeper than Clarissa's competitive concerns.

In the twenties era of her best-known fiction, Woolf employed multitudinous approaches to dress style. The fashion concerns in Mrs Dalloway (1925) are, as many critics have noted, overwhelmingly commoditized, linked to shop windows, price, and class.[13] And yet Clarissa's torn green dress constitutes a nicely complex image for her own torn emotions and the rending of her complacent world. We also have Clarissa's memories of her youthful love for Sally, deliberately parodying traditional first love: "'if it were now to die 'twere now to be most happy.' That was her feeling ... all because she was coming down to dinner in a white frock to meet Sally Seton!" It is a cliché for the woman's dress in love encounters to be remembered—but since these are two women, the moment describes both dresses: "[Sally] was wearing pink gauze—was that possible? She *seemed*, anyhow, all light, glowing, like some bird or air ball that had flown in" (51). Sally's remembered dress is purely about Clarissa's feelings. That this objectification of the loved one reflects traditional romantic imagery, as well as suggesting a less traditional sexuality, should not blind us to its stylistic vagaries. *Is* it possible that Sally wore pink gauze? Such a gown would have meant a transparent veiling over a pink or white underdress—but all Clarissa recalls is the gauze, the exterior cloud that both beautifies and mystifies. It is an ecstasy of the gaze: where a women conscious of her clothed self, such as Jinny in silk, feels her physicality and acknowledges that of others, the ecstatic observer may choose the mystery of *seeming*, which glosses over the question of where the clothing ends and the body, the person, begins. Thus Clarissa's ecstatic memory echoes

---

12. One use of clothing that Woolf ignores or avoids is the lingerie that so fascinated Joyce. In line with the sexual circumlocution characterizing most of her fiction, Woolf presents clothed—not unclothed—bodies as alluring.

13. See especially Reginald Abbott, "What Miss Kilman's Petticoat Means: Virginia Woolf, Shopping, and Spectacle," Modern Fiction Studies 38.1 (Spring 1992): 193–216; Deirdre Flynn, "Virginia's Women and the Fashionable Elite: On Not Fitting In," Virginia Woolf and Communities: Selected Papers from the Eighth Annual Conference on Virginia Woolf, ed. Jeannette McVicker and Laura Davis (New York: Pace UP, 1994), 167–73; and Laura Gwyn Edson, "Kicking Off Her Knickers."

Baudelaire's fascination with *tulle illusion* and claims illusion as meaning—just as Woolf's impressionist literary style claims the halo along with the streetlamp.

If *Mrs Dalloway* plays with Baudelairean illusionism, *To the Lighthouse* (1927) suggests another commonality between the modern feminist novelist and the nineteenth-century poet. Woolf's most aesthetically concerned novel, *Lighthouse* probably contains fewer significant clothing details than any other of Woolf's novels, because it is about absolute ideals. Mrs. Ramsay's "Greek" perfection, continually alluded to, never is described. Her garb is little mentioned, and never in terms of style: a black dinner dress, for which her children choose the accessories, and a green shawl, with which she covers the boar's skull in the nursery (80, 115).[14] When her longtime admirer William Bankes first saw her, she was wearing "a grey hat" and "she was astonishingly beautiful" (176, 193). Sometimes Mrs. Ramsay's beauty is set off by "something incongruous": "She clapped a deer-stalker's hat on her head; she ran across the lawn in galoshes to snatch a child from mischief" (29). The transitory details of dress style—the man's hat, the galoshes—if not of fashionable style, emphasize the ineffability of her beauty. And beauty's indeterminacy makes up a major theme, which is why Mrs. Ramsay may be reduced in Lily's painting to a "triangular purple shape" (52). In fact, Woolf uses abstraction and generality to forward her theme of ineffable beauty. We glimpse pretty Minta as a rather daring dresser, climbing about on the rocks in "very short skirts and black knickerbockers" (74). But later, when Minta comes in to dinner, Mr. Ramsay admires her because "she w[ears] her golden haze" (98), a vague magnificence that—like Mrs. Ramsay's beauty—transcends dress. Like the generalized Beauty of Baudelaire's poems, feminine beauty in this novel acquires its symbolic power through eschewing stylistic detail.

Woolf did not remain in the Baudelairean aesthetic universe, however; she cared personally about fashionable dress, and she struggled to reconcile this concern with her artistic goals. Not only did she write for British *Vogue* in the twenties but she posed for a photo shoot, noting with a mixture of glee and irony, "*Vogue* . . . is going to take up Mrs Woolf,

---

14. This is not to say that *Lighthouse* lacks general clothing references; R. S. Koppen, as part of her "tropology of garments" in Woolf, reads empty clothing—especially the left-behind garments in "Time Passes"—as highly significant "material hauntings" or even, like that shawl, gestures toward an inhuman natural world (35, 155–57).

to boom her" (*Diary* 2: 319). Her notes and diaries frequently mention clothing, including her anxieties about what she called her "dress mania" (*Diary* 4: 229). Despite Woolf's privileged class, her elegant figure, and her dressmakers, she alternated between insecurity and satisfaction regarding clothing (Cohen 149–50, 162–64). She fretted about whether outfits would be ready in time, whether they would become her, and—after the fact—whether she had looked good in them. That is to say, many of Woolf's private remarks about dress style sound like stereotypical feminine clothing chat, supposedly dull to thinking women. Woolf herself wondered, "Why am I calm & indifferent as to what people say of Night & Day [her latest novel], & fretful for their good opinion of my blue dress?" (*Diary* 1: 284).

Appropriately, then, Woolf endeavored to dissect her own dress concerns: "I must remember to write about my *clothes*. . . . My love of clothes interests me profoundly" (*Diary* 3: 21). She did so in "The New Dress" (1927), in which a single woman attends a party given by that fashion leader Clarissa Dalloway. Unable to afford a fashionable new dress—"fashion meant cut, meant style, meant thirty guineas at least" (170)—Mabel Waring nevertheless has been caught in the fashion paradox discerned by Georg Simmel, who pointed out how fashionable dressing aims both at social inclusion and at making one stand out from the crowd. Woolf precisely spells out the dilemma:

> But why not be original? Why not be herself, anyhow? And getting up, she had taken that old fashion book of her mother's, a Paris fashion book of the time of the Empire, and had thought how much prettier, more dignified, and more womanly they were then, and so set herself—oh, it was foolish—trying to be like them. (170–71)

In her hopes to "be original," Mabel and her dressmaker create a retro-style Empire yellow-silk gown. The dress pleases her when she tries it on in Miss Milan's workroom, creating as transcendent a moment of being as any in *Mrs Dalloway* or *To the Lighthouse*:

> When Miss Milan put the glass in her hand, and she looked at herself with the dress on, finished, an extraordinary bliss shot through her heart. Suffused with light, she sprang into existence . . . the core of herself, the soul of herself. (172)

The dress creates extreme individual delight, but the experience cannot be sustained. At the party, Mabel feels that she is simply wearing an "idiotically old-fashioned silk dress" that suits neither her nor modern society. She concludes miserably that she has only succeeded in standing out from the crowd in the wrong way. And in fact the narrative gives us no impartial way to evaluate Mabel's dress. As Laura Gwyn Edson notes, "Woolf is moving away from a profusion of clothing detail as realistic description to an abstraction of clothing images which reveal psychological depths" (121). The story is not concerned with whether Mabel truly looks good or bad; it focuses upon her "wearing" of the dress. Just as Mabel's initial light-suffused experience of the new dress was deeply interior, so her party experience is filtered through a socially imposed self-consciousness. She becomes convinced that her dress is "hideous" and shows "her own appalling inadequacy" (170). She conceives a Lear-like image of people as flies, and herself as a drowning one (171); she privately rehearses her "weak" and "wobbly" life, resolving to forget about clothes and "become a new person" tomorrow (176). The extremity of Mabel's reaction might be comic, but her self-flagellation allows no space for laughter. That a dress can create one's soul, or drown one like a fly, is horrifying; as Lisa Cohen observes, in this story "clothes make the woman rather than revealing her true character" (157). Mabel Waring is a character truly constituted by *wearing*, and thus she enacts the extreme possibilities of interiorized fashion.[15]

"The New Dress" not only embodies Woolf's efforts to examine her insecure love of clothes, it also makes clear that she recognized a vast divide between male and female perspectives on dress. Mabel finds a female friend's assurance that her dress is "perfectly charming!" satirical, "Rose herself being dressed in the height of fashion, precisely like everybody else, always" (171). Yet she longs for praise from the malicious Charles: "if he had only said, 'Mabel, you're looking charming tonight!' it would have changed her life" (173). The women note the collective fashions,

---

15. The pivotal dress delineates the impressionist aesthetic, which centered on phenomena as received by the individual consciousness (Berrong 204). Burstein agrees with Mabel: "The dress is wrong.... [T]his is a fashion victim.... [I]t is the dress that betrays her" (129). But surely the narrative's tragicomic subjectivity indicates that poor fashion judgment is the least of Mabel's problems. Woolf's literary impressionism does not focus on things in themselves but on how people experience those things. Nor can we be sure that this story shows "the largely antagonistic relationship between women and clothing" (Garrity, "Virginia Woolf and Fashion" 202): it shows one woman's experience of one dress.

but male admiration is what validates one's style. Accordingly, "The New Dress" represents the gulf between women and men. In *A Room of One's Own* (1929), Woolf would warn young women that "it is the masculine values that prevail. Speaking crudely, football and sport are 'important'; the worship of fashion, the buying of clothes 'trivial'" (73). Thus it is important, she observes, that women not merely describe dress style but that they explain its significance: "say what your beauty means to you or your plainness, and what is your relation to the everchanging and turning world of gloves and shoes and stuffs" (88).

Woolf never fully resolved these concerns for herself. Near the end of her life, she confessed, "Everything to do with dress—to be fitted, to come into a room wearing a new dress—still frightens me" ("A Sketch of the Past" 68). Yet in her frankness, and her multiple approaches, Woolf is patron saint for the complexity of this project: fashion and dress, in fiction by modern women, serve as rhetorical instruments for examining desires. Nor is it surprising that the code of fashion style traditionally has been labeled a female enigma, one more version of that famous Freudian question, "What do women want?" Fred Davis has noted that fashion designers presumably succeed by forecasting "what women want" (*Fashion, Culture* 131), but as the following chapters show, modern women's clothing touched deeper desires than the mode of the moment. These writers discovered dress as a potential double-edged weapon, especially useful for the singular modern woman.

PART I
The Singular Modern Woman

MODERNISM CONSISTED OF STRIVING to "Make It New," according to Ezra Pound, but the New Woman was endeavoring to remake her world long before Pound and his friends took the literary world by storm. By Edwardian days this New Woman, the supposed bloomer-wearing, public-smoking, suffragist bluestocking of the late Victorian era, was notorious. Neither Dorothy L. Sayers (1893–1957) nor Jean Rhys (1890–1979) was precisely that archetypal female, but each benefited from the New Woman's example. Certainly independent and single women loomed larger in British culture as they pried open educational and occupational doors—and yet the challenges remained personal and urgent for women such as Sayers and Rhys. While Virginia Woolf mused about what women must lose and what they might retain in order to become independent and significant, the younger novelists discovered the practical difficulties for a female living and writing freely, even in the modern world. Both in their lives and in their fiction, Sayers and Rhys directly confronted the traditional categories for the single girl—saintly spinster, frustrated virgin, dangerous vamp—and they used dress style to signify her struggles.

THE CLOTHING CHANGES OF MODERNITY

Modern modes of dress, hugely changing from 1900 to the 1950s, are not a decorative flourish in the novels of Sayers or of Rhys, nor were they incidental to Britons' evolving views of women's capacities and desires. The stunning style transformations reflected shifting standards for womanhood. In a few decades, feminine fashions moved from the tightly corseted S-shape of the 1890s and early Edwardian era; to loose ragtime tunics and frocks; to shockingly short twenties flapper styles that exposed the knees, worn with shingled hair; to demure full skirts and coiffures in the thirties; to the makeshift homefront fashions of World War II, followed by the postwar New Look. When Sayers and Rhys were little girls, their mothers wore the high, rounded bodices and sleeves above floor-length skirts proper for their class and era. But neither child ever graduated into her mother's magnificence: by the time each was old enough to "let her skirts down," the old expression was nearly passé. Women at Sayers's Oxford wore plain tailored blouses and skirts under academic gowns. Fashionable women dressed in straight, loose sheaths, sometimes as short as schoolgirl dresses, during Rhys's footloose years in England and literary apprenticeship in Paris, and while Sayers worked in London in the twenties. In the thirties, women's dresses emphasized gently curved busts and bottoms, with neatly defined waists. The hemlines for Depression-era dresses, however, hovered just below the knee, so the decade's female silhouette was far from Edwardian grandeur. In fact, most dresses between the two world wars are in recognizably modern styles that, although not particularly fashionable now, would attract little attention if worn on the streets of a Western city today. So each woman experienced enormous shifts in dress style during her first fifty years of life. These changes are appropriate to restless modernity, but also quintessentially modernist in their one-way progression: never again, or so it appears, will women habitually wear the long, flowing skirts that characterized female dress in the West for more than one thousand years. And whatever the beauties of period costumes, the message for young women living through these transitions was optimistic: amazing change is possible, change that your mother could not have foreseen, let alone your grandmother!

Yet human nature does not change easily, and fashions never speak unequivocally. A Victorian grandmother might have warned that a dress style that bares the arms and legs will communicate sexual availability, and certainly an incipient sexual revolution accompanied modernity. Modern womanhood, however, was full of paradoxes. While the New Woman worked for change in women's status, and sometimes for sexual freedom, she was a famously frumpy, practical dresser. Thus Oscar Wilde endeavored, in editing *Woman's World*, to respect intellectual women by spending less space on fashion and more on ideas. Hence too the efforts of early university women to dress unobtrusively, despite their personal interests in stylish clothing as described in Sayers's letters and fiction. So it was not specifically early feminists but stylish women in general who supported the startling and sometimes sexy new fashions. An excellent example appears in the development of modern lingerie, which also suggests modern women's attitudes toward clothing their bodies. As Jennifer Wicke has documented, wispy lace-trimmed pastel underwear became all the rage in the 1890s, replacing traditional plain white linen garments; wealthy upper-class women bought the newly fashionable tidbits from dress designers such as Lucile. The stylish lingerie seems sexually enticing, and certainly the attractive undergarments were applauded by the men lucky enough to see them. But this new underwear was a fashion designed by women, for women, worn by many monogamous women, and never displayed in public (Wicke 27). Thus modern stylish lingerie cannot definitely be linked to modern sexual freedom. Rather, its popularity says something complex about women's relations with their bodies at the beginning of the twentieth century—and it shows how men often misread women's dress.

The meteoric ups and downs of the corset also warn us against oversimplifying what fashions communicate. Since the 1850s, advanced doctors had preached against the dangers of tight lacing, which drastically restricted the torso in order to achieve the fashionably tiny waists required by Victorian styles. Progressive women, from Amelia Bloomer to members of the late nineteenth-century Rational Dress Society, excoriated the discomforts and presumed health risks of the corset, which they also disliked because they believed it showed women's enslavements to fashion and men. Nevertheless, until styles shifted in the years around World War I, modish women continued to wear harshly restrictive corsets: how else to maintain an attractive silhouette? (We might compare the fashion for tight corsets to the medically critiqued but perennially stylish stiletto heels of our own time.) With the looser dresses of the teens and twenties, women still wore shaping undergarments, but of another nature: tiny waists were no longer a goal, but big breasts were unfashionable and just as uncomfortable to suppress. When the waistline returned in the thirties, so did corsets. But these corsets were girdles, gentler and kinder than the earlier stays. The newer foundation garments were not only suited to simpler modern dress but freshly advertised to appeal to independent twentieth-century women: rather than making her a slave to fashion, the modern corset customer was assured "that corsetry *gave women* control of their bodies" (Tinkler and Marsh 131; emphasis in original). Evidently a style that we might assume means "suffering to be beautiful," for men's sake, may appeal to a woman for private reasons, perhaps even reasons involved with managing her own life.

Certainly women needed such control in the changing modern world. Early twentieth-century dress styles occasionally made highly sophisticated modernist statements, but many modern styles arose not as philosophical or aesthetic expressions but as natural outcomes of modernity. As already noted, nineteenth-century industrialization had resulted in more bourgeois households and more upward mobility, thereby prompting more fashion competition, and perhaps the feminizing of fashion. Capitalist endeavors also provided cheaper fabrics, colorful aniline dyes (from the 1880s on), and the sewing machine, which helped create mass-produced clothing. These were material causes for fashion changes, not ideological ones. Likewise, modern history changed clothing: the First World War brought thousands of women, if only temporarily, into the workforce. They needed to dress for the job, whether office, factory, or farm, and many single women in particular suddenly had more disposable income. Again, it was material forces and exigencies that made women's clothing styles an issue during the Great War, as Braybon and Summerfield point out: "As their wages rose, working-class munitions workers bought smart clothes, and would not have dreamed of wearing their work clothes in the street—unlike the Land Girls, who took to wearing their breeches off duty as well" (75). When the war ended, most women lost their jobs, and even their peacetime positions were handed to returning soldiers. But the clothing they had purchased, and the lessons in independence, lingered.

In Queen Victoria's time, strenuous campaigning had brought about not only government schools, resulting in near-universal literacy in Britain, but higher education for women as well. Sayers, a member of the first group of women actually to receive degrees from Oxford in 1920, always considered herself foremost a scholar, beyond gender categories. Yet these early women undergraduates, as Susan Leonardi has documented, were continually critiqued by male students for their dowdiness—and simultaneously blamed for being distractingly seductive (22–25). Early female Oxonians knew that they walked a stylistic tightrope, yet they rejected university authorities' initial decree that women undergraduates must wear a male-oriented, black-and-white skirt suit under their academic gowns: such an ensemble was both ugly and impractical (48–49). Modern women did not dress simply to please men, and yet they cared more about dress than most men did. Each sex had difficulty in comprehending the other's perspectives on dress style, even when they followed the same profession.

Of course women's increased freedom was mirrored in fashions, but often ironically. As women grew in independence, they shrank drastically in bulk and outline. Hollander has pointed out that shorter skirts are not merely, perhaps not primarily, associated with sexual enticement. Rather, along with the very gradual incipience of women's trousers, shortened skirts showed that females have legs and can move under their own power (*Seeing* 153). Where women had been idealized as contemplative figures to inspire and admire, the sartorial unveiling of their legs showed that they could be as active as males (214). At the same time, thin became the ideal modern shape for the fashionable woman, a change that made her overall profile more closely akin to a man's—but also reminded everyone that women generally *are* shorter and smaller than men. In the 1850s, the very wide skirts had meant that a fashionably dressed woman could not enter an ordinary doorway on the arm of a man: he was forced to step back and let her squeeze through first, sometimes tilting her hoops sideways in order to slide by. In the 1890s and the Edwardian era, women's enormous hats had towered above men. By the twenties, however, skirts were short and straight, and hats tended to be tiny cloches. In sum, women's outlines became less imposing as they imposed their active selves on society.

Nevertheless, those active females were not permitted the same style standards as men, despite inching closer to masculine clothing styles. Coco Chanel's first successful designs, in the teens and twenties, were adaptations of male style for females: for her fashionable sportswear she is said to have studied her lovers' clothing rather than traditional women's styles. Even her famous little black dress was a planned equivalent to the male dark suit. Yet the black dress never became a female office uniform as the male suit did for men: women's clothing was seen, and still is seen, differently. Braybon and Summerfield quote a 1934 newspaper headline that used clothing to illustrate gender tensions over women in the workforce: "Better Pay & Smarter Clothes for Women: Unemployment & Patched Pants for Men" (139). The accompanying article suggests that women unfairly steal clerical jobs from the male sex, using their earnings merely to indulge fashion desires—whereas a man simply wants a job and a decent pair of trousers. From another angle, but in the same two-tiered universe, numerous fashion manuals advised women to dress with special care for their office work, since "a man's physical appearance does not affect his mental reactions as it does a woman's" (Horwood 47). And one *Miss Modern* (1932) offered the following anomalous advice: "When a man looks for a wife, she must have a nice taste in dress . . . [because her] clothes are so important to a man's success" (quoted in Horwood 59). On the one hand, women were rebuked for their frivolous obsession with fashion; on the other, they were constantly reminded that they had better dress well. Dress style did matter for them, even in the professional world, in ways that it evidently did not for men. Perhaps it is no wonder, then, that modern women sometimes showed contradictory attitudes toward dress, that Sayers alternated between male-tailored suits and glittery gowns, or that Rhys's fictional alter egos cynically dress to entice men, while wistfully suspecting that stylish clothes really do add value to the woman who wears them. The singular modern woman was not permitted single-mindedness regarding her dress styles.

CHANGING STYLES FOR MODERN WOMEN WRITERS

Modernity also offered an assortment of writing styles, along with a wild range of attitudes toward women as authors. Indeed, in part the range of modern fictional styles may be attributed to the original presence, if not the dominance, of women in early novel writing. Frances Burney, Jane Austen, Emily Brontë, Charlotte Brontë, and George Eliot are the best-known to us now. But hundreds more British women, ranging from the decorous Elizabeth Gaskell to the sensational Ann Radcliffe and Marie Corelli, published novels in the nineteenth century, many with great success. Ironically, women's very success would mean that, while they had been major players on the nineteenth-century field of fiction, they would not be seen as leaders in modernist literature. By the early twentieth century, the novel's status was being reevaluated. Most nineteenth-century novelists, from Austen to Thackeray, from Dickens to Eliot, had entertained frankly,[1] but high-modern writers of fiction endeavored to raise their stock to the awesome level of that poetry which Matthew Arnold had suggested "is capable of saving us."[2] And when fiction became serious art, the second sex was pushed aside—just as male couturiers, when they arose in the later nineteenth century, both raised fashion to a profession and overshadowed the women who traditionally designed dresses. By the fin-de-siècle, the vast outpouring of fiction by women was slotted into "women's novels" by "woman authors."[3] And subsequently the newly anointed literary doyens of modernism seemingly completed the sidelining of female creativity.

A few women writers escaped ghettoizing; after all, the term *highbrow* was applied regularly to the high-modernist Virginia Woolf. And it was another woman, Q. D. Leavis, who in her influential *Fiction and the Reading Public* (1932) most harshly attacked those "middlebrow" novels "in which sympathetic characters of a convincing verisimilitude touch off the warmer emotional responses" (58). By contrast the highbrow novelist, she wrote, creates characters "that do not lend themselves to fantasying but cause disturbing repercussions in the reader's emotional makeup" (60). Leavis's rather harsh categories—if you delight in reading the book, it is shoddily constructed; if it is preoccupied with morality, religion, or "religion substitutes," it is bad for you—do not single out women writers. In fact, she remarks that "the confusion of fiction with life and the demand that fiction should compensate for life prevents enjoyment of Emily Brontë and Jane Austen, among others" (60). The novels of the Brontë sisters and Austen famously have provided romantic fantasies for legions of women. Their appeals to women's desires do not keep those

---

1. A *Spectator* editorialist announced that "undoubtedly George Eliot is the only woman of our time whose writings would be remembered for their humour alone" (Anonymous 43).

2. I. A. Richards's famous summary of Arnold's claims (*Science and Poetry* 74).

3. The basic text for this shift is Rita Felski's *The Gender of Modernity*; for a variety of perspectives, see Ann L. Ardis and Leslie W. Lewis, ed., *Women's Experience of Modernity, 1875–1945* (Baltimore: Johns Hopkins UP, 2003). Regarding genre choices, Jane Eldridge Miller has delineated a striking sequence in the history of late nineteenth-century realism: first claimed in the 1880s by male writers, as a means of masculinizing the novel; then taken over by New Woman novelists in the 1890s, for the purposes of social commentary; subsequently then abandoned by the men, who searched for new ways to free their work from feminine associations (39, 44–45). Although it may be overstatement to conclude that "modernism, like the 'new realism,' was a reaction formation against a feminised mass culture" (Ledger 272), scholars of New Woman history rightly note the links between genre and gender disputes.

fictions from being first-rate novels, but the phenomenon led to modernist contempt for these fictions and has resulted in some popular masculine disdain in our own time.[4] Thus novels by women, which seem to break the rules for great literature, may have assisted in an arbitrary division between fictions that appeal to our desires and fictions that are high art. Yet certain independent-minded women writers gained an outsider's advantage by acknowledging the rhetorical elements of literary fiction—which is to say, they recognized that no text is exempt from issues of desire.

These modern, boundary-breaching women often included both high and low elements in the literature they produced, ignoring those who endeavored to use "brow" terminology to put women in their place. Nicola Humble even has redefined the middlebrow as a consciously feminine literary production, "dependent on the existence of both a high and a low brow for its identity, reworking their structures and aping their insights, while at the same time fastidiously holding its skirts away from lowbrow contamination, and gleefully mocking highbrow intellectual pretensions" (11–12). It is a wonderfully insightful dress-style image for the novelists we will read, who—sometimes in a mock ladylike manner—employ modernist styles eclectically. Of course absolute categories are inadequate for all modern literature, but they especially fall short when evaluating modern literature by women.[5] Women did write lowbrow fiction; most famously, Marie Corelli was despised in equal parts for her Gothic sensationalism, her moralizing, and the vast amounts of money her novels earned. In highbrow territory, Virginia Woolf and Gertrude Stein are only the most famous females; Katherine Mansfield and other women aimed at high-modernist status and often hit the mark. Jean Rhys, writing her early fiction under the tutelage of Ford Madox Ford, belongs to the highbrow club—and yet not perfectly, for she wrote in disconcertingly personal ways about female desire.

Dorothy Sayers, on the other hand, gained her greatest fame through a popular field that women were only beginning to enter. The new genre of

---

4. In *A Room of One's Own*, Woolf comments on the "narrowness of life" for Austen and proclaims Charlotte Brontë a genius "twisted and deformed" by anger (67, 69). As for the twenty-first-century masculine perspective on these great nineteenth-century novelists, one need only survey college-educated men: the very popularity of the various film versions of *Pride and Prejudice* and *Jane Eyre* have labeled their originating texts "chicklit," appealing to female fantasies—and therefore less than great literature.

5. See Janice Rossen, *Women Writing Modern Fiction* 2–4.

detective fiction grew out of the work of nineteenth-century male writers such as Charles Dickens, Wilkie Collins, Edgar Allan Poe, and above all Arthur Conan Doyle. Whether classed as low- or middlebrow by the new literary tribunals, detective fiction was regarded not as serious literature but as entertainment, on a par with the modern British craze for crosswords. Looking back in January 1941, Cyril Connolly would proclaim the literary world before World War II "a world in which, like a long sea voyage, those came to the top who could best kill time. . . . Wodehouse, Dorothy Sayers, Duke Ellington; the hobby dominated the art, the artists were artists in spite of themselves, or worked in second-rate and inartistic material" (*Horizon* 3:13 [January 1941]: 6). Connolly loftily assumed that artists who entertain use their gifts inartistically; in so doing, he demonstrated the limits of modernist categories, which proved too narrow for modern women writers.

THE SINGLE MODERN WOMAN

Modern single women writers were labeled in other, more personal ways, by their publishers and by the reading public. Up to this point, any woman's identity had been defined by her married or unmarried state. The traditional publishers' use of "Mrs." or "Miss" is instructive. "Mrs. [Virginia] Woolf" was a London personage; her marriage to Leonard, with whom she founded a daring small press, was part of her Bloomsbury persona. In her married authorial title, she followed in the steps of the nineteenth-century Mrs. Gaskell, as well as the poetic Mrs. [Elizabeth Barrett] Browning. On the other hand, an unmarried woman novelist of Victorian times might employ a male pseudonym, such as "Currier Bell" or "George Eliot." In the early twentieth century, however, both Sayers and Rhys used their own names, so that although each was married she was called "Miss" by reviewers, interviewers, BBC announcers, and readers. The title was a convention, and might even be taken as a badge of female independence—but the evidence for such a positive interpretation is murky.[6] Film stars such as Vivian Leigh were called "Miss" by way of emphasizing their youth, beauty, and pretended availability, but professional women writers were

---

6. This standard terminology also fed some amusing misapprehensions, particularly in the case of Sayers, who looked like the classic homely maiden lady despite her private life as Mrs. Atherton Fleming.

suspected of not caring overmuch about pleasing men and therefore of dangerously evoking the bluestocking and the spinster.

The spinster, that old-fashioned English character, had been a figure of fun and of pathos in the nineteenth century; yet she also had filled a recognized niche in British society. A Victorian spinster, while regarded as a pitiful anomaly, nevertheless had potential for a fulfilling single life: like Florence Nightingale, she might compensate for her lonely condition through good works. The traditional spinster was assumed to be sexually chaste, an admirable state until modern psychology pronounced it unhealthy. Modernity was ironically hard on the spinster; the new sexual theories placed single women in a bind, and new categories for females emerged. Previous to Havelock Ellis's shocking writings on sexuality, all single women had been called spinsters. In the early twentieth century, however, the spinster and the progressive single woman parted ways: the first was seen as repressed and warped, because she was sexually unfulfilled; she also was an objectionably old-fashioned relic of Victorian days. The other sort of single girl was adventurous, independent, and transgressive. Where celibate spinsterhood had been a badge of pride for some early feminists, a way of declaring their freedom from male tyranny, by the second and third decades of the twentieth century the popular perspective, and perhaps the definition, had changed. As Sheila Jeffreys puts it, "While previously the word spinster had simply meant unmarried woman, it was coming to mean, specifically, women who had not done sexual intercourse with men. Thus 'spinsters' like Stella Browne and Rebecca West were able to use 'spinster' as a dirty word to attack women who were not experienced" (175).

In fact, assumptions regarding sexual repression meant that the modern spinster was not only disdained but feared. In 1933, Winifred Holtby observed sardonically that traditional religious morality told women that if they sought sexual fulfillment outside of marriage, they would be punished in the next world, while "twentieth-century morality teaches them that the retention of virginity dooms them to the horror of insanity in this one" (132). For a case in point, we can see Lytton Strachey's *Eminent Victorians*, which examines Florence Nightingale through a modernist lens. Alternately amusing and shocking in 1918, the biography seems dated now, with its repeated, mock-naïve amazement that Nightingale was an occasionally abrasive "woman of action" (7). It is not surprising today to hear that the revered nurse was no sweet-natured angel but a "demon-possessed" person who dominated the men through whom she accomplished her great tasks (73). But behind Strachey's words lurk the new psychoanalytic assumptions of Bloomsbury, and modernist intellectuals in general: that a warped and repressed sexuality must have fueled the pious, unmarried Nightingale. The titillation lay, for Strachey's original audience, in the clash between residual Victorian beliefs about saintly spinsters and the new sexual theories.

Not that the adventurous single girl had it easy either, in the modern age. Her independence and employment options had increased, but public approval was scanty. The single girl with advanced notions of sexual freedom was censured, as Sayers would illustrate through Harriet Vane in *Strong Poison*: sexual adventuring might have been approved by the avant-garde, but hardly by most Britons. On the other hand, now that sexual continence was scientifically disapproved, a woman who was celibate by choice made both men and women uneasy. Human beings do not feel comfortable with vagueness or lack, and the spinster, writes Laura Doan, "is defined by absence.... What the spinster lacks is an 'other' to be defined against or in relation to" (5–6). Moderns thought they knew all about "bad girls," but what *did* the modern spinster want?[7]

There existed the possibility that she simply wanted traditional romantic fulfillment and that, especially after the Great War's decimation of young men, the modern spinster unhappily found herself one of Britain's two million superfluous women. Virginia Nicholson has recorded the remembrances of many women who lost boyfriends or fiancés in the war and, in consequence, never married. Because the First World War saw an unusually high mortality rate in the officer class, this war created an unusual number of middle- and upper-class spinsters across Britain. According to Nicholson, the phenomenon solidified many women's feelings that war had cheated them of "marriage with Mr. Right. Even women who in time married continued firmly to believe that the cream of their

---

7. Sheila Jeffreys argues for the incipient lesbianism of many nineteenth- and twentieth-century spinsters (106). But the issue is complex. Victorian and modern England contained many more middle-class unmarried women than available men. *Pace* Queen Victoria, modern sex manuals discussed lesbianism, in warning tones; however, the general public (instanced by Sayers and Agatha Christie) seems to have regarded two mutually devoted spinsters as an unproblematic and even charming aspect of English culture. Jeffreys herself points out that Ellis and Freudian analysts were limiting women, rather than offering them greater freedom, in assuming that a woman's single state must be defined by her sexual desires or frustrations.

generation had all died" (66). That generation of enforced single women not only lived long, fulfilled lives but made impressive accomplishments in science, in government, in social work, and in literature—achievements they might not have attempted if the male "cream" had survived. Nevertheless, if Virginia Woolf's Angel in the House still overshadowed modern women, so did the durable ghost of singleness:

> Twenty years into the twentieth century an unmarried woman had possibilities undreamed-of by her spinster aunts. But the aunts, with their wispy buns and ruined hopes, were still there to haunt her. The contempt and humiliation suffered by maiden ladies were an ever-present reminder of the spinster's predicament. (Nicholson 30)

For modern women, these aging spinsters stood as living warning posts for how society might devalue single females, even if attitudes were improving. "Do not tell me," Sayers wrote in 1941, "that things are not better [for women] today than they were. I remember my father's sisters, brought up without education or training, thrown, at my grandfather's death, into a world that had no use for them" (*Letters* 2: 300). And Sayers's fictional spinsters demonstrate how that memory haunted her.

In earlier British fiction as well, the spinster had been sidelined: she might be brave and pathetic, as is Miss Bates of Austen's *Emma*; she might be malevolently twisted by disappointment, as is Miss Haversham of Dickens's *Great Expectations*. But a single woman rarely is the protagonist, unless—like Emma herself, or Jane Eyre—she gets her man in the end. Even in modern literature the stereotype lingered, and in fact the early twentieth-century fictional spinster, bearing the burden of the new psychological prejudices, often is more laughable and superfluous than her older sisters. For example, Miss Charlotte Bartlett of E. M. Forster's *A Room with a View* and the repulsive, evocatively named Miss Kilman of Woolf's *Mrs Dalloway* are archetypal thwarted single women, threatening to warp the lives of the young girls in their care. Nevertheless, modernists were beginning to consider the spinster's perspective: Forster's Charlotte finally accepts the reality of young love, and Adela Quested of *A Passage to India* becomes (we are told) a good, enlightened spinster in the years following her stereotyped sexual panic in the Marabar Caves. Woolf too, after setting up an uneven contest between fulfilled married life and empty spinsterhood in *Dalloway*, celebrates Lily Briscoe's decision not to marry in *To the Lighthouse*. Moreover, at the end of her life Woolf would create the confident, if lonely and stereotyped, artistic spinster Miss La Trobe in *Between the Acts*.

The four modern women novelists of this study surpass the above writers, however, in writing novels centered upon the spinster's or single girl's struggles in society. Sayers, Rhys, Pym, and Spark each depict the single woman as perceiving subject rather than abhorrent or pitiful object; at the same time, each writer overtly addresses the demeaning clichés of singleness. As we turn first to the pre–World War II writers Sayers and Rhys, it is notable that although they were of the "two million surplus" generation, neither lost a romantic partner in the Great War. Nevertheless, they learned to be modern women in the war era, began their fiction writing in the twenties, and in the thirties consolidated their crafts. In the previous century, Sayers herself would have been tailor-made for the role of Victorian spinster: plain, pious, middle-class, and well-educated, she might have taught in a girls' seminary or written poetry and engaged in good deeds, like the literary Victorian spinster Christina Rossetti. But modernity offered more: an Oxford education, and jobs with a publisher and an ad agency, leading to a successful writing career. Modernity also may have prodded Sayers toward the sexual adventures which, prior to her marriage, enabled her to avoid the repressed-spinster stereotype. Still, her books reveal a deep sympathy with traditionally chaste spinsters, as with single girls of all stripes: she repeatedly proclaims that marriage is no longer a watershed for female identity.

In contrast to Sayers's upbringing, Rhys's unconventional colonial childhood in Dominica would have made her the ideal Victorian candidate for fallen woman. Rhys came to England as a teenager, with little intellectual aptitude but a good deal of beauty and adventurous spirit. She tried careers on the stage and as a dress mannequin but lived largely by the support of various male patrons, at least until she began to publish her fiction. Contrary to the ruined-woman stereotypes, Rhys did not remain in the demimonde; in fact, this single girl married three times. Most of her novels, however, describe the desperate lives of solitary women who survive by attracting men, an age-old profession presented in modernist literary style and with a purely modern estimate of the single woman's plight. Rather than marriage as the traditional happy ending, Rhys, like Sayers, focused on the challenges faced by any woman who endeavors to fashion her own life in the modern world.

CHAPTER 2

The Self-Fashioned Dorothy L. Sayers

DOROTHY L. SAYERS may seem an odd spokesperson for the stylish single girl. Sayers was not known for feminine beauty, and her only novels were detective fiction, a popular genre famed for elaborate mental puzzles. Yet detective fiction began in the nineteenth century, just as dress became a serious topic and Aestheticism started celebrating decorative surfaces. For Sayers, those surfaces were paramount. She saw dress primarily as a costume for deliberate performance; she also used writing to fashion herself a costume, aided by the conventions specifically associated with detective fiction and with scholarly work—both masculine genres when she began. Her work was, for Sayers, a refuge from sexual stereotypes: "I belong to a profession in which women suffer from no inferiority," she insisted (*Letters* 2: 368). More broadly, she employed traditional standards of objectivity to avoid intrusions into her private life. To a personal query from a PhD candidate she responded coldly, declaring that books should be read and evaluated independently of the author's biography (*Letters* 4: 16–17). Of course this scholarly ideal also may serve as a defense, and Sayers's gregarious surface masked a very private self, ironically fashioned after the modern male dandy.

Sayers as dandy? The comparison arises because her fascination with dandyism was so intense, and because dress style is frequently discussed and always gendered, sometimes angrily, in Sayers's work. Above all, in counterbalance to Sayers's devotion to convention—in dress, in fiction, and in scholarship—sits the writer's showy, attention-seeking self, always embellishing her fiction with dramatic flair, just as she occasionally indulged her characters and herself with glittery dress. The dandy also is an exhibitionist, though he may be strictly conventional as well: Lord Peter Wimsey's dandyism, which permeates these detective novels, partakes of that Brummellian correctness whose clothes are "a kind of rebuke to the world at large" (*Whose Body* 144). Wimsey also qualifies as a Baudelairean *flâneur* who, as Walter Benjamin noted, may justify his dilettantism by using his observational gifts as a detective (72). While the street-strolling flâneur and the dandy often are conflated, the boulevardier constitutes an observing subject, whereas the dandy stages himself as an object for observation, admiration, and envy. Yet in Wimsey the two roles unite, as in Sayers herself and in her elegant genre fiction. Also in the dandy tradition, Sayers showed deep interest in others' dress, especially the clothing of single girls in her fiction; as Christine Simpson noted, "some of [her] most vivid portraits are of sluts, of 'fast' women or of those masquerading as vamps" (3)— or of traditional spinsters. Eventually Harriet Vane combines the roles of free-living single girl and independent spinster, deliberately dressing for each part as her partner Peter Wimsey had done before her.

THE SINGULAR SAYERS

As Susan Leonardi has observed, the youthful Sayers always dressed to be noticed (52). The indulged only child of an Anglican clergyman, Sayers studied medieval French literature and became one of the first women to graduate from Oxford. She published two volumes of poetry before turning to detective fiction; in midlife, she segued into religious dramas and essays, and (during World War II) back to scholarship, with her Penguin Classics translations of Dante and the *Chanson de Roland*. In her entire literary career, despite the elite status of her first-class university degree, Sayers was a popularizer, not only in writing genre fiction but in her colloquial religious dramas and her translations.

As a girl, Sayers demonstrated a stereotypically feminine enthusiasm for clothes, accompanied by a theatrical streak and a love of cross-dressing.

To read her early correspondence is to be struck by the alternating possibilities of dress as self-revelation and dress as a costume for masquerade. Sayers's schoolgirl letters exclaim over the potential power of feminine style: "How *very* kind of *dear* Mrs Wilde to say I was good-looking!!!! She's completely mistaken.... It's only that when I am properly dressed I give a sort of spurious impression of good looks" (*Letters* 1: 63–64). She also loved dressing as a man for theatrical performances: a photo from her early teens shows the young Dorothy costumed as her favorite Musketeer, Athos, complete with moustache; she played Richard III at school; and at Oxford she became known for impersonating the Bach choir director Sir Hugh Allen. At university Sayers continued gushing about feminine dress: even as she completed outstanding scholarship, she wrote, "We have been ... talking about nothing but clothes all the time" (*Letters* 1: 74). Her biographer notes that during Sayers's Oxford days "the phrase 'my dress was much admired' occurs almost as frequently in her letters as references to her work" (Reynolds 45). This girlish chatter would be reproduced twenty years later in Sayers's proto-feminist novel *Gaudy Night*, where Harriet Vane and other Oxonians critique their fellow scholars' clothing: "that frightful frock like a canary lampshade" or the "awful woman ... dressed in a shocking shade of green" (10, 11). To the news that one Old Girl dabbles in nudism, a friend rather cattily remarks, "And her frock so badly cut. If you can't be naked, be as ill-dressed as possible" (24). To be not ill-dressed but "much admired" clearly mattered to the youthful Sayers, even to the point of exhibitionism: she was rebuked by the college administrators for appearing with a "scarlet riband" in her hair and large dangling earrings, each of which portrayed a red-and-green parrot in a cage (Brittain 106; Leonardi 52). In her early life, then, the role of properly dressed woman alternated with Sayers's playful enjoyment of costume's shock potential.

As she matured, the young writer became more deliberate in self-staging, occasionally adopting a dandyish assumed insouciance. In April 1916 she wrote to her parents,

> I have bought a pair of boots.
>   This is the real news of the week. A zeppelin has been brought down in the Thames, and my poems have been accepted by Blackwell, but the importance of both these events is eclipsed by my boots.
>   They have a black patent galosh, and elegant fawn cloth tops. (*Letters* 1: 122)

She lightly mentions war news and casually announces her first book deal—because, in the tradition of dandies from Brummell on, glorifying one's personal dangers or triumphs simply isn't done. Instead, one chats about clothing trivia. In fact, Sayers is consciously, playfully joining two opposed stereotypes: one, that of the small-minded woman who, no matter what earth-shaking events transpire, only cares about dress; the other, that of the dandy who pretends to be as trivial-minded as a woman while knowing full well that his sex entails an understanding of deeper matters. She confidently anticipates that her parents will file her comments in the second category. She does not need to tell them how excited she is about her poems' publication, any more than she later bothered to interrupt the dons' fashion chats, in *Gaudy Night*, to assure us of their scholarly credentials. As female dandy, Sayers upends stereotypes.

Nevertheless, the young Sayers was no coldly collected George Brummell. Certain early disappointments increased her use of clothing as protective cover. After Oxford, she experienced a period of poverty before her detective novels took off in the twenties. During this period, she dressed thriftily and a series of romantic disappointments permanently changed the ways she regarded the world, herself, and men. "I haven't had an evening gown for six years at least!" she confides to her parents in 1919 (*Letters* 1: 148). She might have mentioned that she was immersed in unrequited love—but clothes were easier to forefront: "The colour-scheme—passed with applause by Captain Whelpton—is most exciting—blue frock—red cloak lined with primrose, and black fur. By the way, I don't believe I ever told you about Whelpton . . ." (1: 151). Similarly two years later she masked the pain of her rejection by novelist John Cournos by cheerfully lumping together all her frustrations: "I can't get the work I want, nor the money I want, nor (consequently) the clothes I want, nor the holiday I want, nor the man I want!!" (*Letters* 1: 178). And in the midst of dispiritedly reporting on Cournos's lukewarm affections, Sayers pauses to explain her economical efforts at dress: "I've been having 'remnant mania' rather badly . . . I'm going to make delightful underclothing, all over little purple parrots!" (1: 179). This description typifies Sayers's growing association of income and clothing style. These comments also suggest an increasingly eccentric taste, as her fiction, her letters, and her essays from here on join financial, sexual, and sartorial independence. But the change was not easy. Long after their break-up she wrote reproachfully to Cournos, "If I saw you, I should probably only cry—and I've been crying for about 3 years now" (1: 218). For most of those three years she also had been creating clever detective stories, writing witty advertising copy, and constructing chatty epistles to her family. Her final letters to Cournos—unhappy, angry, and (unusually for Sayers) logically disordered—are nearly her last extant comments on her interior life, although she would live and write voluminously for another thirty-three years.

More than most modern writers, male or female, Sayers kept her private and public lives utterly separate. From Cournos, she rebounded into an affair resulting in an illegitimate son. While supporting her child financially, she kept his existence secret from her pious parents and from close friends, despite eventually marrying journalist Atherton Fleming, officially adopting her son, and attaining reasonable success and prosperity. Similarly, few of Sayers's many friends would know her husband well, even before he descended into mental illness and alcoholism, although she cared for him at home until he died in 1950. And her true relation to her adopted son, John Anthony Fleming, remained practically unknown until a researcher uncovered his birth certificate in the seventies, long after her death. Throughout Sayers's life, disappointment and pain were covered over with layers of social cheerfulness and industrious writing—as many layers as a conservative, well-dressed Englishwoman might wear. Not that Sayers's career, or her outward cheerfulness, were mere façades. In fact, her creative zest remained high, whether she was inventing advertising slogans for mustard or improvising costumes for her cathedral plays. But after Cournos, she ceased to confide her feelings: in letters, essays, and books she writes zestfully of criminology, politics, scholarship, or theology—anything but her private self.

Meanwhile Sayers's clothing style was evolving, in a two-pronged trajectory that suggests that to costume oneself may be a profound piece of self-fashioning. She always possessed a terse, supremely confident writing voice, identified by more than one reader as male.[1] Now a successful author in the 1930s, she began regularly to wear severe tailored suits complete with tie. Such attire had been an Edwardian New Woman style and remained acceptable if not fashionable garb for modern career women, but Miss Sayers's masculine dress seemed extreme. As Michael Gilbert recalls, a fellow Detection Club member would say after a meeting, "'Oh Lord,

---

1. Sayers cheerfully accepted compliments on her "masculine" talent, while maintaining that "the mind bears no distinguishable mark of sex" (*Letters* 3: 324 fn, 383). See Lewis's panegyric, quoted below.

one of the men has left his hat'—only to discover that it was one of Dorothy's many items of male attire" (16–17). Reynolds describes the middle-aged Sayers: "Large, square, mannish in dress (except on gala occasions)—flat shoes, tailor-made suits, a pork-pie or a wide-brimmed felt hat—her appearance from her fifties on disconcerted friends and foes alike" (349). In his 1950 painting of her, Sir William Hutchison shows Sayers not only in suit and tie but with masculine accessories of watch fob and chain, signet ring, and cigarette. With her monumental shape and short gray hair, she looks like a junior Gertrude Stein. Perhaps that is why her closest friends felt compelled to defend her heterosexuality, largely by noting that on gala occasions she still appeared in dramatic, glittery, feminine gowns (McLaughlin, Lambourne, and Reynolds 14–15). For every associate who recalls Sayers as wide, plain, and masculine, there is another to remember her in floor-length "shimmering silver," red, or dark-blue velvet gowns, with glittering earrings.[2] Other acquaintances endeavored to apologize for her unwomanly mien. Even C. S. Lewis, who knew Sayers largely through correspondence, at her funeral praised "the richly feminine qualities which showed through a port and manner superficially masculine" ("Panegyric" 108). Scholar Carolyn Heilbrun concluded that Sayers in later years simply felt "free to disdain . . . efforts of dress, cosmetics, and hairdressing," and costume designer Norah Lambourne recalls Sayers saying, "With my size and shape I am only fit to wear a tailormade suit" ("Biography" 8; McLaughlin, Lambourne, and Reynolds 15). But these explanations elide Sayers's comprehension of clothing rhetorics.

Both the suits and the glamorous gowns aided intentionally staged personae. Certainly the masculine attire in Sayers's portrait constitutes a deliberate statement to the world. In a 1938 essay, Sayers had used clothing to critique men's tendency to view women through the lens of sex:

> It is true that [trousers] are unbecoming. Even on men they are remarkably unattractive. But . . . they are comfortable, they do not get in the way of one's activities like skirts, and they protect the wearer from draughts about the ankles. As a human being, I like comfort and dislike draughts. If the trousers do not attract you, so much the worse; for the moment I do not want to attract you. ("Are Women Human?" 108–9)

---

2. See Josephine Bell (57); Mary Ellen Chase, as quoted in Heilbrun, "Biography" (8); and Reynolds's memories in McLaughlin, Lambourne, and Reynolds (9).

FIGURE 3. Dorothy Leigh Sayers by Sir William Hutchison. © National Portrait Gallery, London.

Although usually Sayers herself did not wear trousers in public, her comments explain one aspect of her mature self-staging: "I do not want to attract you." In middle age she aimed to avoid rather than to signal sexuality, which had not brought her happiness and which she increasingly identified with derogatory stereotyping. Indeed, although Sayers seems to have been attracted only to men, as she aged and as her marriage became difficult, she dropped that interest. She turned outward, to public writing and social friendships, evidently closing herself off from intimacy.

Her desires to avoid intimacy and gender stereotyping, however, did not preclude Sayers's lifelong interests in performative clothing. She eagerly participated in the costuming of her own dramas: planning, scrounging for materials in wartime, donating her own costume jewelry, and even sewing (McLaughlin, Lambourne, and Reynolds 4, 9, 10; *Letters* 4: 36–37). Her childlike enthusiasm for dramatic dress-up often went hand-in-glove with a dispassionate self-evaluation. To a request from Doris Langley Moore, founder of the Bath Costume Institute, she responded happily, "I will certainly 'sit' for you some day, if I should be any good; I've always adored dressing-up. I am rising 57 and rather bulgy in the tum, so I shouldn't do for anything elegant" (*Letters* 3: 483). Sayers listed parts she might play, including "a stout chaperon . . . in evening dress" or "an early Higher-Educated woman with a starched linen collar and tie and primaeval coat and skirt." She concluded cheerfully, "I should not in the least mind the costume's being unbecoming, provided it was something suitable to a stout middle-aged person" (484).³ For the performing Sayers, it seems all the world was a comic stage.

And for the dramatist Sayers, as Talia Schaeffer observes of the dramatist Oscar Wilde, "there was no difference between clothing and costume. Clothing was a way of dressing oneself for an audience, not a way of revealing one's inner traits" (45). In fact, Sayers's love of costuming resembles Wilde's dandyish theatricality. Like Sayers, Wilde loved to incorporate romanticized history—velvet knee-breeches, Cavalier hats—into his more outrageous youthful dandyisms (Schaeffer 43). Similarly, Sayers was fascinated with the historical details of dress. She clothed several of her fictional women in a medieval woman's style of flowing gown with long, tight sleeves and a square-cut bodice (Sayers and Eustace, *Documents* 46–47; *Five Red* 163; *Gaudy* 7); most notably, Harriet Vane wears a gold-tissue version by Worth on her wedding day (*Busman's* 11, 24). Like Wilde, Sayers drew no hard-and-fast line between drama and everyday

---

3. Eventually she posed as a suffragette in "formidable Edwardian hat and mantle" (*Letters* 3: 523 fn) in Moore's historical fashion show. A reporter described Sayers's costume as "the nearest approach to manly styles in feminine guise that could then be devised" (Winefride Jackson, n. pag.).

dress: when she spied a "magnificent full length coat of beige with fur trimming" worn in a production of *Volpone*, she "rushed and bought it" for herself afterwards (McLaughlin, Lambourne, and Reynolds 15). Her delight in dressing dramatically persisted to her life's end.

WHOSE BODY? LORD PETER'S DANDYISM

How, then, did Sayers dress up her fiction? "The dandies of literature," writes Jessica Feldman, "are often created by artists who are also dandies," such as Lord Byron or Oscar Wilde (3). Again, both Sayers's performative instincts and her masking uses of clothing style suggest dandyism. So do her endeavors to avoid intimacy, and the ways that she used dress to undercut gender categories. Moreover, her insistently asexual writing persona meant that she easily adopted what most readers assumed was a male voice. Feldman sums up: the dandy "is neither spirit nor flesh, nature nor artifice, ethical nor aesthetic, active nor passive, male nor female. He is the figure who casts into doubt, even while he underscores, the very binary oppositions by which his culture lives" (4). No one real person can be always showily feminine and über-male, purely individualistic and exuberantly social, exquisitely accessorized and yet perfectly unself-conscious in public. So while the dandy may cast into doubt his culture's polarities, he also projects his own longed-for self into a fictional ideal.

From the start, Sayers's detective Lord Peter Wimsey was "so exquisite a work of art... his spats, light trousers, and exquisitely polished shoes formed a tone-symphony in monochrome" ("The Entertaining Episode" 27–28). But Wimsey also acted a central role in Sayers's novels, and that in itself was new; for if the Victorian spinster had been a risible, pathetic, or sinister supporting actor in literature, so with the Victorian dandy. Only in the twentieth century did novelists begin to play these single figures for protagonists and the dandy become a figure of serious fantasy, with a mind deeper than trivia and a body beneath his sartorial splendor. While the historical dandy tried to reclaim for the male sex the self-fashioning made possible by dress, and often to disclaim any need for the opposite sex, in the early twentieth century the fictional dandy became a romantic ideal. The independent New Woman had long doubted that a masculine brute was the most desirable mate; accordingly a fresh, possibly effete but charming and nonthreatening hero appeared in literature, capable of winning over the most disgruntled woman. This mass-market romantic dandy usually was either a sexless, harmless Bertie Wooster or a manly man who, like Baroness Orczy's Scarlet Pimpernel, masked himself as a dandy to disguise his heroic derring-do. It was Sayers's genius to create a combined dandy and masculine hero who, if not perfectly plausible, complicated the new type. Sayers's hero possesses all the dandy virtues, minus the dandy drawbacks of narcissism and coldness toward women. Wimsey's wit and social graces, perhaps even his fashion expertise, make him an entertaining companion. But he is avowedly attracted to women, and his fashion concerns usually are presented as a playful performativity, like those of Sayers herself. As a bonus, Wimsey's noble family and riches constituted an especially alluring fantasy by the end of the twenties. And he is a multifaceted Romantic archetype, both damaged and desirable. Permanently marked by shell shock (from heroic action during the war), hampered by a super-sensitive intelligence, Peter Wimsey's flaws are believable while his gifts are incredible: first-class scholar, wealthy nobleman, linguist, musician, poet, criminologist, cricket player, diver, and international statesman—plus those superior powers in hand-to-hand fighting displayed by most detectives from Sherlock Holmes on—and, as he modestly tells Harriet Vane, not a bad lover either (*Strong Poison* 34).

Wimsey was not created as Sayers's own dream lover, however; originally he seems to have been her fantasy self. She claimed that she made him wealthy because as a young writer she was so poor: "It gave me pleasure to spend [Wimsey's] fortune for him. . . . When my cheap rug got a hole in it, I ordered him an Aubusson carpet" (*Letters* 1: 185 fn). Surely the luxurious security of Wimsey's lifestyle is part of his daydream appeal for many readers (as well as his repulsiveness for others[4]). And in his unfathomable wealth, along with his noble connections, Wimsey also breaks with historical dandyism. Most real dandies, from Brummell to Wilde, were self-made gentlemen who struggled with debt, a natural result of their expensive tastes. The original dandy even may be read, along with the rise of the dark suit, as an ironic marker of democracy. But Lord Peter

---

4. "Snobbish" is Julian Symons's adjective for both Sayers and her protagonist (108, 110), and see Ian Stuart on Wimsey's "ghastly glamour" (30). Not only socially conscious readers but many male critics deeply dislike Wimsey, which probably confirms the erotic elements of his fey dandyism.

Wimsey rejoined material substance and style, and in this he was both more real and more fantastic than his predecessors.

In Sayers's debuting *Whose Body?* (1923), Wimsey plays a foolish-seeming fop who cannot stop talking (e.g., 35–36). But the novel contains the full Wimsey in embryo: his self-mockery, his consciously artistic use of dress, and his vulnerabilities. Moreover, even the plot, which begins with an unknown male body in a bathtub and the disappearance of an important financier, suggests the ways Sayers joins dress and literary styles. The mystery plays upon the idea that all undressed bodies of like sex, size, and age are similar—a theme that ironizes the careful ways that Wimsey adorns his own body. He self-consciously prattles about dress, wondering whether to visit the corpse "in a top-hat and frock-coat? . . . A grey suit, I fancy, neat but not gaudy, with a hat to tone, suits my other self better. Exit the amateur of first editions . . . enter Sherlock Holmes, disguised as a walking gentleman" (13). Wimsey's self-mockery extends to deliberately costuming himself as a fictional detective. Sayers exuberantly dresses her dandy's language as he dresses his body, with innumerable small details and trivial witticisms that yet serve a practical point: "I feel so happy, I shall explode. O Sugg, Sugg, how art thou suggified! Bunter, my shoes. I say, Parker, I suppose yours are rubber-soled?" (35–36). His prattling monologues seem both self-skewering and vulnerable, excessive decoration rather than Brummellian negation. Crystal Downing has linked Wimsey's playful linguistic style with Sayers's own playful dress, as parallel forms of subversion: "While his creator spectacularizes the performances of the 'literal' by the way she dresses her body, Peter spectacularizes the performance of the 'figurative' by the way he dresses his language, often subverting serious conversation by throwing in garbled bits of songs, clichés, and verse" (50). Chatter typifies the modern dandy, and here it indicates that Sayers's detective is trivial-minded and silly. Moreover, Wimsey's chatter epitomizes his creator's decorative writing style, the verbal equivalent of those parrot-in-a-cage earrings: a glossy, colorful surface over an extremely conventional framework.

Those conventions required that a detective possess insights far beyond those of law enforcement officers or the general public; thus Sayers takes pains to emphasize that Wimsey uses dress to play the effete gentleman—a pose, as Heilbrun noted, intended to fool criminals and stupid, "manly" investigators (*Hamlet's Mother* 247–48). He also employs his style expertise to interpret the mixed signals of the body in the bathtub. Although naked, the unknown man is superficially well-styled: "The hair... had been cut and parted by a master hand, and exuded a faint violet perfume" (16). Observing the manicured fingernails, Lord Peter comments, "Bit of a dandy, your visitor, what?" As a connoisseur of male style, however, Wimsey soon notes opposing characteristics, including badly decayed teeth, ears full of wax, and "filthy black toenails" (30–31), which suggest the body of an impoverished workingman. Similarly throughout the novel, he observes salient details such as the color of a hair in a hat, or whether discarded clothes are folded neatly, in order to deduce whose body is whose.

Yet if this were all, Wimsey the dandy hardly could compete with the purely comic creations of P. G. Wodehouse, and Wimsey the detective would be another forgotten Golden Age sleuth, a one- or two-dimensional logic machine. Lord Peter, like Sherlock Holmes and Miss Marple, has become one of the immortals, ironically through his human weaknesses. Sayers's detective consistently demonstrates two vulnerabilities: a hypersensitivity, and recurring nightmares from shell shock. His sensitivity appears early in *Whose Body?* As Wimsey begins to deduce that something gruesome has happened to the missing Sir Reuben Levy, he first quotes a nursery rhyme and then proposes quitting: "Here's a poor old buffer spirited away—such a joke.... D'you know, Parker, I don't care frightfully about this case after all." Detective Parker responds shortly that Peter can leave if he wishes, "but you forget I do this for my bread and butter" (55). Dandyish dilettantes make witty jokes about death—but Wimsey, who will not quit, has a heart beneath his shirtfront. Later, Parker lectures Peter on his posturing: "You want to be consistent, you want to look pretty, you want to swagger debonairly through a comedy of puppets.... You want to be elegant and detached? That's all right, if you find the truth out that way, but it hasn't any value in itself" (121). Parker's speech morally dissects Wimsey's self-staging: elegant detachment is fine if it works, but dandy style has no intrinsic substance, no "value in itself." Yet it is suggested that Wimsey's insouciant mask is part of his complex self, and in fact the dandy's prattle suggests his ideal version of the world.

For even Sayers's fictional world is not ideal. Throughout all the novels, the hypersensitive Wimsey is haunted by knowing that the murderers he identifies will be sent to the gallows. In *Whose Body?* he hesitates when it appears that the culprit is a brilliant doctor who helps charity patients. Concurrently, Wimsey is plagued by nightmares of trench warfare, stemming from his war service (130–31, 162) where as an officer he sent men to their deaths. His squeamishness about capital punishment makes up part of Wimsey's androgynous sensitivity and in fact is highly unusual in a fictional sleuth of that era. No other famous detective—Sherlock Holmes, Hercule Poirot, or even Miss Marple—is so troubled by the likely fate of the murderers he or she discovers.[5] And Sayers frequently balances Wimsey's concern with calls for justice for victims: for instance, Inspector Parker argues that Sir Reuben was "an innocent and lovable man" (120). Yet this tension will characterize Wimsey to the very end of his recorded history: the last Wimsey novel, *Busman's Honeymoon*, concludes with him weeping in the arms of his bride, at the thought that he has brought another human being to death.

If this emotional pattern seems unmanly, so is the very realistic shell-shock motif. By the Great War's end, as Elaine Showalter describes, doctors had diagnosed 80,000 cases of shell shock in soldiers (168). The original descriptions of shell shock saw it as emasculating, making battle veterans weak, hysterical, and intermittently cowardly: "This parade of emotionally incapacitated men was in itself a shocking contrast to the heroic visions and masculinist fantasies that had preceded it. . . . Indeed, emotional repression was an essential aspect of the British masculine ideal" (169). The very phenomenon of shell shock shocked traditional British culture. But Sayers herself critiqued her culture's repressed masculine ideal: "The idea that a strong man should react to great personal and national calamities by a slight compression of the lips and by silently throwing his cigarette into the fireplace is of very recent origin" (*Song of Roland* 15). She insisted that men may show emotion without being unmanned.

Nevertheless, for most readers Wimsey's shell shock implied, as Gill Plain remarks, a bisexual ambiguity:

> As a victim of war, the Peter beneath the mask retains the emotional state loosely defined as feminine. His silly-ass persona, while outwardly effeminate, served as adequate protection against unwelcome intrusions, making it in effect a typically masculine defence against the danger of being seen to be less than appropriately stoical. (55)

---

5. For example, "'Sanders was hanged,' said Miss Marple crisply. 'And a good job too. . . . I've no patience with modern humanitarian scruples about capital punishments'" (Christie 165).

And clearly the complex gender welter augments Wimsey's appeal. To join masculine action with feminine response is to contain worlds within oneself: if weeping over condemned murderers is womanly, hunting them down is a ruthless male project. Likewise, if shell shock as a response and a condition seemed effeminate, going to war and surviving the trenches was the ultimate masculine adventure, and an unhappily real one for Sayers's original readers. In fact, Wimsey's symptoms are more realistic than many of his other attributes. Showalter describes the striking ways in which the condition fell out according to class divisions: "Symptoms of hysteria—paralysis, blindness, deafness, contracture of a limb, mutism, limping—appeared primarily among the regular soldiers, while neurasthenic symptoms, such as nightmares, insomnia, heart palpitations, dizziness, depression, or disorientation, were more common among officers" (174). As a former officer, Wimsey suffers so precisely from the second set of symptoms that we might wonder if his creator had studied medical records.[6] But shell shock was a famous scourge in post–Great War Britain, and the syndrome became a significant literary motif for examining masculinity and postwar culture, as in Woolf's *Mrs Dalloway* (1925). Likewise in Sayers's *Unpleasantness at the Bellona Club* (1928), George Fentiman is a damaged war veteran who must live upon his wife's salary; accordingly, his marriage is foundering upon his insecure sense of masculinity. Modern women writers observed that modern horrors were undermining traditional gender verities.

Not cold self-sustainer, but hypersensitive veteran; not empty-headed butterfly, but consummate player of the dandy role: *Whose Body?* holds the seeds of a later, complex Lord Peter Wimsey. In any case, if dandyism is about performance and ostensible insouciance, is it truly about clothes? Is it even about gender definition? Despite raising these questions, the

---

6. Or if personal experience played a part: depictions of Wimsey's shell shock often are attributed to Sayers's life with her husband, Atherton ("Mac") Fleming, who had been gassed during the war. But she met and married Fleming several years after introducing Lord Peter to the world.

Ariela Freedman finds that Sayers employs shell shock to confound "distinctions between doctor and patient, detective and criminal, hero and villain, virility and vulnerability, and the pursuit of good and evil" (366)—an overstatement, since Wimsey remains the traditional hero and Sayers's novels very much about good versus evil. Nor is it clear that Wimsey's damaged condition suggests "a social critique of war" (372), any more than his sensitivity to the execution of murderers meant that Sayers herself opposed capital punishment (see *Letters* 3: 164). But certainly shell shock was a common shorthand for the ways that World War I changed masculinity (see Humble 198).

early Wimsey remained a stereotype, an entertaining comic character. That Sayers's dandy detective would grow as the novels progressed, and grow into a person rather than a fantasy figure, was unexpected. Yet Sayers herself was changing as she wrote her novels. As she changed her clothes and masked her feelings, she wrote with more serious intent—and her dandy hero revealed more of his inner life, through the influence of a single girl.

SINGLE GIRLS AND SPINSTERS: *UNNATURAL DEATH* VERSUS MISERABLE MARRIAGE

> Why then do we associate spinsterhood with frustration? Bachelors are not presumed to be frustrated. Rather they are regarded as lucky dogs evading their responsibilities.
>
> —Winifred Holtby, "Are Spinsters Frustrated?" (1935)

To compare the dandy to the spinster may seem a study in opposites. The dandy was stylishly clothed; the spinster was traditionally dowdy. The dandy, whatever his exigencies, lived and dressed as a leisure-class member; the spinster, with few financial resources, often was impoverished. And, as Holtby's query implies, the bachelor (a category encompassing most dandies) might enjoy society's double standard regarding sexual mores, while the spinster was not only constrained by the rules of morality but then disdained for that very constraint. Single women knew, of course, that they were not sexless, however plain or aged. Sayers, even as she spotlighted her rich dandy, created numerous single girls and spinsters who are more realistic than the early Lord Peter. Yet they share some characteristics with the detective. Sayers's single females, whether artistic young Bohemians or conservative older spinsters, dress consciously for effect and often are hyperaware of themselves as performers—like Wimsey, and like Sayers herself. It is the married people in her novels who sink into oppressive relationships.

Sayers's earliest examination of single girls is in *Unnatural Death* (1927), originally titled "The Singular Case of the Three Spinsters," which not only features numerous single women (all three victims and the murderer herself) but introduces Wimsey's sidekick, Miss Climpson. This lady, in her pious imperturbability, prefigures Christie's Miss Marple as one of the first spinster sleuths in English literature.[7] However, while Miss Marple is white-haired, fluffy, and elderly—presumed beyond sex or politics—Miss Climpson is middle-aged, and she frequently refers to her own single state and the plight of aging spinsters: "I should have made a very good lawyer but... when I was young, girls didn't have the education or the *opportunities* they get nowadays... my dear father didn't believe in it" (*Unnatural* 26; all emphases Miss Climpson's). The spinster-detectives are similarly serene in the face of lurid crimes and possess a wealth of feminine trivia. "You will *excuse* the mention of *underwear*," Miss Climpson writes to Wimsey, "but wool is so expensive nowadays, and it is necessary that every detail of my equipment should be suitable to my (supposed!) position in life" (30–31). Although delicate lingerie has been available for decades, she knows that the well-to-do spinster she impersonates would wear traditional woolen undergarments (undergarments that Miss Climpson, herself a middle-class spinster, apparently does not own). To have a spinster masquerade as another spinster explodes a cliché: evidently all spinsters do not dress alike. The irony is important; as Sayers commented, the few women detectives in print by the twenties had so far "not been very successful.... Marriage... looms too large in their view of life; which is not surprising, for they are all young and beautiful" (Introduction 15). Obviously, Miss Climpson avoided the pitfalls of youth and glamour. The spinster detective, like the ostensibly effete male sleuth, showed unexpected resources and strength: she was "successful, daring, and unusual, [and therefore] the exact opposite of what society had deemed 'old maids' to be" (Kungl 82).

Old maids pervade *Unnatural Death*: the plot turns upon older women who live and die unmarried. A wealthy spinster dies in her bed, and murder is suspected even though the death seems natural. Chief suspect is the dead woman's heir, Mary Whittaker, a strong-minded nurse. As Wimsey, Inspector Parker, and Miss Climpson investigate, they repeatedly are puzzled by the lack of a murder method; along the way, two more single women are killed, a former housemaid and a young friend of Miss Whittaker. Various masquerades ensue, with both the detectives and the culprit playing elaborate parts. The only significant married character, the

---

7. Miss Marple debuted in a short story, "The Tuesday Night Club," in *The Royal Magazine* 350 (December 1927); *Unnatural Death* had appeared in print three months earlier.

mysterious, seductive Mrs. Forrest, turns out to be the unmarried Miss Whittaker in spectacular disguise. Miss Climpson elaborately plays her nosy-spinster role, ultimately nearly getting herself killed. And Wimsey rushes in to save his spinster sidekick just in time, staging a climactic dénouement that usually is stereotyped for the romantic female lead.

In fact, Miss Climpson as romantic protagonist is a running joke. Wimsey introduces her in a way that leads both Detective-Inspector Parker and the reader to assume that she is his mistress: "quite comfortably fixed in a little flat in Pimlico . . . the arrangement's only been going a few months" (21–22). Much to the relief of the strait-laced Parker, Wimsey's kept woman turns out to be a thin, middle-aged person with iron-grey hair "under a net, in the style fashionable in the reign of the late King Edward" (23). Obviously her utility is not sexual, and Wimsey explains in a speech excoriating "the wasteful way in which this country is run. . . . Thousands of old maids, simply bursting with useful energy, forced by our stupid social system into hydros and hotels and communities and hostels and posts as companions" (28). He has organized and bankrolled a detective agency called the "Cattery" (another sex joke), made up of single women and headed by Miss Climpson. Her secret talent is the spinster style that masks her detection, a style summed up by Wimsey as "a long, woolly jumper on knitting needles and jingly things round her neck. Of course she asks questions—everyone expects it." Still, he persistently jokes about the spinster as erotic object. "One of these days they will put up a statue to me, with an inscription," he says:

> To the Man who Made
> Thousands of Superfluous Women Happy
> Without Injury to their Modesty
> or Exertion to Himself. (29)

Again, Sayers raises the issue of single women's sexuality: is it so absent that one can make jokes upon it? That very absence becomes the novel's theme.

For if sexual desire is present in a spinster, is it (as scientists of the day had it) an unnatural sexual bent? *Unnatural Death* alone among Sayers's novels depicts lesbians frankly, especially for a popular novel of the twenties. The murderer is lesbian, insofar as she exhibits any sexual tendencies, and in recent years critics have inquired whether Sayers makes Miss

Whittaker especially monstrous because of her sexuality.[8] The novel's perspective on homosexuality is mixed. Miss Climpson warns young Vera of the dangers of being *schwärmerisch:* "I cannot help feeling that it is more natural—more proper, in a sense—for a man and woman to be all in all to one another than for two persons of the same sex" (171). Vera ignores her and proceeds with her plans to live with Miss Whittaker, who then callously murders her young companion. But the novel complicates this ugly picture by also depicting a devoted pair of older women. The initial murder victim, Agatha Dawson, had been the surviving partner. Agatha and Clara are remembered as "a remarkable pair of old ladies," and an elderly countryman sums up his attitude toward such women: "The Lord makes a few on 'em that way to suit 'Is own purposes" (125, 128). Miss Climpson writes tolerantly, "In her day [Clara] was considered very 'advanced' and *not quite nice* (!) because she *refused* several *good offers*, cut her hair SHORT(!!) and set up in business for herself as a HORSE-BREEDER!!! Of course, *nowadays*, nobody would think anything of it" (77). By focusing on details of style, Miss Climpson can celebrate the Victorian spinster Clara's independence from men as a sign of approaching modernity.

Lesbianism in the novel makes up only one facet of Sayers's study of "superfluous women": if the spinster is defined by what she lacks, *nothing* is this spinster-novel's theme, and the key to the murders. "I can't manufacture evidence out of nothing," Wimsey protests near the end. "I've built you up a case out of nothing" (202). In fact, the elusive murder method turns out to be "nothing"—a bubble of air in a syringe, which kills quickly and leaves no traces. The real-life efficacy of this method has been debated, but as symbol, "nothing" in the syringe is effective. In the climactic scene where the murderer-spinster Whittaker, disguised as Mrs. Forrest, tries to murder the detective-spinster Climpson with a syringe, Wimsey explains dramatically, "There is—nothing in it" (261), referring to more than the hypodermic. Mrs. Forrest has been an enigma to the sleuths, comically unrecognizable as their chief suspect. Where Mary Whittaker wears "beautifully tailored" suits (45), the ostensible divorcée is showy and tasteless, "over-dressed, musquash and those abbreviated sort of shoes with jeweled heels and hardly any uppers" (66). Crucially for the plot, however, not even the style-sensitive Wimsey sees until

---

8. See Leonardi (64); Morris, "Arsenic and Blue Lace: Sayers' Criminal Women," *passim;* and Kenney (128).

the end that Mrs. Forrest herself is nothing, a false identity created by costume, makeup, and wig. The mental disjunction created by two opposing female styles has been cemented in their minds by a similar disconnect between single girl and married woman—even though Wimsey already had discovered that Mrs. Forrest is not the experienced woman she plays. He senses that, despite her seductive costume and behavior, she is "spinsterish," and his impression is confirmed when he kisses her and feels her shrink in revulsion (163, 164). Wimsey concludes that "the Great It" is lacking in her; she is "something essentially sexless" (163)—which is to say, a woman without interest in men lacks a vital ingredient.

Finally, *Unnatural Death* asks what is natural and unnatural: In death (since death from a bubble of air might seem very natural)? In sexuality? In female behavior? "When a woman is wicked and unscrupulous," Parker sermonizes, "she is . . . fifty times worse than a man" (226). Although Mary Whittaker is described as "well-educated" (7), she is a nurse and did not matriculate in a university; at one point the exasperated Wimsey refers to the suspect as "this half-trained girl out of a hospital" (252). Nevertheless, *Unnatural Death* is all about the "Woman Question" (Kenney 128), which includes heavily fraught issues of sexuality. Lesbian or not, the woman lacking a man is presented as an unnatural being—despite assurances from Wimsey that spinsters can be intelligent and useful. Still, the novel cannot draw any conclusions but anxiety and despair over the condition of society.

Appropriately, then, the plot concludes with the self-strangled body of Mary Whittaker and two opposing summations about the unnatural. The conventional Parker remarks, "An evil woman, if ever there was one," but his comment is not the final word. "Wimsey said nothing. He felt cold and sick" (264). As *nothing* was the mystery's key, so nothing can be pronounced in conclusion. In this final paragraph, Sayers's detective is developing his customary post-case jitters when an unexpected event abruptly ends the narrative. They step outside "into a wan and awful darkness," which leads the overwrought Wimsey to ask if the world is coming to an end. No, Parker reassures him, it is merely a solar eclipse. Where the death of the murderer, one of Sayers's most bloody-minded culprits, might be cathartic, it leads instead to apocalyptic darkness. Miss Climpson, whose insights and courage finally cracked the mystery, has disappeared with no final word—appropriately, perhaps. For the spinster detective, like all single girls, is outside the normal framework of her society: she may help cure its ills, but she also unsettles it. As Marion Shaw and Sabine

Vanacker have noted, even cozy Miss Marple may inspire fear: "The spinster is moral arbiter, curb of license and disorder, and image of repression; she is also what lies outside the normal expectations of a woman's life as it is lived in patriarchal society and although this diminishes her it also gives her the power of the abnormal over the normal, to threaten, to judge, to undermine and to destroy" (43). This sense of nemesis is implicit in *Unnatural Death*'s concluding eclipse, an unnatural natural phenomenon.

If the spinster remains unnatural in Sayers's early fictional world (despite Wimsey's efforts to employ surplus women), is marriage, then, the ideal state? Surprisingly Sayers's novels of the late twenties, all written during her early married life, feature miserable, mismatched, and even murderous marriages. *Clouds of Witness* (1927) leads up to the spectacular murder trial of Wimsey's hapless older brother, the Duke of Denver, married to "a long-necked, long-backed woman who disciplined her children and her hair" (36). Their marriage is unhappy, but the situation of the Duke's mistress, tied to an abusive husband, is more dire. Moreover, the case turns on the death of a man who had been planning a *mariage de convenance* with Wimsey's sister Mary. In this novel, human beings appear remarkably inept at choosing partners. So with her husband gone at the end, the Duke's beautiful, battered mistress simply walks away from him, into a London shop to buy new clothes, "her own woman at last" (285, 286). Likewise *The Unpleasantness at the Bellona Club*, along with the miserable Fentiman marriage, introduces plain, capable Ann Dorland, whose hopes of love are thwarted when the murderer accuses her of stalking him because of her "mania about sex" (308). Probably Sayers's most painful depiction of her younger self, this single girl is pitiable but not likable, and Wimsey is kind but implausible when he assures her that she will some day find a "man of the world" who will appreciate her intelligence (322). More convincing is his remark about the Fentimans: "It always gives me the pip to see how rude people are when they're married. I suppose it's inevitable" (105). And married people may be worse than rude: in *The Documents in the Case* (1930), a silly wife manipulates her lover into poisoning her husband. Sayers peripherally suggests progressive ideals for marriage: the Gentile Freddy Arbuthnot espouses Rachel Levy, and middle-class Detective Parker courts Wimsey's aristocratic sister. Most significantly, *Documents* is narrated through epistles from a writer to his novelist fiancée, whose interchanges suggest a marriage of equals. Sayers was considering "marrying Peter off"—to a single girl who would change his style.

SINGLE GIRL CHANGES DANDY'S CLOTHES: FROM *STRONG POISON* TO *GAUDY NIGHT*

Both detective fiction and fashionable dress fascinate their audiences through a sophisticated use of viewpoint, one of the classic detective writer's most important skills. The mystery writer designs her fictions' surfaces for manipulation of perspective, an effect that Sayers claimed involved "the whole artistic ethos of the detective story" (Introduction 14). She refers to the ways in which clues are laid out fairly, while the detective's insights remain hidden until the mystery's dénouement. But in the world of fashion, the gulf between viewer and object remains sacrosanct: a dressed figure keeps her secrets, since the value of sartorial style lies in its surfaces. We do not inquire into what the runway model thinks of the dress buyer, whatever our personal self-consciousness about clothing. Like the detective's ratiocinations, much of the model's appeal lies in her evident perfection, that impenetrable veneer very close to the higher plane where the dandy dwells. And we know that Sayers enjoyed displaying glittering surfaces, in dress and in fiction.

What happens, however, when the object of awe changes, when the dandy strips or the detective bares his soul? This disconcerting display is what Sayers achieved in the Wimsey-Vane books. In style, these novels become more complex, less smoothly conventional entertainment. In content, they satirize the modes often presumed to characterize the thirties: a socially conservative reemphasis on marriage for women, and a commensurate return to more "womanly" fashions (Rowbotham 120–25; Buckley and Fawcett 93–95). For single girls, career ambitions or job necessities warred with traditionalist trends, and they persisted despite male grumbles. "The ladies were most adorable," complains a chief clerk in *Strong Poison*, "when they adorned and inspired and did not take an active part in affairs." Wimsey accurately interprets his remark to mean that the clerk is "anti-sex-appeal" and likely to hire a typist with skirts "the regulation four inches below the knee" (75). Likewise Harriet, a long-liberated single girl, observes retrogressive feminine styles on the dance floor with a jaded eye:

> Long skirts and costumes of the 'seventies were in evidence—and even ostrich feathers and fans... but it was so obviously an imitation. The slender-seeming waists were made so, not by savage tight-lacing, but by sheer expensive dressmaking. To-morrow, on the tennis-court, the short,

loose tunic-frock would reveal them as the waists of muscular young women of the day, despising all bonds . . . masks, only. If this was the "return to womanliness" hailed by the fashion-correspondents, it was to a quite different kind of womanliness—set on a basis of economic independence. (*Have His Carcase* 37–38)

Harriet sees the decade's return to conservative feminine style as playacting, or perhaps a gender contest with marriage as the goal.

Harriet starts as a detective-story writer living in 1920s Bloomsbury. As a mystery writer, she is so obviously a version of Sayers herself—for instance, not pretty but possessing a beautiful voice[9]—that the author has been suspected of inventing a fantasy means to wed her beloved detective. But in fact, Sayers initially found Peter unworthy of her single girl. She confessed later that she had planned to use *Strong Poison* (1930) to marry off Wimsey and so be rid of him, in the best marriage-plot tradition. Instead, Sayers found that her "puppets" could not be forced: "I could not marry Peter off to the young woman he had (in the conventional Perseus manner) rescued from death and infamy, because I could find no form of words in which she could accept him without loss of self-respect" ("Gaudy Night" 79). Harriet Vane herself, once animated, was a character too independent for a fairy tale. Rather, in several more novels, Sayers's characters inched toward marriage over a real-time period of seven years, during which she changed both Wimsey and her readers' perspectives.

Accordingly, change is a theme throughout *Strong Poison*: changes in point of view intertwine with changes in clothing style in ways that make Wimsey less a dandy and more a fully characterized man. The typical dandy may seem to sympathize with women better than the average man, but he is slumming in the feminine world. As Rita Felski observes of the modernist Aesthete, his "playful subversion of gender norms and adoption of feminine traits paradoxically reinforce his distance from and superiority to women, whose nature renders them incapable of this kind of free-floating semiotic mobility" (106). He does not have to worry about the constraints that affect women. But Wimsey learns to take those constraints seriously when he undertakes to defend Harriet against murder charges. She is on trial for poisoning her former lover, novelist Philip Boyes; she is in danger

---

9. See *Strong Poison* 41; Heilbrun, "Biography" 8.

of being convicted, largely because of public disdain for her morals and because most men do not understand her independent spirit. Although already on Harriet's side, since he is in love with her, Wimsey comes to experience the helplessness that accompanies unacknowledged gender stereotypes, and he relinquishes the careless impermeability of the dandy.

When Harriet appears, the narrative emphasis on Wimsey's clothing lessens, while we gradually hear more of her personal style. Even Lord Peter's person seems to change. In *Whose Body?* Sayers had introduced him as comically repulsive: "His long, amiable face looked as if it had generated spontaneously from his top hat, as white maggots breed from Gorgonzola" (7). But at their initial meeting, Harriet assures Peter that he doesn't "remind [her] of white slugs" (*Strong Poison* 39). Still, in light of his newfound passion, Wimsey sees his whole person as inadequate. From his first interview with Harriet, when he comes away exclaiming to himself, "Her skin is like honey—she ought to wear dark red and old garnets—" (47), he changes from an entertaining object to a perceiving subject, more interested in dressing her than himself. Descriptions of Wimsey's personal style in this novel reverberate with a new self-criticism. "I know I've got a silly face," he tells Harriet apologetically; he has dressed with great care to meet her, and he casts his courtship comically in terms of style: "I'll come in a different set of garments each time, so as to give you a good all-round idea of the subject" (45, 47). As the newly in-love dandy leaves the jail, he stops to view himself in a shop window: "I wonder if Bunter was right about this suit." He sees instead a sign, "ONE MONTH ONLY," and is sharply returned to Harriet and her plight (48). Never again will Wimsey idly display himself along the boulevards, enjoying his mirrored reflection. No longer does he perform as upon a stage: now the reader alternately moves in and out of his mind, observing his insecurities. After Bunter discloses that he knows Wimsey is in love, the detective hurries to gaze at himself in a mirror, muttering, "I can't see anything" (79). He dresses with anxiety. "Please don't alter yourself in any particular," says Harriet politely (47), and Wimsey's friend Marjorie urges him to remain the insouciant dandy: "Don't alter, will you?" Wimsey's response is to quote—but, significantly, only in his head—a poisoned character from Renaissance tragedy: "Oh, I am changing, changing, fearfully changing" (89). The allusion makes clear that "strong poison" refers not only to arsenical murder but to Wimsey's new-felt love. And the mirror recurs significantly, in another solitary scene where Wimsey views himself as object:

> He saw a fair, foolish face, with straw-colored hair sleeked back; a monocle clinging incongruously under a ludicrously twitching brow; a chin shaved to perfection, hairless, epicene; a rather high collar, faultlessly starched, a tie elegantly knotted and matching in color the handkerchief which peeped coyly from the breast-pocket of an expensive Savile-Row-tailored suit. (162)

For the first and last time, terms such as *ludicrous* and *epicene* are applied to Wimsey. He wants to smash the mirror, destroying his own futile image—but Sayers will do that for him.

Strong Poison reveals more self-doubt in Wimsey than any of the other novels: before emerging as fully rounded, he must be stripped of confidence and experience a traditionally feminine vulnerability. Meanwhile, as Wimsey wallows in frustrated helplessness, his "Harem" for old maids' wasted talents seems to run itself, with little control from the patron (40), and Miss Climpson and her deputy Miss Murchison handle most of the detective work. Glorying in the clichés, Miss Climpson adopts an elderly spinster ugliness, wearing a mackintosh and black petticoats with pockets, "garments . . . of a useful and old-fashioned kind" (36, 207, 213). Like other eccentric, independent women of the time pretending to be a medium, Miss Climpson stages an elaborate séance in order to find a missing will, hiding a spiritualist's devices under those useful petticoats. Meanwhile, in equally exuberant self-parody, Miss Murchison chews gum, plays with purses, and generally pretends to be an ignorant typist in order to secretly search her boss's office. Thus *Strong Poison* reverses gender stereotypes: Sayers's detective hero is passive and vulnerable, while the women run the investigation and his "helpless" beloved refuses to marry him. Yet Wimsey becomes more fully developed even as Harriet comes to the forefront.

Have His Carcass (1932) sustains that disjunction between the would-be lovers, through an emphasis on bodies and dressing for display. It opens with Harriet on a solitary walking tour, simultaneously demonstrating her emotional and her financial independence. Since she prefers "convenience to outward display," she wears a sensible skirt and sweater, while carrying no skin creams or silk frocks in her pack (10). Yet this novel continually challenges that sensible independence, in a mystery that turns upon lonely aging women, gigolos, and the issues of money and independence that rule them. When Harriet discovers the "rather over-elegant" Paul

Alexis with his throat cut, we are given shadow images for Wimsey and herself: the overdressed gigolo and his pathetic older fiancée versus tastefully dressed Peter and nonpathetic Harriet. Alexis, a poor, good-looking professional dancer, is a vulgar dandy, with "pale mauve socks" and tie, and shoes explicitly condemned by Wimsey: "Foul color and worse shape. Hand-made, so that the horrid appearance is due to malice aforethought" (13, 16, 49). Harriet's view of the wealthy, widowed Mrs. Weldon is more ambivalent than Wimsey's disdain for Alexis: from initial revulsion at the "predatory hag . . . dressed in an exaggeration of the fashion," Harriet quickly examines herself: "Did it come to this, then, if one did not marry? . . . [But s]ingle, married, widowed, divorced, one came to the same end" (38, 39)—that is, anxiously awaiting a man. Although the wealthy Wimsey is no gigolo, Harriet dreads becoming a dependent women.

The novel emphasizes dress as costume, significant for women more than men. A relational milestone is reached when Harriet buys the wine-colored dress Peter has recommended: "Wimsey considered, rightly, that when a woman takes a man's advice about the purchase of clothes, it is a sign that she is not indifferent to his opinion" (128). But Wimsey is touched, rather than seduced, when Harriet dresses to impress him; it is the chauvinistic suspect Henry Weldon that Harriet vamps by dressing in a "clingy," impractical Georgian costume including "a corsage which outlined the figure and a skirt which waved tempestuously around the ankles" and a similarly old-fashioned "oversized hat of which one side obscured her face" (186, 185). That female style can deceive stupid men is a given in Sayers's world. And male costume now appears purely as the play it always was, for the dandy. Wimsey too dresses for the vulgar: "I wish to appear in my famous impersonation of the perfect Lounge Lizard," he tells Bunter, who immediately suggests "the fawn-colored suit we do not care for, with the autumn-leaf socks and our out-sized amber cigarette holder" (322). It may seem surprising "that he (or Bunter) had taken, all the way to Wilvercombe, a suit they did not 'care for'" (Scowcroft 20). But in pursuit of evidence the detective previously has worn "an aged Norfolk suit, stockings, with sober tops, an ancient hat" (*Clouds of Witness* 138), and also "an easy lounge suit . . . a trifle more pronounced in colour and pattern than Wimsey usually permitted himself" (*Unpleasantness* 237). Wimsey collects imperfect outfits for play-acting. In this novel, however, he costumes himself for amusement: there is no reason to make the hard-boiled Leila believe he is a gigolo, since she is quite willing to be impressed by his rank and money (94). Where Harriet's dress obviously influences Weldon, in line with the novel's observations about modern women's manipulative costuming, male dress has become chiefly a detachable source of self-entertainment. Moreover, in contrast to *Strong Poison*, in *Carcase* Wimsey is not "foolish-seeming." Rather, he amazes Harriet with his answer to the mystery: "You're right, Peter . . . you must be" (347). And in the climactic *Gaudy Night*, these trends are solidified: women's clothes are detailed, not men's, and nearly the entire novel is presented from Harriet's perspective, yet it is Wimsey who becomes the supreme object of desire.

When she conceived *Gaudy Night* (1936), Sayers recalled, she was considering a straight novel about an Oxford woman graduate returning to "the creative life of the intellect" ("Gaudy" 81). She soon became convinced that academia was a place where Harriet Vane could stand equal to Peter Wimsey, and that the theme of intellectual integrity was ideal both for a "love-interest" and for a detective story (82). The plot follows Harriet visiting her woman's college at Oxford, the college's reputation being threatened by a mysterious poison-pen writer who clearly is an unbalanced female, and Wimsey joining Harriet in solving the mystery and finally persuading her to marry him. As a novel of ideas, the narrative is permeated with both discussion and images representing various life options for women: the intellectual spinster-scholar in her ivory tower, the married woman endeavoring to balance relationships with work, the homemaker who believes she follows the only womanly calling. As a detective novel, *Gaudy Night* employs those concepts, including current theories about repressed spinsters, as red herrings to distract the reader from the guilty party, a "traditional" woman who fears and hates educated women.

Sayers's most ambitious novel has both delighted and repelled readers since its publication. Prominent feminists including Nina Auerbach and Carolyn Heilbrun have written about their appreciation for Sayers's fiction and also their discomfort at feeling drawn to *Gaudy Night*'s ideal: a "unique and encouraging" scholarly community of females (Heilbrun, *Hamlet's* 239); an independent, successful woman; and a brilliant but enlightened man, who finally marries Harriet on her own terms. That the book has inspired such emotion among educated women suggests not only that Sayers's topics strike sensitive nerves but that the novel itself limns out discomfiting conflicts in modern female desires. We are introduced to a community of women, happily doing intellectual work together apart from men, but as the mystery heats up that community fills with suspicion and jealousy. Academic women are reassured to find that the poison-pen writer and nighttime stalker is a woman with immoderate devotion to a man and scorn for intellectual integrity. Yet the ethics are less than clearly defined. As Nina Auerbach points out, "The stereotype of the 'crazy spinster' is both the serpent in the garden and the pivot of the mystery, and Sayers depends on her readers' complicity in it" (189). It "might even be one of ourselves," murmurs the Warden, "elderly virgins and all that" (*Gaudy* 74). And after the mystery is solved, the Shrewsbury College dons believe they failed: the culprit Annie lectures them for three pages about sterile females whose ivory-tower existence takes no account of human "lives and happiness," while her audience sits in meek, stunned silence (443). Miss de Vine, the most magnificently objective scholar of all, can only say vaguely, "I do blame myself. . . . One ought to take some thought for other people" (446–47). So while the mystery's conclusion displays the potential danger of personal commitments, it does not unequivocally celebrate academic detachment or female independence.

Moreover, Wimsey's superiority complicates any feminist reading. Although the entire novel is narrated from Harriet's perspective, it is Wimsey the hero who consistently affirms both integrity and love, however they appear to clash. Thus while Harriet finds she can do satisfying work and exist without a man, it is symbolically proper that she finally agrees to marry him: he outranks her. While Harriet is respected in her small sphere, Wimsey does not appear for nearly three hundred pages (he is away doing mysterious, international diplomacy). But he then solves the mystery when the women cannot, as the culprit Annie notes contemptuously (444).[10] It is true that Wimsey makes a valedictory speech repenting of his "vanity" and "windy self-importance" (452). Yet this confession also demonstrates his laudable sensitivity; moreover, his intelligence is superior even in Harriet's own sphere: he tops her sonnet (360–61), and he gives her wise advice for her writer's block (301–3). As Harriet realizes, he's "not a man but a miracle" (215).

In many respects, *Gaudy Night* heavily revises Sayers's formula; until then, despite broadening characterizations, she had continued producing

---

10. Heilbrun insists that Wimsey's success "is not only necessary but wholly correct historically. . . . For it is women, even women like Harriet Vane, who internalize" the sexual myths that obscure a correct reading of the clues (*Hamlet's* 240). Whatever the necessity, the male detective's triumph qualifies Sayers's portrayal of independent women.

solidly conventional detective plots with brightly decorated surfaces. Certainly this book did not follow mystery standards: no murder, and no concluding communal *Schadenfreude*, only increased uncertainty and anxiety when the culprit is revealed. Sayers's opus also makes a more-than-passable claim to be a novel of ideas. But one central factor still precludes its being realistic fiction, even by milder, twentieth-century middlebrow standards: Lord Peter Wimsey, while more fully characterized, yet remains a glittering fantasy figure. Harriet's colleagues admire and desire Wimsey (increasing her desire for him, of course) in several scenes that ironically reverse the objectifying male gaze (Heilbrun, *Hamlet's* 257). The women eye Peter as he strolls across their quadrangle (323), and in a repeated but expressive metaphor, he serves as "dynamite in a powder factory" (61, 370–72, 407), sparking jealous tensions among the dons. On their river outing, Harriet studies the details of Peter's face from the "glitter of close-cropped hair" down to the "little hollow above the points of the collar-bone": fifteen lines of lyrical and sensuous description (292) that utterly remake the original foolish-looking Wimsey whose face was compared to white maggots (*Whose Body* 7). The contrast between the high-spirited, vivid simile of Sayers's first novel and the carefully realistic small details in her romantic description encapsulates the significant, parallel changes in her writing style—and in Wimsey's person: yet the ultimate effect is less realism than generic romantic fiction, although of an intellectual order. Certainly the body is not the sum of this hero's attractions. In the river scene, with Wimsey's traits "magnified as it were by some glass in her own mind" (291), Harriet's imaginal lens intellectualizes even the physical. It is a significant reversal because it involves a woman's gaze objectifying a man—even though, as Kenney has commented, Harriet's observation is from the neck up, emphasizing the "passionate intellect" (92). Nevertheless, even as object, Wimsey dominates.

Ironically too, *Gaudy Night* uses dress style to denigrate feminine expertise. Here the dandy's objectivity, whether regarding his own performative dress or his knowledge of others' fashions, contrasts favorably with women's clothing fusses. Where Wimsey merely remains "tailored to swooning point" (57), we are treated to an eight-line description of Harriet's Gaudy dress, whose "dull surface effaced itself, not out-shining the dull gleam of the academic poplin" (7). Dull, indeed. The women scholars gossip about others' clothes, and they dress anxiously when Lord Peter is coming to dinner (323). They do focus their knowledge of female styles on a dress found on the dummy hanged in effigy: "Who, by the way, owns a black semi-evening crêpe de Chine, figured with bunches of red and green poppies, with a draped cross-over front, deep hip-yoke and flared skirt and sleeves about three years out of date?" (145). No one, it seems; the women cannot determine the owner. Wimsey, on the other hand, always deduces correctly through his style knowledge: he specifies the kind of woman's shoe (Cuban heel, not French) that smashed Harriet's chessmen, thereby exonerating one suspect (410–11).

Finally, however, Sayers employs clothing to support her ideally egalitarian intellectual world. When Harriet borrows Peter's scarf (398–99), and he her academic gown, it signals not only their intimacy but their equality in the university. "Bless the man," Harriet thinks, "if he hasn't taken my gown instead of his own! Oh, well . . . it's exactly the same thing" (292). The scene paves the way for Sayers's comic romantic conclusion, played out with her lovers dressed in similar scholars' gowns and caps: "If Senior Members of the University chose to stand—in their gowns, too!—closely and passionately embracing in New College Lane right under the Warden's windows, [the scandalized Proctor] was powerless to prevent it" (457). In their concluding embrace, Harriet and Peter cannot be distinguished by sex, but their dress signifies the intellectual equality of their union. So Sayers concludes with an image representing a concept dear to her heart: the perfectly androgynous style of the mind.

THE CINDERELLA OF LITERATURE

Clearly the issue of women's place in society engaged Sayers throughout her life, as did writing style, and the two concerns were intertwined in her re-dressing of the novel. Her concern, that quickly marrying Peter to Harriet would be "false and degrading," is both stylistic and feminist ("Gaudy" 208, 211). That hurried, clichéd ending would have ruined Sayers's hopes for a detective novel of manners—and it also would have degraded Harriet into a traditional dependent heroine. Sayers made no sharp distinctions between stylistic and gender-based hypocrisies. Moreover, despite her expressed anger about societal stereotypes of women, she was essentially hopeful about the transformative powers of education and a clear writing style, a stance that frustrates scholars who wish to pigeonhole her. For instance, *Gaudy Night* shows Sayers's belief that a university is fundamentally about the disinterested search for truth; Lillian Robinson countered that universities are too invested in maintaining the power of white males ever to provide an intellectual platform on which women may stand equal to men (230–31). But Sayers was thoroughly versed in the prejudices of universities: although she achieved a First Class on her exams in 1915, with special commendation, the Oxford administrators did not consent to award degrees to women until 1920. Nevertheless, she maintained a huge faith in the powers of logical thought and well-written prose. In *The Mind of the Maker* she argues that, for the writer, evil is stylistic, "bad art"—whereas "'good' is good craftsmanship, 'beauty' is artistic beauty, and 'truth' is structural truth" (99). Writing style, then, was not an optional veneer but a virtue and a gesture of hope for humanity, especially women. In a profound way, then, Sayers might have claimed that style makes the woman: beautiful surfaces cannot redeem corrupt substances, but they may aid in transforming reality.

If the detective novel brought Sayers prosperity and fame, it was also for her crusading spirit a cause to uphold. In 1937, Q. D. Leavis would extend her push against lowbrow fiction with a scornful review of *Gaudy Night*. Leavis, in addition to resenting what she viewed as Sayers's romanticizing of the English university, was reduced to incredulous disgust by a scene in which Shrewsbury College's faculty assure Harriet that they all love her detective fiction. Real scholars—or at least real people of taste—simply cannot enjoy detective novels, Leavis fumed ("The Case" 338). Her critique is, perhaps, hyperprotective of women's literary reputation. In the early twentieth century, all writers and readers agreed that detective and suspense stories were entertainments, and Sayers herself would not have demurred: she defended detective fiction merely by pointing out that it was both written and read by educated people. In fact, the mystery novel had risen with the bourgeoisie, as more leisure reading was required for an increasingly literate population. Thus in 1948 W. H. Auden described the typical mystery reader as "a fairly successful professional man with intellectual interests" ("The Guilty Vicarage" 409). Fifty years later, Jacques Barzun directly asserted that modern "detective stories were written by and for highbrows," naming intellectual male fans from Bertrand Russell to J. L. Borges and Pablo Neruda. Yet, as Barzun acknowledges, the most prominent Golden Age detective novelists were women (739). Sayers herself emphasized the mystery writer's educated status. In her introduction to the classic *Trent's Last Case*, she described E. C. Bentley as "an educated man, with the whole tradition of European letters behind him, who was not ashamed to lay his gifts of culture at the feet of that Cinderella of literature, the mystery novel" (Bentley xi). The fairy-tale metaphor suggests that Sayers foresaw the detective novel's rise in stock. And although she had no expressed interest in gendering the genre, the image makes the classically educated author (like Sayers herself) a percipient prince, honoring the disdained drudge.

Sayers saw style as key to the detective novel's value. She insisted that the

> most intricate plot ever woven will never carry bad writing; but good writing will often carry a thin plot and really inspired writing will carry almost anything. That is why, in reviewing crime stories for an intelligent paper, I lay what some people may consider an exaggerated emphasis on style. ("Style in Crime Stories" 9)

Her theory sounds close to the high-literary Flaubert's ideal of a book about nothing, carried by absolute style. But in truth, Golden Age detective fiction also heavily depended on plot, as Sayers knew. As a ball gown reveals the poor drudge's beauty, so excellent writing style was simply the dress that enabled an intelligent audience to appreciate the Cinderella of literature.

Nevertheless, if she claimed intelligence for her readers, Sayers also insisted upon what she called, in a 1936 lecture, "The Importance of Being Vulgar." This defense of popular writing was prompted by a hostile review of *Gaudy Night*. Sayers begins by gleefully paraphrasing the reviewer's verdict: "I am really a very vulgar writer, only rather smarter" (5). Then she stakes her claim: "To have the soul of the commonest man or woman and to be able to express it in noble language, ordered and controlled by the intellect, is the only recipe I know for the highest and most enduring kind of greatness" (6). The homely cooking metaphor itself evokes Sayers's common style. And she goes further, claiming Shakespeare as the supremely vulgar writer, since "anyone who wants to write as greatly as Shakespeare *must* begin by feeling like Tom, Dick and Harry" (17). She responds to accusations of snobbery by arguing that she "loves a lord" because of her "sheer unmitigated commonness.... I am myself as common as mud in my likes and dislikes" (16). The approachable content of vulgar genre literature, presented in intelligent, "noble language," summarizes the aesthetic that powered Sayers's entertaining prewar fiction.

In 1940, Sayers observed, "War is the breaking up of security and habit, and the letting-in of energy upon the things that had become static and corrupt" (*Begin* 14). By then she essentially had written all of the Wimsey stories. And she began to question the detective genre's absolutist formula, which "softly persuades [readers] that love and hatred, poverty and unemployment, finance and international politics, are problems capable of being dealt with and solved in the same manner as the Death in the Library" (*Mind* 175). She retained her fascination with style, and she continued to insist upon the importance of the vulgar—though her scholarship might be said to flip the categories. Her plays and translations presented famous and exalted material in everyday English, for a lay audience. Her radio play *The Man Born to Be King* created a national furor by using slang to retell the Gospel story, with a nervous BBC trying to defend against organized protests from conservative groups (*Letters* 2: 335). "What is depressing," Sayers commented, "is the attitude of the pious who dislike having the *actuality* of the Gospel forced upon their notice. . . . [For them] the brutal Roman gallows [is] a pattern stamped in gilt on the cover of a prayer-book. 'The play,' said one correspondent angrily, 'seemed to bring God down to earth'" (*Letters* 2: 340). "Actuality" and "bring[ing] down to earth" were key concepts for Sayers: her final project endeavored to translate Dante's vulgar dialect. She was both highly critical of carelessly written English and highly skeptical of overly rarefied language.

Sayers also grew more exercised about women's position in society. She had believed that education and the occupations were fully opened to women, and she had fashioned her life into a production in which it was work that mattered most of all. But if the substance of women's battles had been won, the details—males' assumptions about females—still left much to be desired. Thus, in "Are Women Human?" (1938), she had used the wearing of trousers to signify a rational unconcern with the sexual attraction often assumed to motivate women's dressing. Three years later, in the much angrier "Human-Not-Quite-Human," it becomes evident that "wearing the trousers" is not a worn metaphor for Sayers. She points out that in certain Asian countries women wear trousers, while men dress in "skirts," but everywhere, she says, "Man dresses as he pleases, and the Woman to please him; and if Woman says she ever does otherwise, he knows better." How would a man feel, she inquires mockingly, "if the center of his dress-consciousness were the codpiece . . . his interests held to be natural only in so far as they were sexual"? (117). Sayers's satirical speculations are humorous, but she does not bother to mask her anger over the narrow roles forced upon women, roles she sees epitomized in clothing conventions. And while she endeavored to be seen simply as a person, without regard to sex, she inevitably skewed toward the masculine in her own dress and writing styles. She learned to employ dress to artistically present herself to the world—as her character Peter Wimsey always had used it. She could become a kind of female dandy, however, only when she was in a position both to dispassionately view herself and to know that she was not an object of sexual interest to men. Hence, where Lord Peter's early dress signifies a cold guard against intimacy, Sayers's suggested erotic readiness; where his later deemphasis on dress suggests his new emotional openness, her later enjoyment of her costuming options tells us that she had closed herself off.

Sayers, herself a Cinderella of literature, recognized the dangers of self-fashioning. Of her dandy precursor Oscar Wilde she wrote that "he posed so much in everything he did that it is difficult to distinguish the pose from the reality, and he was probably the last person in the world to know" (*Letters* 3: 525). Sayers's own postures had clear goals: her love of drama alternated with her desire to be seen as a serious human being. Both personae required conscious costumes—glamorous gowns and tailored suits—which served as different facets of a carefully constructed surface, impermeable to the end. On the day of her sudden death, Sayers had shopped in London by herself. Her editor records that just before returning to her house, where she would experience a fatal heart attack, the writer stopped by an art gallery, where "she looked for a time at the portrait of herself by Sir William Hutchison" (*Letters* 4: 426 fn). We too may see that painting, in the National Portrait Gallery. But we cannot know what Sayers saw or thought, when she studied the self that she had so deliberately fashioned.

CHAPTER 3

Jean Rhys and Modeling for Men

A T FIRST BLUSH, Jean Rhys (1890–1979) seems a drastic opposite to Dorothy L. Sayers. Where Sayers was a plain and loudly confident university graduate, Rhys began as a pretty, insecure, and lightly educated chorus girl, the sort of woman that Sayers's Lord Peter Wimsey might term "a little bit of fluff." While Sayers wrote popular detective novels, along with religious drama, theology, and learned translations, Rhys published grim modernist fiction, in avant-garde venues: in contrast to Sayers's glittering genre fiction, Rhys's literary impressionism delved into stark emotion through unconventional modes. As to their lives, while Sayers won public fame, Rhys sank into an alcoholic poverty so obscure that, until her miraculous late-life revival with *Wide Sargasso Sea* (1966), many fans and even her publisher assumed she was dead. Yet the two women shared not only an age (Rhys was three years older) and an era (the twenties and thirties) but a deep sympathy with the modern single girl and a complex approach to dress. Like the detective novelist, Rhys had been used by men and then deserted. But where Sayers suppressed and objectified her anger into public essays about misogyny, Rhys's fury simmered in all her novels. For Jean Rhys, objectification—a lesson taught by men, in more than one sense—was a dirty if useful weapon. One could wield it through displaying one's attractive self, preferably in expensive new fashions. Or one might employ it in modernist fiction.

This chapter describes the ways in which Jean Rhys developed her impressionist writing style, through which she presented her life of modeling for men as an object for examination, while also divulging her own complicity in that life. Rhys may be read as champion of the colonialist victim, or as the writer who gave a voice to the madwoman in the attic. But these labels obscure her hard road to modernism, as a single girl displaying her attributes. In her novels, modernism and *la mode* are not linked through intellectual theories. Instead Rhys, who had worked not only as a chorus girl but as an artist's model and in haute-couture shops, brought an intimate perspective very different from that of the theorists of modernity and fashion. Ultimately, her youthful experiences, including the convergence of sex and literature in her relationship with the influential modernist writer Ford Madox Ford, taught her that both clothing and language offer means through which desires are mediated between men and women.

As a patronized female in literary modernism, Rhys wrote scathingly about her conflicted life. That Ford was her writing master, and she his sexual mistress, is not only a literary cliché but a typical modernist irony, seen in the careers of other women ranging from H. D. to Zelda Fitzgerald: the supposedly liberating modern ethos pressed women into very traditional roles, even in their artistic apprenticeships. In any case, while Rhys came of age in a world that stripped literature and clothing of inessential details, her Paris remained an environ in which men presumed that women's clothing spoke sexually: poet Blaise Cendrars observed of a futurist design by Sonia Delaunay, "Sur la robe elle a un corps" (l.10) [On her dress, she has a body]. Modern fashion also remained a field in which Jean Patou, *couturier* for the liberated flapper, could brag, "My gowns please men ... [and they] say to their wives, 'At last you are dressed according to my taste'" (Etherington-Smith 72). Rhys learned both to fear and to satirize those masculine tastes, and her fiction displays her knowledge of what clothing means for women. In modeling for men, Rhys (like her single girls) performed in order to please—but also to strike back at—the male sex.

MANNEQUIN FOR MEN

Female modernists were particularly hard-hit by modern style's anomalous combination of old and new. In the chorus line of Gaiety shows, Rhys dressed in comic, frilly, or suggestive styles, as required by her manager and admired by men. As an independent young woman on the street, however, she learned to simplify the elements of dress style, from multiple layers to a few necessary items such as her character Julia's "black dress and hat and very dark grey stockings" (*After Leaving* 182). Likewise, she developed a hard minimalist narrative style for her fiction, a "cold deliberation" in cutting excess from her stories (Ford, "Preface" 26). Yet her rhetoric always expresses longing, and she maintained a sexual economics of dress learned in her chorus-girl days, as voiced by Anna in *Voyage in the Dark:* "You look at your hideous underclothes and you think, 'All right, I'll do anything for good clothes. Anything—anything for clothes'" (22). How could this age-old relation to men, and to clothing, accompany the "terrifying insight" and "singular instinct for form" that Ford praised in her stories ("Preface" 24, 25)?

The first answers lie in Rhys's early life, which like modernism itself joined twentieth-century freedom to premodern content. The perennial outsider, Ella Gwendolen Rees Williams was born a white colonial in West Indian Dominica, daughter of an impoverished Welsh doctor. As a young girl she was sent to school in England, where teachers and students mocked her Creole accent and she was miserable in the cold, gray climate. A voracious reader but a bashful talker, she often appeared ignorant, with nothing but youth and beauty to recommend her. By age eighteen, the shy young Gwen Williams had quit her girls' school to study drama. Seemingly resourceless, told that she would never succeed in classical theatre, she secretly signed a contract to perform in the chorus of a traveling musical. With news of her father's death in Dominica, the aunt serving as her guardian threw up her hands, and Gwen slipped into the demimonde.

The demimonde, a shadowy class of women who are neither fully prostitutes nor entirely respectable, provides the dominant mythology for Rhys's personal and literary worlds—but *mythology* is here a key word. The demimonde itself was a fantasy, of women for sale who were not sordid streetwalkers but glamorous performers, often actresses, dancers, or singers; who exerted seductive power over the men maintaining them; who reaped rewards in the form of expensive clothing and jewelry. That a few such historical women existed does not validate the mythology, as identified by French novelist Alexander Dumas *fils* and celebrated by avant-garde writers from Charles Baudelaire to Ernest Dowson to Marcel Proust. It is perhaps significant that the most famous half-worlds, *demimondaines*, and their praisers were French, and that Rhys loved Paris all her life. Moreover, most writers romanticizing the demimonde were male, although novelist Colette, with *Gigi* (1942), is a memorable exception. Rhys would learn firsthand the potential misery of the kept woman, yet she never quite relinquished her hope that another man or another dress might transform her existence.

Rhys, like her fellow chorus girls, was susceptible to demimonde myths: as a girl she may have poured over Filson Young's *Sands of Pleasure* (1905), about a young engineer's obsession with a Continental courtesan (Pizzichini 39). Accordingly, her *Voyage in the Dark* (1934) opens with its chorus-girl protagonist Anna reading *Nana*, Émile Zola's 1880 novel about a power-mongering prostitute. Anna's roommate Maudie warns her that it's "a dirty book," noting shrewdly, "I bet you a man writing a book about a tart tells a lot of lies" (9). But Maudie also helps Anna pick up the man who will become her first lover, for the girls share the romanticized hope of becoming one of those rare kept women who marries well and lives happily ever after.[1] Anna recalls a headline trumpeting, "Chorus-Girl Marries Peer's Son" (64). The chorus girls' inconsistent worldliness characterizes the demimonde myth, on both sides of the male-female gulf, and Rhys's own life reflects this mythologizing: scholars struggle to disentangle her biography from her autobiographical fictions. We do not know the details or extent of her life as a prostitute, as an artist's model, as a mannequin, or in other temporary, marginalized jobs.[2] Rhys was not necessarily

---

1. In *British Modernism and Censorship*, Celia Marshik concludes that Rhys's novels "cannot imagine alternatives to bourgeois womanhood despite the satire they direct at the purity movement, which rested upon bourgeois sexual identity" (240, fn 136). In fact Rhys, with her experience in "amateur prostitution," knew that world from the inside, unlike other anticensorship writers such as Virginia Woolf, G. B. Shaw, and James Joyce. Marshik may not sufficiently credit Anna's desire for fairy-tale love and permanence: as described here, Rhys's accounts of her early life compellingly dovetail with Anna's detailed experiences in *Voyage*, which in my reading include a fatally uncritical acceptance of demimonde myths.

2. Early Rhys scholars tended to speak of "the Rhys woman," as if her protagonists Anna, Julia, Marya, Sasha, and even Antoinette of *Wide Sargasso Sea* were manifestations of the same person; moreover, Lillian Pizzichini's *The Blue Hour* often simply recounts incidents from the novels as if they happened to Rhys herself. Clearly this is not always the case—yet Rhys inarguably used many scenes, characters, and even bits of dialogue from her own experience.

truthful in her personal reminiscences, she did not always recall distant memories correctly, and she was uninterested in logically successive histories. Consequently, Carole Angier's biography moves constantly between the fiction, the evidence, and speculation about what we can know of this writer's life, especially in the space between 1909 and 1919.

In those ten speculative years, during a brutal Great War and large shifts in cultural mores, the girl who used various names—"Gwen Williams" at school, "Vivien," "Emma," "Ella," or "Olga Gray" on the stage and in her shadowy street life (Angier 57)—learnt the paradoxical use of modern dress and the female body. This unsentimental education began in the choruses of Gaiety shows, which were the forerunners of the twentieth-century musical comedy. In 1909 and 1910, Rhys performed in travelling productions of the hit Gaiety musical *Our Miss Gibbs*, with a brief abortive sojourn in a music-hall revue called *Chanteclair*, a "Feathered Fantasy in Three Fits." Late in life, Rhys recalled *Chanteclair* as a barely rehearsed show that featured "a girl in tights walking across the stage, dropping an egg and clucking loudly" (*Smile* 86). Contrasting with the vulgar amusements of *Chanteclair*, the premier Gaiety show *Our Miss Gibbs* offered a coherent and almost perfectly decorous romantic story, adorned by clothing that wealthy, stylish women aspired to wear themselves. Gaiety musicals presented two foci of desire: first, the ambition of marrying above one's station (a feat frequently enacted in the plots of such shows, and occasionally in the actual lives of their stars); second, the goal of acquiring beautiful clothes and displaying them for admiration. Both of these desires dominate women's demimonde myths, and Rhys—who nearly stopped reading books during her chorus career, since the other chorus girls did not read—spent a year or more "reading" *Miss Gibbs*: daily, nightly, and in her dreams. The show's heroine, Mary Gibbs, is a beautiful and virtuous Yorkshire lass who has come to London to work in "Garrods" department store. Mary is in love with a young bank clerk who actually is the disguised heir to an earldom. When she discovers his deception, she breaks off their relationship, but after many comic plot twists and several spectacular song-and-dance numbers, they reunite and are wedded. This Cinderella marriage plot was echoed in many musicals of the period, such as *The Shop Girl* (1894) and *The Earl and the Girl* (1903), and *The Count of Luxembourg* (1911), which Rhys played in as well. Equally compelling, for the girls in the choruses, was the fairy-tale reality of Gaiety performers who wed rich and titled men. Famously, Rosie Boote, an illegitimate child of vaudeville, became a Gaiety star and then Marchioness of Headfort in 1901. In addition, Gertie Millar, who starred in the London production of *Miss Gibbs*, would wind up the Countess of Dudley; Gladys Cooper, with a smaller part in the same *Miss Gibbs* production, not only became a famous actress but married a baronet; and even from the touring *Miss Gibbs* company, Rhys's friend Nancy Erwin became Lady Dalrymple-Champneys. The famed beauty Lily Elsie, star of *The Count of Luxembourg*, left that show midseason to marry a wealthy man. For the young Rhys, Cinderella lived; she did not discern the thin guardrail between "happily ever after" and the abyss of prostitution.

The Gaiety shows themselves walked a tightrope in terms of sexual enticement. Modern theatre critic W. J. Macqueen-Pope praised the new decorum of the Gaiety Theatre, explaining that in 1893 founder George Edwardes did away with "lavish display of feminine limb.... Skirts replaced tights, and mystery, deep, alluring and irresistible, surrounded the female form" (11). Moreover, Macqueen-Pope recalled nostalgically, "To know a Gaiety Girl, to take her out to sup, that was a cachet about town" (392). The performers and the shows were considered perfectly decorous yet skirted the edge of provocation. In *Miss Gibbs* a knowing girl sings,

> I am sure your education
> Is not complete at present, girls,
> Till you've met with one sensation
> That's really rather pleasant, girls,
> Get some man who's young and handsome
> To grasp you tightly....
> ....
> Arms and the man,
> Arms and the man,
> Ev'ry man has two,
> That will surely do,
> Is it enough for you?
> You feel a thrill all through. (Caryll and Monckton 158–61)

In this ditty, Lady Betty's advice teeters between innocence and sexual knowledge, as did other Gaiety songs. In *The Sunshine Girl* (1912), the heroine Delia specifically advises a balancing act between modest and seductive dress: "Just a little touch will often be enough . . . Just in case young Lord Tom Noddy comes to call!" Rather than "display of feminine limb," she recommends a glimpse of lingerie: "Just a frilly frou-frou, / Not so very much; / What they see of you / Will 'frill' them 'frou and frou.' . . ." (Rubens n. pag.). Obviously, the styles that fascinated the ladies in the audience also caught the interest of men.

Certainly both Gaiety shows and early live-fashion displays were intimately connected, and fashion shows were known to attract male viewers who did not care about the clothing. The use of live models may have started with Charles Frederick Worth, but mannequin shows as performances began in 1890s London, at the same time as Edwardes's Gaiety Theatre (Evans 125). Dress designer Lucile claimed credit for the first runway parades, in which the models emerged from behind a curtain and walked a ramp, and which encouraged male attendance (Kaplan and Stowell 116, 119). The women came to see the clothing, the men frankly to ogle the women inside the dresses. And while Lucile and French *couturier* Paul Poiret continued their private mannequin shows as the twentieth century began, they also staged and sold new fashions through public theatre performances (Rappaport 185). Lucile dressed Gaiety stars such as Lily Elsie for *Count* (Kaplan and Stowell 115); consequently, reviewers often focused on the clothing, even helpfully identifying the designer and informing women which costumes were available ready-made from which department stores (Booth and Kaplan 53). Accordingly, a review entitled "Frocks and Frills" termed *Count*'s opening a "brilliant success," supporting that claim merely by describing, scene by scene, the assorted "charming" costumes (Detmold n. pag.). Even the popular *Our Miss Gibbs* was especially known for its spectacular hats created by Maison Lewis (Macqueen-Pope 424). "That's the last Parisian hat!" Garrods' *modiste* Madame Jeanne and the chorus sang. "Men will wait outside on the mat, / If you have that hat!" (Caryll and Monckton 39–40). Men did wait outside for Gaiety Girls, with varying intentions.

Undeniably, Gaiety musicals sold new clothing styles and (at least in fantasy) the girls inside them (Rappaport 192). Most ominously for Rhys, the shows preached sexual attraction as a bankable possession, and dress as the mutual currency of exchange. While the shop-girl comedies presented sex as a commodity, albeit part of a decorous marital settlement, *Miss Gibbs* also taught young women that clothing was both the exorbitant price of, and the reward for, seduction. For the real-life girls, this

FIGURE 4. Gertie Millar as Mary Gibbs in "Our Miss Gibbs" by Rita Martin; published by J. Beagles & Co (bromide postcard print, 1909). © National Portrait Gallery, London.

suggested that—as implied by reviewers—the fashionable dresses were the most important items on stage. In *Voyage in the Dark*, Rhys would describe a businessman musing, "Have you ever thought that a girl's clothes cost more than the girl inside them? . . . You can get a very nice girl for five pounds, a very nice girl indeed. . . . But you can't get a very nice costume for her for five pounds. . . ." Obviously, then, the chorus girl Maudie cheerfully concludes, "People are much cheaper than things" (40). In line with Gaiety-song philosophy, Rhys's fictional alter egos dress to entice men, but they tend to believe that stylish clothes really do add value to the woman who wears them.

Not surprisingly, the Gaiety Girl who would become the writer Rhys was seduced and supported by a wealthy, well-connected Englishman. For about eighteen months she lived a demimonde fantasy, spending most weeknights in Lancelot Grey Hugh Smith's mansion and her days shopping for dresses or taking singing lessons, while occasionally still performing in a show. Smith paid her rent and for her classes, took her to dinner, and bought her clothing. In fact, it seems the first money her lover gave her was for new stockings (Angier 66). The young Rhys hoped that Smith would marry her, and when he ended the affair she was devastated: the fairy tale had failed. For the next seven years, she drifted in a shadowy, true demimonde for which details are murky. She lived with, and worked for, a woman who advertised herself as a Swedish masseuse; she also stayed with Shirley, a showgirl friend who had become a high-priced call girl. In each venue, Rhys probably sexually served men and gave a cut of her pay to her hostess. From Shirley she seems to have learned that, as the protagonists of her first four novels attest, the more stylish your clothes, the higher class of man you can attract. Eventually Rhys became pregnant and in desperation contacted Lancelot Smith. In accordance with his chivalrous name, Smith sent money for an illegal abortion and thereafter paid her a small monthly stipend—from afar, through a lawyer. The glamorous demimonde life, the Cinderella Gaiety Girl conclusion: both turned for Rhys into lonely, desperate circumstances.

"What was the difference between Nancy [Erwin] and me?" Rhys recalled asking herself when her first love affair ended. Erwin, the showgirl-become-baroness, "was ruthless and I wasn't" (*Smile* 94). But Rhys knew it was something further: "Some [chorus girls] were very ambitious, determined to make a good marriage . . . and if you imagine they ever did anything which might interfere with that you don't know the type" (88). Rhys herself had lacked that steely determination, and so she allowed herself to slip from chorus girl to paid woman. Looking back, she mused, "It seems to me now that the whole business of money and sex is mixed up with something very primitive and deep. When you take money directly from someone you love it becomes not money but a symbol.... It is at once humiliating and exciting" (97). Lancelot Smith had unwittingly given her a major theme for her fiction: the humiliating excitement of modeling for men—along with the suppressed anger that underlies such a relationship.

Smith's stipend enabled Rhys to buy some notebooks and brightly colored pens that attracted her in a shop window, and she used them to record her pain and rage (*Smile* 103–4). Yet that record, as well as the anger, remained hidden for several years. Rhys continued to take jobs related to displaying one's self and one's clothing. She posed as a nude artist's model in London but refused, she claimed, to sleep with her employers. She also, with another girl, rented a corner of a Bond Street dress shop, where they endeavored to sell hats (*Letters* 294). In Paris of 1923–24, she gained the mannequin experience fictionalized in her stories and in *After Leaving Mr Mackenzie* (26); in the later twenties, she evidently worked as a receptionist "in a smart dress shop near the Avenue Marigny" (Angier 125–27). The French jobs are vividly, repeatedly depicted in her fiction. And so are the more verifiable next events in her life: marriage, to a man who chose her dresses, and an affair, with a man who guided her literary style.

IMPRESSIONS FOR MEN: *THE LEFT BANK* AND *QUARTET*

"He criticized her clothes with authority and this enchanted her," Rhys wrote in her first novel. In *Quartet* (1928), the mysterious Stephan Zelli promises to pay for Marya's dress and then comments, "It's not worth that.... Not that it is ugly, but it has no chic. I expect your dressmaker cheats you" (18, 19). He offers to support her financially; he critiques her magisterially. Zelli is very like Rhys's first husband, Jean (John) Lenglet. Having turned down at least two chances of marriage in London from 1914 to 1917, Rhys agreed to marry a secretive Dutchman of whom she knew only that he did not demand sex without marriage, he would choose her clothing, and he would help her escape chilly London (Angier 98–99). She trusted that Lenglet, a sometime journalist and *chansonnier*—also a spy and a thief—would pet her, patronize her, and buy her dresses. And in 1919, when Rhys embarked for the Continent to marry Lenglet, she needed clothing: her dressmaker retained her trunk of dresses, in lieu of unpaid bills (*Smile* 114). She was moving from illicit relations with men to legal marriage, but she still possessed the dependent mentality of the kept woman, and that mind-set would ironically prepare Rhys to be inducted into modernism.

Her willingness, perhaps her desire, to be patronized showed in Rhys's dress. By 1920, Western women's styles were less layered and more unified than they had been for several centuries, and simplicity and easy movement were imperative for the footloose, cosmopolitan life Rhys increasingly led. But that simple unity also enabled women to try out peculiar styles, such as Mary Pickford's childlike look, as described by Hollander: "The vulnerable neck (now bare), the fluffy curls (now free), together with the short skirt, flat bust and high waist all lent themselves to a new look of attractive immaturity—not the attractions of a ripe young virgin but of a little girl" ("Women and Fashion" 115). Long before Vladimir Nabokov's *Lolita*, the Victorian sentimentalizing of childhood had engendered a penchant for child-women, a taste for which some women learned to cater. Accordingly, Pickford (1892–1979) played little girls and ingénues until her career fizzled at the end of the twenties. Certainly the little-girl role appealed to Rhys: she often had dressed that way for Lancelot Smith, who may have called her a baby, as Walter terms Anna in *Voyage in the Dark* (Angier 66; *Voyage* 44). And Rhys's women sometimes reflect that style through infantile diction, especially when remembering the good times with men who supported them: "I'd darling muslin frocks covered with frills and floppy hats—or a little peasant dress and no hat," recalls the narrator of Rhys's early story "Vienne." This thinly disguised alter ego uses nursery speech to evoke "the spending phase" of Rhys's life with Lenglet: "Nice to have lots of money—nice, nice. Goody to have a car, a big chauffeur, rings, and as many frocks as I liked" (*Left Bank* 202, 221). As a woman whose beloved father died just when she needed help, Rhys played the child to certain father figures: Smith and Lenglet, who made love to her and dressed her, and then Ford Madox Ford, who made love to her and promoted her fiction. Even when married she acted the helpless young girl, and when Lenglet's money-making schemes collapsed, Rhys leant elsewhere for support—specifically on Ford, then at the height of his influence as a literary impressionist.

FIGURE 5. Ella Gwendolen Rees Williams, aka Jean Rhys (1890–1979), English writer, here c. 1921. Photo by Pearl Freeman / Bridgeman Images.

British literary impressionism, exemplified in Ford and his friend Joseph Conrad, should not be confused with the earlier nineteenth-century Impressionism led by French painters, which predated Ford's theories. "We accepted without much protest the stigma 'Impressionists' that was thrown at us," Ford recalled. "We saw that Life did not narrate, but made impressions on our brains. We in turn, if we wished to produce in you an effect of life, must not narrate but render impressions" (*Joseph Conrad* 194–95). As Todd Bender summarized it, "Impressionist writers aim to record the way impressions impinge on consciousness to make that 'shimmering haze' which is life" (46). In their evocations of light and mist, literary impressionists such as Virginia Woolf did echo Impressionist painters such as Claude Monet; however, the novelists also emphasized the chronology of perception, demonstrating that the often random order in which we observe events differs from traditional narrative plotting (Berrong 205). Both the use of style to influence perceptions and the unsettling of artistic norms came naturally to Rhys, with her experience in dressing for men and in the fallacies of traditional plotlines—as we shall see.

Of Rhys's apprenticeship and affair with Ford, we have multiple biased accounts. Ford's companion Stella Bowen described the relationship grimly in her memoir *Drawn from Life* (1941); Ford portrayed it luridly in his novel *When the Wicked Man* (1932), where Rhys becomes the drunken Creole vamp Lola; even the cuckolded Lenglet would have his say in a 1933 novel titled *Sous les Verrous*. Each narrative contains verifiable elements of Rhys's *Quartet*, where a young impoverished couple in Paris sees the husband arrested and imprisoned for financial malfeasance. The pretty, helpless wife meets an older, well-to-do artistic couple and is taken into their home, only to have an affair with the husband that destroys her marriage and embitters all four actors. In Rhys's novel, blame is freely assigned but surprisingly little attention is paid to literary mentoring as a factor. Yet both Ford and Rhys knew that she never would have been a writer without his guidance; in fact, they never would have met if not for her writing. In need of money, Rhys had taken some essays written by her husband to H. Pearl Adam, an influential English journalist working in Paris. Mrs. Adam was not interested in Jean Lenglet's articles but asked Lenglet's wife if she had written anything herself. Madame Lenglet produced her notebooks with the accounts of her chorus-girl life, seduction, and downward spiral. Mrs. Adam cut, edited, and typed the fragmented scribbles; she showed them to Ford, who subsequently trained, published, and renamed the author Jean Rhys.

Although much more attention has been paid to Rhys's sexual affair with Ford than to the literary training he gave her, the one cannot be understood without the other. Ford's literary impressionism, which affirmed the sensitive, passive consciousness (Kronegger 14), dovetailed with Rhys's peculiar mixture of passivity and passion in response to masterful men. Rhys's writing would evoke modernist fascinations with the semiotic: because her fiction lacked traditional form, and because it focused upon women's private lives, it appeared naturalistic, even primitive, with her West Indian roots providing an additional exotic attraction. Likewise, the telegraphic jottings of her private diary, little inhibited by formal punctuation or syntactical linkage, easily fit modernist ambitions of destroying convention—as did her seamy descriptions of a young woman's sexual degradation.[3] Ford affirmed her writing and her self, since he believed that "all art must be the expression of an ego" ("On Impressionism" 167). But he also taught Rhys to shape and cut, translating her English stories into French (Angier 134–35), in the service of artistic writing. More frankly than any other high modernist, Ford famously preached the paradox of artistic expression: "The Impressionist author is sedulous to avoid letting his personality appear in the course of his book. On the other hand, his whole book, his whole poem is merely an expression of his personality" ("On Impressionism: Second" 323). This enigma of disciplined self-expression especially amazes in Rhys's fiction, since she showed little inclination for self-discipline in any other area of life.

But she always had worked hard at one area, that of pleasing men. And she must have thought of her demimonde days, if Ford gave her his standard advice for young writers:

> You will seek to capture [your reader's] interest; you will seek to hold his interest. You will do this by methods of surprise, of fatigue, by passages of sweetness in your language . . . you will alternate . . . seek to exasperate so that you may the better enchant. You will, in short, employ all the devices of the prostitute. ("On Impressionism: Second" 333)

---

3. Sheila Kineke observes how, when Ford praised Rhys's "singular instinct for form," he reiterated "instinct" where he might have said "craft," thereby reducing Rhys "to a sort of passionate primitive" (Kineke 287).

These lines, written ten years before Ford met Rhys, nonetheless seem to evoke her need to attract men's attention. She may have undertaken, in her relations with Ford, the same sort of posing for men, in exchange for support, that she had practiced with Smith and with other, unknown lovers in her shadowy years: seeking at all costs, and by various devices, to hold his interest. Still, their relationship ultimately was more about writing than about sex, and in two surprising ways this affair differed from any other love affair for Rhys.

First, Ford—unlike Rhys's previous lovers—does not seem to have cared about dressing her. Oddly enough, that role was filled by Stella Bowen, who recalled of their young protégée, "Ford gave her invaluable help with her writing, and I tried to help her with her clothes" (166). In *Quartet* Lois Heidler (based upon Bowen) regularly critiques Marya's clothing, although she herself wears gaudy, tasteless outfits in contrast to the younger woman's fashionable simplicity (115). Lois buys Marya a lace collar, "to cheer your black dress up"; after the affair has begun, she begins publicly proclaiming Marya's need for a new hat: "'She must be chic . . . She must do us credit.' She might have been discussing the dressing of a doll" (79, 85). Hugh Heidler's interest in Marya's clothes extends only to noting "the shape of her breasts under the thin silk dress she wore—a dark-coloured, closely fitting dress that suited her" (130). So Lois, just as she half-acts as procurer for her husband, also dresses his mistress for him; in so doing, she underlines the demeaning aspects of such an exchange.

Perhaps a slippage in the term *chic*, as Rhys's narrative progresses, indicates Marya's (and Rhys's) growing cynicism about being dressed like a doll. In the first part of the novel, being chic means being stylishly dressed, as indicated in the speech of both Stephen and Lois (19, 85). But this standard usage slides into a more colloquial meaning as Marya spirals downward: too late, she thinks nostalgically of her husband, "He was kind to me. He was awfully chic with me" (125). If chic describes not style but kindness between individuals, not appearance but actions, it has acquired an ethical significance. Yet the possibilities of this transformation—from stylistic valuation to moral trait—swiftly are undercut. When Marya tells the imprisoned Stephen that the Heidlers have lent her money, he comments, "They're chic" (126). We know that they are not kind; they merely put on an appearance of kindness, as important to them as a chic dress might be to others.

In any case, although Ford may have encouraged his protégée to "employ all the devices of a prostitute" in her writing, she did not. A second striking aspect of Rhys's affair with Ford was her ability to remain independent of him in her fiction. In this one area, she seemed able to take advice but avoid slavish efforts to please. When men dressed her, Rhys accepted their guidance; even late in life, she wrote, "I am not chic or elegant. I'm grotesque except somebody else dresses me and advises me. I was all right sometimes in Paris because Jean [Lenglet] bought all my clothes" (*Letters* 77). Writing, however, was a different matter: "I was *dragged* into writing by a series of coincidences—Mrs Adam, Ford, Paris—need for money" (65). Although originally she worked at it partially to please her lover and father figure, even prior to the breakup she refused to model her writing after a man's stipulations. All her life, she would remember Ford's preaching on precision and discipline. Yet her fiction, even that written under his tutelage, sometimes veered away from his recommendations. In his preface to *The Left Bank*, Ford complained that when he tried to get Rhys to introduce "an atmosphere . . . some sort of topography" describing the Rive Gauche, she cut material instead (25–26). Rhys's novels would steadfastly remain "the expression of an ego," and indeed the assertion of an ego, as opposed to any courtesan-like appeal to the reader. Likewise, her early stories, written under Ford's guidance, show women modeling for men but stubbornly holding themselves apart.

In puzzling over what he saw as Rhys's refusal to include "descriptive passage[s]" in her *Left Bank* stories (1927), Ford had concluded, "Her business was with passion, hardship, emotions: the locality in which these things are endured is immaterial" ("Preface" 26). He overlooked Rhys's very material, although minimalist, evocation of Montparnasse, evinced in certain ironic parallels between high modernism and modern haute couture, between the pyrotechnic surfaces of aesthetic fiction and the rich fashions covering all-too-material bodies. This is the point at which clothing style and writing style coalesce in Rhys's life and novels. In his rarefied fiction, Gustave Flaubert had boasted, subject does not matter: style may become "une manière absolue de voir les choses" (345) [an absolute manner of seeing things]. But Rhys knew all too well the sexual economy in which both men and women value women more highly if their clothing—their style—seems valuable. Hence she employed that Flaubertian aesthetic of high style ironically, to assert the primacy of the subject, the woman inside the clothing.

In two early stories, "Mannequin" and "Illusion," Rhys defines women's relations to clothing, first in youth and then in age. "Mannequin" simply describes a day's work *chez Jeanne Veron* for a new young model. Anna is oppressed by the cold rooms and "the cold eyes" of buyers, as well as the other mannequins, whose selves are encased in the archetypes they portray: the *jeune fille*, the *gamine*, the *femme fatale*, the *garçonne*, the *blonde enfant*—and the "frankly ugly" star with the "chic of the devil" (*Left Bank* 61, 64–65). The magisterial Madame Veron rules; her models must follow her aesthetic tastes. Consequently their day, like their job of wearing clothes not their own, is numbed and static. "One asks oneself: Why? For what good? It is all *idiot*," Anna's friend remarks (69). It is only when Anna walks out into the Paris street at day's end that she feels "happy in her beautifully cut tailor made and a beret." As all the models emerge, they take aesthetic joy in the epiphanic brief moment in which they are "gay and beautiful as beds of flowers" (69, 70). Although they resent the pressure to be automata for the high-fashion system, the young women assume that their clothing is inseparable from their selves, that their beautiful surfaces constitute an organic whole. The sketch offers no explanation or reconciliation for the mannequins' contradictions: it simply describes.

"Illusion," by contrast, presents a deliberate overanalysis of an older woman's relation to dress. Unlike the young models, whose garments are for display, the homely, "gentlemanly" spinster-painter Miss Bruce secretly collects a closetful of beautiful garments in which she claims a detached aesthetic interest. To the unnamed narrator, who discovers the contents of Miss Bruce's closet while its owner is in the hospital, the dresses constitute "everything that one did not expect" from an unobtrusive Englishwoman (*Left Bank* 3). The friend describes the gowns in sensuous detail: "a riot of soft silks . . . an evening gown of a very beautiful shade of old gold: near it another of flame colour: of two black dresses the one was touched with silver, the other with a jaunty embroidery of emerald and blue" (3). In fact, these brilliant clothes are unusual in Rhys's fiction, reminiscent of Sayers's fascination with dramatic gold-tissue dress and glittering surfaces; they may indicate a plain woman's desire for attention (less necessary for the attractive, fashionably simple "Rhys woman" of the novels). Certainly the narrator believes that Miss Bruce's collection shows her "perpetual hunger to be beautiful and that thirst to be loved which is the real curse of Eve" (4); that is, the middle-aged artist surely collects dresses because she has a secret desire to attract men. Soon the narrator builds a speculative fantasy about

Miss Bruce's sad, illusory search for "the perfect Dress, beautiful, beautifying," and the dresses themselves are personified, shrugging their silken Gallic shoulders over the impossibility of making the spinster beautiful. The vignette swiftly concludes with Miss Bruce's own defensive response: "Why should I not collect frocks? They fascinate me. The colour and all that" (5). If we believe her, the gorgeous dresses indicate a purely aesthetic taste. But the damage is done, because her friend maintains that the spinster longs to wear her dresses and (though the reader may suspect that Miss Bruce is a lesbian) to wear them for men. Rhys never indicates who holds the titular "Illusion," Miss Bruce or her friend. But it is clear that, while the young mannequins may be overidentified with their clothing, we indulge such illusions; on the other hand, a single woman who claims a detached interest in clothes is regarded with deep suspicion. Either one models for men, or one refuses to "dress" at all. Thus these stories use clothing to question both haute-couture tradition and high-modern aestheticism.

Nevertheless, Rhys's novels demonstrate her continued affinities for modernism and fashion. As Ford inadvertently taught her when he loved her, encouraged her writing, and then abandoned her, absence and obliquity merely show up the desires they cannot fulfill. In *Quartet* (originally *Postures*), both dress and literature are occluded by absence: all Marya's beautiful clothing is in the past, sponsored by her disgraced husband. When Stephan is arrested, Marya sells her dresses with the aid of her landlady, who accurately identifies the nature of her wardrobe: "'This, for instance, this *robe de soirée* . . .' She pointed out the gem of the collection: 'Who would buy it? Nobody. Except a woman *qui fait la noce*.'" It is "not a practical dress," Madame Hautchamp explains, but "a fantasy" (37). The overglamorous evening gown in fact characterizes Marya as a woman who dresses for men. And that the gown should be sold marks the destruction of her fantasy world. Near the novel's end, with both affair and marriage essentially over, Marya daydreams about "stupid things like a yellow dress that Stephan had bought her once at Ostend. . . . It had been fun to wear beautiful clothes and to feel fresh and young and like a flower" (164). Once, like the mannequins in Rhys's earlier story, she had felt an organic continuity with her attractive garments, "like a flower," but this passage makes clear that Marya feels the loss cruelly because the clothing is tied to the absence of a man's love and financial protection. Also absent from *Quartet* is any autobiographical echo of literary gifts, whether Rhys's or her lover's. Hugh Heidler is not a writer, let alone an influential literary spokesman. Rather, he is an "English picture-dealer man," described vaguely as "a very important person in his way" (6, 9). He and his wife Lois (who paints) are constantly portrayed in terms of middle-class conventionality rather than aesthetic interests. Ironically, the shady Stephan Zelli also deals in art, in his way: he first introduces himself to Marya as a "*commissionaire d'objets d'art*," telling her that he sells "pictures and other things" (17). The substitution of art-dealing for writing makes Heidler a mere commodifier, scarcely better than Zelli, who fences stolen artifacts. Heidler also manipulates others' creative gifts: he has "made discoveries. He helped the young men," Marya is told (9). Clearly Rhys changed her lover's profession as an insult to Ford, in order to present him, like Zelli, as parasitical: each manipulates and merchandizes others' creations.

But the absence of literature also redounds upon Marya who, although a former chorus girl, is strikingly unskilled in any direction except making herself attractive—a living *objet d'art* to be bought, sold, or stolen. "She's a decorative little person—decorative but strangely pathetic" her friend Miss De Solla thinks (7). Marya always waits to be acted upon, never acting herself. She has been the "petted, cherished child" in her marriage; when she moves into the Heidler household, she continues to play that role (22). No wonder, then, that Heidler's first amorous advances evoke the "fright of a child" in her, along with queasiness in the reader, since he creeps into Marya's bedroom like a father intent on molesting a daughter (90). And no wonder that Lois, the mother surrogate, not only attempts to dress her but manifests her resentment as jocular child abuse: "Let's go to Luna-park after dinner," she suggests. "We'll put Mado on the joy wheel, and watch her being banged about a bit" (85). Marya already has seen her surrogate riding the merry-go-round to the strains of "*Je vous aime*": "a little frail, blond girl, who careered past, holding tightly on to the neck of her steed, her face tense and strained with delight" (57). Clearly, a little girl cannot prevail over Heidler or his wife—and an object cannot help being manipulated.

Marya's extreme passivity not only makes her vulnerable to the confident, slightly predatory Heidlers, it lessens the novel's impact. *Quartet* is noticeably less accomplished than Rhys's other novels, probably because the author's pain and anger were too fresh for her to admit any complicity.[4]

---

4. Sean Latham insists correctly that, despite Marya's seeming masochism, the writing and publication of *Quartet* was "an act of aggression" against Ford and Bowen (*Art of Scandal* 163). But Rhys paints an unsympathetic—or honest—portrait of her alter ego, too.

In order to make her surrogate—who, like Rhys herself, sleeps with her hostess's husband and deserts her imprisoned spouse—perfectly innocent, the author must make her perfectly helpless. Furthermore, Rhys's efforts to play with perspective all hinge on Marya as victim. She is like "L'Enfant Perdu or the Babe in the Wood" to her friend Cairn (92); Heidler himself thinks that she cries touchingly, "quietly, all soft and quivering, her little breasts heaving up and down in painful, regular jerks" (129). The unattractive characterization may be autobiographical: Bowen remembered Rhys as "very pretty and gifted" but possessing "a complete absence of any desire for independence" (166). And ironically, it is Marya's own dependent nature that leaves her solitary at the novel's end. In contrast to Sayers's women, for whom satisfying work is the key to happy singleness, Rhys's single girls never escape their longings for love or for nice clothing, two troublesome desires that became increasingly conflated in her fiction.

STREET-WALKING WOMEN: *AFTER LEAVING MR MACKENZIE* AND *VOYAGE IN THE DARK*

In *After Leaving Mr Mackenzie* (1931) Rhys again recalled the Ford affair, but this second novel is much less about the former lover and much more about clothes, aging, and female desperation. The narrative focuses entirely on the breakup's aftermath and ways of compensating for lost love. In characterization, *Mackenzie* constitutes an extreme swing of the pendulum: where Marya was passive and vulnerable, Julia is active, aggressive, and even violent. While Marya lives first with her husband and then with the Heidlers, Julia is solitary, despite sporadic efforts to reconnect with her family or with a man. Where Marya was continually characterized by her youth, Julia's dominant—and only pathetic—trait is her aging appearance. And where Heidler of *Quartet* was masterful and egotistical, Mr Mackenzie is passive, even when Julia makes a scene and strikes him in public. He is a shadowy and largely absent businessman who possesses no attractions except money; it is "of new clothes" that Julia thinks "with passion, with voluptuousness" (20).

Rhys used *Mackenzie* as a means of artistically shaping her own continuing anger: this novel, in contrast to the free-flowing *Quartet*, is stringently organized to emphasize irony. In Paris, Julia receives a sort of severance check from her former lover Mr Mackenzie, through his lawyer; she watches his house and pursues him to a restaurant, where she makes a scene and slaps his face with her glove. A young Englishman, Horsfield, observes her actions. He follows Julia, befriends her, and gives her enough money to travel to London. On her ten-day trip (the heart of the novel) Julia visits her unsympathetic relatives, her mother's deathbed, and the subsequent funeral. She calls upon another wealthy former lover, who gives her money; she reencounters Horsfield, who gives her more money and sleeps with her. Because she will not believe that Horsfield truly cares for her, she returns to Paris, where she accidentally runs into Mr Mackenzie again. He buys her a drink and gives her money once more, as the novel ends.

Julia is a conundrum: both Mackenzie and Horsfield puzzle over whether she is responsible for her own descent into semiprostitution. Her self-awareness unsettles Mackenzie:

> She had been an artist's model. At one time she had been a mannequin. But it was obvious that she had been principally living on the money given to her by various men. . . . One day she had said to him, "It's a very easy habit to acquire. . . ."
>
> [But] he had not quite agreed with her. There would have been no end to the consequences of whole-hearted agreement. (26)

Mackenzie soon stops asking "intimate questions," being unwilling "to go too far or too deep" into Julia's point of view (27). The kindlier Horsfield, however, is "curious to speculate about the life of a woman like that and to wonder what she appeared to herself to be—when she looked in the glass, for instance . . . she must have some pretty pathetic illusions about herself or she would not be able to go on living" (91). Thus Rhys cogently sums up male assumptions about fallen women: one man does not want to see the woman's side, in case his smug worldview is shaken; the other, while sympathetic, assumes that appearances must be all—at least for "a woman like that." In any case, their alternating perspectives demonstrate Rhys's increased mastery of modernist style—which she uses comically, to conjure sympathy for Julia. Her public altercation with Mackenzie, narrated from his perspective, alternates in short paragraphs between "She said" and his unvoiced response:

> She said that Maître Legros had bullied her. . . .
> Well, he probably had. . . .

She said that she had begun to cry. . . .
Well, in all careers one must be prepared to take the rough with the smooth.
She said that she had been determined never to accept the money. . . .
"Well, well," thought Mr Mackenzie. "*Tiens, tiens.*" (31–32)

The more we see of Mackenzie's inner self, the less we like him: Rhys adapts a modernist technique (free indirect narration, which usually induces sympathy with the owner of the revealed consciousness) for her own ends.

And how complicit is Julia in her own fate? She appears active; she is a *flâneuse*, a female stroller of the Parisian and London boulevards. Yet this role in itself is a paradoxical one. The original flâneurs, as Charles Baudelaire envisioned them, were detached observers of the urban scene. For a single woman, however, streetwalking traditionally implied prostitution, although modernity complicated that interpretation. In the late nineteenth century, window-shopping had become a respectable activity for solitary women, but dress, place, and mien continued to distinguish the virtuous shopper from the prostitute. Independent female streetwalking even might "be interpreted as an attempt to identify and place the self in the uncertain environment of modernity" (Parsons 41).[5] When Julia streetwalks, she is both displaying herself—and she is very aware of the possibilities of picking up men—and objectively observing her world. But she cannot correctly combine the roles. Julia tells Horsfield that she left home "with just the same feeling a boy has when he wants to run away to sea. . . . Only, in my adventure, men were mixed up, because of course they had to be. . . . Do you understand that a girl might have that feeling?" (51). Horsfield pities her, but he cannot understand. Nor does Julia wholly reject traditional interpretations of her street wandering: men "had to be" mixed up in it. Early in the novel, a man follows Julia, only to be repudiated; at the end, another man accosts her and then, when he looks closely into her tired face, recoils: "Ah, *non, alors*" (187). Perhaps after all she is more traditional streetwalker than free-spirited observer. As Deborah Parsons has pointed out, Rhys's "mannequins, models, show-girls, and prostitutes . . . are problematically uncertain realizations of the urban

---

5. For more on modern *flânerie*, see Janet Wolff, "The Invisible Flâneuse: Women and the Literature of Modernity," *Theory, Culture and Society* 2.3 (1985): 37–46; Walter Benjamin, *The Arcades Project* (Cambridge, MA: The Belknap Press, 1999).

woman as model for emancipated identity" (144). Julia provides a tragic alternative to the educated, independent New Woman who confidently walks the streets.

In each of her protagonists' tragedies, Rhys denies the too-easy assumptions of modernity, that we may leave history behind: just as her women are restrained by traditional stereotypes, so they are haunted by their personal pasts. "Every day is a new day; every day you are a new person. What have you to do with the day before?" Julia tells herself—shortly before returning to Mackenzie and his grudging support (157). Twice, she sees the ghost of her youthful well-dressed self: first in London, wearing "a long, very tight check skirt, a short dark-blue coat, and a bunch of violets bought from the man in Woburn Square," and later in Paris, where an old menu reminds her of wearing "a white crêpe de Chine dress, and red slippers" (180). The clothing carries, for Julia, nostalgic associations of past happiness. But to her former lovers, her actual reappearances seem ghostly and distasteful; she haunts Mackenzie, he feels, "as an ungenerous action does haunt one" (28). And to her first lover Neil (based on Lancelot Smith), Julia knows she must appear "an importunate ghost" (66). For the men, her reappearance suggests, not the glamorously dressed woman of the past, but an expectation that she wants money—an expectation that Julia inevitably fulfills. This equation of stylish dress (Julia's recollections) with money (her patrons' memories of paying for her clothes) is precise, if metaphorical. The men paid for her costumes as a way of buying sex with her; she bought the clothing as a means of attracting the men, in hopes of gaining both money and love—entities that are disastrously close together in this novel. Certainly Julia's love affair with clothing may be read as a mistaking of style for substance. Repeatedly throughout the novel she hopes to recreate herself through dress. Her first response when she needs cash is the thought, "I must get some new clothes" (19). The narrative begins and ends with Julia, having received a little money from a grudging man, planning to spend it on dress (58, 182). And by the conclusion, it seems that she equates clothing with love, or at least sees it as a way to obtain love: "She began to imagine herself in a new black dress and a little black hat with a veil that just shadowed her eyes. After all, why give up hope when so many people had loved her?" (181–82). Moreover, the plot seems to validate that equation. Clothing and appearance indeed rule Julia's society: "People thought twice before they were rude to anybody wearing a good fur coat" (80).

In *After Leaving Mr Mackenzie*, the past is not dead enough for the men, while it is too much past for women. And it was through a return to the past, and a new voice, that Rhys finally achieved her mature style. Rhys's third and fourth novels, *Voyage in the Dark* (1934) and *Good Morning, Midnight* (1939), show a notable growth in writing skill. In moving from third-person to first-person narration, she found a more effective style for her brand of literary impressionism. In the earlier fictions, she had struggled to encompass both the passivity and the anger reflected in her two favored costumes, a little-girl dress and a sleek, simplistic modern style. As noted, the frills of an infantile presentation did not win Marya the sympathy Rhys might have expected. She moved to the other extreme with the mature, sarcastic Julia of *Mackenzie* but still struggled to master the heavy ironies of her protagonist's situation. Each of Rhys's novels opposes plot to point of view, as Celia Marshik delineates (175). But while the first two novels' endings are sad and deflationary, it is the conclusions of *Voyage* and *Midnight* that directly re-dress the fairy-tale marriage plot: no shining prince or happy life (*Voyage*) and a "yes" not to marital relations but to a grotesque semi-rape (*Midnight*). In fact, Rhys's matured narrative style reflects the increased simplicity of her characters' preferred monochromatic outfits (black, dark blue). Each of these later two novels uses the first-person voice to capture the holistic perceptions of one unfortunate single girl.

In *Voyage in the Dark* (1934), the writer recalled her chorus-girl days and initial seduction, from twenty years' vantage point. This third, very autobiographical novel is not about Ford at all, yet it most effectively demonstrates the lessons he taught her. The shaped and cut ego displayed in this fiction is as jarring and as compelling as a stripped body and, despite its young narrator and "words of one syllable" (*Letters* 24), the novel is as mature as one of Chanel's little black dresses. More impressionist than ever, this narrative remains almost entirely within its protagonist's point of view; yet as she receives her unhappy sentimental education, the childlike Anna like her creator learns to objectify feminine grief through a broadened vision of dress and the inescapable self.

Youth dominates *Voyage*, which begins with birth imagery and ends with an abortion. The birth motif corresponds to Anna's daydreams of her childhood: unlike Rhys's first two novels, *Voyage* is filled with memories of Dominica, and its protagonist, like Rhys herself, was born in the West Indies. In certain ways, the narrative is consciously childish, "like a kitten mewing," Rhys commented (*Letters* 24). The kitten image is appropriate, since the vulnerable Anna frequently is seen as too young for her predicament. Her lover Walter Jeffries (a full portrayal of Lancelot Smith) questions her age when he first meets her (12). And his love-talk assumes her naïveté: "You rum child, you rum little devil" (48). To coldhearted cousin Julian, who will persuade him to break off the affair, she is "infantile Anna" (69). Walter, he remarks, "has been doing a bit of babysnatching" (73). Moreover, Anna is first depicted with a childlike fixation on dress: "When I thought about my clothes I was too sad to cry" (21). She longs for beautiful clothes, and when she wears black it is because she has read that "men delighted in that sable colour" (19). With the first money Walter sends her, she hurries to Cohen's dress shop in Shaftesbury Avenue, where the proprietors dress her as if she "were a doll." Her outfit resembles the clothing worn by Julia's younger ghost-self, dark blue with a long, tight skirt "so that when I moved in it I saw the shape of my thighs" (25). Whether Anna recognizes the style's sexuality is unclear. Her excited response again evokes birth: "*This is a beginning. . . . Out of this warm room that smells of fur I'll go to all the lovely places I've ever dreamt of*" (25; emphasis in original).

Anna trusts in clothing to create her new life, but the plot skewers her faith in modeling for men. By the narrative's midpoint, Walter has broken off the affair and in so doing inadvertently breaks Anna's clothing dependence. Far from having Julia's "voluptuous" obsession with clothing, the disillusioned Anna exhibits a freedom from dress concerns startling in the girl who earlier had "want[ed] pretty clothes like hell" (22). She learns both to analyze and to sympathize with other modern women on the street. She observes "a black velvet dress in a shop window, with the skirt slit up so that you could see the light stocking. A girl could look lovely in that, like a flower or doll." The familiar imagery first suggests Anna's sisterhood with Rhys's other dress-conscious women: black again, sexualized again, and aiming to resemble a beautiful inanimate object. But Anna carries the observation further by acknowledging others' perspectives: "The clothes of most of the women who passed were like caricatures of the clothes in the shop-windows, but when they stopped to look you saw that their eyes were fixed on the future" (111). Equal parts dispassionate criticism and pity, Anna's summation is very mature, as is her subsequent commentary. "Keep hope alive and you can do anything," she observes, acknowledging her own hopelessness. New clothes no longer equal love—only hope.

For Anna personally, the novel's end offers little hope; rather, the narrative points up the impossibility of escaping one's past. When, like Rhys herself, Anna becomes pregnant by one of the unknown men she has picked up, she sells the fur coat her former lover gave her but also writes to him requesting help (144). Walter's intermediary Julian appears, assuring Anna that wanting the baby is "nonsense" and that they will pay for an abortion. Then she must try to "start fresh. . . . You'll forget it and it'll be just as though it had never happened" (147). Likewise a doctor, called in after the abortion is botched, laughs: "She'll be all right. . . . Ready to start all over again in no time, I've no doubt." Originally Rhys ended the novel with Anna's death, but her publisher persuaded her to create a supposedly more hopeful conclusion.

Rhys's growth in artistry becomes clear when we compare this conclusion with that of *Quartet*, her previous novel featuring a childlike woman calling for our sympathy. The final pages of the earlier book proceed in abrupt jerks from Marya's perspective to Stephan's. Newly released from prison, Stephan becomes angry when Marya rejects him physically and taunts him with her affair with Heidler. They quarrel, and he snatches a gun and—when Marya tries to stop him from leaving the apartment—knocks her down. In our last glimpse of the protagonist, she is probably not dead but "crumpled up and l[ying] still" (185)—and surprisingly unpitiful. Stephan walks out, is picked up by a female acquaintance, and follows her, thinking, "*Encore une grue*" (186) [Another whore]. The effect is not merely distancing irony but a dismembered narrative, both too distant and clumsily fragmented. By contrast, *Voyage* concludes with a more subtle reference to the protagonist's prostitution—and yet clearer, since the cynical doctor's comments are embedded in her perspective. Anna lies in bed, hearing his words and thinking "about starting all over again, all over again . . ." (158). The repetition points up the hopeless cycle in which the young *demimondaine* is caught.

Likewise, Rhys's novels featuring mature women—*Leaving Mr Mackenzie* and *Good Morning, Midnight*—show how she increased her powerful effects when she began to cut her narratives from the whole cloth of single perspective. Both Julia and Sasha are sarcastic and self-destructive, and *Mackenzie* provides a clear, ironic commentary on male misunderstandings of the single girl. But its conclusion is, like the entire narrative, coldly distanced. First Julia, returned to Paris, is accosted as a prostitute and then rejected when her suitor looks more closely at her (187). Then we are given (as in *Quartet*) a final short chapter from a man's perspective. Mackenzie, unexpectedly encountering Julia once more, finds the "romantic side of his nature assert[ing] itself.... 'I'm not a bad sort,'" he tells himself. "Who says that I'm a bad sort?... How many of them would give a drink to a woman who had smacked them in the face in public?" (190). His self-congratulatory generosity subsides into melancholy, as Julia accepts his money without thanks or comment. He escapes into the street for Rhys's smashing concluding line: "It was the hour between dog and wolf, as they say" (191). The twilight image might be stretched to describe Rhys's experience of the thirties; it also prefigures the bestial and lupine imagery of *Midnight*, which moves beyond *Mackenzie*'s skilled ironies to become the masterpiece of Rhys's first career. More fragmented, more symbolic, and more experimental than her earlier works, this fourth, overtly prewar novel also presents her most convincing and most culpable protagonist.

STYLING PREWAR PARIS: *GOOD MORNING, MIDNIGHT*

Having established herself as a modern novelist, and having taken her third protagonist into the dark, Rhys greeted stark night in her fourth, and nearly final, novel. *Good Morning, Midnight* turns both the modern woman and the modernist novel inside out. The narrative voice is gruesomely frank, describing hallucinations of a mechanized society, bestial imagery, and cruel objectifications of both sexes. Through her protagonist Sasha, Rhys punctures not only the traditional marriage plot but its male modernist revision, since the book concludes with a horrifying, ironic play upon Molly Bloom's famous "Yes." It was sixteen years since, in the conclusion to James Joyce's *Ulysses* (1922), Molly had welcomed her husband to her bed, thereby reaffirming her commitment to their marriage. And not only had high modernism aged, but those promises of modernity had gone terribly wrong. That *Midnight* bears a sense that "the night is coming," is unsurprising, in war-threatened Paris. What shocks is that Sasha embraces the impending doom: "May you tear each other to bits, you damned hyenas, and the quicker the better.... Let it be destroyed. Let it happen" (173).

This bitterest novel also suggests Rhys's surprising response to a happier life. In the thirties, her writing found critical success and, unlike her downward-spiraling single girls, she remarried. Rhys had lived with her literary agent, Leslie Tilden Smith, since 1928; when she finally obtained a divorce from Jean Lenglet, they wed. Smith devotedly typed and encouraged her writing until his death at the war's end—after which Rhys married his cousin, Max Hamer. But despite the long-suffering support of two patient husbands, these marriages were not unqualified successes. Rhys had become an alcoholic, and often a violently quarrelsome one; moreover, neither husband was rich, and frequently the struggle for money overwhelmed all else. Perhaps Rhys truly owned her single girls' perspectives, in which love and money are intertwined: after all, a fairy tale includes both an ideal marriage and untold riches. The same sexual economics dominate the traditional Victorian novel's marriage plot, which ultimately Rhys would explode in *Wide Sargasso Sea*. And perhaps her personal disillusionment explains the anger with which she styles prewar Paris, a city she always had loved, and turns a cynical eye on any claim of disinterested sympathy.

Moreover, in a direct assault on high-modernist verities, Sasha fixates on a single, lost garment she had coveted when working in an haute-couture shop: "I have tried it on; I have seen myself in it. It is a black dress with wide sleeves embroidered in vivid colours—red, green, blue, purple. It is my dress. If I had been wearing it I should never have stammered or been stupid" (28). Most Rhys women love little black dresses, but this longed-for garment is a big black dress, with dramatic, brightly decorated sleeves in Schiaparelli fashion. Notably, Sasha sees this "power dress" as intimately related to herself, a garment that would have enabled her to respond brilliantly to her sneering supervisor. The classic black embellished with colors harks back to Miss Bruce's claim that beautiful clothing constitutes an aesthetic pleasure—and certainly for Sasha this longed-for dress has nothing to do with modeling for men. Perhaps it represents the lost modernist myth of salvific art (see T. Miller, *Late Modernism* 14); however, the longing for perfect style is hopeless in the aging world of late-thirties Europe.

Sasha is the oldest, most self-aware, and most hopeless single woman in Rhys's canon. Like Marya and Julia, she has a failed marriage and wistful memories colored by beautiful clothes; like Julia too, she mourns a baby that died a few days after birth. Unlike Anna, she has no expectation that she will "do it all over again." She has come to Paris on a solitary trip, with funds borrowed from a friend, for "a change" and to get "some new clothes" (11–12). But the clothes do not inspire hope: Sasha claims little interest in dressing to attract men and no confidence that any man wants her. She thinks frequently of suicide and sardonically about her survival to this point: "Saved, rescued, fished-up, half-drowned, out of the deep, dark river, dry clothes, hair shampooed and set. Nobody would know I had ever been in it" (10). She is by far the most objective self-evaluator of Rhys's women.

Yet Sasha also possesses a radically divided self. As Carol Dell'Amico has noted, *Midnight* above all is "a flâneur novel" that "bespeaks a subjectivity in crisis" (8, 9). Even more than Julia in *Mackenzie*, Sasha wanders the streets, but Julia at her story's end still hopes that new clothes may gain her love. Sasha nurses no ambition of picking up a beneficial man: she is harshly pessimistic about her own value and future. But her other side is quakingly self-conscious: "My life, which seems so simple and monotonous, is really a complicated affair of cafés where they like me and cafés where they don't . . . looking-glasses I look nice in, looking-glasses I don't, dresses that will be lucky, dresses that won't" (46). She spends her cash on a daily round of drinks, in establishments where she suspects that others despise her. She responds by getting her hair dyed: "First it must be bleached, that is to say, its own colour must be taken out of it—and then it must be dyed, that is to say, another colour must be imposed on it" (52). The hair process suggests the self-reaming required for psychic survival, as does the dichotomy Sasha employs when addressing her beloved Paris: "You are looking very nice tonight, my beautiful, my darling, and oh what a bitch you can be! But you didn't kill me after all" (16).

In fact, this woman's true spoiled love affair is with Paris, which binds the narration together. The metropolis is a significant aspect of modernism[6] that yet, as Tyrus Miller describes, in undermining individualism made it "increasingly difficult for authors to achieve some sort of synoptic vision, to discover some place from which to narrate the whole" (39–40). But Rhys through her fictional Sasha achieves such a vision: the once-loved city provides an inclusive framework for presenting the modern fragmentation of subjectivity. This novel's plot may be read as a street walk in which the narrator confronts animate places, such as Paris and her hotel room; memories; and occasional human beings. Sasha's impressions merge past and present, inanimate and human, since she addresses each entity as if it were living. Sometimes inanimate objects speak, as in the novel's opening words: "'Quite like old times,' the room says. 'Yes? No?'"

---

6. See Williams (10) and also David Harvey, who reads Georg Simmel's "The Metropolis and Mental Life" (1918) as a contemporary representation of a connection between the urban experience and modernist thought (282).

(9)—voicing its occupant's divided self. In the street Sasha encounters a few men who try to pick her up, or simply to befriend her: a young Russian is kind—but once she notices that he is anxious about paying for a taxi or drinks, Sasha has no interest in him. The painter Serge sympathizes when she cries—but after all, he wants her to purchase his painting. Meanwhile, Sasha is haunted by unpleasant remarks overheard in cafés and by her next-door neighbor, a cadaverous *commis* (traveling salesman) who makes passes at her, dressed in a white robe. The *commis*, who follows her and comes to her door uninvited, "looks like a priest . . . of some obscene, half-understood religion," or perhaps he is "a paper man, a ghost, something that doesn't exist." In any case, he frightens Sasha: of all the unpleasant or cruel people in Rhys's repertoire, he is the closest to inhuman. She regularly retreats from him, and all the others, into her room, "a place where you hide from the wolves outside" (38).

Yet she finds wolves in her memories of human cruelty as well, particularly in her past job in a Parisian couture shop. "I would feel as if I were drugged, sitting there, watching those damned dolls, thinking what a success they would have made of their lives if they had been women. Satin skin, silk hair, velvet eyes, sawdust heart—all complete" (18). Although Sasha herself has been a live mannequin, she sees the artificial figures in the shop windows as ironically perfect women, beautiful objects unable to feel. She recalls how a "sturdy old lady with gay, bold eyes" entered with her daughter and began to try hats on her perfectly bald head. But when they left, Sasha heard the daughter abusing her mother for making a fool of herself and glimpsed the old lady's "face reflected in a mirror, her eyes still undaunted but something about her mouth and chin collapsing" (22–23). Struck with compassion—and with identification—Sasha mentally accused the daughter of "bloodless[ly] killing" her mother.

The weight of human contempt, and the desirability of being an insensate object, are underlined by Sasha's second recollection, about her treatment at the hands of the visiting English manager. In an episode that presumably led to her dismissal, "Mr. Blank" questions Sasha about her facility in German, flustering her so that she can only respond in her head, in a babble: "Homo homini lupus, aus meinen grossen Schmerzen mach ich die kleinen Lieder" (24) [Man is a wolf to man, out of my great pains I make the little songs].[7] Unquestionably humans are cruel to one another,

---

7. The classical tag is from Plautus but was famously used by Sigmund Freud in *Civilization and Its Discontents*; the second line is from Heinrich Heine's "Lyrical Intermezzo."

in Sasha's view and in Rhys's as well. Yet Sasha, recalling how Mr. Blank badgered her until she cried, defends herself eloquently in retrospect:

> You, who represent Society, have the right to pay me four hundred francs a month. That's my market value, for I am an inefficient member of Society.... So you have the right to pay me four hundred francs a month, to lodge me in a small, dark room, to clothe me shabbily, to harass me with worry and monotony and unsatisfied longings till you get me to the point when I blush at a look, cry at a word.... Let's say that you have this mystical right to cut my legs off. But the right to ridicule me afterwards because I am a cripple—no, that I think you haven't got. (29)

There is nothing akin to this speech in all of Rhys's writing: a sustained argument about the wolves ruling society and their relations to weak and "inefficient" single girls. Through Sasha, Rhys condemns not only the English manager but all powerful, abusive men for assuming a sadistic gender-capitalism: whatever the market—that is, women—will bear is right. An unprofitable worker becomes a barely useful object, to be mistreated in accordance with her low value. Sasha speaks these words in hindsight, with an aged sense of her own worthlessness, to men or to anybody. Yet the memory of her boss's objectification is matched by the way in which Sasha objectifies him, refusing even to allow him a name: "Now, strangely enough, I am no longer afraid of Mr Blank. He is one thing and I am another" (28). Still, escaping into objectification, of oneself or others, proves dangerous for Sasha: man is a wolf to man.

Perhaps a growing wolfishness stems from the prewar atmosphere. Sasha remembers the joyful early twenties: "The war is over. No more war—never, never, never" (114). In retrospect, that false promise points up the impermanence of her youthful marriage and happiness. And she recalls friends singing popular songs with rather ominous clothing metonymies: "That funny kind of dress you wear / Leaves all your back and your shoulders bare."[8] Sasha's husband Enno sang a ditty capturing his hand-to-mouth philosophy: "Quand on n'a pas de chaussures.... On prend une voiture, / On ne vois voit pas les pieds!" (116) [When we don't have shoes, we will ride in a car so no one sees our feet!]. Even clothing in her

---

8. R. P. Weston and F. J. Barnes, "In These Hard Times" (1915).

past, for this Rhys woman, evokes scantiness and lack: "shabby clothes, worn-out shoes, circles under your eyes, your hair getting straight and lanky" (121). And in Sasha's present, while Rhys's other women yearn for transformative clothes, desirable dress exists only as a lost possibility. Likewise Enno's promise, "when we get to Paris," becomes a leitmotif in her memories (115, 117, 119, 120). But beautiful Paris is no longer available; Sasha is through with modeling for men, and she anticipates "the next war, or something like that. Nothing to cry about" (39). Stylish Paris and the displayed, stylish self already are lost to Sasha; why, then, should she weep over further destruction?

Sasha believes she has finished being an object of male desire, but she has not realized the complications of objectification. One casual encounter proves different: a handsome young man pursues her, inexplicably to Sasha until she realizes that he is a gigolo who believes she is wealthy. She is alternately amused and bemused to find the tables turned: "He isn't trying to size me up, as [men] usually do—he is exhibiting himself, his own person" (72). The gigolo René provides a mirror image for Sasha's own modeling for men: "I have done this so often myself that it is amusing to watch somebody else doing it" (73). She suspects that he is deceived by her fur coat and she half-encourages his advances, thinking, "I might be able to get some of my own back" (72). Yet despite herself, she is drawn into companionship with him: it is not merely that he shares her habits of using sexual attraction for money, but like her, René is lonely and world-weary: "I'm not always so fond of human beings, either" (77). Gradually she is drawn into hoping that he really wants her, not her supposed money.

At the book's end, she allows René into her hotel room. They quarrel, and he responds with wolf-like sexual violence and insults—until Sasha says, "You can have the money right away" (183). To her shock, he immediately gets up, puts on his clothes, and leaves. Her mirror image appears to have enacted the most crass possibility of Rhys's single girls: the prostitute who truly wants only money not love. Sasha is devastated, yet Rhys does not end with this simple ironic reversal, that the objectified woman has turned a man into an object. When Sasha in amazement sees that René did not take her money, she celebrates by drinking, and her subsequent hallucination merges "Madame Venus" with voices saying "Femmes, femmes, femmes, femmes" and a train saying "Paris, Paris, Paris, Paris." The goddess of love joins with a vanishing Paris, creating a huge steel machine with long, thin arms: "At the end of each arm is an eye, the eyelashes stiff with mascara. When I look more closely I see that only some of the arms have these eyes—others have lights." Paris herself has become a modern object, a "very beautiful" one (187). And if the City of Light herself is styled a machine, then people are either objects or beasts: "Who wouldn't be afraid of a pack of damned hyenas?" (173). So if the ethical grounds of thirties modernism strive to reject "the efficient robot" and the mechanized body (T. Miller, *Late Modernism* 24), then Sasha's climactic nightmare suggests the machine has won.

Finally, her wish for destruction, both personal and national, culminates. As she longs for René to come back, she pictures him turning around and walking up the stairs. She undresses and lies on her bed, waiting. But when her door opens, the man who enters is not Rene but the sinister *commis* from next door. That Sasha embraces her rapist, pulling him down on the bed, "despis[ing] another poor devil of a human being for the last time," has been read as a compassionate broadening on her part, a return to seeing others as human beings, not objects. But the effect is horrific, as is her final "Yes—yes—yes . . ." (189). As Mary Lou Emery noted, Sasha is echoing her submission to the bullying Mr. Blank: "Just a hopeless, helpless little fool, aren't you?" "Yes, yes, yes, yes. Oh, yes" (*Midnight* 28). Thus, if "this final scene suggests birth [of a reunified self, for Sasha], it is that of a machine with mascaraed eyes, an artificial woman like the shop dummies Sasha has cynically admired" (Emery 171). She is embracing death, perhaps literally; she is making herself an object; and she is inviting degradation as she earlier prayed for war to end it all: stripped, prone, and welcoming midnight.

"I can abstract myself from my body," Rhys once remarked to a shocked Frenchman in Paris (*Smile* 95). If so, it is because she felt she must learn to strip off her self as one would strip clothes from one's body—and her characters struggle to do the same. But if in fact clothes are "inseparable from the self" (Hollander, *Seeing* 451), Rhys nevertheless depicted women's strategies for comprehending and managing that inseparability. Certainly the writer used her often retrograde dependence upon men and clothes in the service of a pared modernist style. So if clothing served as a metonymy for the tragic dependence of women modeling for men, the literary impressionism modeled by men had offered a way for Jean Rhys to "write back." But in any case, high modernism—including literary impressionism—was dying. War was coming, and Paris, fashion, literature, and Rhys herself would be buried beneath its floods.

PART II
The Homefront Style

The War in *Vogue* and Literature

T O DESCRIBE A WAR'S PROGRESS through a fashion magazine seems the essence of triviality. But the Second World War, conducted so extensively against civilians, was a war of incongruities, where trivial material facts played their part in life and death. In Britain, women were urged to recycle lipstick holders and to have their corsets reconditioned rather than replaced, but they also suffered real hardship in the loss of homes, possessions, loved ones, and life. British *Vogue* photographed theatre-goers in full evening dress, taking refuge from bombs in the London Underground, while in the next few years tens of thousands of Londoners died from bombs. Families at home ate their dinners off Morrison bomb shelters, and then crawled underneath those makeshift dining tables to sleep at night. Women were patronizingly encouraged to "preserve the arts of peace" by maintaining their "feminine interests" in beauty and dress, this being their "best contribution . . . to national defence" (*Vogue* 9/20/39: 23).[1]

---

1. British *Vogue*, while containing some of the material in the American edition, differed substantially during the war. All subsequent references to British *Vogue* magazine are by date: page number.

But women, especially single women, also played active and vital military roles in the Battle of Britain, during D-Day, and throughout the war. *Vogue* itself, which in 1939 had reluctantly made "The Case for Slacks," would in 1945 publish pictures of naked concentration-camp victims (5/17/39: 57; 5/45: 42–43). Incongruity, combined with defiant triviality, became a hallmark of British courage: the homefront style.

Like fashion, high-art literature seemed a trivial occupation in the face of Fascist threats to life, liberty, and Western civilization. In truth, the heirs of high modernism were so accustomed to believing in art as the meaning of life that they were flummoxed by the downgrading of their highest values. Most notably, Cyril Connolly founded his literary journal *Horizon* in order to uphold ideals of high culture in wartime England. And wartime literature did flourish, but in ways that put a period to the era of sacred literary art. High seriousness was reserved for grim political fictions by authors such as Arthur Koestler and George Orwell. The most successful male novelists of the thirties, Graham Greene and Evelyn Waugh, sought war posts in the forties, thoroughly enjoying the life-and-death excitement and using their experiences in popular middlebrow novels. Female novelists also changed their lives: Dorothy L. Sayers turned permanently from detective fiction to religious drama and scholarship, and Jean Rhys, whose modernist novels had promised so much, receded into a twenty-year obscurity. For some women writers, the war eventually validated a homefront style where domestic and personal trivia took on new significances. Overall, most serious fiction focused upon small-scale, realistic depictions of wartime life, but often dependent upon content rather than style. Despite Connolly's hopes, the exigencies of war pushed literary style into an auxiliary role. British literature was aging out of modernism, and what it would become had not yet appeared.

Nevertheless, supporters of literature found its marginalization harder to bear than did the fashion promoters, who were accustomed to speaking of their wares with light irony. As a *Vogue* editor cheerfully wrote, "We are not surprised, but inordinately pleased, to learn that so stern a thing as the will to conquer can be made of such fragile stuff as a frock" (9/20/39: 26). Some literary writers, on the other hand, were quite surprised to learn that their work could be seen as "fragile stuff." But those who spent the war writing discovered that the ironic understatement fashionable in wartime provided a workable style for literary art. Finally, then, the war—its challenges, its deprivations, and its grim revelations—brought permanent changes in the styles of fashion and of literature. Both Britain's dress and her literature became signs of her stiff upper lip and a small nation's insistence upon the value of small things, although what began as courage would end, in the later forties, in a culture of minimalism.

CHAPTER 4

How *Vogue* Changed Clothes in War

IN A PROPHETIC 1939 EDITORIAL, British *Vogue* claimed that "fashion, like the woman it clothes, is proving no goodtime girl, thrown into confusion by the shock of war, but a staunch support, an invaluable ally" (9/39: 20). In a vast war, fashion's reputation for triviality was both challenged and reinforced by its material nature. As early theorists recognized, fashion encodes both our inner longings and our outer social relations. Add to those encoded meanings the economic implications of a certain dress or hat, implications that became stark with wartime shortages, and Britons could not deny that how one dresses matters. What remained debatable was the question of degree: how much of clothing's importance was symbolic, and how much of it was starkly economic? By the end of World War II, the debate would crystallize in two unexpected and discomfiting areas: one, the shockingly un-English response of Frenchwomen and French couturiers to wartime occupation and deprivations; the other, the British response to continued postwar shortages and rationing, as seen in the New Look.

SERIOUS *VOGUE*

Vogue has been scorned as a source for fashion history, for ignoring the class distinctions in dress that would persist into the postwar period (McNeil, "Put Your Best Face" 283). But the premier fashion magazine offers plenty of evidence, through its articles and its advertisements, for an incipient democratizing of dress. Wartime strains told alike on couture and everyday British dress, and shortages, rationing, and political implications all are reflected accurately through a progression of wartime *Vogues*.[1] It is true that those who earned a living through fashion always had walked a tightrope between heavy meaning and gossamer transience. But to speak, in uncertain times, with delicate irony of serious topics was both to entertain and to assure readers that they still might leaven their fears with humor. Thus editors joked: "She says she won't be seen dead in her gas mask. I say she probably will be, anyhow" (5/3/39: 41). And as war threatened in the summer of 1939, Alan Stewart in *Vogue* advised women on appropriate table talk:

> It seems there is a situation in Europe, and you can't cling to the dim convention that Foreign Affairs are a purely masculine foible. Since everybody talks politics, it is a social necessity to know about these things . . . and make a success of this new and exciting game. (6/28/39: 52)

The facetious tone aims at a fashionably careless stance, rather than giving genuine advice: very few readers thought of European affairs merely as an "exciting game." Just a few weeks earlier, the magazine's editors had admitted that "it takes the very young or the very tough, those who cannot remember the last war, or those who are not too appalled at the thought of another, to find much real distraction . . . just now" (5/3/39: 45). Yet their writers endeavored to distract, and more: even as *Vogue* made light of serious issues, it spoke seriously of fashion:

> We put our faith in fashion . . . [as] fashion is no surface frivolity but a profound instinct. . . . Wars, revolutions, social changes have altered its

---

1. Unlike the World War I period, where *Vogue* maintained its upper-class, haute-couture identity (see Buckley and Fawcett 71–76), the homefront war on citizens stretched British *Vogue* (nicknamed "Brogue") in surprising directions, as this chapter describes.

course, but not extinguished it—nor will war do so now.... How explain such unswerving purpose, such superb assurance, except on the thesis that fashion is part of an irresistible Life Force? (2/40: 11)

Vogue's credo here appeals to a transcendent rationale, using a rhetoric both fatuous and loftily abstract. How else to justify a fashion magazine in wartime? A more down-to-earth justification also appeared in 1940, in the words of Edna Woolman Chase, Vogue's American editor in chief: "You think that Vogue is enormously concerned with matters which, to you, seem utterly fantastic. We believe ... that they have, if taken in their sum total, large importance in developing the outward and visible graces of a civilized way of life." Chase's claim, that fashion is among the civilized "causes for which this war is waged" (Chase and Chase 329), would be repeated by others later in the war. So would the pragmatic economic details of all the little people and industries that fashion magazines and designers supported. Both defenses are plausible, but they lack the glamorous archness employed by Vogue as the war began.

In early-war Vogue, the editorial tone is complacent but ironic. Certain pronouncements deliberately join the trivial and the momentous: "Do your beauty exercises ... and keep your hair and complexion in good trim. It would be an added calamity if war turned us into a nation of frights and slovens" (9/20/39: 26). This exhortation, shortly following Britain's declaration of war, may be read as shallow, as naive, or as gallantly winking. In the same issue, women are informed that "no spirit, however strong, can survive an unrelieved diet of khaki and war talk. Determine, then—in this European jungle—to dress for dinner" (44). To dress for dinner was to insist that the protocols of British civilization, protocols representing the traditions of the upper and wealthy classes for which Vogue was created, were eternal verities. That "dressing for dinner," carried out in literal jungles throughout the empire, bore a special symbolism is clear from its thematic persistence in modern literature: from Clarissa Dalloway in Woolf's *The Voyage Out* (46) to the beleaguered aristocrats of Evelyn Waugh's wartime *Brideshead Revisited,* the old-fashioned fashionable had insisted on donning special evening clothes to dine. And the war did sound the death knell for that custom, as Vogue eventually would admit.

The war would not kill fashion, however, though Vogue's editorial staff learned to rein in their casual ironies. The joking of late 1939 reflects the

"Bore War" or "Phoney War" period, where British soldiers and civilians alike prepared for action, waited for attack—and then became skeptical as nothing happened. As Angus Calder recalled, during the Bore War "the belts of the well-to-do did not tighten very much" (70). By the spring of 1940, however, it was becoming evident that appeasement had failed. Accordingly, *Vogue*'s tone shifted to a less flippant language that implicitly acknowledged present dangers, deprivations, and—fully as important, in light of Britain's future—an incipient democratized society. The June 1940 issue, prepared just before the evacuation at Dunkirk, included an editorial headed "Things Are Different," which mixes equal parts of concession and self-congratulation:

> This is a season with a difference.... We have lost splendor, but gained spontaneity; lost formality, but gained friendliness.... [D]ressed up for afternoon (precious service leave time): dressed down for evening.... The need for simpler entertaining, fewer servants, has brought us down to doll's house living, miniature and gay. (6/40: 27)

Things were different, all right: many society women were working for the WVS (Women's Voluntary Service) or had actual service jobs, and government restrictions were beginning to limit the expenditures of the wealthy. Still, the writer concludes airily: "Instead of poor little rich girls there are rich little poor girls, who . . . are glad things are—different."

In two months, no one would be glad. The Dutch army already had been defeated; Brussels fell. In June Mussolini declared war and Hitler's troops entered Paris. The evacuation of British forces from Dunkirk was cause for equal parts pride and shame, but Britons had scant time to meditate upon it, with the Battle of Britain beginning. "Britain is fighting for her life: we are all involved," wrote *Vogue* editor Leslie Blanch in September 1940; her language is notably subdued and straightforward in contrast to earlier wartime editorials (36). The fashion magazine remained a fashion magazine: the same issue includes news of Paris fashion houses closing, along with patterns for "the new straighter silhouette" (27, 28–29). And a self-advertisement assures the reader that "wherever freedom survives— Vogue lives and flourishes. Vogue is still published in London and New York. . . . Now, more than ever, Vogue has a mission: to preserve the art of civilized living" (66). *Vogue* continued to celebrate itself and its focuses, but without metaphysics or coy ironies. From here out, the war-style jokes would be consciously brave or defiant, as in an advertisement that boasts, after months of heavy bombing, "Luftwaffe Cannot Interrupt an Otherwise Permanent Wave" (2/41: 10). Things are different now, indeed.

If the language of fashionable style changed as the war got under way, dress styles too took unexpected paths. Late-thirties couture fashions had been excessive in their feminine silhouettes, excessive in their use of materials, and often excessive in the demands they put upon the wearer. As recently as January 1939, a Vogue headline had dictated "Nipped-in Waists: Dresses Demand It, Corsets Contrive It" (1/11/39: 34). The war nipped that incipient style in the bud, along with full skirts and long silken evening gowns. Nobody needed extra discomfort while engaged in war work, and no extra materials were available. Suffering to be beautiful fell out of fashion: British women were suffering enough.

Likewise, the war largely suspended a flirtation between modernist artists and high fashion. Since its start, Vogue had used stylized covers, and in the twenties and thirties those covers were created by avant-garde artists such as Salvador Dali, Eduardo Garcia Benito, and Georges Lapape. Highmodern art occasionally even influenced modern fashion: in particular, Elsa Schiaparelli's Surrealist designs often were inspired by her friendships with artists. But Schiaparelli spent the war in the United States, and her influence in Britain, like that of other Continental designers, faded during the forties. Surrealist clothing may have seemed silly in wartime, or simply impossible to make and maintain. Even by the late thirties, Vogue's painted covers had given way to commercially oriented photographs that aimed, in the words of Edna Woolman Chase's famous directive, to "Show the dress . . . if that can't be done with art then art be damned" (Chase and Chase 294). By the time the war began, covers did show the dress in a straightforward manner, and if there was a stylized backdrop or design, it was patriotic. British Vogue's wartime photographer Lee Miller may have been the lover of Man Ray and friend of Pablo Picasso, but her photos for the magazine were plain and realistic: in wartime, the real sufficed.

In fact, reality nearly overwhelmed British households during the war. Nothing demonstrates the seriousness of trivial things like the history of clothes rationing in wartime Britain, and here the material bases of fashion come to the fore. Shortages began before actual rationing, for reasons that everyone accepted: British wool was needed for uniforms and silk (usually an artificial "silk") for parachutes. Even the bits of noncloth used in women's foundation garments soon would be in short supply, and the ways that trivial dress details were linked to the monumental war are described in the words of an anonymous wartime ditty: "Ships of steel for even keel / Need tons and tons of corset steel. / Army trucks if they're to hurdle / Need the rubber of the girdle" (Walford 109). Clothing prices rose steeply, more than doubling between September 1939 and May 1941 (42). The WVS collected and distributed free clothing from the United States and Canada. Still, rationing seemed in order, not merely to limit consumption but to prevent the wealthy from buying up what cloth and clothing remained. Such rationing was vehemently opposed by certain government leaders, including Winston Churchill, and veiled in secrecy up to its introduction in June 1941. Modeled upon a rationing scheme created by the Third Reich and stolen by British spies, the plan tried to avoid a last-minute run on the stores by inserting extra margarine coupons at the back of Britons' food-ration booklets. Then the announcement was sprung: citizens must use those coupons when they purchased cloth or clothing, in addition to a green card of forty more clothing coupons. The initial allowance was sixty-six coupons per adult per year, although this ration soon was cut. A man's coat was sixteen coupons; a pair of trousers was five to eight coupons; a woman's coat required from eleven to fourteen coupons, a dress seven to eleven coupons. Pajamas for either sex took eight coupons. Length and material affected the coupon "cost"—for instance, wool trousers or a wool dress used up more coupons than the same garments in cotton. Underwear, socks and stockings, handkerchiefs, ties, and footwear all required coupons. Clothing for small children was coupon-free, and eventually growing adolescents were allowed extra coupons, as were other special cases, including manual laborers, uniformed civilians, and diplomats. But no one luxuriated in an abundant wardrobe. Even if they qualified for supplemental coupons, the ration "gave adults something like half their pre-war consumption of clothing" (Calder 377). That was, of course, if they could pay the sky-high prices. Clothing styles in wartime Britain were shaped and fenced in by material constraints.

Given the restrictions and the obsessive coupon counting required (and granted black-market and illegal coupon-trading practices), the most surprising aspect of wartime rationing is its popularity. Mass Observation surveys found that seven out of eight respondents were pleased by the introduction of clothing rationing, because they felt that it was fair (Calder 275). The wealthy still bought more, and for that matter had more clothing in their closets already. But they too learned to "Make Do and Mend," in the words of the propaganda campaign. The queen set a public example by adhering strictly to wartime restrictions and having her own clothes cut down for the young princesses (Walford 29). In a war for survival, patriotism becomes fashionable, and it was significant for Britain's future that rationing became linked with patriotism in the public mind. *Vogue* jumped on the thrift bandwagon, promising readers at the outbreak of war "a practical and useful magazine . . . [that will] show how to make shillings do the work of pounds." Not incidentally, the same issue warned that *Vogue* would be published monthly rather than fortnightly and that "wartime conditions and transport problems make it impossible for magazines to be available, as before" (9/20/39: 8). Over the next few years, supply shortages would increase *Vogue*'s price and cut its size repeatedly (6/40; 4/42; 7/42). But more substantial changes in the fashion magazine would happen within. Perhaps it is not surprising to find airy support for Sir Kingsley Wood's new purchase tax, or to be told that his "no margin for error" motto resembles "those sound dress maxims that *Vogue* has always preached. How often have we counseled against 'the dress you buy and seldom wear'; how often said: 'Accessories which just miss chic are the ones that cost you more than you can afford'?" (10/40: 33). Certainly *Vogue*-ish thrift retained an unconscious elitism. Some early-war suggestions for thrift might miss the mark for the average housewife, but she hardly could dispute, throughout the forties, *Vogue*'s basic shopping theme: "Money now buys less, so you must make yours do more" (11/40: 8).

Indeed, the magazine adapted itself to new conditions with a celerity appropriate to fashion's changeable nature—and aimed at a broader audience than before. In the July 1941 issue, the first to respond to the rationing scheme, renewed defiance mingles with boosterism:

> It is now said that Fashion's goose is properly cooked and done in, for want of the best butter. . . .
> But Fashion, or elegance, is indestructible, and will survive even margarine coupons, for it is that intangible quality of taste, that sense of discrimination and invention which has lived on through all the clangour and chaos of the world's history. (7/41: 18)

The editorialist cannot resist a snobbish shudder at the linkage of dress with margarine coupons ("a horrid slight")—but she significantly adds that "this apparent knock-out blow to Fashion will prove the making of a wider sense of taste." That inclusive aim would last for the duration of the war because of deprivations that to some degree affected everyone, rich and poor. And to some degree, the solutions were the same for everyone. From summer 1941 on, both fashion photo spreads and advertisements regularly listed the source, the price, and the number of coupons required for each garment. And a feature that had been popular during the Depression years, Vogue-brand dressmaking patterns, became once more enormously important as more women endeavored to make do.[2] Energetic women, whether skilled seamstresses or not, observed that the coupons required for a length of cloth were fewer than those for the same amount made into clothing. *Vogue* prudently announced a possible pattern shortage, requesting patrons to choose from those already in stock; indeed, a month later the *Vogue Pattern Book* was temporarily suspended as the result of a warehouse bombing (6/41: 16; 7/41: 50). By midwar, the thrifty housewife's resort had become the norm, and feature articles on the latest fashions described clothes that one easily could sew oneself (9/43: 36). Indeed, so frequent became articles such as "Suggestions for Saving" and "Wartime Economies" that one suspects that *Vogue* was grateful for a fresh topic to grab its readers' interest, and perhaps to grab new readers, especially since it could no longer showcase extravagant clothing styles.

Was fashion's goose, then, in fact cooked? If dress was no longer exclusive, if clothing styles focused on necessity rather than decoration, did wartime Britain even have fashionable dress? Early in the war, the Board of Trade had implemented Austerity restrictions in order to curtail the unnecessary use of materials and labor: among Austerity's complex ordinances, manufacturers had to limit the pockets, buttons, seams, and pleats on clothing. Lace and decorative trim for infants' and women's clothing (and, eventually, underclothing) were banned, as were double-breasted suits and turn-ups (cuffs) on trousers for men. The laws were arcane and easily circumvented: those sewing their own clothes continued to decorate according to their tastes and means, and bespoke work for rich customers was not subject to the restrictions because those citizens paid a

---

2. *Vogue* had started selling paper dress patterns, for the less affluent, in 1916; however, as Buckley and Fawcett note, these early do-it-yourself patterns were so complex as to require "professional interpretation" (76). By the thirties, home dressmakers' patterns were more user-friendly.

33 percent luxury tax (Walford 54). But the net effect on fashion was depressive: Austerity panels, as Peter McNeil has noted, "did not so much dictate how garments should appear as how they might not" ("Put Your Best Face" 285). This ethos of negation implied that stylish dress had no place in wartime: clothing should be thrifty and functional. It is true that, in an effort to help wartime clothing manufacturers, the board also produced the Utility Clothing Scheme, which instructed certain firms to create attractive clothing following Austerity rules. Dreamed up by couturiers from the new Incorporated Society of London Fashion Designers, the first Utility garments were featured in Vogue, with moderate praise from its editorial staff: they were well-constructed and unmemorable (1/42: 52–53). Utility dresses were good-quality clothes at an excellent (because government-capped) price, but like most wartime clothing, these garments were born of necessity, not desire.

Also born of necessity was Vogue's insistence upon making a virtue of deprivation. When even society women did not choose their clothing from runway shows, they were praised for their plucky individualism: "Each woman wears the things that suit her best, and looks so lovely that she starts a new fashion" (1/41: 11). When midwar Austerity rules constrained decorative trim, an editorial titled "Today's Standard: Fewer, Simpler, Better Clothes" assured its readers that "in these days anything elaborate looks silly" (4/43: 31). The same issue concluded with tips on ways to renovate one's old clothes using Vogue patterns (73–75). In general, fashionable styles were simplified of necessity, so skirts became shorter and slimmer. An extensive photo feature called "Half-Measures" suggests dressing well by using two parts—"blouse and skirt, sweater and skirt"—thus having more options for fresh outfits (3/43: 29–37). Vogue claimed that "fashion [had] slowed into the tempo of a steady marriage, for it takes too many coupons to have clothes with which one falls in and out of love" (11/43: 28). But wartime lifestyles also mitigated fashionable dressing: when a dinner invitation meant staying the night because of the blackout, donning an evening gown (which in any case would be out of date) began to seem unnecessary. When materials for hats were expensive and stockings hard to obtain, wearing either to church became optional, as the Archbishop of Canterbury was obliged to proclaim (Calder 279). "By the middle of the war," Walford concludes, "fashion itself was out of fashion: out-of-date and worn clothes, simple hairstyles, no hats, no jewelry, and low-heeled shoes had become the new, patriotic style" (103).

Not only were low-heeled shoes handy for war work, but they looked better with socks, the legwear most available for most women. The wartime changes in British dress style were striking even to other nations at war. Most notably, American GIs posted to England were given a booklet that warned them not to look down on British civilians for appearing "dowdy and badly-dressed.... The British know that they help war production by wearing an old suit or dress until it cannot be patched any longer. Old clothes are 'good form'" (Longmate, *The G. I.'s* 23)[3]. And dress historian James Lauer sums up: "Clothes-rationing was introduced in June 1941, and fashion almost ceased to exist" (252).

GENDERED *VOGUE*

Nevertheless, feminine style was not dead, and its wartime expression shows intriguing differences between female and male clothing concerns in wartime Britain. Angus Calder explains, "Women in Britain, of all classes ... did their best to keep smart. It was patriotic to be chic." But "the famine of clothes" meant that "fashion sense expressed itself increasingly in elaborate attention to the head and face" (378–79). Hats were not rationed, and women who wished to adorn their heads sported styles ranging from very large cloches to patriotic little "Monty" berets. Likewise, although the factories campaigned to get women workers to cut or pin up their hair, girls still were seen with imitation Veronica Lake tresses: long, curled, drooping across one eye, and utterly impractical. Clearly, some British women went to considerable effort to look appealing, despite the challenges.

A notable feature of *Vogue* advertisements, beginning in 1941, is an aggressive rhetoric of apology for shortages. The tone is occasionally preachy, as in this prim announcement from Peter Scott Sportswear: "Patrons realizing that scarcity is a step to victory will exercise patriotic patience when confronted with difficulties in obtaining supplies"

---

3. Some GIs used the dress shortages to their own advantage. One veteran recalled that a gift of nylon stockings "got you a weekend in bed" and became known as "shack-up material." A young Englishwoman described a less-successful effort to sexually capitalize on material desires, seen in an American soldier who approached women in the street, inquiring, "How would you like a parachute? Pure silk. Yards and yards. I've booked a room in a hotel...." (Longmate, *The G. I.'s* 273).

(5/41: 76). Other companies went on the offensive, as instanced by this Yardley header: "What! No powder? It's not the shopkeeper's fault!" (5/41: 18). The customer was not to whine: there was a war on. Some manufacturers created repair services: Braemar knitwear invited patrons to send their holey woolies to the "Braemar 'Stitch-in-Time' service," and both Berlei and J. Roussel, makers of foundation garments, encouraged women to bring in their worn corsets for "reconditioning." Soon new notices followed, announcing that there had been such a demand for corset repairs that the process had been slowed. Still other advertisements frankly manipulated the situation:

> If you feel tired and aching after the morning's shopping you definitely need a good modern foundation, and the very best you can buy is a Berlei.... So you ought to have a Berlei but, to be brutally frank, you may not be able to get one, for our production is strictly limited. (7/41: 9)

British women, already talented at queuing, were encouraged first to desire, and then to strain toward attaining, a now-rare Berlei corset. In the words of another tantalizing advertisement on the same page, for Sanforized woolens, "The Thrill is in the Chase." Clearly, in certain ways wartime shortages stimulated style—and not only regarding necessary commodities.

To chase down needed woolens or a corset-repair service might be rational, if not thrilling. However, many of these announcements concerned cosmetics, especially lipstick. Lipstick, that nonessential essential, provides an excellent indicator of a ground shift in, along with the wartime permutations of, a particular style. Once the province of flappers, motion-picture stars, and fast girls, by the late thirties painted lips were becoming typical of women of all classes (Horwood 68–69). Perhaps it is fitting, then, that *Vogue* advertisements for Tattoo lipstick were notably declassé in comparison to the tasteful restraint of other ads in the magazine. Tattoo's ads featured sultry models in exotic locations, evoking cinema glamour rather than upper-class dignity: "Cleopatra couldn't hold a Roman candle to you ... now your lips are by Tattoo!" (2/22/39: back cover). The prewar spreads also inched toward erotic suggestion: "Lips that open like a flower to love ... in soft, sweet surrender ... by Tattoo!" (4/19/39: 139). In May 1939, Tattoo unveiled its daring new lipstick holder, featuring a naked woman and flowers in relief, meant to set off "the flaming romantic redness of the Hibiscus flower!" (5/17/39: back cover). Soon, however, many of these holders would be recycled in the war quest for scrap metal, and advertisements would proffer lipstick refills rather than brand-new tubes.[4] South Seas exotica gave way to new, businesslike colors such as Helena Rubenstein's Regimental Red and Cyclax of London's "Auxiliary Red, the Lipstick for Service Women" (9/39: 67; 12/39: 58). Women donning dreary, unfeminine uniforms hoped to span the beauty gap with makeup, and lipstick offered bright color at a relatively low cost. Nevertheless, shortages were felt: "What! No lipstick?" begins a Yardley ad, which scolds, "Economy in the use of your Beauty Preparations is just one more sacrifice you must make" (4/41: 26). *Vogue* itself campaigned stoutly for women's right to cosmetics. A 1942 editorial is headed "It Must Go On": the writer seriously discusses not military campaigns but why women need cosmetics, and why their production (already at 25 percent of peacetime manufacture) must not be curtailed further (8/42: 31). The Board of Trade agreed and made efforts to keep beauty supplies available (Walford 95). The triviality that is cosmetics was deemed significant for women's morale—and, women persistently argued, for that of men as well. The irrepressible Tattoo creators paraphrased Admiral Nelson: "England expects these days that every woman shall be a beauty" (5/40: 106).[5] Despite the waning of high fashion in wartime, women still wanted to look good.

So did men, although their clothing concerns were for convention and comfort. Austerity regulations for men's trousers and suits prompted editorial complaints in the *Times*. Evidently men were unhappy without watch pockets and back straps on their vests—the latter of which, it was claimed, helped stout men appear more slender. The de rigueur shorter socks meant that male calves were chilly, and many men simply resented the order against trouser turn-ups. A coalition of businessmen protested, and in 1943 MPs even mentioned on the floor of Parliament the "serious

---

4. The wartime use of lipstick refills was not limited to Britain. In 1945, when *Vogue* correspondent Lee Miller wandered through the deserted Munich villa that had belonged to Eva Braun and her sister, she noted especially the supply of Elizabeth Arden lipstick refills on Braun's dressing table (*Lee Miller's War* 198).

5. Adolf Hitler saw it rather differently, commenting glumly after discussing beauty-products manufacturing with Eva Braun: "The moment one tries to lay a hand on a woman's beauty care, she becomes his enemy." He secretly stopped production, anyway. Benito Mussolini, a more fashion-conscious Fascist, was amused by Nazi attempts to ban cosmetics, philosophizing, "Any power whatsoever is destined to fail before fashion" (Walford 95, 12).

dissatisfaction" the "regulations were causing to business and professional men." Initially the government stood firm, with Board of Trade President Hugh Dalton responding in typical wartime irony: "There can be no equality of sacrifice in this war. Some must lose lives and limbs; others only the turn-ups on their trousers" (Longmate, *How We Lived* 249). But the next year, with victory in sight, restrictions were loosened, making the manufacture of cuffed trousers and pleated skirts legal once more. In a delighted article headed "Achilles' Heel Has Turn-Ups," *Vogue* mocked male vanity: "And no more talk of trivialities, please. . . . Men have shown their hand. They, too, are fashion conscious" (3/44: 29). Was it, however, a matter of fashion? Certainly some men proved more self-conscious than women about their dress. As Dalton commented, in loosening Austerity restrictions, "we have done something to lift . . . the morale of the men. The morale of women has always been high, but that of the men has been depressed by not having enough pockets" (Calder 280). Perhaps one would not call this a male fashion consciousness, but convenience or even habit: since the standard suit had been expected menswear for 120 years, consistency in dress had become very important to middle-class men. Even at the war's end, when troops were demobilized and issued civilian clothing, many soldiers complained about their makeshift new suits. "I was the recipient of a repellent brown number with tiny white dots," actor Peter Ustinov recalled, and it possessed a "lining made of old pyjamas stitched together" (Hall 7). Perhaps the men had reason for complaint.

So did women, who, in the midst of wartime dress exigencies, remained anxious to distinguish themselves from men. As might be surmised from the popularity of lipstick among women in the forces, efforts to remain feminine abounded, abetted by *Vogue*, which published articles proffering "Points of fit and fashion to make you at ease in your uniform" (12/41: 55,70). But one surprising nonchange regarded trousers for women. Trousered females were a topic of considerable discussion in the war period, when many Britons seem to have expected that, with world war threatening civilization, women soon would breach the gender barriers by wearing trousers as frequently and casually as men. Novelist Evelyn Waugh complained that midwar London was "shabbier and shoddier," inhabited by "horrible groups of soldiers . . . lounging about with girls in trousers and high heels and filmstar coiffures," sourly adding, "I never saw so many really ugly girls making themselves conspicuous" (*Diaries* 536: 15 March 1943). Women novelists reveled in the comic and catty potential of what most considered an unbecoming trend, perhaps thereby reflecting their own anxieties over changing women's roles. E. M. Delafield's eponymous *Provincial Lady in Wartime* (1940), in London seeking a job, continually associates "trousered women" with war work. The obnoxiously peppy Pussy Winter-Gammon, she notes, "cannot possibly be less than sixty-six, but has put herself into diminutive pair of blue trousers" (55). The Lady's own resistance to trouser-wearing is softened by the good taste of her young friend Serena ("Trousers brown"), who informs her that "this war is really being won on coffee and cigarettes, by women in trousers" (61, 64). Eventually the Lady herself, after resolving to be "strong-minded" enough to resist the trend, chooses "a very nice pair of navy-blue slacks, thinking that I look well in them" (111). Looking well is the question too in Angela Thirkell's *Cheerfulness Breaks In* (1940), where lovely, empty-headed Rose Birkett appears in grey flannel slacks for a golf outing with her fiancé. Lieutenant Fairweather corrects her dress masterfully: "You can't come like that, my girl. Four minutes and a half to put on some decent clothes" (6). Rose quickly changes into a skirt. Indeed, in Thirkell's fiction it is not the fashionable young things who object to breeches but the women uninterested in traditional femininity. Mannish Miss Hampton, who wears "an extremely well-cut black coat and skirt, a gentlemanly white silk shirt with collar and tie, and neat legs in silk stockings and brogues, holding a cigarette in a very long black holder," tows a companion, Miss Bent, "a rather flabby edition of Miss Hampton" (82, 84). Yet—in intended comic irony—Miss Hampton rejects the new trouser look, remarking, "Can't abide those women who go about in slacks trying to look like men. Drove an ambulance all over the North of France myself in the War and never once thought of trousers" (87). Later she fosters a debate with Mrs. Phelps over "those ridiculous trousers." "I know exactly what I'd look like," Miss Hampton declares, "neither a man nor a woman." To which the pot-valiant Mrs. Phelps retorts, "Well, that's exactly what you look like now" (196–97). Thirkell, throughout her rather trouser-obsessed novel, seems anxious to show that only the most feminine women—glamorous Rose, and Mrs. Phelps with "her abundant bosom" (165)—dare try men's clothing, which for them accentuates the sexual differences. The worst thing of all would be to look like "neither a man nor a woman."

In fact *Vogue* evidence suggests that although more women were wearing trousers to work, and some observers like Waugh noted an increasing use of slacks in young women (Calder 334–35; Walford 31–32), they did not become a true fashion. A Cecil Beaton photo spread, "The Way We Dress These Days," included only one "slack suit," despite the title (3/43: 44–45). Even the stocking shortage did not induce stylish women to swathe their legs, it seemed, and women forced to wear trousers or austere uniforms on the job sought to compensate through lipstick and fingernail polish (12/40: 22). When cosmetics ran low, most women still endeavored to curl their hair and even to sabotage the perceived masculinizing effects of uniforms, such as those assigned for farmwork: as Vita Sackville-West noted critically, the Land Girls' "green jerseys, brown breeches, brown felt slouch hats and khaki overcoats" often were worn with nonissue garments such as a flowered frock or a magenta jumper (Calder 428–29). *Vogue* itself initially had condemned those "slackers in slacks," "who think war is also declared on all the elegance and artifices of our beauty-conscious age" (9/39: 19). But eighteen months later, the magazine featured rather preposterous "Fashions for Factories": "streamlined, uncompromising chic fitted for a vital job" (6/41: 54). And the cover for the October 1941 issue actually showed a model in a pantsuit, although the theme was the cyclical nature of fashion (33–36). Fashion was, the editors argued in their first "rationing" issue, associated peculiarly with "fundamental feminine finesse, as opposed to masculine force" (7/41: 18). Fashion would outlast the chaos of war and war clothing: when the men had tired of fighting, feminine style would remain.

The same theme resonates throughout wartime *Vogue*, despite occasional gender-crossing styles. More than one wartime ad offers a woman's suit expressly "Tailored by a Man's House"—in Argyll Street, Sloane Street, or Savile Row (see 6/40: inside cover, 6, 7). One also may view certain wartime hat styles, such as the Monty beret, as miniature "mannish" headgear (Walford 49). But it is nothing new for women to wear patriotic decorations, and tiny hats required less material. *Vogue* mentions two mid-war cross-dressing trends, first a "Beau Brummell" style for women (4/42: 42–45) and then a "Byronic air," achieved by bringing out "your husband's white waistcoat, adapt[ing] it to your slimmer figure and wear[ing] it with a grey flannel suit" (4/43: 54–55). However, each fad stemmed from wartime austerities, as is made clear: "The limitations [Brummell] imposed, as arbiter elegantium, are forced on us by circumstances. But . . . we welcome . . . the perfection of simplicity" (4/42: 45). The Byronic style's subtext too is the forced need to cut down old clothes and make do. Insofar as these passing trends make gender statements, they express the ongoing belief that men's clothes are characterized by limitations and simplicity; therefore, male dress is temporarily useful for women enduring home-style rationing.

Women's Utility clothing arguably resembled the traditional male suit at its best. These well-made, well-bred designs boasted simple sleek lines and a total lack of unnecessary ornament, characteristics that might have been praised by Brummell himself. The Utility ideal encapsulated his rhetoric of negation. But Utility styles were not sought-after fashions, and like uniforms or trousers for factory work they would be abandoned by

FIGURE 6. World War II Utility dress: A model stands on a Bloomsbury rooftop, showing off her pale blue and black wool Atrima dress, costing eleven coupons. (Ministry of Information Photo Division Photographer, 1943.) © Imperial War Museum (D 14844).

women once the war's end made more elaborate dress available. We may observe this embrace, and subsequent relinquishment, of masculine style in a progression of Vogue advertisements for GOR-RAY skirts. In April 1943 the ads began proclaiming, "We women want a 'man style' pocket" (inside back cover). When the war was over, however, after a prolonged campaign along the lines of "Why let the men have all the good pockets?" GOR-RAY dropped the overt gender references in favor of a tacit appeal to male-style freedom: "It's so cleverly cut—it lets you stride as you will, down country lane or office corridor" (4/46: 105). And even that advertising approach disappeared within a few months, in favor of an emphasis on the garment's slenderizing aspects: "Figures always balance in this beautifully tailored GOR-RAY skirt. Cleverly cut pleats subtract from the waistline and add to the charm" (9/46: 105; 11/46: 105; 12/46: 105). Not only were more pleats permitted after the war, but the average British woman for the first time in years enjoyed the luxury of resuming that traditional feminine preoccupation, her weight. So much for imitation male styles; they had sufficed only for the artificially imposed clothing of wartime.

SERIOUS COUTURE

Seriousness was not just a style but a national mind-set in wartime, as seen in Vogue's refocused articles. Certainly Vogue had published nonfashion pieces earlier, for example in the 1920s when it included reviews of high modernist poetry and fiction by T. S. Eliot, James Joyce, Ezra Pound, and Virginia Woolf (Garrity, "Virginia Woolf, Intellectual Harlotry" 189). But during the Second World War, the intensity of real-world affairs overwhelmed everything else. Initially the magazine published occasional photo features on women doing war work, especially the high-status Wrens (11/41: 56–57, 92; 9/43: 50–53). Increasingly, however, in the early to mid-forties, Vogue presented essays about the war's progress that were not specifically about women and certainly not about clothing. Artist Paul Nash described "The Personality of Planes"; Eve Curie, from her home in France, wrote "I Saw the Nazis Fall Back"; Lt. John G. Stewart of the U.S. Air Force told about "what the men in the ground crew go through" when one of their pilots or planes is hit (7/44: 52, 82). As the war wound up, Vogue essays would cover the war in the east, various commanding officers (including an interview with Douglas MacArthur), and the election of Clement Atlee over Winston Churchill (7/45: 23, 46–47, 65; 9/45: 28–29, 34–35, 40–41). Male writers included A. L. Rowse and Harold Nicholson. Women reported from overseas too, describing postwar conditions in Czechoslovakia and Holland (8/46: 61, 97–98; 61, 91). The level of analysis in these news essays was not high, and they may reflect an effort to attract a more general, middle-class audience. The fact remains that, increasingly throughout the war, Vogue used big topics, events, and names to fill its previously narrow-focused magazine.

Along those lines, two Vogue photographers especially refashioned their careers for wartime. High-society and fashion photographer Cecil Beaton wrote and snapped pictures of the Royal Air Force in England and of British troops on the "Jungle Front" in southeast Asia (7/41: 29–31, 60; 6/44: 76). And his postwar fashion spreads, showing models posed against ruined Paris walls, would offer the first inkling of later trends toward ironically edgy Vogue pictures (11/45: 46, 53). Above all, however, it is in Lee Miller's photos and reporting that we see the startling effects of war upon the Vogue woman. Miller, the adventurous daughter of a prosperous New England family, was well acquainted with Europe. She spent part of her youth in Paris with the Lost Generation; she modeled for Condé Nast, studied art, and married first a wealthy Egyptian and eventually an English painter. During the war, she served as a photographer for British Vogue, alternating fashion shoots with photos of the Blitz and other wartime rigors. When American troops were stationed in Britain, she acquired U.S. press credentials and traveled to France to report on the Normandy invasion. Many of her Continental photo essays were published in Vogue itself, including accounts of medical staff on Omaha Beach (9/44: 34–35, 82, 85) and "St. Malo: The Siege and the Assault"—an illustrated article, hugely long by Vogue's standards, based on Miller's own experiences while embedded with the army (10/44: 50–51, 80, 84, 90, 96). She also delivered reports on the liberation of Paris (especially interesting to the magazine's readers) and Brussels; on moving with the troops through the Alsace Campaign (4/45: 50–53, 80, 83–84, 86, 90); and subsequently on her observations regarding "Germany—The War That Is Won" (6/45: 40–43, 84, 86, 89). But it is Miller's pictures from Germany that became most famous, and especially for being printed in Vogue. Her photo of dead concentration camp victims at Buchenwald is very small in British Vogue, but the printed text is unequivocal: "The six hundred bodies stacked in the courtyard of the crematorium, because they had run out of coal the last five days, had been carted away until only a hundred were left" (6/45: 43). And Miller's contemptuous anger at German civilians, who act as if "they are liberated instead of conquered people" (84), is corrosive and nearly constant throughout her accounts of Germany, and nearly as shocking and indecorous for *Vogue* as her photos.

However, the most notorious of Miller's wartime photos does not show atrocities. She stayed in Hitler's private apartment in Munich (taken over by the 179th Regiment) immediately after touring Dachau; her subsequent evocation of the ordinary, trivial surroundings of the dictator's life, combined with the horrors of his deeds, produced an almost unspeakable dissonance. In her dispatch to *Vogue*, Miller describes the atrocities of the prison camp in several paragraphs and then returns to Hitler's home. "We spent the night there, using Hitler's toilet and taking his bath and generally making ourselves at home with a very swell bunch of guys," soldiers from the 45th Division (*Lee Miller's War* 188–89). The famous photos of this evening, of Miller in Hitler's bathtub, are symbolic rather than revelatory. As she recalled, the entire apartment was devoid of personal touches, apart from banal bourgeois luxuries marked with "A. H." and swastikas. The bathroom itself "could have been bought from a furnishing catalogue" (192). It does not reveal anything grand about its former user. Rather, in posing herself naked in Hitler's erstwhile bath, Miller created an image of the ironically trivial bases of civilized twentieth-century humanity. Framed between an artfully placed photo of Hitler on the tub's edge and an uninspired female nude statuette gazing across the bathroom, Miller sponges herself amid gleaming chrome and tile. Her grimly weary bathing seems light years away from *Vogue*: where is fashionable dress and society now? The only clothing, apart from Hitler's uniform in the photo, is Miller's discarded, crumpled military fatigues—and her muddy army boots, discoloring the pale-yellow bathmat with dirt from Dachau. The only society evoked is the recent memory of the Reich's dead, naked victims, and the nearly dead in their striped pajamas. It is the apogee of the Second World War's negation of style: Hitler's bathtub offers a potent image for the ways in which the war stripped all concerned to the skin, beyond clothing (fashionable or not), beyond the veneers of civilized living. Not, however, beyond sex. The picture was not, as some thought, self-posed but taken by Miller's lover, American photographer David Scherman, and though the photo is not erotic, she clearly is an attractive woman. Moreover the mysterious nude figurine, gazing across the water

FIGURE 7. Miller in Hitler's Bath [David E. Scherman] / [The LIFE Picture Collection] / Getty Images.

past the dead "monster" Hitler, suggests a gulf between the sexes all the greater for the strippings of war. The war did not end gender divisions any more than it ended the wearing of clothing: soon Miller would get out of that tub and dress once again.

For that matter, she remained style-conscious throughout the war. Scherman recalled that in wartime France, Miller, the formerly "fastidious, obsessive clothes-horse," soon looked like "an unmade, unwashed bed" (10). But Miller herself wrote to her editor Audrey Withers, as she and the American troops approached Paris, "There they are already wearing swell uniforms like London—and I have only battle dress. Would you find an almost finished uniform of mine at French Kilgour & Stanburg and send it?" (*Lee Miller's War* 65). In later cover letters she commented self-consciously on her disheveled state and apologized for the camera film "soaked in melted lip rouge" (159). And in her reports, Miller used clothing for metonymic characterization. Of the inhabitants of the bombed German city Aachen she reported, "The people lived in cellars and vaults, but wore fur coats, silk stockings, and fiercely ugly hats" (*Vogue* 6/45: 84).[6] From Miller's style-conscious perspective, the luxurious dress showed the obtuse stubbornness of Hitler's defeated followers, and German women's inability to realize that their head adornments were "fiercely ugly" signified both aesthetic and moral ignorance. As *Vogue* representative, she read clothing with political and ethical seriousness.

Most difficult to interpret was the end-of-war style flaunted by liberated Frenchwomen, a style that initially flummoxed the liberating British and American soldiers. In entering Paris, we "expected ill-clad gray mice," Scherman recalled; what they found was "cork-shod, balloon-skirted, high-coiffed beauties" (10). In her *Vogue* report, Miller went into more detail about the French "girls in flippant clothes": "Their silhouette was very queer and fascinating to me after utility and austerity England. Full floating skirts, tiny waist-lines. They were top-heavy with built-up pompadour front hair-dos and waving tresses; weighted to the ground with clumsy, fancy thick-soled wedge shoes" (10/44: 27). Miller describes the nonutilitarian and un-austere Parisian styles, in which the emphasis is on a fullness—full skirts, full sleeves—unknown in rationed, rational Britain for several years. She judiciously notes that deprivation necessitated some styles, for instance, the awkward cork or wooden shoes. She also defends French wartime stylishness, in terms that both *Vogue* editors and French couturiers would echo:

[Frenchwomen] deliberately organized this style of dressing and living as a taunt to the Huns, whose clumsy, serious women, dressed in grey uniforms, were known as the "souris gris." If the Germans wore cropped hair,

---

6. This description contrasts with other accounts, for example, Walford on "women wearing two different shoes, torn and dirty military jackets, and bits of rope and cord acting as belts on oversized trousers.... Fashion [had not been a concern] for most German women for a very long time" (179).

the French grew theirs long. If three yards of material were specified for a dress—they found fifteen for a skirt alone. Saving material and labour meant help to the Germans—and it was their duty to waste instead of save. (78)

In Britain it may have been "patriotic to be chic," as Calder claimed, but it was even more patriotic to follow Austerity rules and make do. In occupied France, because the rules were imposed by the enemy, it was thought patriotic to break them whenever possible. The English understood this difference in theory, although often it was hard to comprehend the vastly different war experiences of London and Paris. Paris had not been bombed nightly, like London; Parisian women had not been obliged to cut their hair and don uniforms for war work. Rather, occupied Paris was a very dangerous place for those involved in Resistance work (including many young girls), and for those with wealth or aristocratic or Jewish connections. Moreover, the shortages in Paris went far beyond wool, silk, or leather; unlike in England, hunger was prevalent in France. (When Parisian couturiers resumed their international fashion show the next autumn, viewers would be struck by the models' thinness.) Perhaps for these very reasons, the French insistence on remaining stylish grated on many practical Britons. In one *Vogue* article, Carmel Benito explained, "We just had to show the Germans our spirits wouldn't fail. . . . We were prepared to do without food, fuel, light, soap, servants . . . but we wouldn't look shabby and worn-out. After all, we were Parisiennes" (10/44: 36). That last line sums up the implicit arrogance of wartime French style, an arrogance resented not only by the German occupiers but subsequently by France's British rescuers. France had abandoned her Maginot Line and been conquered—or at least the British thought so; to then defy their conquerors through dress simply confirmed English traditions about French frivolity.

Fashion had been a long-time area of mutual criticism between the two nations, from the late Middle Ages on. The French saw English clothing, and Englishwomen, as plain, if not uncouth; the English scorned the frivolity of French fashions, linking these tendencies with supposed Gallic effeminacy. Yet French influences over British fashion had increased, at least for women, throughout the nineteenth century. It was in France that Worth rose as the first artistic couturier, and the seminal fashion displays at the Universal Exposition of Paris in 1900 seemed to solidify the reputation of Paris as the twentieth-century's fashion authority (Angeletti and Oliva 44). The swift change for Britons may be reflected in Osbert Sitwell's recollections that in 1900 "very few women—apart from the American contingent who thereby gained an unfair advantage over the rest—obtained" their clothes in Paris, "though within a few years every woman who could afford to do so was following the American example" (267–68). In the late twenties and thirties, Parisian influence had gained an added fillip, as women designers including Chanel and Vionnet became glamorous influences upon fashionable females. Chanel in particular expanded the appeal, and therefore the power, of French fashion through her "poor chic" style (Angeletti and Oliva 94–95). Even as war approached, it seemed hard to gainsay the cheerful generalization offered by *Time* magazine regarding the autumn 1939 Paris collections: "Whoever runs the world, Paris intends to go on making his wife's clothes" (8/21/39).

And therein lay the true gall: revelations at the war's end suggested that Paris *had* continued to clothe the wives of those in power, whoever they might be.[7] Even before that, however, British *Vogue* had confronted the old question, most ephemeral and most serious, of whether Britain might free herself from *la mode Parisienne*. London designers felt the unfairness of always being deemed second- or third-rate (queued after Italy, which still insisted upon its Renaissance reputation as a fashion leader). In hopeful prewar articles such as "London Takes the Lead," *Vogue* patriotically had proclaimed, "Never before have the London Collections been so strongly individual, so little influenced by Paris" (3/22/39: 57). Throughout the war, praise of French gallantry alternated with gleeful claims that "Paris is in eclipse," making it London's opportunity to shine. In January 1941, an editorial celebrated the fact that several Parisian couturiers—Molyneux, Paquin, Worth—had moved to London: since Englishwomen had clothing restrictions, these designers would produce fashions primarily for export and draw needed money to Britain. Still, *Vogue* insisted that their fashions "spr[ang] from the fertile soil of English life" (27). As the war advanced, casual references suggested a popular assumption that French fashion was passé. From an advertisement for "French Cologne Made in England" to a Moss Brothers commercial remarking, "The French

---

7. Certainly Margherita Sarfatti, glamorous writer and mistress of Mussolini, went to Paris for her dresses, although she patriotically patronized the couture of Elsa Schiaparelli (Paulicelli 55). Once the war started, German propaganda asserted the superiority of "Gretchen" styles; nevertheless, Emma Göring seems to have ordered twenty Occupation-made gowns from Paquin in Paris (Walford 148).

had a word for it" (*chic*), the past tense was assumed for French products and style (2/42: 16; 3/43: 25). Before Paris was liberated, one would have thought that French style was finished.

No wonder that the liberating Allies were stunned to see what Frenchwomen had accomplished on meager rations. Moreover, there were persistent rumors of collusion. Couturier Lucien Lelong, president of the Chambre Syndicale de la Haute Couture, had bargained repeatedly with German authorities, first to keep the fashion houses open, then to keep them in Paris rather than Berlin or Vienna. He also begged extra material allowances for high-fashion purposes. His reward was to see as many as one hundred houses of haute couture continue through the Occupation— and then to be accused of cooperating with the enemy (Taylor 135). After the war, accusations and defenses were traded vigorously. It was not until Dominique Veillon's *La mode sous l'Occupation* (1990)[8] that historians were given a dispassionate, balanced account of couturiers' activities in Occupied France. In the years after World War II, fashion houses were accused of marketing their wares to German officers' wives—and some had. They were accused of catering to collaborators—and some had. They were blamed for selling to the black-market nouveau riche, and most of the couture houses had done that, although with snobbish reluctance (Veillon 121). French designers' reputations were not helped by Coco Chanel's wartime love affair with a German officer (ironically, Chanel survived this public-relations disaster to become even more famous and successful in the fifties). The extent of collaboration between Parisian couturiers and the occupying forces is not determinable, although evidence suggests that most of the dress houses' customers from 1940 to 1944 were, as always, wealthy Frenchwomen.[9] For other Allies the question was, did French fashion houses collaborate with the enemy? But for many French people the couturiers' crimes, if such they were, were crimes of class: "High society rubbed shoulders with Germans" (Veillon 110). In an

---

8. First published in English, revised and updated as *Fashion under the Occupation* (2002). References to Veillon are to the English edition.

9. Of the up to twenty thousand special couture ration cards issued each year by the Third Reich, only two hundred were allotted to German customers (Veillon 116–17). The two hundred cards do not include Vichy government connections or black-market wealth, but they do suggest that the rumors of fashion shows exclusively attended by Nazi officers' wives may be mythical.

atmosphere of wartime fear and deprivation, the classism of haute couture stood out as never before.

The conflict over Occupation couture reflects the debates that arose with modernism over the utility of art. Certainly in this instance "good taste" had very different meanings for wartime French and wartime Britons—the one aesthetic, the other ethical. For many Britons on the homefront, the French insistence on remaining style-conscious seemed simply tasteless and unbecoming behavior in a conquered people that had, once again, required rescue from doughtier nations. Moreover, wartime styles in France held an element of frivolity that encapsulated all of fashion's most objectionable qualities: Those ridiculous hats! The wasteful use of materials! The same *Vogue* issue that contained Miller's descriptions of entering Paris included the French houses' fall collections, which appeared shockingly full and luxurious; they went far beyond what could be sold to British or even American customers during a war not yet won. *Vogue* felt obliged to follow up in its next issue with an editorial admonition to the British Board of Trade, to abolish Austerity as soon as possible (11/44: 25). Lee Miller chimed in, with the assurance that the French

> regard [fashion] in the nature of an art exhibition.... Each dressmaker wants to express some sort of *joie*. They know there is no question of "buyers" from abroad (it is no longer patriotic to flaunt new clothes, as in the face of the Germans). But the workroom people need work and wages. (36, 78)

True, when the war began, more than twenty thousand people were employed in couture industries in Paris alone (Walford 34). But economic necessity is an afterthought in Miller's explanation; rather it is the art of fashion, the "joy" expressed thereby, that comes first to her pen. Similarly Lelong, forced publically to defend the 1944 Autumn Collections, first explained that the designers actually had lessened the amounts of material used in each garment, creating "simple suits and coats which we felt better suited . . . France's official re-entry into the War at the side of the Allies." It was merely French couturiers' great talent, Lelong claimed tactlessly, that made "three yards appear to be six" yards of material. He added that the collection's elaborate evening dresses were shown only for effect and would be sold off "to the wives of neutral diplomats" (*Vogue* 12/44: 33, 78). Then the designer hastily cited both the French economy and the reputation of *la haute couture Parisienne* as justification for all his efforts to keep the fashion houses alive throughout the Occupation (78). Once again the ephemeral and the material, art and necessity, vied as explanatory myths for fashion.

The next spring's collections were frankly conciliatory in their moderation and simplicity: "clothes are more functional, less exuberant, than in the 'Liberation' showings [of autumn]," commented *Vogue* (5/45: 29). These newer designs constituted an implicit apology from the French couturiers—but they also seemed to signal the assured reascendancy of French fashion, "Paris Regained." Within two years, Christian Dior would be catapulted into fame and, on both sides of the Channel as across the Atlantic, the "homefront style," though so different in England and in France, would mutate into the luxuriant New Look. Despite continued shortages and postwar rationing in Britain, and despite the debate over what constitutes tasteful wartime fashion, France again would define stylish dress—or so it seemed. Evidently the war had changed nothing in the protocols of fashion.

Yet the world had changed, as *Vogue* editor Lesley Blanch would argue—or at least British women's dress habits had changed. In a postwar editorial, Blanch claims that "our ideas of luxury are changed, and so we buy necessities as luxuries" (5/46: 69). It is not that women will not continue to buy clothes, she says, but they will want "clothes with lovely colours and comfortable textures, which stand up to wear and tear and do not require much keeping in order." These changes are specifically gendered, in Blanch's view, but in the area of obligatory evening dress she seems to speak for both sexes: "I very much resent being compelled to dress one way or another. . . . I want there to be as much fluidity in our way of living and eating and dressing, as in our way of thinking" (97). *Vogue* itself had changed, on the necessity of changing for dinner. Now one was free to exercise one's options in clothing. *Change* was the mantra of the times.

For that matter, the New Look was a change far more complicated than a return to French fashion. Did this famous style, which for a time made Christian Dior the world's most successful designer, truly represent a retriumph of French couture? Its combination of full blouse, tiny waist, and longer, fuller skirt made a sensation when introduced by Dior's new fashion house in February 1947. Yet as early as 1945, *Vogue* had commented, "The wind is changing . . . away from masterly severity, towards a gentler femininity," toward tightly belted waists, rounded hips, gathers, padding, and bloused backs—that is, toward many features that still were prohibited or simply impossible under wartime rationing of materials (3/45: 29, 33). In the Autumn Collections from Paris, a few months later, some Lelong creations came close to Dior's upcoming style (Vogue 9/46: 43). The public did not want any more of Lucien Lelong, with his unfortunate wartime associations—and yet, it seemed, women still yearned for that French imprimatur. Dior had worked for Lelong until he opened his own fashion house. Still, the vision was Dior's, and his stress on decorative femininity, and on bringing back an art from the past, raises further questions. Was the New Look a step backward for women? Was it even new? The second question is easier to answer: no. The New Look constituted a refashioning of Edwardian styles; it also echoed the full skirts and corseted waists that designers had attempted to introduce in 1939, just before the war.

Did British women's embrace of the New Look, then, demonstrate their longings to return to secure, domestic prewar roles? Certainly they adopted the style enthusiastically, despite continuing material shortages, rationing, and Austerity rules. But the psychological incentives may have lain more in Britons' general feelings than women's self-images. British women, who had been thrifty and patriotic, mended and made do throughout the war, were weary of the struggle and eager to celebrate victory with a little luxury—even if it involved defying their stingy government, as Frenchwomen under the Occupation were said to have defied their conquerors with illogically wasteful styles. Labour MP Bessie Braddock might snort at the New Look style as "the ridiculous whim of idle people" (Walford 197), but Britons in general were ready for an idle holiday. They could not get it in Britain of the later forties, with problems of homelessness, joblessness, and sky-high taxation. Nor did continued clothing restrictions cheer. (Not until 1949 did most fashions in Britain become coupon-free.) Ever-helpful Vogue published an essay in which Cambridge economist Louis Stanley explained why England must export her best goods (2/46: 70, 88). But the British had cast off their wartime government, and they now reacted against lingering clothing rationing and Utility rules (retained until 1952) as well. They had become accustomed to queuing, and they were willing to do so to ensure more equitable distribution of food and health care for their fellow citizens. Restrictions on clothing, however, now seemed like rationing without rationale—and

FIGURE 8. Dior "Bar" Suit, 1947. The Metropolitan Museum of Art, gift of Mrs. John Chambers Hughes, 1958 (C. I.58.34.30); gift of Christian Dior, 1969 (C. I.69.40). © The Metropolitan Museum of Art. Reproduction of any kind is prohibited without express written permission in advance from The Metropolitan Museum of Art.

some of the French and *Vogue* creeds began to appeal. The same social-leveling instincts that voted in Clement Atlee's government told citizens that it was only fair they enjoyed a bit of life. After all, as Dior himself said of the war, "Everything that goes beyond the simple fact of food, clothing, and shelter is luxury. Our civilization is a luxury, and it is that we are defending" (Beaton 298). And Harry Hopkins points out that Dior's designs appeared during the fuel crisis of February 1947, just when *Daily Express* headlines screamed "LESS . . . LESS . . . LESS" (91). In rebellious response, women seemed to demand, "MORE . . . MORE . . . MORE!" The New Look required more cloth, and dreary material necessity might militate against such a fashion. Nevertheless, women were pulled irresistibly toward a style all the more engaging for its impracticability.

It is therefore doubtful that the wearers of Dior's look intended to signal their approval of the role of the *hausfrau* (a despised term, after Hitler). Despite the necessity of corseting for the less than slender, and hipette padding for the underendowed, it was the New Look's luxurious aura that attracted women in postwar, still-Austerity Britain. They also liked the option of more specifically feminine garments that, after years of uniforms or factory trousers, seemed a freedom, not a constraint. Eventually this increased emphasis on freedom would lead to eclecticism in dress styles in the Western world, and even in the immediate postwar milieu lay the seeds of consumerist fashion. Freedom from the dictatorship of designers beckoned: despite their love of Dior's style, women remembered that they had made do, sometimes attractively, without expensive designer dresses. Significantly, Hopkins records that the New Look's ubiquity in Britain by 1948 was due not to Parisian haute-couture sales but to mass-produced imitations (94). And the prewar beginnings of prêt-à-porter swelled in the forties and fifties into our present mass production of clothing, where to sew one's own clothing is a special hobby, and to have it made is a costly exception. Even a designer dress now need not mean a garment hand-fitted in the shop of the eponymous creator. Ironically, the seemingly retrograde New Look was indeed new, in that it marked the birth of freedom and choice in dress styles.

As to traditional femininity, the war's end meant for many women the loss of wartime jobs and a return to domestic roles, but the changes in gender assumptions were profound, as were the stylistic milestones. The next chapter examines the literature of the homefront, which marked the beginnings of understated postwar writing. In wartime, literature like clothing is frivolous, if not of solid material use—and in fact, war demonstrates the potential frivolity of all style, whether linguistic or sartorial. Just as the era of serious *Vogue* affirmed the staying power of fashion but lessened its authority, so writers would find that wartime sustained literary creation but also multiplied schools and styles.

CHAPTER 5

Literature in Wartime

WORLD WAR II undermined many foundations in London, one of those great cities that Raymond Williams describes as essential to the formation of modernism (7). War's exigencies blew up the pretended necessity of high style; even Christian Dior had observed that beyond basic food, clothing, and shelter, all is luxury. And luxuries vary: while clothing style bears an appeal both popular and elitist, literary art in modern Britain interested only a small minority. Moreover, where fashion was identified primarily as female, high modernists had labored to create a literature that was, to paraphrase James Joyce, no longer for the ladies (T. Connolly, *Scribbledehobble* 15). Consequently, in wartime the sharp divisions of highbrow and middlebrow literatures faded, avant-garde writing appeared effete, and the fictions taken most seriously provided realistic, understated descriptions of contemporary life.

The war raised serious questions as to whether literary art could even survive. Thirties writers and thinkers frequently had described highmodern aesthetics as an "ivory tower" (MacKay 135), and with the onset of war this trope resurfaced. In 1939 C. S. Lewis addressed Oxford undergraduates on "Learning in War-time," in a famous lecture that also suggests the conditions of literature in wartime. What is the point, Lewis asked, of remaining in the university's ivory tower with life and liberty in the balance? His answer was twofold: First, "The war creates no absolutely new situation: it simply aggravates the permanent human situation [inevitable death] so that we can no longer ignore it" (27). Second, he praised the humanist tradition of intellectual and creative endeavor while on the brink of disaster. People "propound mathematical theorems in beleaguered cities, conduct metaphysical arguments in condemned cells, make jokes on scaffolds, discuss the last new poem while advancing to the walls of Quebec, and comb their hair at Thermopylae" (28). Even under extreme circumstances it is human nature to think and create—or at least, like the Spartans arranging their long hair before certain death, to invoke the lighter arts of self-styling. Nevertheless, while the history of human resilience offered hope for Britons' dark days, these images also evoke their desperate situation: "beleaguered cities," "condemned cells," and "scaffolds" were not exaggerated fears for those who opposed Hitler. Furthermore, the war did create a new situation, precisely in reminding people that "life has always been lived on the edge of a precipice" (27). It forced not only scholars but fiction writers to justify their endeavors rather than hiding in an ivory tower.

The threat of another world war also provoked some writers, especially men, to grandiose pronouncements: In "September 1, 1939," W. H. Auden proposed dramatically that moderns either "love one another or die" (1.88). A few months later, George Orwell announced that "from now onwards the all-important fact for the creative writer is going to be that this is not a writer's world" ("Inside the Whale" 197). But Auden revised his poem, and wartime Britain turned out to be a very good writer's world for Orwell, giving him material for numerous essays and literary reviews as well as inspiration for *Animal Farm* (1945) and *1984* (1949). Evelyn Waugh had been more prescient, if more frankly self-centered:

> My inclinations are all to join the army as a private. . . . I have to consider thirty years of novel-writing ahead of me. Nothing would be more likely than work in a government office to finish me as a writer; nothing more likely to stimulate me than a complete change of habit. There is a symbolic difference between fighting as a soldier and serving as a civilian, even if the civilian is more valuable. (*Diaries* 438: 27 August 1939)

Waugh's tone is detached, but his assumption about the superiority of "fighting as a soldier" indicates a romanticism shared by all but the most pacifist of men in the Phoney War period. Ultimately Waugh, like Orwell, enjoyed a most stimulating war, publishing a novella and two novels while gathering material for *Sword of Honour* (1952–61).

Women writers, on the other hand, were more cautious in pronouncement and more modest in expectation. As detective writer Margery Allingham, enthralled to gas-mask distribution and the billeting of evacuees in her English village, recalled the summer of 1939, "I had taken a look at my own work and decided it was beyond me, probably for ever" (85). This self-dismissal did not long prevent her from resuming her current novel, or from storing its precious manuscript in a biscuit tin in an effort to protect it from the anticipated blitzkrieg (174). In a more philosophical vein, Elizabeth Bowen tried to explain why she could not produce novels during this war: "One cannot reflect, or reflect on, what is not wholly in view. These years rebuff the imagination as much by being fragmentary as by being violent" ("Contemporary" 340). In striking contrast to Waugh's confidently anticipated stimulation, than which "nothing would be more likely," Bowen found that the fragmented wartime conditions produced radical uncertainty. Accordingly she wrote no novels during the war years, although she later used her homefront experiences in *The Heat of the Day* (1948). During the war, Bowen published a memoir, a family history, and many short stories.

What none of the novelists realized is that literature would continue, throughout and following the war; however, as with dress styles, the watchword would be *change*. Lewis was correct that war created no absolutely new situation; nevertheless, the joke on the scaffold differs considerably from a joke uttered in domestic tranquility. Consequently, the life-and-death drama of war, whether experienced in uniform or civilian attire, changed its actors permanently and in so doing permanently changed British fiction. At the time, no one knew whether writers and readers were witnessing the death of ivory-tower modernism or the long, difficult gestation of a new style. As things turned out, it was both.

Just as *Vogue* demonstrated the war-induced changes in homefront fashions, so Cyril Connolly's putative high-art journal *Horizon* came to exemplify a growing literary pragmatism. Initially, this chapter examines the public devolution of high modernism into Connolly's precious, nostalgic aestheticism. In the thirties and forties the accepted modernist canon—such as it was—fell apart: boundaries, chronologies, and styles all proved their definitional inadequacy, and arguably their irrelevance in wartime. Accordingly, rather than undertaking a full history of wartime literature I highlight writers whose work offers milestones for a literary shift toward a postwar new style. Evelyn Waugh's wartime fictions saliently comprehend the death of the old style, while novels by Arthur Koestler, Rex Warner, and Philip Larkin signal incipient changes in literary values. These male authors provide a foil for Elizabeth Bowen, whose wartime stories more overtly use dress details to lay the ghosts of prewar styles and to elegize the marriage plot. As in dress styles, neither art nor pragmatics triumphed fully: literature would emerge from the war with style again significant and transformed into a literary New Look.

BETWEEN THE OLD STYLE AND THE NEW: *HORIZON*

In *A Purgatorial Flame* (1990), Sebastian Knowles suggested an overarching image for the state of British literature during the war, that of Dante's Purgatory. He noted the many writers whose careers were arrested and refocused during this period; he also described the numerous ghosts of wartime fiction, including the master-poet phantom in T. S. Eliot's "Little Gidding." Eliot's ghost-poet suggests the unknown quality of future literatures—and also that Eliot's own time is past (ll. 65–66, 76ff). The great modernist cannot tell whether this Purgatory will conclude in Paradise or in Hell. In a similar spirit, most wartime literature falls into one of two categories: the old style, which mourns the end of modernism, or the new, heralding the beginning of a new age.

High modernism never intended to become old. But its leaders, already middle-aged in the twenties, began to die as the war started: W. B. Yeats, Virginia Woolf, James Joyce—all were gone by the end of 1941. D. H. Lawrence, though younger, had died in 1930. By the late thirties, Ezra Pound was self-exiled in Italy and busily exiling himself further through his eccentric Fascism. Eliot himself would survive in body and in reputation, but as *Four Quartets* shows he had placidly accepted his status as the Grand Old Man of modernism. Younger poets—W. H. Auden, Stephen Spender—already had challenged modernist elitism and aestheticism through their political engagements in the Red Thirties. As for fiction, all the most influential avant-garde novels, by Joyce, Woolf, Lawrence, Ford, and Wyndham Lewis, were published by 1930. If modernism was not in decline by the thirties and forties, that period sometimes termed "late modernism," it surely had mutated. "In the empty spaces left by high modernism's dissolution," Tyrus Miller writes, "late modernists reassembled fragments into disfigured likenesses of modernist masterpieces: the unlovely allegories of a world's end" (14). The apocalyptic image is just, but it also applies to many not-so-avant-garde writers of the period, such as Waugh and Orwell, who do not fit comfortably into present critical narratives of modernism. Not only high modernism but its often rigid categories were dying away.[1]

By World War II, British literature exhibited a modernist complex (in all senses) that belied simple labels, as shown by recent endeavors to categorize Elizabeth Bowen. Indubitably an artistic writer, Bowen's interest in domestic furnishings and clothing slots her handily into both realist and women's camps—neither acceptably late modernist if Samuel Beckett remains the touchstone.[2] But if modernism ever had been monolithic, it was shattered first by women's writing and then by time, as the children inherited and moved beyond their elders' world. Marina MacKay notes that when the *Times* published its famous editorial proclaiming the "Eclipse of the Highbrow," the succeeding debate was significantly deflated by publisher Geoffrey Faber's observation that many modernist stylistic innovations had become the established norm (MacKay 118–19). Accordingly the rising novelists of the thirties, Waugh and Greene, claimed to admire monuments such as Joyce's *Ulysses* and Eliot's *Waste Land*—yet they remained middlebrow, interested in artistic creation but also in making a living.[3]

---

1. The rigidity of those categories, like many aspects of modernism, remains under debate. Some current scholars limit late modernism to avant-garde style and/or radical politics: Samuel Beckett, Mina Loy, Djuna Barnes, and Wyndham Lewis, for Miller; high modernists in their final productions, for the "happily biased" Jane Goldman (211) as for Jed Esty (9). However, these later experimental modern writers, like the last works by major modernists, do not fully represent future literary directions and so are not very useful for my more inclusive study.

2. Nicola Humble painstakingly places Bowen's novels "at the highbrow end of the middlebrow" (13, fn 78), and Vike Martina Plock points out that both Virginia Woolf and Agatha Christie served Bowen as mentors (288). Both critics demonstrate the inadequacies of strict classification for modern women writers.

3. See, for example, "The Books You Read" (1930), where Waugh cites both *Ulysses* and *The Waste Land* as standards for the up-and-coming young writer.

If high modernism was an oldster's game for many younger writers, its defenders often narrowed it down to nostalgic aestheticism and a rather effortful evasion of politics—in short, to that insular ivory tower. As such, this late-modernist aestheticism did not give up the ghost without a struggle, and it is largely due to Cyril Connolly that this struggle is recalled as the center of British wartime literature. By 1939 Connolly already viewed himself as a failure, for his cherished ambition had been to become a high-modernist writer. Like Waugh thirty-six years old when the war began, Connolly had produced a novel about the artistic life, *The Rock Pool* (1935), soon followed by *Enemies of Promise* (1938), which brooded upon the obstacles facing high-minded novelists. Near the war's end, he would publish a book of meditations on life and art titled, in keeping with the wartime popularity of revenant spirits, *The Unquiet Grave* (1945). But Connolly was unhappily correct that he would be remembered as a commentator upon literature. For literary historians he is significant because he founded and edited the wartime literary journal *Horizon* (1940–1949), aiming to "give to writers a place to express themselves, and to readers the best writing we can obtain. Our standards are aesthetic, and our politics are in abeyance" (*Horizon* 1/40: 5).[4] Connolly's manifesto gestured toward standard modernist ideals, in which style rules content. Nevertheless, in seeking to preserve high modernism he inadvertently lumped himself with nostalgic fogies who longed to escape the difficult present by returning to a beautiful past. Even the conservative Waugh would satirize *Horizon*'s ideals in *Put Out More Flags* (1942): "Art for Art's sake, Geoffrey. Back to the lily and the lotus" (138). Waugh mocked Connolly by portraying him as the sensitive aesthete Ambrose Silk, who pseudonymously composes most of the material for his esoteric journal *Ivory Tower*. The parody was extreme, but the parallels were obvious: *Horizon* was the only wartime literary journal in London willing to defend aestheticism and, like Ambrose, proclaim its disgust with politically influenced literature. Or so Connolly's opening editorials went; to his disappointment, the actual magazine ranged far from "the lily and the lotus."

Of course Waugh himself participated, more overtly than Connolly, in the nostalgic wartime aestheticism that constituted a literary "old look." Its spirit was summarized frankly by Osbert Sitwell in 1944, as he

---

4. All subsequent references to *Horizon* are cited within the text, by month/year: page number.

introduced his leisurely memoir: "In this cruel and meaningless epoch, between the bars of which I now write, neither past nor future seems to have any existence; only the present which contains the dead ashes of the past" (vii). Therefore, Sitwell continues, "I *want* my memories to be old-fashioned and extravagant.... I *want* this to be gothic, complicated in surface and crowned with turrets and with pinnacles, for that is its nature" (xiii). In content and elaborate verbiage, this nostalgic old style shows how modes had changed: high-art writing reverted in wartime to a fin-de-siècle mode, "old-fashioned and extravagant"—not thirties or twenties, but from the era of Sitwell's privileged youth.

Following a similar style, Waugh shocked his fans when he published *Brideshead Revisited* (1944). Some hitherto admiring readers protested not only *Brideshead*'s frank Catholicism but its luxuriantly worded nostalgia, so unlike the author's previous cruel, spare fictions. Yet the romanticized images of Oxford in the twenties, of beautiful young people (no longer satirically capitalized), of rich, noble houses replete with faithful servants—everything far from war-torn England—made *Brideshead* a huge hit in both Britain and the United States. Especially popular were the narrator's leisurely memories of wining and dining:

> I rejoiced in the Burgundy. How can I describe it? The Pathetic Fallacy resounds in all our praise of wine. For centuries every language has been strained to define its beauty, and has produced only wild conceits or the stock epithets of the trade. This Burgundy seemed to me, then, serene and triumphant, a reminder that the world was an older and better place. (175)

This decorative rhetoric implies world enough and time for enjoyment, of language and of gracious living rooted in the past. It also epitomizes the wartime literature of nostalgic old style, a mode that, as Bernard Bergonzi notes, actually was "not nostalgia for many but pure fantasy" (39). Waugh himself later blamed both *Brideshead*'s style and some of its content on wartime deprivations, commenting that "the book is infused with a kind of gluttony, for food and wine, for the splendours of the recent past, and for rhetorical and ornamental language" (Preface 7). Yet at the time he noted confidently, "I think perhaps it is the first of my novels rather than my last" (*Diaries* 566: 30 May 1944). And he was correct: while *Brideshead* did mourn a lost era, the wartime Purgatory also took Waugh beyond satire to a fuller narrative style.

Not only disappointed aesthetes and conservative novelists indulged in nostalgia; war-weary readers also longed for comfortable, secure literary worlds. Accordingly the bookshops hardly could keep fiction in stock, especially classic novels by Jane Austen, Charles Dickens, and Anthony Trollope. In part this was because of reduced print runs, and paper restrictions meant that publishers were limited to 60 percent, then to 40 percent, of prewar production. The result was that, as Calder notes, "new books generally became shorter" (511). New books also became less new: while publishers sold piles of classics, often in inexpensive, recently created Penguin editions, the number of freshly written novels fell off sharply. Bergonzi records that published new novels in England dropped from 4,222 in 1939 to 1,179 in 1945, concluding that it was "not a good period for the novel" (27). But paper shortages were not the major problem. The real shortfall lay in content: many writers were in military service and had time to pen only short stories or sketches. Others, like Bowen, felt they could not concentrate on large projects while survival hung in the balance: "If at present we cannot write, and our friends cannot write, we can read" ("Contemporary" 340). The requisite blackouts boosted the popularity of reading, while both readers and writers sought comfort and escape in nostalgic old style.[5]

Comfort, coziness, and nostalgia were far from Connolly's hopes. *Horizon* was meant to be avant-garde, although its stated purposes—to defend art, to support the artist—were preservative and therefore redolent of the past. The reputations of both Connolly and *Horizon* have suffered from misapprehensions, because of Waugh's mockery and because critics have taken Connolly's editorial "Comments" at face value, assuming that he stuffed his issues with esoteric art. Historians usually contrast *Horizon* with *Penguin New Writing*, a periodical anthology of realistic wartime stories, sketches, and criticism that appeared throughout the forties. According to this opposition, *Penguin New Writing* represents the realist tradition, concerned with grimy details of wartime life at home and on the battlefield, while *Horizon* constitutes a literary ivory tower. "Connolly was certainly an escapist, and proud of it," wrote Calder. But at least he was "an intellectual escapist" (515, 516). Meanwhile, in *New Writing*,

---

5. Or in lowbrow fiction such as James Hadley Chase's sensational *No Orchids for Miss Blandish* (1939), a favorite read during the Battle of Britain, according to Orwell ("Raffles and Miss Blandish" 236).

"the [politically committed] young writer kept faith by his commitment if he merely described, in lame prose or bald verse, exactly what he himself was doing" (514). In fact, the literatures of each are considered unmemorable. Paul Fussell concludes, despite his approval of Connolly's aesthetic aims, that

> disappointment threatens anyone searching in published wartime writing for a use of language that could be called literary.... What one finds, rather, is the gush, waffle, and cliché occasioned by high-mindedness, the impulse to sound portentous, and the slumbering of the critical spirit. (251)

"Gush, waffle, and cliché" might apply to Connolly's own confiding editorials, in which he championed "the delayed-action art and literature which survives indifference and slowly dominates" (4/40: 233). But intention and outcome are two very different things, and *Horizon* became a magazine whose aims, like those of *Vogue*, adjusted to and were adjusted by war.

Horizon's insular repute is belied by its complex contents, which have been surprisingly little analyzed.[6] Despite Connolly's promise of politics "in abeyance," every issue contained political commentary along with poems, short stories, and reviews. Several times, too, Connolly printed summary Mass Observation reports describing the "impact of war upon the civilian mind and mood" (7/41: 13)—and one hardly could find a purer documentary form than these sociological surveys. The journal's war commentary appears most strikingly in a recurrent "War Symposium": "a series of contributions dealing directly with the war ... consist[ing] of stories, essays, letters, or *reportage*" (2/41: 92). Yet even in the magazine's creative offerings, war persistently popped up. Despite later assertions that only *Penguin New Writing* published realistic war fiction, Connolly's journal included William Sansom's "The Wall," with detailed reportage about London firefighting (7/41: 24–27), and J. Maclaren-Ross's "I had to go sick" (8/42: 113–27) and "This Mortal Coil" (12/42: 416–21)—each story almost itself a mass-observation record. A war story by poet Alun Lewis (12/43: 392–405), in addition to his poetry, seemed, as Connolly remarked, "to suggest army life as it really is."

---

6. Mark Rawlinson discusses *Horizon*'s many soldier and putative-soldier contributions (150–53, 158–60), but he is in the minority.

In fact, Connolly proved unexpectedly inclusive and pragmatic. "Where are our war poets?" he inquired rhetorically. "The answer (not usually given) is 'under your nose' . . . they are only peace poets who have assimilated the material of war" (1/41: 5). And he printed the poetry and art under his nose, much of it dealing with war, such as Geoffrey Matthews's "Poem for a Friend Joining the RAF" (1/41: 14), illustrated by an interleaf photograph of the bombed ruins of Coventry Cathedral. Stephen Spender's "Air Raid" seems a starkly documentary poem, describing the horrifying and mundane details of a family bombed inside their house:

Then the inside made outside faces the street.
Rubble decently buries the human meat.
Piled above it, a bath, cupboards, books, telephone,
Though all who could answer its ringing have gone. (2/41: 94: ll.25–28)

Realism triumphed in Connolly's late-modernist journal.

And pragmatics necessitated the publication of art far outside any ivory tower. For several years, Connolly would both scrimp on paper, sometimes eliminating poems or his editorials, and scrounge for good content. He did not jettison his literary standards; in November 1941 he would complain, "*Horizon* receives a hundred poems a week. Why are they so bad?" (299). Rather than bad poems, he printed journalism or realistic art, such as Cecil Beaton's photos of British war ruins (5/41: 352–53) and desert warfare (9/42: 162–63), arguably less artworks than reportage. The same might be said of "Prisoner of War" by Captain Robin Campbell, DSO (3/44: 152–61). Most memorably, *Horizon* published a controversial excerpt from Arthur Koestler's 1943 novel *Arrival and Departure* (10/43: 244–51), controversial because it described the transport and massacre of Polish Jews by SS forces. Despite its ostensibly fictional form, Koestler's vivid, haunting depiction provoked anger and skepticism in some readers, answered by a scathing rejoinder from the author (12/43: 433). The readers did not want to believe that pogroms could happen in modern Europe, Koestler was outraged by their doubt—and both parties forgot the fictional framework. The boundaries between art and life were breached, not as an aesthetic experiment but as a consequence of war.

In fact, although he yearned to be avant-garde, Connolly held a middle-way perspective on the war. And both the editor's political moderation and his flexibility gave the journal an engaging breadth: as did British *Vogue*, *Horizon* adjusted its styles in order to survive. Ironically also like *Vogue*, Connolly's journal exuded an aesthetically based reverence for all things French, a reverence that stemmed from a barely hidden inferiority complex in respect to British style. Just as *Vogue* published reports from the occupied country, *Horizon* eagerly would print long "Letters from France" by an anonymous "talented lady" (3/41: 187–200; 11/41: 341–58). Eventually the journal even reflected *Vogue* in having its own mini-controversy over rumored complicity with the Nazis, on the part of certain respected French writers.[7] Moreover, during and after the Liberation of Paris, British writers would hotly debate the relative value of contemporary French versus English literatures. Philip Toynbee reported admiringly on the "tough continuity" he saw in liberated Paris, adding, "For an Englishman it is both humiliating and invigorating to discover that the creative energy of French writers has easily defied four years of clumsy Teutonic interdiction" (11/44: 295, 296). But many British readers and writers disliked being told that they should feel humiliated by French creativity. John Lehmann indignantly responded that Toynbee in his rush to praise the French had disregarded Britain's own fine literary output. Lehmann's defense of English literature reflects similar tensions to those between style-proud Parisiennes and clothing-rationed Londoners in 1944–45:

> Mr. Toynbee speaks, with just respect, of the period of privations, obstacles and tragedies with which French writers had to contend; but for a period which in Britain was marked by similar difficulties, accentuated—as most of our French friends will agree—by total mobilization for the continuance of the war (and the liberation of France) it seems to me a matter of legitimate pride to be able to point to such works of outstanding scholarship, original thought, and literary brilliance as [Lehmann's list of notable British books, 1940–1944]. (1/45: 5–6)

Connolly happily printed Lehmann's pugilistic letter under the title of "The Battle of the Books," followed by his own pacifistic note: "That the

---

7. See "Correspondence" in *Horizon* 3/45: 218; 5/45: 362; 7/45: 72.

French should think our books better than theirs, and that we should hold the opposite opinion is part of the sweet mirage of propinquity which is such a fortunate symptom in two countries who in culture, and in historical predicament, are really one" (7). It is hard to find evidence of that so-called sweet propinquity or oneness outside of Connolly's head; in the cultural arena, the war increased tensions between the two nations. And literary Londoners were divided between an obsequious Francophilia and a bellicose defense of plain, honest English writing.

Both nostalgia and snobbery characterized the British Francophiles, to a greater extent than with their counterparts in fashion. Certainly in both *Vogue* and *Horizon* admiration for French artistry was elitist. Only those with sufficient money to travel to Paris, and to buy couture clothing, aspired to the "Made in France" label. Likewise a high level of education, if not money, enabled the well-to-do to enjoy French literature and culture. After a late-war fact-finding trip, Connolly reported that the "three weeks spent recently in France were amongst the happiest in my life," admitting that his reaction "may well be annoying to the English reader unprivileged to travel" (7/45: 5). At least in the area of fashion, women who could not afford the clothing might gaze at the magazine images and dream, or purchase ready-made imitations; lovers of French literature and culture had to acknowledge that they constituted a privileged coterie.

But of course this literary fascination with French modes represented longing for the prewar era and frustration with ways in which the war had cramped British style. Connolly's own characteristically labile references to French literature are mingled with concern for the state of English letters. He acknowledged that French literature seemed ideal because it was out of reach: "Critical articles [in *Horizon*] tend to be predominantly French. This is not because Horizon is pro-French, but because, at a time when France is inaccessible, so many critics are fascinated by French literature" (1/44: 5). He then complained of poor submissions in English, indicating *Horizon*'s desire to publish more polished fictions:

> Horizon will always publish stories of pure realism, but we take the line that experiences connected with the blitz, the shopping queues, the home front, deserted wives, deceived husbands, broken homes, dull jobs . . . are so much a picture of our ordinary lives that unless the workmanship is outstanding we are prejudiced against them. (5)

Connolly seems to express a prejudice against the domestic settings that typify most women's literature.[8] His stated bias, however, is against depictions of "ordinary lives" on the homefront, and toward that which seems exotic and unavailable, including France.

Accordingly, as the European war wound down, *Horizon* continued its unstable mix of reverence for French achievement and apology for homefront mediocrity. The May 1945 issue boasted "NEWS OUT OF FRANCE," featuring a twelve-page Comment praising Occupation and Resistance literature. Writings by Jean-Paul Sartre and Paul Valéry appeared (307–12; 312–17), followed by a "Letter from Paris" by Nancy Cunard mentioning "those hats on the women" and "their fanciful high wooden-soled wedge shoes" (397). *Horizon's* Gallic feast after famine provoked complaints, answered by partial retractions. Even Connolly tempered the description of his "happiest" weeks in France by remarking that the English are more honest, "whereas in France everyone cheats, everyone distrusts" in response to the German occupation (7/45: 5). Eventually he resolved "to have fewer French articles" in *Horizon* (12/45: 365). But then he could not resist a screed on contemporary English literary lacks: "And what is the matter with the young? And the B. B. C.? And America? Why are its serious writers so very pretentious and its popular writers so bad?" Connolly pledged himself to continue to work "for a new humanism which considers human life vulgar but sacred. . . . And to uphold the belief that Art is an end in itself, with a life of its own and rewards of its own" (366). *Horizon's* editor never abandoned his aestheticism, although he claimed it was non-elitist and apolitical. And his "vulgar but sacred" ideal is a problem that high modernism had struggled with, and a late-modern oxymoron vividly illustrated by Connolly's own *Unquiet Grave*.

Evelyn Waugh termed *The Unquiet Grave* "an authentic breath of Bloomsbury air" (*Diaries* 616: 9 January 1945); the comment was not intended to be laudatory. Originally serialized in *Horizon*, this small book locks in the wartime connection between revenant modernism and self-indulgent aesthetic old style. Connolly's mixture of penseés and memoir

---

8. Both Jenny Hartley (8) and Gill Plain (40) single out this Connolly quotation for evidence of his antifeminine bias. But although one could not call Connolly a feminist, these words should be read in the context of his many loose-lipped wartime "Comments." *Horizon* published several of Elizabeth Bowen's stories, on precisely these homefront topics.

contains all the fragmented high-modern allusion, the large proclamations about life and love and art, that he must have longed to put in *Horizon*, interspersed with sensuous personal memories of prewar France, its weather, food, and sea. He clearly rejoices in using original allusions and untranslated quotations from other languages—mostly French and Latin, but also Greek and Spanish. He constantly alludes to the past and critiques the present "decline of fiction": "Flaubert, Henry James, Proust, Joyce, and Virginia Woolf have finished off the novel" (22). He reverently quotes Eliot: "the progress of the artist is a continual self-sacrifice, a continual extinction of personality" (96–97). He intersperses confidences about his own obesity and love affairs with longings for a lost France: "Rue de Chanaleilles. Summer night, limes in flower; old houses, with large gardens enclosed by high walls, silent in the leafy heart of the Faubourg: sensation of what is lost; lost love, lost youth, lost Paris,—remorse and folly. Aïe!" (26, 61; 26).

Connolly also offers inadvertent evidence for the triumph of the vulgar over the sacred in literary art, as seen in his aggrandized longing for prewar life on the *Rive Gauche*: "For an angora pullover, for a red scarf, for a beret and some brown shoes I am bleeding to death; my heart is dry as a kidney" (87). His memories of pet ferrets and lemurs resort to unintentional comic grandeur: "When I think of lemurs depression engulfs me 'à peu que le coeur ne me fend'" (118). But for the most part, Connolly's language slips back into cozy English pet-love, vulgar in more than Sayers's populist sense:

> [Our pet ferrets] pursued oranges and eggs and ping-pong balls, and wore harness with little bells; and from among them there came forth a queen, the tawny, docile Norfolk beauty whom we named the English Rose, who performed her cycle of eating, playing, sleeping and relieving herself, and who saw three continents from a warm sleeve. (114–15)

Topically far from epic modernism, the sentences remain cast in nostalgic old style. Yet the telling small details, and the refusal to aim for the stars, foreshadow postwar literatures that would eschew drama and grandeur for the trivial and the mundane.

From sacred to vulgar, *The Unquiet Grave* reflects its author's acknowledgement that the literary era he adores has ended. The framing device, Aeneas's deceased helmsman Palinurus, is a classical ghost. His body lies unburied on an Italian beach while his spirit meets Aeneas in the underworld, in a Roman purgatory. Connolly's book ends with the ancient debate: was the helmsman willfully negligent, colluding in his own death? The author concludes that Palinurus "stands for a certain will-to-failure or repugnance-to-success, a desire to give up at the last moment, an urge towards loneliness, isolation and obscurity" (146). Since Palinurus represents the modern writer, to blame the victim in this way is to blame artists themselves for modernism's demise. Connolly's verdict also acknowledges that the ghost *is* a ghost, and that prewar modernism finally can expect nothing but a decent burial.

BURYING LITERARY OLD STYLE: WAUGH, KOESTLER, WARNER, LARKIN

To describe wartime literature is, inevitably, to select certain exemplars out of many. Since I am not recounting an inclusive history but rather laying a foundation for discussing postwar "re-dressings" of the novel, I pass over intriguing fictions by writers such as Henry Green and Rosamond Lehmann in order briefly to spotlight a few significant markers along the road to postwar literature, in novels by Arthur Koestler, Rex Warner, and Philip Larkin. This discussion begins, however, with Evelyn Waugh, whose satirical distance and deep nostalgia made him a highly conscious commentator on wartime's literary Purgatory.

If Connolly miserably suspected that modernism was over, his friend Waugh was fully, cynically cognizant of that fact. As MacKay has noted, both *Put Out More Flags* and *Brideshead Revisited* are "largely novels about modernism and very self-consciously after modernism, and in neither is there anything to compensate for what has been lost, culturally and artistically" (126). These two war novels mingle mockery and elegy regarding Britain's dead modernism. Other nostalgic writers, such as Osbert Sitwell, purely mourned for the loss of a more gracious world and literature—or, like poets Edith Sitwell and Dylan Thomas, stubbornly continued producing the luxuriant lines they valued. But Waugh refused to wallow. Unlike Connolly, he always had mocked and despised the high-modern cult of the artist, despite his own predilections for aestheticism and for modernist cinematic narration: he already was expert in spare, understated fiction. That he began in wartime to undertake an elaborately decorative prose is due in part to characteristic contrarianism, and in part to a suppressed Romanticism and midlife crisis, but also to a deliberate decision to dissect his own era and desires. Thus, while *Brideshead* indeed exemplifies nostalgic old style, it also insists that the prewar world is gone, old style is passé, and a dreary new England must be faced.[9]

In confronting this drab new world Waugh, like Orwell, was impelled by a dramatic conviction that the conditions of literature in Britain were changing permanently. Waugh's odd little early-war "Work Suspended" includes his first use of a long, periodic sentence style for fiction. The narrator, John Plant, is a smug middle-aged writer living in Morocco. His careful solitary life is interrupted by the death of his father, an artist who did "English painting as it might have been, had there not been any Aesthetic Movement" (157). Although busy with his eighth detective novel, Plant returns home to wrap up his father's affairs. While in England, he falls in love with a friend's wife. But the would-be love affair—like his writing, and the narrative itself—is suspended abruptly: "Our story, like my novel, remained unfinished—a heap of neglected foolscap at the back of a drawer" (234). That the war meant turning a permanent corner is underscored not only by this inconclusive conclusion but by Waugh's frequently expressed regrets. He seemed unable either to resume or to forget his suspended novel.[10] When congratulated later on *Put Out More Flags*, he claimed it was "minor," whereas "Work Suspended" "was the major work" (*Letters* 158: 5 December 1941). Connolly printed one chapter, "In My Father's House," in *Horizon* (11/41: 329–41), appropriately since John Plant's descriptions of his father's life, paintings, and death covertly commented on the wartime literary scene. The death of an older generation, and the selling-up of outmoded works of art, might pretend to relate to aged parents—but middle-aged modernists knew better. For the less insightful, there was the heavy symbolism of the senior Plant's last, unfinished painting, which "was to have been called 'Again?' and

---

9. Despite MacKay's highly insightful readings of *Put Out* and *Brideshead,* she overidentifies the nostalgia of Waugh's fictional Charles Ryder with that of Waugh himself (see MacKay 128). As many extraliterary comments show (including the lines quoted above, regarding wartime "gluttony," and below, on Ryder's mediocrity), Waugh was highly critical of his character's values, and that criticism included, but did not equate to, self-critique.

10. He sent a chapter to John Betjeman in September 1939, remarking that he had "discontinued" it; he confided to another friend that it was "jolly well done" and he would continue it if he couldn't find a war job; then, in February 1940, he announced to his agent, "I shall not resume my novel for the duration" (*Letters* 127, 137).

represented a one-armed veteran of the First World War meditating over a German helmet" (143). While Waugh probably intended the painting to mock bathetic art, it perpetuated a standard homefront theme: the dead past returns to haunt us.

Appropriately, then, the dedication for *Put Out More Flags* (1942) refers to "a race of ghosts, the survivors of the world we both knew ten years ago . . . no longer contemporary in sympathy" (np). In this comic novel, set in Bore-War England, Waugh tidily killed off or exiled the relics of modernism, especially aesthetically oriented characters. Two old-style aesthetes, Ambrose Silk and Cedric Lyne, are done in through war, cuckolded in different ways by the adventurer Basil Seal. Ambrose, after founding the high-art journal *Ivory Tower*, is manipulated by Basil into fleeing supposed anti-Semitic persecution. By the end he is hiding out in a remote Irish village, writing "absolutely nothing" (282), while the triumphant Basil enjoys Ambrose's comfortable flat, assigning his new girlfriend to pick the embroidered initials out of the aesthete's silk underwear and replace them with Basil's own. Cedric's end is just as harsh. The shy architect husband of Basil's long-standing mistress Angela, he occupies himself designing eighteenth-century grottoes. Finally he is called up and through a series of military blunders dies, freeing Angela to marry Basil at last. But even the conquering Basil's triumph is ambiguous: as the story concludes, he has accepted a dangerous mission on the Continent. Respectable marriage and real heroism being outside Seal's rascally character, Waugh wrote no more Basil Seal novels; Basil too was a prewar ghost, "no longer contemporary in sympathy."[11]

Brideshead Revisited goes beyond burying the past, to disown the present and cast a grim eye on Britain's future. Waugh had looked forward to the inspiration of war, working hard to win a soldiering job. But by midwar he was writing in his diary,

> I dislike the Army. I want to get to work again. I do not want any more experiences . . . to influence opinions or events, or expose humbug or anything of that kind. I don't want to be of service to anyone or anything. I simply want to do my work as an artist. (548: 29 August 1943)

---

11. Waugh did publish a limited-edition forty-nine-page novella, *Basil Seal Rides Again* (1963), a labored resurrection of an aged character as passé as the Lord Peter of Sayers's few late stories.

A few months later he began *Brideshead* which like *More Flags* puts paid to prewar styles, though in more complex, less comic ways. Waugh painstakingly constructs a prewar idyll and then destroys it, through three aesthetically oriented university students: the aristocrat Sebastian Flyte, who seeks a beautiful life in the Paterian sense; Anthony Blanche, the purely modernist aesthete; and Charles Ryder, who under their tutelage becomes a painter. As modernism ages in the thirties, the promise of each young man is punctured. From Charvat ties and champagne, Flyte declines to an alcoholic beggar in exile. Blanche, who as a student championed *The Waste Land*, remains an astute critic but far out of the mainstream, in London's gay underground; he has not become an artist himself. And Ryder, who finds success in painting great houses about to be demolished, must face the fact that even his best art is only "playing tigers" (273). "[Ryder] was a bad painter," Waugh wrote to Nancy Mitford. "Well he was as bad at painting as Osbert [Sitwell] is at writing" (*Letters* 196: 7 January 1945). Waugh begs Mitford not to repeat the simile, but it is telling: whatever his own predilections, he condemned self-indulgent aestheticism and nostalgia.

It is the war, however, that in *Brideshead* forces the end of nostalgic old style. The middle-aged Ryder is a commissioned cog in an army that has no use for art, and like his creator sick of soldiering. He returns to the beautiful Brideshead estate to witness its desecration. Even the murals he painted there in the twenties—"modern work," comments the quartering commandant, "but the prettiest in the place"—have been vandalized by soldiers (347). Ryder has only the "small red flame" of religious faith for comfort, since both his memories of and his ambitions for beautiful art have been shot down. Appropriately, then, the contemporary "Prologue" and "Epilogue" sections that bookend the novel appear in simpler, less florid style than the narrative in between. And *Brideshead*'s concluding line is deliberately bland: "'You're looking unusually cheerful to-day,' said the second-in-command" (351).

No style to cherish, no deathless art: these were bitter pills for the heirs of modernism. Neither Waugh nor Connolly believed that literature should "influence opinions or events" or "be of service to anyone or anything." Yet the realist fiction that would inaugurate a new literary style did not share this disdain. The postwar New Look in literature would include minimalism, comic litotes, and a distrust of high artistic claims: it had not yet arrived, but its seeds are clear in the rise of wartime novels that—against all sound modernist doctrine—preached overt political messages and often were lauded for doing so. In particular, these writers experimented with democratic ideals, even in their plots undercutting the elitism of high-modernist style. Three very different novels demonstrate coming postwar styles and subjects, along with the passing of traditional aestheticism: Arthur Koestler's *Darkness at Noon* (1940), Rex Warner's *Aerodrome* (1941), and Philip Larkin's *Jill* (1946).

Like Orwell, Koestler was concerned with blindness, on the part of the British Left, to the perils of Communist totalitarianism. *Darkness at Noon*, a terse account of a Stalinist official caught in a web of his own weaving, compellingly confirmed for many Britons the Soviet evils suggested by the early-war Russian-German alliance. But it is not only its content that makes *Darkness* memorable; as Orwell would do in *1984*, Koestler captured in his prose the sense of a smothering solitude, in which the protagonist's ethical dilemmas are epitomized by the ways language is used. In his prison cell, Rubashov is haunted by memories of those he has betrayed, blaming his own tendency to see the other person's point of view—a dangerous tendency for a revolutionary (23–24). Rubashov broods upon a useless mental habit he has acquired, that of a divided self that signifies one's useless sympathy for others (154). Foreshadowing postwar novels' overt play with subject-object narration, in *Darkness* the protagonist often addresses himself in the second person (108). The solipsism that so fascinated high modernists—"Let us go then, you and I," says Eliot's Prufrock to himself (l.1)—now found itself pinned and dissected on the page. Talking to oneself is both an effective and a problematic narrative strategy, but it was the late moderns rather than high modernists who would fully investigate the complications of calling oneself both "you" and "I." Koestler's fiction showed that saying farewell to high modernism need not mean simplification, any more than political significance need preclude timelessness.

Nevertheless, political statement does not guarantee stylistic sophistication. In *The Aerodrome: A Love Story*, Warner produced a memorable dystopia despite two-dimensional characterization and a clunky plot. Young Roy, inhabitant of a dreary English village, is fascinated by the flashy military inhabitants of the large modern aerodrome which threatens the village's traditional life. Soon he discovers that he was adopted as an infant and becomes alienated from the parents who raised him. Various erotic entanglements complicate Roy's rise as a pilot in training, despite the special patronage of the cold-voiced Air Vice-Marshall. Meanwhile, the village decays as traditional English leaders, the Rector and the Squire, pass away. Eventually, the Air Vice-Marshall's corruption is revealed, the secret of Roy's parentage is untangled, and survivors are left with a vague hope for the future.

The Aerodrome's best-selling popularity may be attributed to two ways in which the novel struck a nerve with war-fraught readers. First, Warner's fable presents a world in which traditional Britain and its modernized future exist together in an irreducible tension—or rather are so much at odds that they cannot coexist for long. For those nostalgic for prewar days, the novel justified their dislike of crass futurism: forget your backgrounds, the evil Air Vice-Marshall urges the neophyte pilots, and forget those parents "who have served in most cases as channels or conduits through which you have all in varying degree been infected with the stupidity, the ugliness, and the servility of historical tradition" (178). As in Waugh's "Work Suspended," parents signify the past that one would leave behind, and here that past seems indeed crude, dull, and irretrievable. Not that the future, as seen in the overt power-mongering of the Aerodrome's inhabitants, attracts. For the second fascinating aspect of Warner's novel lay in its self-centered narrator Roy, who offered a new sort of confessional realism as he frankly described jettisoning family, friends, and lovers in his efforts to climb to the top of the heap. Indeed, Roy prefigures the ordinary, nonheroic "blokes" who would populate much fifties fiction, horrifying and fascinating the reader with their crass grabs for pleasure and prestige.[12]

Self-consciousness, overturned tradition (including the tradition of a sympathetic protagonist), and comic minimalism: all are part of Larkin's *Jill*, which unlike the two previously mentioned novels did not deal overtly with politics or cause a big splash when it appeared at the war's end. Indeed, when the war began, Larkin still was an undergraduate and had yet to realize the métier that would make him the most prominent British poet of the later twentieth century. As part of the Movement, he would employ a plain yet precise language intended to deflate the

---

12. *The Aerodrome* strikingly resembles John Braine's *Room at the Top* (1957), about an ambitious young accountant on the make. Braine's novel echoed *Aerodrome* both in narrative voice and in plot, down to the climactic death of the bloke's attractive older mistress and his slightly chastened conclusion. The Lewis Gilbert film *Alfie* (1966), starring Michael Caine, would follow a similar pattern.

pretensions of both Romantic and high-modernist poetry. Prefiguring this new style, *Jill* serves as the anti-*Brideshead*, in language and in plot. Like Waugh's Ryder, John Kemp, a scholarship student at Oxford, is bedazzled by a handsome, wealthy fellow undergraduate, his roommate Christopher. But Larkin's protagonist enjoys no prewar idyll: the lordly Chris and his upper-class crowd alternately use and neglect Kemp, who endeavors to impress his roommate by inventing an attractive younger sister named Jill. Jill becomes a "hallucination of innocence" (135) for her creator, who writes letters from her to himself, composes a diary recounting her schooldays, and eventually begins to stalk a young girl named Gillian. One hardly could find a narrative more distant in style or content from Waugh's romantic opus—except that, like Ryder's aspirations, Kemp's pathetic delusions end badly. His hoped-for friends desert him and he is hospitalized with pneumonia, forced to face his own worst dreams:

> All his life he had imagined people were hostile to him and wanted to hurt him; now he knew he had been right and all the worst fears of childhood were realized. He was used to humiliating memories, but these seemed different, they had really existed. (203)

Larkin's comically blunt narration utilizes a litotes appropriate to his protagonist's masochistic meekness. It also foreshadows the postwar undercutting of elaborate language. "They had really existed" appropriately concludes the sentence, by trailing off into a banal abstraction that typifies Kemp's own failed personality. In his unattractive self, John Kemp—although very different from Rex Warner's cocky Roy—like him serves to bury the traditional literary protagonist. In his insecurities Kemp too prefigures the fifties bloke who, an upstart in a still class-conscious Britain, constantly worries about money. The admired Chris, no Sebastian Flyte, borrows money, asks his roommate to write his essays for him, and generally lacks noblesse oblige. The ideals of nostalgic old style cannot survive Larkin's wartime world.

Jill also looks ahead to postwar fiction's subject-object concerns, in scenes showing Kemp's willing self-abasement. When Chris and his friends use Kemp's tea dishes without inviting him to join them, Kemp is "acutely conscious of being referred to in the third person, but it express[es] his mood" (32). And Larkin's most extreme play with point of view appears in Kemp's obsession with seeing through a girl's eyes, such that clothing is more of a marker in *Jill* than in most male-penned fiction. In a brief bout of delusional self-confidence, Kemp tries, as a Rhys woman might, to transform himself through dress. Depressed "by the sudden reflection of himself in a hatshop window," Kemp determines to remake himself:

> It would be splendid to go into a tailor's and order a dozen new suits, in tweed, with fob pockets and leather buttons. The idea of spending money took hold of his mind, and he began considering what he could buy, something he could wear to show his good humour: a really smart tie, for instance. In fact, a bow-tie. (97)

That Larkin penned this sartorial fantasy in 1943, when few had new suits with fob pockets and leather buttons, suggests his character's alienation from the actual limits of dress in wartime. It then is fully appropriate that when Kemp dares to buy a bow tie, his self-making fails: "He was so nervous when he emerged that for all practical purposes he was a walking bow-tie" (98). The first female acquaintance he encounters insists upon retying it for him. His brief interest in transformative dress becomes one more sign of his faulty manhood.

These wartime novels by men, whether nostalgic for or bitter toward Britain's customs and literature, do not for all their cogency celebrate a rising new order. Romanticism and nostalgia are satirized, traditions are critiqued, democracy is inevitable—yet seems as dreary as the old hierarchies. Waugh, Koestler, Warner, and Larkin write more about failure, fear, and the end of an era than about hope for the future. As for literary styles, *Brideshead*'s luxuriant prose was heavily critiqued, even by its author; *Darkness at Noon* and *The Aerodrome* engaged readers through political significance, and *Jill*'s careful style of small things was little noted at the time. What would become the comic minimalism of postwar literature is grim; realism is sometimes psychological, sometimes political, sometimes the recording of small details—but rarely all three. One might have expected war to prompt realistically detailed military accounts or great homefront dramas. But the dominant homefront style in fiction was, like the homefront style in dress, tapered down. And as traditional great literature ended in Britain, no one realized that it was the beginning of something new, especially for women.

ELIZABETH BOWEN'S HAUNTED HOMEFRONT

In 1940, *Vogue*'s Lesley Blanch had asked whether women would use their wartime opportunities to become ersatz men: "What is this Amazonian spirit? Is it an expression of abnormality? Or is it an extravagant expression of aggression, born of centuries of repression—in short a desire to 'wear the trousers'?" (9/40: 36). Women wearing trousers was, as I have noted, a fertile wartime topic. For Sayers, trousers showed how men misread feminine style; in novels by Delafield and Thirkell, the donning of trousers illustrated women's own wartime struggles over gender roles. But Blanch uses the expression to delineate key differences between the sexes. Women, she says, do not see war as a game; rather, "women are harsh realists: not for us the palliating sports-idiom by which the gentlemen of the press doll up the news" (36, 78).

Women's harsh realism dominates Elizabeth Bowen's fictional homefront: female or male, each of her characters is haunted by a past that reveals itself under the extreme conditions of wartime. Bowen herself, as an Anglo-Irishwoman, understood her own end-of-era status; as a well-known novelist, she teetered on the brink of high modernism; as an air-raid warden, she filled a homefront job often held by men. Using the abbreviated style of the short story, even as homefront skirts, dresses, and fashion itself were trimmed by necessity, Bowen did not praise but sought to bury prewar nostalgia. Her stories are not avant-garde but middlebrow, using romance and trivial details, including those of dress. Thus, whatever her high literary gifts and her ability to do a man's job, Bowen writes as a woman who comprehends what she termed "a rising tide of hallucination" on the homefront. She describes those hallucinations as compensatory, realistic, and unrelated to mental illness: "We all lived in a state of lucid abnormality" (Preface ix). Bowen's protagonists may be psychically damaged, but the damage occurred before the present war. The conditions of blitzed London wash these problems to the surface, and the author carefully depicts them through small details: "Through the particular, in wartime, I felt the high-voltage current of the general pass" (Preface xiv). Those particular details suggest incommensurable divisions between the sexes.

Famously interested in interior decoration, Bowen details clothing as a form of domestic accessory in which exteriors reveal interior states.

Plock has described Bowen's novelistic use of clothing details as peculiarly modernist, not only denoting human relations but employing fashion's instability to represent moderns' fluidity of emotions and identity (288–91, 298). I would add that in Bowen's wartime stories ghosts repeatedly, through dress details, evoke a richer yet insubstantial past, suggesting that history and traditional gender relations (Bowen draws no distinction between the entities) attract us but are deeply problematic.

Bowen regularly reworked the Edwardian ghost story to signify an irrepressible dead past. During the Great War, battlefield tales of ghosts—from the legend of Mons to the return of Napoleon—had been common, and Jay Winter has shown that they served to process grief for loved ones (129). Wartime ghosts provided a striking juxtaposition of brutal realities with a desperate insistence upon the spiritual. Yet in Great War accounts, revenant phantoms are overwhelmingly beneficent, whereas they are unwelcome and frightening in World War II stories: even resurrected loved ones carry with them the evil reek of war. Accordingly, the late-modern ghost story laid modern nostalgia to rest. Bowen's ghosts are sometimes amusing, but they never serve as emblems of healthy mourning or suggest that the past can save us.

In Bowen's best-known story, "The Demon Lover," the demon menaces a hapless woman rather than enticing her. Yet this title piece translates all the others: every revenant, no matter how benign-seeming or even humorous, is horrific. In taking the old tale of the supernatural lover who returns to claim a promise and setting it in the deserted streets of blitzed London, Bowen provides a potent symbol for the return of the repressed and the revenge of history, as well as a delicately literal horror story hinged on trivial details. Mrs. Drover, a respectable middle-aged wife and mother, has stopped by her London home to retrieve a few items. Her shut-up house is described in plausible, frightening terms of violence:

> the yellow smoke-stain up the white marble mantelpiece, the ring left by a vase on the top of the escritoire; the bruise in the wallpaper where, on the door being thrown open widely, the china handle had always hit the wall. The piano . . . had left what looked like claw-marks on its part of the parquet. (661)

The small details confirm the veiled threat of an unsigned letter she finds inside her locked house: "You will not have forgotten that today is our anniversary, and the day we said. The years have gone by at once slowly and fast.... I shall rely upon you to keep your promise" (662). When Kathleen Drover reads the letter, even "her lips, beneath the remains of lipstick," begin to turn white, and she hurries to the mirror to study "the change in her own face." Her appearance is characterized by disengagement, from her "carelessly pulled down" hat brim and lack of face powder, to her husband's pearls hanging "loose round her now rather thinner throat, slipping in the V of the pink wool jumper her sister knitted last autumn" (662). As Bowen has used the domestic trivia of ordinary furnishings to symbolize the demon lover's threatening approach, so she details her protagonist's middle-class personal style to suggest the "complete dislocation from everything" (664) that Kathleen has undergone since parting from her soldier-fiancé in the Great War. In becoming an ordinary housewife, she also has turned into an empty shell ripe for possession. Kathleen's fearful memory of her boyfriend is threefold: "He was never kind," and she remembers him pressing her hand upon his uniform button so hard that it left a mark on her palm; he extracted an "unnatural promise" from her, that they would meet again in twenty-five years, dead or alive; and *"under no conditions* could she remember his face" (665; emphasis in original). Appropriately, at the story's conclusion when Mrs. Drover tries to escape in a taxi, she finds herself "eye to eye" with its mysterious driver—but his face remains blank, and he never speaks. The story ends with Kathleen beating with "gloved hands" on the glass as the taxi, "accelerating without mercy," carries her off into the suburbs—not usually a terrifying destination. It is an archetypal nightmare of absolute male power enacted on a helpless female, underlined by banal details. The wartime setting merely intensifies the conditions of a traditional theme. Bowen's narrative teeters between a supernatural demonic tale and a barely possible realism, wherein a shell-shocked, obsessive veteran stalks his long-ago love. But the literal truth does not matter: as a Great War revenant, Kathleen's fiancé symbolizes the horror of another colossal war; as a figure from her girlhood, he links her "energetic and calm" middle-aged exterior with dark elements of her younger self. Whether demonic or human, he possesses her only through fear and force: "He was set on me," she recalls, "that was what it was, not love" (665). So Bowen's title piece emblematizes the extreme alienation of the sexes underlying many of these wartime stories. Most are not frightening, but all play with characters' blinded perspectives, and all employ small details to invoke a repressed past.

"Ivy Gripped the Steps" is not a ghost story, yet the protagonist Gavin is haunted, by memories of a childhood infatuation with his mother's glamorous friend. In carelessly amusing herself by flirting with the preteen boy in her care, Mrs. Nicholson has warped Gavin's sexuality, making him a solitary "amorist" (689). As World War II concludes, the middle-aged Gavin returns to the seaside resort of his childhood and finds Mrs. Nicholson's house covered with a near-diabolical ivy: "There was something brutal about its fecundity . . . one could have convinced oneself that the ivy must be feeding on something inside the house" (686). The glamorous owner has been dead since 1912, along with her lover Admiral Concannon, who predicted the Great War and died in it. The gulf between little Gavin's fantasy, of having a special relationship with his beautiful hostess, and the reality, of militant history personified in the admiral, is crystallized in Mrs. Nicholson's fatuous refusal to acknowledge a coming war: "After all, we live in the present day! . . . I never even cared for history at school; I was glad when we came to the end of it" (695). She insists that European war is at odds with her civilized female life. She came "to the end of history," she tells the admiral flirtatiously, in the "year I put up my hair." Her repeated word for war is "silly":

> Civilized countries are polite to each other, just as you and I are to the people we know, and uncivilized countries are put down—but, if one thinks, there are beautifully few of those. Even savages really prefer wearing hats and coats. Once people wear hats and coats and can turn on electric light, they would no more want to be silly than you or I do.—Or *do* you want to be silly? (696)

Her reasoning itself expresses a silly Edwardian optimism that will die with World War I. But the patently false image of coat-wearing savages also suggests the ways in which, for Mrs. Nicholson's generation, clothing occludes differences they want to hide.

Mrs. Nicholson's own clothing impels the young Gavin's enchanted disenchantment—and demonstrates Bowen's repeated uses of dress to signify a rich yet insubstantial past. Mrs. Nicholson is both enticing and untouchable: "Her *coiffeur* was like spun sugar" and her dress characterized by "summery" fullness, with skirts that flowed down "to dissipate and spread where they touched the floor" (690). The contrast between the artificial luxuries of Edwardian style and later wartime austerity hardly could be greater. Mrs. Nicholson favors accessories such as gauze scarves and transparent silk parasols (693, 694); her personal style partakes of the filmy vagueness that so fascinated Baudelaire in describing Woman as an idol. Not surprisingly, Gavin develops a fetish for his idol's clothing, making his dowdy mother uneasy when he fingers her satin hand-me-downs from Mrs. Nicholson (697). At a dinner party where she outshines the other ladies, he cannot take his eyes off her "most beautiful dress," whose "quick stuff" like "her delinquency . . . gave out a sort of shimmer" (702, 701). The simile suggests that even the boy Gavin senses duplicity in Mrs. Nicholson's style; likewise, in their last intimate conversation, the fringed Kashmir shawl that he fingers (705) evokes the British empire in its final complacencies. All these small details emphasize not only the unreality of the boy's romantic dreams but the untrustworthiness of the now-dead Mrs. Nicholson and Britain's past. In concluding, the story cuts between the perspectives of the older Gavin and a young girl he tries to pick up. Gavin appears one moment to be a pathetic victim of his past and the next to be "wolfish." He is, the girl concludes at last, "a preyer. But who had said, preyers are preyed upon?" (711). Power does not indwell any person absolutely, and Gavin's inability to form a mature erotic relationship makes him both wolf and victim in a history-damaged world.

Middle-aged Gavin is imprisoned by his childhood family romance, as Maud Ellmann has observed (174 fn 32), yet the excruciations of wartime gender relations break the standard forms. Where a common feminist interpretation follows Virginia Woolf in suspecting "domestic fascism" on the homefront, in certain war fictions "it is both men and women," says John Mephim, "whose obsessions, infantile fixations and manipulating, egotistic self-absorption lead to pathological and dysfunctional relations" (63). Mephim applies this equal-opportunity domestic tyrannizing to Bowen's *The Heat of the Day* (1948), but it also occurs in her wartime stories. The unnamed woman narrating "Songs My Father Sang Me" was wounded by her father's desertion when she was seven years old. But he had been damaged by her mother's treatment of him; the narrator in turn hurts her listener, who may be a lover or a casual date. Although she sits with him in a nightclub, she is barely aware of him except as an audience for her recollections. "Have I hurt your feelings? But you haven't got any feelings about me," she says. To which he quickly responds, "Only because you haven't got any feelings about me" (651). It is the common condition of gender relations in Bowen's world.

This woman is haunted by her father as was Mrs. Drover by her demon lover; like Kathleen Drover, she has been numbed by youthful relations with a powerful male. Although the narrator's father seems more benign than a demon lover, he too is a Great War revenant, "one of the young men who were not killed in the last war" (651). During the war he had courted and married her mother, who their daughter describes as one of "the pin-ups *de ses jours*." The mother's personal style followed the deceptively girlish Georgian look:

> My mother was dark and fluffy and as slim as a wraith; a great *glacé* ribbon bow tied her hair back and stood out like a calyx behind her face, and her hair itself hung down in a plume so long that it tickled my father's hand while he held her while they were dancing. (651)

The mother's childish style is key to the daughter's subsequent experience. On the day he deserted the family, the father drove the child to a hillside, bought a comb to untangle her hair, and bade her gaze down at "England. I thought I'd like to see her again" (657). Then he enigmatically studies the little girl, finally banishing an idea: "'No; it wouldn't work,' he said. 'It simply couldn't be done. You can wait for me if you want. I can't wait for you'" (658). The seven-year-old is puzzled, and her adult self does not comment directly on his semiseductive actions. The father, who never moved beyond his Great War experiences to find success in civilian life, nostalgically identifies his first-war love affair with a lost England. Their joint memory of the "flapper" mother, with her infantilized personal style, taints the father-daughter relationship that Bishop presents as another image for dysfunctional prewar nostalgia. The daughter has indeed remained a little girl waiting for her father, frozen in time. Because "People don't, on the whole, come back," she can cherish her damaged memories, crystallized in her father's "last war" songs that—like revenants themselves—remind her of the past and alienate her from men in the present.

In most of Bowen's supernatural wartime stories, hopes for romantic union are not merely questioned but dismissed as impossible. Bowen, writes Maud Ellmann, regularly "evades the traditional marriage-plot, often by killing off the would-be groom" (166). Are love and marriage passé, then? And why cannot wartime lovers console each other? Bowen does not conclude, but in "Green Holly" she offered an amusing, style-based answer to the long-standing masculine conundrum, "What do women want?" In this comic ghost tale, bored young men and women, engaged in secret war work in an isolated country house, tire of romancing one another and fall in love with phantoms. With its country house location, its melodramatic ghosts, and its Yuletide setting, the story follows English ghost-tale conventions. Yet in tone and outcome it is far from "The Demon Lover," which focused on the controlling abuser of World War I. In "Green Holly" the men are passive and indifferent, and it is women who feel and act. Miss Bates, having tried and discarded the available men, dreams of a perfect lover in perfect clothing: only a ghost will do. Alluring insubstantiality has been extended to the male sex.

The opening sentence evokes Dickensian phantoms: "Mr Rankstock entered the room with a dragging tread: nobody looked up or took any notice" (719). He moves like an activated corpse, like Marley's ghost, but attracts no attention. Once, we are told, the workers were on a first-name basis; once they were romantically entangled. As they lost interest, they reverted to "Mr." and "Miss." Now they seem to have been together "for forty years," and friends on the outside see them as ghostly (719). Even when Mr. Winterslow, originally engaged to Miss Bates, confides that he's "got a ghost," the others do not immediately attend. They show enthusiasm only in singing about "the green holly: / Most friendship is feigning, most loving mere folly" (721). Finally, after their Shakespearean affirmation of cynicism, they question Mr. Winterslow about his ghost. "She was marvelous," he confides, and she wore a feather boa.

The narrative avoids private perspectives, reporting what the Military Intelligence workers say and do but nothing of their inward selves. Rather, Bowen recounts the thoughts of her frivolous, glamorous phantom—appropriately enough, since the ghost's very existence depends upon subjectivity, her own and that of others. She always manifests herself, we are told, with the mingled anxiety and exhibitionism of a woman about to make a grand entrance, but for her "it was not merely a matter of, how was she? but of, *was* she—tonight—at all?" (723). Utterly dependent upon others' gazes, the ghost fashions her seductive feminine style from "the limbo that [is] her wardrobe now." Thus her dress is not described by color or cut but in terms of effect:

> Her own person haunted her—above her forehead, the crisped springy weight of her pompadour; round her feet the frou-frou of her skirts on a

thick carpet; in her nostrils the scent from her corsage; up and down her forearm the glittery slipping of bracelets warmed by her own blood. It is the haunted who haunt. (723)

That the ghost is haunted by herself—not by her companion phantom on the floor, who has blown out his brains for love of her—emphasizes her bewitching vanity. She chooses now to love hapless Winterslow, ignoring his unattractive "handwoven tie, his coat pockets shapeless as saddle-bags, the bulging knees of his flannel trousers," because she needs an object for her subjectivity: "the illusion was all" (724).

The story might reach an horrific traditional climax, in which a beautiful phantom entices a man to his death. But Miss Bates comically deflates traditional expectations, turning the gender tables in the story's unexpected conclusion. As Mr. Winterslow is a realistic, nonideal male, so Miss Bates evokes Jane Austen's spinster. In fact, her personal style, from long legs in "ribbed scarlet sports stockings" to nicotine-stained fingers and hair in a snood (721, 726), raises the specter of the single girl who threatens to "wear the trousers." Asking Winterslow if he has "come over funny," she then rebukes him for his "Romantic, nostalgic" fascination with a ghost in preference to the real-life women around him. However, Miss Bates adds, on entering the hall her own attention was caught by Winterslow's "enchanting inverse . . . the man of my dreams." She has spied a second ghost, the dead man at the bottom of the stairs. And just as the female ghost offers an enticing contrast to unseductive real women, so the male ghost constitutes Miss Bates's romantic ideal—based on his style:

> From his attitude, it was clear he had died for love. There were three pearl studs in his boiled shirt, and his white tie must have been tied in heaven. . . . The destruction of his features, before I saw them, made their former perfection certain, where I am concerned.—And here I am, left, left, left, to watch dust gather on Mr. Rankstock and you; to watch—yes, I who saw in a flash the ink-black perfection of *his* tailoring—mildew form on those clothes that you never change. (726)

Like the female ghost's feather boa, the male ghost's tuxedo epitomizes romantic glamour; his perfect dress suggests that he died for love, that hackneyed, idealized link between male and female in Western culture.

Yet it is not the ideal that Miss Bates regrets; rather, she wants the power to evoke such a tragedy: "'But who was *she*, your feathered friend, to deceive him? . . . I could be fatal,' moaned Miss Bates, pacing the drawing-room. 'I could be fatal—only give me a break!'" (727). Her comic frustration is more self-knowing than Mr. Winterslow's infatuation, yet both suggest the estrangement of women and men. Each ghost seems invisible to his or her own sex, as is appropriate for an embodied, or rather disembodied, erotic longing. Why should dress details matter, in depicting this alienation? The feather-wearing female ghost is feather-headed; the suicided lover is a Prince Charming waxwork, adored for his clothes, not his self. These portraits suggest the shallowness of the details that seduce us, along with a surprising comic equation. The glamorous woman is the clichéd femme fatale, whose clothes are part of her fascination. But we are disconcerted to hear a woman gush over a man's perfect dress.

Finally, the inability of Bowen's characters to form or maintain stable erotic relationships—never mind marriages—echoes her perception of the fragmentary nature of homefront existence, and therefore of literature in wartime. Her stories acknowledge women's complicated fantasies of a happy past, whether involving a father's love or a perfectly turned-out lover who kills himself for you. Always there is that final, ominous twist to those nostalgic dreams, and an unhappy cynicism regarding human relations: "Most friendship is feigning, most loving mere folly."

Were dreams and cynicism, then, the future of gender relations? If many Britons believed that the war's end signaled a reversion to business as usual in male and female roles, just as Dior's New Look seemed to return women to a traditional feminine shape, they were not wholly mistaken. But it would prove impossible either to fully recapture prewar gender roles or to stay in the suspended hallucinatory state depicted in Bowen's stories. During the war, short stories such as Bowen's were popular, Rod Mengham has observed, because they "prompted a method of reading that would tolerate incompleteness, fragmentariness, on the understanding that a real and satisfying completeness would eventually supervene" (126). When that completeness finally emerged, it was in a very different vein and style.

PART III
Stylish Spinsters in a Postwar World

"THE POSITION OF THE UNMARRIED WOMAN—unless, of course, she is somebody's mistress, is of no interest whatsoever to the reader of modern fiction." So commented Barbara Pym in her journal, adding cheerfully, "The beginning of a novel?" (*Very Private* 269).[1] Certainly by the mid-twentieth century the classic British spinster seemed a relic associated, as George Orwell put it, with a nostalgic England of "old maids biking to Holy Communion through the mists of the autumn morning" ("Lion" 75). And yet unmarried women, including spinsters, abound in late-modern fiction by women. This surprising mild renaissance of the spinster is in keeping with Britain's postwar world, where traditional labels were confounded. No longer could a woman permanently be labeled "married" or "single," nor might a quick glance on the street ascertain one's class. Even Dior's luxuriant New Look was purchased in mass-produced versions tempered by ongoing Austerity, enabling feminine style to say more for less. Postwar literature also endeavored to say more for less, using fewer words and emphasizing restraint and understatement, irony rather

---

1. Pym eventually revised the line for *Quartet in Autumn* (3).

than tragedy, and comedy rather than drama. Certainly comedy's necessary self-objectification was amply illustrated when the spinster, that unromantic object of pity, neglect, or scorn, became the subject of a novel; and in novels by Pym and by Muriel Spark, the spinster's clothing—also traditionally pitiable—offered a rich field for demonstrating the dissolution of categories in the postwar world.

In postwar Britain, the Movement poets developed a leveling aesthetic that employed an ostensibly shallow surface over a deep structure of protest. Apart from these writers' recognizably flat ironies, apparent in fifties novels as well, later modern and postmodern fiction would not sort easily into recognizable schools of style. The social shattering caused by war—which signaled an end for some writers and a beginning for others—also fractured the tidy categories and prescriptions that had ruled literary art.

In particular, an assortment of female novelists such as Elizabeth Taylor and Olivia Manning found themselves freer than before. And Pym and Spark, each of whom had toiled for years to win literary recognition, finally began to prosper. Single themselves, they wrote fictions mapping out the position of the unmarried woman. Whether voicing the thoughts of chaste spinsters, free-living single girls, or—occasionally—wedded women, Pym and Spark pointedly satirized traditional beliefs that marriage saves, defines, or even changes a woman very much. Other forces worked more powerfully upon women, including time, employment, and the recent crucible of war.

WHAT THE WAR TEACHES WOMEN

In a *Vogue* essay near the war's end, Dorothy Parker had speculated on what it might be like for soldiers returning to their wives after the war: "He has touched the horizons; he comes home to your delightful little drawing room. He has seen the world aflame; he comes back to your new red dress" (12/44: 88). The assumption that military wives in 1944, on either side of the Atlantic, possessed "delightful" drawing rooms, or new dresses, is optimistic. But the contest between broad horizons and narrow domestic interiors clearly is no contest, Parker implies: women must widen their interests in order to deal with their changed men. Yet—though sophisticated female writers still employed dress imagery—women had not remained static, as their history and literature testify.

For many observers, wartime brought shocking changes in relations between the sexes. As men absented themselves from the British homefront, or moved in and out irregularly according to their military assignments, and as most married women took jobs outside the home in contrast to their prewar roles, the lines between married and single women blurred. The war saw a record number of marriages and, perhaps in consequence, by 1945 the yearly divorce rate had more than doubled. Births to unwed mothers increased, including a record number of babies born to middle-aged spinsters (Braybon and Summerfield 215, 212; Calder 312–13). These social changes were not trivial in scope or in effect.

Did the war change women permanently? Susan Gubar has argued that women in World War II learned that relations between the sexes always will be a power struggle: "What the war teaches women is that they must relinquish any dreams they may have had about joining forces with men" (256). Her evaluation of wartime literatures followed suit: "Concerned less with military maneuvers and more with sexual antagonism, the literature women wrote about World War II needs to be understood as a documentation of women's sense that the war was a blitz on them" (258). For Gubar, the war created stringent disappointment in women, who had hoped finally to be put on a level with men. It is a striking evaluation, but narrowly conceived. Certainly an alienation between the sexes, as depicted in Elizabeth Bowen's stories, was sharpened by war. On the other hand, approximately sixty thousand British civilians were killed in air raids during the Second World War (Hopkins 22). For homefront Londoners, the war was a blitz on everyone, and it is unlikely that job equity was a first concern for women who were experiencing the loss of property, friends, and family—and anticipating further horrors, should Hitler conquer Britain. Therefore, as Gill Plain observes, the issue of the war's effects on British women is very complex. Since the Luftwaffe attacked the civilian population, "sacrifice was universalized, and the hierarchies of suffering established by the First World War became an anachronism in this new age of total war" (9). Inequities did appear; the British government originally assigned to women injured or killed in war operations a compensatory value of 50 to 75 percent of the monetary value attached to a man. But public outcry resulted in corrections to this policy in 1943 (Calder 400). Plenty of evidence also exists for employers' initial resistance to hiring women workers for their factories and farms (Riley 260; Braybon and Summerfield 157–58). Nevertheless, Britain's wartime conscription policies impelled an overwhelming change in hiring practices. Nine out of 10 single women and 8 out of 10 married ones, between the ages of 18 and 40, were employed in the armed forces or in industry during the war (Calder 331). Women did all sorts of hitherto male work, ranging from farm labor to highly skilled technical jobs and classified code-breaking tasks. "Eventually," Calder points out, "fifty percent of all workers in aero-engine factories, and a considerably higher proportion in the aircraft factories proper, were women and girls" (152). And they were making more money—not as much as men in similar positions but "fabulous sums" compared to their pay in prewar women's jobs such as domestic service, stitchery, and shop clerking (Braybon and Summerfield 185). That many women would lose those jobs to men as the war ended, or willingly relinquish them for the domestic hearth, does not negate a certain net gain from the experience. As Calder observes, the Second World War was most significant in its effect on the attitudes of, not toward, women (400). Those changed attitudes gradually emerged over the next two decades.

Residual stereotypes remained. Postwar Britain saw an outward return to domestic yearnings, which some observers saw embodied in Dior's New Look. Women and men both searched for spouses, resulting in a "strange postwar boom" in matchmaking services (Hopkins 141). And, not surprisingly, conservative psychologists and educators encouraged women to return to their natural careers as wives and mothers (E. Wilson, *Only Halfway* 33). In sociological postwar discussions of women's workplace roles, as Niamh Baker remarks, "the invisibility of women who were not attached to a husband is remarkable" (16). Above all, the psychosexual stereotyping of the spinster hardened. According to Elizabeth Wilson, sex and marriage manuals of the forties and fifties all "betrayed a horror of celibacy." Moreover, some writers went further to blame the spinster herself, suggesting that "for a woman to be living alone was not only the path to loneliness, bitterness, and frumpiness, but was likely to be the lot of women who were selfish and egocentric" (*Only Halfway* 94). Evidently frumpiness was an assumed evil of singleness, along with other miseries. These attitudes revived the modernist avant-garde beliefs about celibate spinsterhood, now filtered down to pop psychology and distilled in a stronger, cruder spirit. Yet this postwar prejudice against spinsters was essentially modern, since the Victorian spinster had been accepted as a natural if sad aspect of British society. Nevertheless, in a key difference, now the spinster might live alone rather than as part of an extended family—and she might even choose to do so while supporting herself. Clearly, just as the New Look did not truly revive the Edwardian dress of Christian Dior's mother, so postwar women, men, and society could not return to tidily circumscribed, prewar gender roles—such as they were.

Did women in fact learn, as Gubar writes, to despair of ever being accepted as equals by men? Pym and Spark found that they could bypass bigotry by aiming for the larger issues signified by the personal. Plain has concluded that "war creates a situation in which the gender debate is subsumed by a meta-narrative of power" (20). Under the guise of personal issues, then, questions of what is power, who holds power, and how much power is a good thing had predominated in Elizabeth Bowen's stories and would continue in postwar women's novels. From the war's onset, women had gazed at their new opportunities and asked what it was they wanted from employment, from social freedom, and indeed from men. Their answers tended to affirm their own sex's traditional gifts but not their sex's traditional constraints.

WHAT THE WAR TAUGHT WRITERS

After the war, new novels avoiding grand themes, written by men bent on dismantling elitism, jostled fictions centered upon domestic trivia, written by women who seemed no longer to care what men thought. A literature of small things was not unprecedented. Despite Cyril Connolly's stated prejudice against stories about "the blitz, the shopping queues, the home front, deserted wives, deceived husbands, broken homes, dull jobs" (*Horizon* 1/44: 5), the majority of Bowen's wartime stories concerned these domestic topics, and Connolly printed them. Social changes were part of the wartime experience. And women knew that even a love story might signify more than a traditional feminine preoccupation. Karen Schneider explains, "British women writing the Second World War excavate[d] the metonymic aptness of romance as a trope for war to its deepest roots" (8). Not that women ceased to care about romance for its own sake, but they had learned to used their sequestered status—as middlebrow, focusing upon people and events, rather than highbrow, overtly writing about ideas—to their own advantage: Pym and Spark would employ romance as trope for all sorts of meanings. Moreover, the fact that women's literature was a secondary category offered a liberating detachment to women writers. For example, although Connolly published Bowen's work, the highbrow *Horizon* was overwhelmingly, proudly male-authored and male-read (4/41: 292)—but few female writers seemed to care, and *Horizon* ended in 1949. Most women were not closely identified with aesthetically oriented modernism; they observed its life and demise from a distance. Thus the war taught women writers a certain cynical observation of male literary values and a steely-eyed unconcern with male approval—again, perspectives that Pym and Spark would excel in.

Although only a few short years separate most of Sayers's and Rhys's novels from those authored by newly emerging postwar writers, the space is more than chronological. In contrast to the understated postwar novels of Pym and Spark, Dorothy Sayers's fiction seems chained by genre conventions and Jean Rhys's prewar novels saturated with modernist drama. The older women—who were not elderly in the forties but middle-aged, and might have written many more novels—did not merely experience a hiatus but a full arrest of their prewar writing careers. In certain ways the generic categories, high or low, themselves were confounded through war. In 1941, Sayers confirmed what recent critics have termed the death of the Golden Age of detective fiction:[2] "It has been borne in upon me that people are getting rather too much of the detective story attitude to life—a sort of assumption that there is a nice, neat solution for every imaginable problem" (*Letters* 2: 241). In wartime even readers of genre fiction could not safely find refuge in predictable patterns. As for Rhys, when eventually she published *Wide Sargasso Sea* (1966), it proved an amalgam of her prewar single-girl narratives, Old Style nostalgia, and a proto-postmodern experimentalism. Its artistic success did not make it less of a sport in the sixties, because the war years changed permanently the conditions of literary creation and reception.

The new literature of rhetorical minimalism, often associated with Larkin, Kingsley Amis, and the "Angry Young Men" or Movement poets of the fifties, employed a deliberately anti-eloquent language especially suited to leveling, comic fictions. High modernism had professed to be anti-Romantic, while retaining epic ambitions and expressing tragic regret for lost verities. But the Movement writers made an art of flat negation, of—in the title of a poem by D. J. Enright—"Saying No." I am not concerned here with questions of the label's validity; as Blake Morrison demonstrated in his foundational study, Movement poets and novelists did

---

2. See Knowles (174) and Julian Symons (131–42).

share common backgrounds, subjects, and writing styles. Their rhetorics used hesitation, apology, and qualifiers that implied a modest "emphasis on the fallibility of the poet" (Morrison 102). For the Movement's typical literary subjects, one need only think of Larkin's most famous topoi: empty churches where "there's nothing going on" ("Church Going" l. 1), or a cold and lonely sexual revolution, in which "Talking in Bed" descends to a quest for words "not untrue and not unkind" (l. 12)—phrases that also capture the group's stylistic uses of linguistic negation.

"Style" itself was a fraught concept for the Movement. From lyric poets to Alan Sillitoe's working-class *Saturday Night and Sunday Morning* (1958), British literature turned away from high-modern experimentalism, which postwar writers saw as grandiose and even sentimental. Early twentieth-century writers like Joyce's Dedalus had claimed that they "drew less pleasure from the reflection of the glowing sensible world . . . than from the contemplation of an inner world of individual emotions mirrored perfectly in a lucid supple periodic prose" (*Portrait* 180–81). For the high-modern aesthete, style *was* a valid subject in itself. But by 1954, Kingsley Amis was critiquing the "nostalgia for style nowadays among people of oldster age-group," by which he meant "a personal style, a distinguished style . . . with wow from imagery, syntax, and diction" (Rabinovitz 899). In truth the Movement did not disdain careful style but the overblown importance some writers attached to high-modernist tenets, and to the recent war's nostalgic Old Style: "What is needed," *Poetry London* concluded in 1950, "is not so much the inspired poem as a revival of style: first-class workmanship" (Bergonzi 160). Postwar literature, in keeping with its writers' diminished expectations, punctured, mocked, and scrupulously refused to elaborate upon its arts.

The Movement is rarely referenced in analyses of postwar women's fiction, yet women writers also developed a leveling aesthetic, the ostensibly shallow surface of a deep structure of protest. For a summary of the Movement's philosophy, and a prose exemplar of its anti-eloquent eloquence, one hardly could do better than the musings of Barbara Pym's Letty upon her own spinsterhood: "Might not the experience of 'not having' be regarded as something with its own validity?" (*Quartet in Autumn* 25). As Michael Cotsell noted, Pym's fiction typifies mid-twentieth-century British self-perception: "the 'minor events in minor lives' . . . belong to the postwar context in which 'something major—Britain—became minor'" (Cotsell 33; quoted in Little 78). Certainly "becoming minor" characterized both the content and the style of much postwar fiction.

In detail and in usage, the new postwar literary style often paralleled the new sartorial styles in their cool understatement, as in their insistently quotidian texture. Also like postwar literature, postwar dress style was less monolithic, and full of quiet contradictions. Dior's New Look might have represented a return to domestic femininity, but it also showed British women rebelling against dull, homefront-impelled Utility styles. Likewise spinsterhood was deemed pathological, yet the postwar period saw more independent, single working women than ever. Throughout the fifties, conformity in dress seemed the norm, with reticent, rigid men's suits and curved, unbusinesslike, submissive women's clothing (Hollander, *Sex and Suits* 166). But Valerie Steele suggests that the most significant fifties couture was not the famed New Look but Coco Chanel's sweater suit (*Paris Fashion* 251). Resurrected from wartime disgrace, the House of Chanel revived its signature look: women's cardigan suits that were structured but feminine, emphasizing strings of pearls that, democratically, might be costume jewelry. Functional, flattering, flat-chested: the Chanel suit demonstrated that women could dress in a mode both businesslike and feminine, not to mention affordable. In any case, by the sixties even young celebrities avoided high fashion; as French actress Leslie Caron recalled, "You looked really old-fashioned if you wore couture dresses" (Thomas 33). Perhaps not coincidentally, male couturiers had regained the field in the fifties and continued to dominate the business throughout the twentieth century (Steele, *Women of Fashion* 9, 116–17). Democracy, understatement, eclecticism—the aesthetically approved styles for literature and for dress resembled one another most strikingly in this: fewer people heeded aesthetic mavens, in fashion or in literature. And women especially were freer than before.

The postwar burgeoning of options for style suggests why Pym and Spark can be read as sisters beneath the skin, despite the apples-and-oranges aspects of comparing their fiction. Pym, beloved by her fans, is admired by certain scholars and fellow writers. Yet even following a famous, Cinderella-style comeback in the 1970s, after Philip Larkin and Lord David Cecil pronounced her the "most underrated novelist of the twentieth century," she remains underrated by academics and pigeonholed as a woman who wrote for women (*Times Literary Supplement*, 21 January 1977; quoted in Holt 251). On the other hand, Spark, who contended fiercely with male writers and publishers, aimed at and gained international fame as a literary artist. Spark has been despised, defended, and discussed by squadrons of readers, scholars, and critics, especially because of the brevity and comic rhetoric in her many novels. In the world after modernism, there exists no authoritative playbook for the literary artist.

Nevertheless, the parallels between minimized, pared-down postwar dress styles and minimized, pared-down postwar literary styles not only are evident but offer cogent evidence for a continuing gulf between female and male novelists. For example, Spark's and Pym's uses of negation and trivia include dress details, still a typically feminine emphasis in fiction; and negation and trivia also typify Movement novels, which celebrate the ordinary life of the average bloke and employ negation with comic élan (Morrison 174). Kingsley Amis's Dixon finally lands his dream job because of his negatives rather than his plusses. "It's not that you've got the qualifications, for this or any other work," his millionaire employer remarks. "You haven't got the disqualifications, though, and that's much rarer" (*Lucky Jim* 234). Amis's gleeful celebration of absence is not so different from the nonevidence provided by Miss Jean Brodie's nightdress of crêpe de chine, which damns her in the eyes of her fellow teachers—not by its presence under her lover's pillow but through its subsequent disappearance: "She's that brazen" (Spark, *Prime* 99). Not so different, that is, except that the one instance involves a man's career and the other a woman's love affair, substantiated through details of dress. So these novels' similarities raise a question: Even if dress in the twentieth century remained largely a woman's domain—because it was both commonplace and ephemeral, concerned with surface rather than depth—why could not a literature that deliberately spoke a quotidian vernacular become, at last, equally the possession of men and women?

In sum, the postwar, male-led relinquishment of epic grandeur might have enabled a full appreciation of feminine trivia as well. Yet that "might" did not take place. The divergent responses to these authors' styles, in male-authored Movement fiction and in postwar novels by Spark and Pym, point up the still-large gulfs between male and female understandings of literature and the sexes. Furthermore, each woman's comic treatment of the stylish spinster—needlessly fashionable, the men insist, since she lacks a man—demonstrates their awareness of those discrepancies. Not even in the feminist seventies would the sexes fully agree upon the relation of glamour to aging, loss, and death: when Spark and Pym endeavored to objectify those grim themes, their creations continued to delicately mock all male expectations of female style.

CHAPTER 6

Pym, Spark, and the Postwar Comedy of the Object

O N THE SURFACE, few fictional characters look less alike than self-dramatizing Jean Brodie and modest Mildred Lathbury. Where Muriel Spark's famous novel described *The Prime of Miss Jean Brodie*, Barbara Pym allowed her humble spinster to be filed under the dull label of *Excellent Women*. The very titles describe both a personal and a narrative style: Jean Brodie is in her "prime," suggesting a peak of excitement; Mildred is "excellent," of straightforward, consistent quality. Where Miss Brodie celebrates her prime, Mildred pours tea and observes the romantic vicissitudes of others. And where Jean Brodie romanticizes her own sex, in a kind of myth-making gigantism, Mildred engages in comic deflation of all pretensions—including all idealized gender stereotypes. Nevertheless, each woman is a spinster surprised by her own longings. And just as the style of each spinster presages her substance, whether Miss Brodie's dramatic "Roman profile" or Mildred's "mousy" plainness, so in these postwar novels female self-presentation through dress serves as a cameo for each narrative's style.

Similarly, astringent pyrotechnic Muriel Spark (1918–2006) and cozy understated Barbara Pym (1913–1980) rarely inhabit the same critical page. Yet they shared more than an era and subject: each satirized modern gender relations by writing novels in a style that I have dubbed "the comedy of the object." The comedy of the object employs trivial details and negation to satirize the ways that human beings objectify one another, a long-standing interest for women writers. Modernism too was deeply interested in subject-object relations, so both linguistically and topically Spark and Pym follow a trajectory begun decades earlier and crystallized in the thirties. As Tyrus Miller describes it, late-modern writers saw an increasing mechanization of the human, which they perceived as a "compulsory lowering of the threshold of difference between subjects and objects." This grim subject-object blurring led writers to rethink "a whole series of precepts central to earlier modernism"—including, first and foremost, the "heroic subjectivity of the innovating artist" (43, 45). The undermining of the heroic artist, however, enabled the nonheroic protagonist, which is one reason that postwar writers constructed comedies in contrast to tragic narratives such as Rhys's prewar novels.

The comedy of the object naturally fit postwar women: as women they were accustomed to being objectified, and they knew how to value small details of personal style. The power of this approach lies in the frisson between the serious and the trivial, along with the decision to laugh. A century previous, Charles Baudelaire had identified a profound link between comedy and self-objectification, writing that the wise man who slips and falls can observe himself from a distance and therefore laugh. Baudelaire acknowledged the hazard in this process by dubbing it "dédoublement," a term used by nineteenth-century doctors for dissociative identity disorder ("De l'essence du rire" 379–80). The odd interweaving of the profound and the trivial proved ideal for these modern women, encompassing as it did the familiar, frequently scorned female trope of dress. After all, as Karen Hanson has explained, a self-objectification similar to dédoublement is necessary for following fashion: "A personal interest in dress and open responsiveness to the changing whims of fashion depend upon a recognition that one is seen, that one is—among other things—an object of others' sight, others' cognition" (70). Accordingly, postwar women employed dress to humorously objectify the self: not in the free indirect discourse that privileged the modernist hero, but through a pared-down grammar as wittily understated as any Movement poem, as chilly, and as funny.

Given the mid-century changes in marital mores, and these two authors' very different lives, one might expect to trace strikingly divergent paths for their single girls. Yet whether sexually experienced or virginal, the women of Pym and Spark possess similar attitudes toward life and toward men. In the personal lives of both authors, the marriage plot had proved false and subsequently became comic fodder. Each writer found dress style personally engaging, but clothing also served each woman as a means of self-presentation that had less and less to do with men as she aged. And each woman overtly minimized literary style in her novels; yet, because of the brevity of these narratives, the style becomes the thing. Their late-modern spinsters and single girls use slyly understated voices, which signal the multitudinous ways that the rest of the world—the married and the men—underestimate them.

POSTWAR SINGLE GIRLS

The three novels discussed in this chapter review history: Spark's *Miss Jean Brodie* (1961) is set largely in the thirties and her *Girls of Slender Means* (1963) in wartime London, while Pym's *Excellent Women* (1952) takes place in the immediate postwar world of austerity, queues, and bombed-out churches. Thus the lens of the past offers additional objective perspective on the styles of postwar single womanhood. After the war, young women faced fewer jobs, fewer marriageable men, and more urgings to marry. The New Look epitomized the general female dilemma: return to graceful femininity, but (with continuing Austerity regulations) do it with fewer materials. This near-literal imperative, to make bricks without straw, was especially acute for women but also typified the country's frustrations: the romance was over, the Empire was shrinking, Britain's finest hour was past. Of course, some individual Britons' best hours were yet to come; for instance, writers such as Pym and Spark, who previously had struggled, began to stand out. Serendipitously, each woman used her growing experience of gender differences in her fiction. Thus these postwar novels, while overtly nostalgic, subtly reframed the past.

All her life, Barbara Pym employed a double approach of nostalgia and critique. Born into the middle classes, an Oxford-educated lifelong spinster, she both fulfilled and transcended spinster stereotypes. As an early female graduate, Pym might seem at first glance to resemble Dorothy L. Sayers. Like Sayers, she recorded more dress than academic details of her university life—but Pym clearly did care more about the clothes and the fun: "I worked at Old English for about 1½ hours after breakfast," she writes in a typical diary entry. "Really it gave me the pip. After lunch I started to make a summer frock (deep orangey-pink and white check gingham—5¾ a yard!) I think it should be rather nice" (*Very* 25: 29 July 1933). Unlike the high-performing Sayers, Pym earned a Second, which seems to have satisfied her (*Very* 44). Furthermore, and startlingly for a woman who eventually would epitomize decorous Anglican spinsterhood, she cultivated an Oxford reputation as a boy-crazy, forward young female, not only gushing about beautiful young men but energetically pursuing them: "I saw my darling Lorenzo today. Just a fleeting glimpse of his profile—but so divine" (*Very* 20: 27 April 1933). Young Barbara probably also acquired some unspinsterish sexual experience, although such references are modestly elided in her diary.[1] Yet as Henry Harvey ("Lorenzo"), Pym's early objet d'amour, recalled, "In spite of chasing people who took her fancy and having no apparent inhibitions . . . [Barbara's] passions, in so far as they were not kept back to being pretend play passions, stayed in her head and heart" (Holt 49). The young writer already was experimenting with the varieties of female experience and recording her own trivia-mindedness humorously: "At Marks and Spencer's I bought a peach coloured vest and trollies to match with insertions of lace. Disgraceful I know but I can't help choosing my underwear with a view to it being seen!" (*Very* 33: 8 January 1934).

Nevertheless Pym used her education well, in her novels and in various jobs. Her characters frequently quote poetry wittily, and obscure poetic allusions furnished titles for several novels. Moreover, Pym's later correspondence with Philip Larkin shows that she read extensively in modern literature. After earning her BA in 1935, she worked diligently at her novels: writing, submitting to publishers, and revising when they were rejected. She also traveled to Hungary and Germany several times, visiting a German boyfriend, and worked briefly as a governess in Poland. As war approached, she was called up and assigned to the censorship office. At that time Pym also experienced what was probably her last serious romance, unhappily with a married man. In an effort to heal her heart, she joined the Women's Royal Naval Service, the WRNS or Wrens, and spent the rest of

---

1. "Today I must always remember I suppose. I went to tea with Rupert . . . —and he with all his charm, eloquence and masculine wiles, persuaded [several pages torn out]"; "I went and [Henry] was extremely nice—but Jockie came in and caught us reading 'Samson Agonistes' in bed with nothing on. Really rather funny" (*Very* 17, 40).

FIGURE 9. Barbara Pym with Henry Harvey ("Lorenzo"), early 1930s (Barbara Pym Estate).

the war in Italy. After demobilization, she took a job at the London-based International African Institute, where she would serve as assistant editor of the scholarly journal *Africa* until her retirement in 1974. Thus Pym's education helped her earn a livelihood while her jobs provided grist for the fiction mill, ranging from *Excellent Women*'s charming naval attaché Rocky to the many Africa-obsessed anthropologists throughout her novels.

Despite her man-chasing youth, Pym's personal writings suggest equivocal feelings about marriage. In 1945 Pym and her sister Hilary took a London flat; Hilary, who worked for the BBC, had contracted a war marriage and quick divorce. The sisters would live together, two single women, for the rest of Barbara's life. As scholars have noted, Pym's mature domestic arrangements fulfilled her youthful prophecies. At age twenty-one she had recorded,

> I began writing a story about Hilary and me as spinsters of fiftyish. Henry, Jock and all of us appeared in it. I sent it to them and they liked it very much.... It is of course "for Henry," and in it I seem able to say what I cannot in the ordinary course of events. (*Very* 44: 1 September 1934)

The story, which became her first published novel, *Some Tame Gazelle* (1950), featured a pair of middle-aged sisters living together in an English village, each nursing an innocent devotion to an unworthy man: "Some tame gazelle . . . oh, something to love!" Belinda, Barbara's surrogate, loves the pompous, self-centered but charming Archdeacon Hoccleve, who is married to her long-ago rival Agatha but happy to bask in his old girlfriend's admiration. At first glance, this fiction—sent in chapters to Henry and other Oxford friends—seems another piece of exhibitionism, confessing and mocking Pym's own unreciprocated attachment. Yet as she revised and resubmitted her manuscript over the years, she indeed seemed to write "for Henry" what she could not say in person, and the message was not entirely affectionate. Pym took her publisher's advice to "make it more malicious" (Holt 144), and in final published form the archdeacon is both insensitive and exploitive of Belinda, who protests her doormat status only in secret thought. Also in secret, Belinda acknowledges that she has no desire to change her pleasant spinster life. During the novel's concluding wedding—which, to Belinda's relief, is neither hers nor her sister's—she realizes not only that it is "so much easier to bear the burden of one's own pathos than that of somebody else" but that "perhaps the very recognition of [pathos] in oneself meant that it didn't really exist" (*Gazelle* 248). The slyly affirmative negation suggests the doubling quality of Pym's spinsters, who possess the gift of observing society as outsiders while also viewing their own selves as comic, pathetic objects—or not.

To cast herself as spinster from such an early age shows that Pym shared in the secret contrariety of her outwardly meek, conventional women. Her friend and biographer Hazel Holt concludes that in fact Pym had less ambition to marry than to have love affairs—or simply to love

(148–49). Certainly Pym did not seek marriage at all costs. She refused a couple of proposals, even commenting of the adored Henry at one point, "I love him too, but don't want him for my very own yet awhile" (*Very* 44: 18 July 1934). Her stance may be defensive pride, but it puzzled Pym's male friends, as she acknowledged in a fictional scenario sent to Robert Liddell after Henry eventually married another woman:

> "Oh, fancy if all passion should not be spent! . . . It is more than I can bear," said Mr Liddell. . . .
> "Well, well," said Miss Pym, coming into the room. "Two old men bearing an imaginary burden, that is what I see. It must be the more heavy because it is not real."
> "So there is no burden?" said Mr Liddell, rising to his feet.
> "I will not say that," said Miss Pym, in a quiet thoughtful tone, "but you do not have to bear it." (*Very* 75: 12 April 1938)

The mockery here is of the males, who think that the "burden" of a spinster's unspent passion must be unbearable. Pym refused, as do her fictional spinsters, to fit tidily into patronizing male categories. In fact, as she developed her characters, she turned the tables. In the early-written *Crampton Hodnet*, drab little Jessie Morrow receives a surprising marriage proposal from a self-centered curate and—surprising him in turn—declines: "For she wanted love. . . . And then, how much more sensible it was to satisfy one's springlike impulses by buying a new dress in an unaccustomed and thoroughly unsuitable colour than by embarking on a marriage without love" (94). Miss Morrow does buy an "unsuitable" green dress, which garners much satisfying attention. Her rationale—that stylish dress is safer than loveless marriage—does not contradict her actions in a later novel, where she deliberately dresses in order to trap the handsome, vapid widower Fabian into marriage. She is "not the person to cherish a hopeless romantic love for a man, especially if he were free and lived next door" (*Jane and Prudence* 139). A blue velvet dress, originally belonging to Fabian's dead wife, does the trick. It also suggests the stupidity of men, however attractive, and turns the tables: who is patronizing whom? Like most of Pym's self-aware single women, Jessie Morrow's inner life diverges from her outwardly meek demeanor: she knows how she appears to others, and she employs her double nature to advantage. Stylish dress provides secret comfort and satisfaction —but it also may prove a useful instrument.

Pym's life illustrates her divided self. While yearning for romance, she also wrote, persistently and diligently. "I want Liebe," she told her diary, "but would be satisfied if my novel could be published" (*Very* 55: 29 December 1935). She sometimes objectified her romantic longings through a sharp-eyed attention to men's clothes: "Henry was absolutely at his best. He wore his grey flannel suit, a bright blue silk shirt with a darker blue tie and blue socks" (*Very* 52: 25 August 1935). Appropriately then, her first-attempted novel, inspired by reading Aldous Huxley's *Chrome Yellow* when she was sixteen, had been titled *Young Men in Fancy Dress*. That fascination, with attractive young men and their stylish attire, became a cool-eyed critique in the opening lines of *Some Tame Gazelle*: "The new curate seemed quite a nice young man, but what a pity it was that his combinations showed, tucked carelessly into his socks, when he sat down" (7). The critical perspective is Belinda's, for the curate is her sister's object of affection. And in general Pym's novels employ this double gaze, including a satirical but not jaundiced eye for male style—because the unglamorous protagonist, typically a middle-aged spinster, herself cherishes an attachment to one of those ridiculous men. Pym men may be unworthy, but they are the only show in town for a single girl seeking love.

World War II changed Pym's prospects, discouraging her romantically but eventually launching her writing career. She entered it as a marriageable young woman; by 1945, she considered herself on the shelf. After the breakup of her last serious romance, she began seriously to call herself a spinster: "nothing will be quite as good, there will be no intense joy but small compensations, spinsterish delights" (*Very* 120: 29 March 1943). She even temporarily lost interest in clothing: "I went into Bright's and looked vaguely at materials—red spotted chiffon for a spinsterish nightdress" (*Very* 124: 13 April 1943). The contrast—between the young Pym's earlier delight in choosing underwear "with a view to it being seen" and the thirtyish Pym's apathy—appears also in *Excellent Women*, when Mildred comments that her washing contains "just the sort of underclothes a person like me might wear . . . so there is no need to describe them" (75). In other words, to be a spinster is to wear underwear that no one will ever see. Mildred (like her creator) will revise this attitude—Pym mocks the idea that stylish dress is only to please men—but it colors the novels nonetheless, starting with *Some Tame Gazelle* in 1950. *Excellent Women* appeared in 1952, and four more novels within a decade. Pym became known for gentle, understated comedies of manners; if *Liebe* failed her, a postwar writing career seemed assured.

Muriel Spark also achieved postwar literary success, but through a more fiercely focused career trajectory. Scottish-born Muriel Camberg, she grew up in a marginal position she eventually relished: she was part Jewish, and her parents teetered on the line between middle and working class. Sent to James Gillespie's School for Girls, a fee-paying but not exclusive school that would inspire *The Prime of Miss Jean Brodie*, young Muriel won prizes for poetry but left at sixteen to train as a secretary. Even then she planned to become a writer. But she also sought independence and experience, both of which she swiftly gained when she traveled to Africa in 1937 to marry schoolmaster Sydney Oswald Spark. At age nineteen, the young poet found herself isolated in colonial Rhodesia, pregnant and dependent upon a violent, mentally unstable man. Over the next six years she would separate from Spark (keeping his name) and move about Africa, working to support herself, her incapable husband, and their infant son. Eventually obtaining a divorce, she journeyed back to Britain on a troopship, weaving through U-boat-infested seas in 1944. Her exile and survival in Africa gave Spark material for striking short stories and poetry while also cementing her outsider status. Neither black nor a typical white colonial, neither fully Jewish nor Christian, not Scottish enough to stay in Edinburgh for long, soon after her return Spark moved to London to pursue a literary career. In the metropolis she found herself competing with literary men from relatively affluent and Oxbridge backgrounds. She was still an outsider, but one who was learning the powers of persistence and resistance. Like many a modern artist, Spark would move from place to place in a kind of self-exile all her life, living in London, New York, and finally Italy. Unlike famous expatriates such as James Joyce, however, she did not write exclusively about her home country: her novels are set, like her own life, in many different places. And her marginal status, less willful than involuntary, made her the queen of detached objectivity.

Spark's professional life was a workaholic whirlwind. In the 1940s, she published poetry, short stories, and literary biographies. She also edited poetry reviews and took various jobs to support herself, including a wartime stint as secretary in the Foreign Office's "Black Propaganda" office. By the 1950s, Spark had become a significant player in the New Romantic literary revival. Her fame in fiction began when she won a 1951 short-story contest sponsored by *The Observer*; editor Philip Toynbee told her, "We thought it was written by a man until we opened the envelope" (Spark, *Curriculum* 199). She was moving toward a Roman Catholic conversion in 1954, a change that underscored her fiercely independent nature. A subsequent breakdown from overwork and Dexedrine spurred her first, semiautobiographical novel, *The Comforters* (1957). Following its critical success, Spark began to turn out novels quickly: *The Prime of Miss Jean Brodie* (1961) was her sixth and *The Girls of Slender Means* (1963) her seventh. Her stock would rise meteorically: she received an OBE in 1967 and other honors, British, French, and Italian, in the following decades.

Spark's personal life became a monument to her single-minded devotion to literary art. The epitome of the modern single girl, after her unhappy short-lived marriage she experienced motherhood not unlike Dorothy L. Sayers, bearing a son whom she supported but did not raise herself. Also like Sayers, she evolved into a tough writer consciously competing with men. As a struggling young editor, poet, and critic, she engaged in two serious love affairs. The second of these affairs, with literary partner Derek Stanford, might have concluded in marriage but for Spark's Christian conversion, which Stanford did not share. Very pretty, charming, frequently gregarious, Spark eventually realized that men attracted by her did not necessarily consider her their equal. As her character Fleur Talbot says of her literary lover, "He often liked what I wrote but disliked my thoughts of being a published writer" (*Loitering with Intent* 53). Frequently Spark ended up feeling betrayed by family members, lovers, and friends, and breaking off relations. Like Jean Rhys, she could speak from a unique international perspective and wide experience of unreliable men. Unlike Rhys, Spark's fiction never parades the author's vulnerabilities; rather, gleaming surfaces pave over any lingering injuries.

Spark became a new New Woman, a kind of reborn spinster oddly like Pym in her fictional deployments of gender, dress, and dédoublement. This is not to ignore the differences: Pym's single girls long for love, if not marriage, experiences toward which Spark's women are ambivalent at best. In *Loitering* Fleur explains, "I write poetry. I want to write. Marriage would interfere"—an attitude that seems unnatural to her female acquaintances but "in fact was quite natural to me" (28). As David Goldie concludes, "In [Spark's] world marriage is commonly a condition of limitation involving either erosion of self or grounds for powerful mutual resentment" (12). Though a few of Spark's heroines do marry hastily at their stories' ends, marriage signifies restraint for them; by contrast, Pym's women's narratives often conclude with a hope for marriage or at least for emotional connection. Perhaps the difference stems from their single girls, usually virginal in Pym but sexually experienced in Spark's fiction. Still, in both writers' novels, men tend to prove second-rate.

If the end of a single girl's life is not blissful marriage, why then should she care about stylish dress? Spark, like Pym, found several answers to this question. In life, dress served Spark as an aesthetic ideal. From childhood she had been fascinated with clothing trivia. In her memoir, she lists the details of her grandmother's Victorian attire, describing chemises, stays, drawers, petticoats, and stockings before arriving at outerwear and a crowning memory of a blue silk brocade dress nicknamed "Bluebell." Early in life, Muriel's grandmother had worn it to a fancy-dress party and won a prize; over sixty years later Spark wrote, "I have never seen anything quite so beautiful, nor touched anything so sensuous before or since" (*Curriculum* 89). What fascinated young (and old) Muriel was the dress's sensuous feel, not any interest in how others would view its wearer. As if to drive the point home, early in her career she named her beautiful long-haired cat "Bluebell": a surprising conversion from the seeming sociality of dress to an introverted domestic pleasure—and also a talisman for potent art. A single striking garment or two often suffices her short novels, serving as emblem for the text: so the Schiaparelli dress in *The Girls of Slender Means* captures the savagery and enticing self-absorption of its youthful subjects. And so Lise's disturbing "psychedelic" ensemble, in *The Driver's Seat*, depicts the disparate elements of Spark's most unsettling novel.[2]

Both Spark and Pym used modernism's self-doubling propensities to create a comedy of the object. Self-doubling may be both funny and serious. Baudelaire wrote of comic dédoublement that "ce n'est point l'homme qui tombe qui rit de sa propre chute, à moins qu'il ne soit un philosopher, un homme qui ait acquis, par habitude, la force de se dédoubler rapidement et d'assister comme spectateur désintéressé aux phénomènes de son *moi*" ("De l'essence du rire" 379–80, emphasis in original) [it is never the man who falls who laughs at his own tumble, unless he be a philosopher, a man who has acquired through habit the power of quickly dividing himself and acting as a disinterested spectator of the phenomenon of his *self*]. This complex self-splitting was explained further by Théophile Gautier,

---

2. Spark herself would purchase expensive designer dresses, even when she could ill afford them, if she felt the need to raise her spirits or—on one memorable occasion—to impress her publishers (Stannard 194, 239). She used adornment as the sign of a successful, independent woman: after hearing that her longtime lover Stanford was marrying someone else, she took some of her royalties and bought herself a diamond ring (Stannard 201).

commenting on Baudelaire's *Fleurs du mal*, as espionage: "Every sensation he experiences has to be analysed by him; involuntarily he separates his two selves [il se dédouble], and when he lacks any other subject takes to spying upon himself" (32). Such a clear-eyed self-observation appears particularly in comic form in Pym's fiction. But her spinsters also enjoy spying on others: "Ah, you ladies! Always on the spot when there's something happening!" (*Excellent Women* 5). Such nosiness becomes more sinister and culpable in Spark's fiction. Her protagonists participate in an authorial observational stance that—far from the traditional omniscient narrator—evokes Graham Greene's claim that "every novelist has something in common with a spy: he watches, he overhears, he seeks motives and analyzes character, and in his attempt to serve literature he is unscrupulous" (143). Even to live life as a detached observer is to evoke suspicions of betrayal, a frequent theme in Spark's life as well as her fiction. The links between self-splitting and betrayal appear in many Spark novels, including *Miss Jean Brodie*, where Sandy serves as a spy and a double agent.

However, while covert operations and self-doubling may typify modern and late-modern literature, the comedy of the object is an especially female genre because women traditionally have been objectified. Therefore, in the feminist truism, they are accustomed to objectifying themselves; as John Berger observed succinctly: "Men look at women. Women watch themselves being looked at.... Thus she turns herself into an object" (47). Both their customary interest in fashion and their status as the second sex gave women an advantage in dédoublement, as this chapter demonstrates through Pym's *Excellent Women* and Spark's *Prime of Miss Jean Brodie*. Despite their evidently different styles, Pym and Spark in their most famous novels took the subject-object dilemma to new heights. Subsequently, Spark's *Girls of Slender Means* used the comedy of the object to put paid to the succession of proud louses that populate the postwar Britain of male-authored fiction.

BRITANNIA DIMINISHED: *MISS JEAN BRODIE* PAST HER PRIME

The question of why Spark in particular has not been regarded as a Movement novelist, despite her use of an ironic, understated style, may be answered through examining her use of dress and personal trivia, both to celebrate individual female perception and to satirize traditionally grand literary ideals. Her biographer Martin Stannard observes that Spark's fiction presents "no message" or social conscience, as in Angry-Young-Man novels (211–12), and this is true if we expect an overt social lesson. Then too, Spark was part of the New Romantic poetic movement—yet her chiseled fiction is far from the lush self-indulgence despised by Movement writers. Even her use of symbols is double-edged to the point of satire: her trim novels both enact and mock the ideal of a perfect objet d'art. If Spark has one message throughout her fiction, it is about the dual rewards and dangers of aestheticizing experience, as abundantly demonstrated in *The Prime of Miss Jean Brodie*.

Jean Brodie seems to aestheticize herself without the concomitant spying upon herself, the dédoublement. The narrative never tells us the spinster teacher's thoughts, always showing her through the speculations of her young students or a bemused larger world. So perhaps Amis's denigratory "wow" quite well describes Jean Brodie's melodramatic personal style, "head up, like Sybil Thorndike, her nose arched and proud" (see Rabinovitz 899; *Prime* 27). But such a label ignores the novel's complex sympathy for the doomed teacher. Miss Brodie, so ostensibly the risible object rather than the narrating subject, triumphs through her overtly ridiculous, vivid style: "I wore my silk dress with the large red poppies which is just right for my colouring," she tells her girls. "Mussolini is one of the greatest men in the world" (46). The inappropriate non sequitur shows the teacher's delusive charm, and the book's double perspectives of fascination and condemnation. If modern dress style promises "to annul the fragmented condition of modernity with the imposition of a coherent subjectivity" (Finkelstein 47), then Jean Brodie, in choosing her red dress and magisterially announcing its effects, imposes her subjective self-vision upon her students and thus controls her body as perceived object. Likewise Spark, in a pared-down prose studded with bright images, uses allusion and juxtaposition to shape how we read not only the novel but Miss Brodie's dated aesthetic dogma.

Jean Brodie was inspired by Spark's charismatic teacher Miss Christina Kay, one of the "clever academically trained women who had lost their sweethearts in the 1914–1918 war . . . a veritable generation of spinsters" (*Curriculum* 61–62). Miss Kay's red dress with poppies, her passions for Mussolini and for the arts, her amusing non sequiturs—all led to Spark's fiction of a spinster teacher who acts out her passions, enthralling her students and offending the authorities. In describing Miss Kay, Spark quotes John Steinbeck: "I have come to believe that a great teacher is a great artist" (*Curriculum* 67). And in inventing Miss Brodie, descendent of a famously creative Edinburgh criminal, Spark created a spinster whose efforts to style her own life result in being hoisted by her own petard. (Deacon Brodie was, according to the legend, hung upon a gallows he himself had constructed.) Jean Brodie's self-styling project includes overt affirmations of her own singleness: "If I were to receive a proposal of marriage tomorrow from the Lord Lyon King-of-Arms I would decline it," she tells her girls. "I am dedicated to you in my prime" (22). Despite her overt sensuality, she regards and retains her single state as integral to her "prime." Her little girls sense a paradox; they have observed that their parents "don't have primes"—"they have sexual intercourse" (15). As it turns out, Miss Brodie has sexual intercourse too, but she also is, the narrator explains, one of Edinburgh's "legions" of single women "who crowded their war-bereaved spinsterhood with voyages of discovery." In affirming the negation that is her spinsterhood she is not unusual; she is unusual in choosing to teach, in dedicating her "prime" to her students (43). And there too lies her downfall: not her affair with the singing master, or her secret love for the art teacher, but her eventual efforts to use her girls as sexual and political surrogates impel her student Sandy to betray her.

Spark's novel is postwar not only in plot but in denying its titular heroine any traditional romantic conclusion: Miss Brodie may be in love with Teddy Lloyd, the married art master, but she must settle for less. Her personal history verges on political allegory, since the teacher's most cherished memories are of the Great War, where her fiancé Hugh died. Young Sandy and Jenny fantasize that Hugh has secretly survived the war and returned to haunt the moors, an ominous revenant very like Bowen's "Demon Lover"—and with similar implications of the revenge of history. But imagining herself perfectly free, their teacher flourishes as a spinster of the thirties, with fewer men available but more independence than previously, while naively celebrating the rise of Continental fascism. Appropriately for the historical analogy, Jean Brodie's downfall occurs in 1939 and she dies of cancer in 1946. If the first war serves as locus of the Romantic for Spark's teacher, the second delineates the destruction of Britain's glory, and Miss Brodie's. Early on, she sits "nobly like Britannia with her legs apart" in Mr. Lloyd's art class (50). However, she will hunch "shriveled and betrayed" after the war's end (58). Like Cotsell's Britain, and like most postwar fiction, she is "something major . . . becoming minor" (Cotsell 33).

From the start, the novel poses questions about the fate of the single girl. The school's founder, Marcia Blaine, hangs in portrait in the great hall, with an open Bible and marked passage below: "O where shall I find a virtuous woman?" (2). The verse from Proverbs 31:10 is loosely paraphrased, adding the Romantic "O" to emphasize the question. Must a virtuous woman be a wife (as in the biblical passage)? Does a truly virtuous woman exist? As an introduction to Miss Brodie and her methods, the query hangs in the air, soon complicated by quotations from "The Lady of Shalott" (3, 20). Jean Brodie loves Victorian Aestheticism—she also quotes Walter Pater on the Mona Lisa—and romanticized art. Tennyson's legendary Lady makes the error of leaving her sheltered castle and esoteric weaving (an art, but in a properly feminine sphere). She leaves her loom, she eyes the handsome Lancelot, and she seeks the world of love, Camelot. The Lady is an isolated priestess of art who tries to pursue love in the real world—and so is Jean Brodie, who, as Patricia Waugh notes, aestheticizes most human experience by imposing her artificially resolved narratives on history (89). But these allusions suggest that Miss Brodie cannot survive her encounters with actual history—and that her students cannot become perfectly virtuous women.

Their teacher's inveterate self-aestheticizing is nonetheless fascinating and fateful: "I went with my friends for an audience with the Pope. . . . I wore a long black gown with a lace mantilla, and looked magnificent" (45–46). The frankly subjective rhetoric, the mixing of the momentous and the trivial, is part of Miss Brodie's art but also part of Spark's deflationary, mock-epic humor. The dress details incongruously center the papal audience around the "magnificent"-looking Miss Brodie, which is what Spark's narrative does as a whole: the book stubbornly remains "about" Jean Brodie, however her students—or Spark's readers—endeavor to resist. As Sandy perceives, the teacher powerfully uses her personal style to create fiction, "making patterns of facts" (76). In imitation, Sandy and her friend Jenny secretly compose fictions about the revenant fiancé Hugh making "his abode in a mountain eyrie," and about Jean's actual lover Mr. Lowther (17, 77–78). Sandy also creates her own private literary fantasies, interjecting herself into classic Romantic novels so that she sits in a garden with Mr. Rochester, or bears secret epistles "o'er the heather" for

Robert Lewis Stevenson's Alan Breck (60–61, 28). Like the teacher's own speeches, the little girls' stories both satirize and honor Miss Brodie's art.

Sandy herself leads "a double life of her own in order never to be bored" (20)—and it is this self-doubling talent that leads Miss Brodie rightly to predict that Sandy will make "a great spy" (116–17). Unlike her teacher, Sandy possesses the self-objectifying ability to dédouble, and she can move easily between art and life without confusing the two. From listening to Hugh's story "with double ears" (76) to studying Teddy Lloyd's paintings, in which all the girls double as representations of Jean Brodie (105ff), she perceives that Miss Brodie cannot separate herself from her own fictions. The teacher cannot view herself as an object; having a "defective sense of self-criticism," she has "elected herself to grace" (91, 116). In endeavoring to induce her girls to act out her desires she becomes dangerous, and her final manipulations prompt Sandy to betray her to the authorities.

Yet Sandy belatedly admits that the teacher's supreme confidence had "its beneficent and enlarging effects" (91), effects that Spark parallels when she uses trivial details to characterize the grandiose Miss Brodie. The novel's imagery, like Miss Brodie herself, is both enchanting and ironically twisted. Again, in Spark's spare style, one detail presents a world of meaning in miniature. So those bright poppies on the teacher's dress, the color of passion, also evoke drugs—and death: as we know, the poppies bloom on Flanders Field, where Jean's youthful lover Hugh "fell like an autumn leaf" (9). And it is her grand affinities with Mussolini and with Caesar, as Miss Brodie flattens those who scorn her "beneath the chariot wheels of her superiority" (56), that bring Sandy to betray her to the school authorities—and yet also put Sandy behind iron bars at the novel's end. Spark's fiction plays with signification, in the fondly ominous way that she claimed to play with her characters: "I love them most intensely, like a cat loves a bird. You know cats do love birds; they love to fondle them" (Stannard 129). Likewise she fondles the trivia, always with an ironic edge. As Ian Gregson comments, "The pleasures of her fictions arise from the consequent fun she has with the incongruous weight which her characters attach to trivia" (5–6). So the peripheral is made to appear important, and the most significant pushed to the margins. "I'm not really interested in world affairs," Sandy tells the headmistress, "only in putting a stop to Miss Brodie" (134). But we know that Sandy should be concerned with world affairs, in contrast to which the affairs of Miss Brodie are trivial indeed.

Trivia is synecdoche in Spark's novel: the part stands for the whole. Miss Brodie stands for fascism, for Mussolini and Caesar. In other words, the trivial does (like Jean Brodie herself) possess a significant ideology here, because it comprises a true style of small things, with not only social and philosophic significance but aesthetic roots. Like Ezra Pound's Image, the trivial detail "presents an intellectual and emotional complex in an instant of time" (Pound 253). So, in accordance with modernist Imagism, Spark employs small metaphors for large meanings; as another modernist poet put it, "For all the history of grief / An empty doorway and a maple leaf" (MacLeish, "Ars Poetica" ll. 19–20). In fact a leaf stands for Jean Brodie's dramatized history of grief: as Mary Schneider noted, the teacher's account of Hugh's death (which sets her class weeping) is permeated with references to autumn leaves (424). Miss Brodie quotes from Keats's ode "To Autumn" and then says that her lover "fell like an autumn leaf," and when the headmistress unexpectedly appears, the errant teacher catches "a falling leaf neatly in her hand" (9, 10). This insistent image is not only a textbook exemplar of New Critical aesthetics. It is also, in its overdetermination, slyly humorous, suggesting the totalitarian potential of an airtight formalism. We do not cry with the little girls; we merely notice that Miss Brodie herself is in a mellow and fruitful autumn—another implication of the leaf, and one that she cannot control. In another ironically multifaceted image, Jean Brodie in her prime begins to wear newer clothes and "a glowing amber necklace" with magnetic properties that she demonstrates to her girls (55). Her own attraction for the two male teachers at the school is a patent analogy. But we also know what amber truly is, and that Miss Brodie is caught, surely as any insect, in a grotesquely frozen beauty. In staging herself as "prime" object of desire, she inadvertently wears the signs of her desires' ultimate end; thus Spark reworks and mocks high-modern artistic tenets.

Finally, Jean Brodie is defeated through her paradoxical project of affirming her spinster-state while also playing perpetual romantic lead. "If I wished I could marry him tomorrow," she boasts of her neglected lover Gordon Lowther—just before he announces his engagement to another woman (120). She never will marry, and in the end a stereotypical spinster style suggests the futility of Miss Brodie's much-vaunted prime. She sits "shriveled and betrayed in her long-preserved dark musquash coat," admitting "I am past my prime" and "Hitler *was* rather naughty" (58, 131). This final dress detail, a once-stylish fur coat, like the other fashion markers sprinkled throughout Spark's brief novel encapsulates her subject's belated condition. And now the non sequitur is pathetic, not comic—and less of a non sequitur to our understanding. Miss Brodie may be artistic, but she does not fully comprehend, or acknowledge, her double nature—and so she betrays herself, over and over, as much as her student Sandy does. Spark's complex narrative concludes in the 1950s with Miss Brodie in her grave and Sandy, no perfect virtuous woman either, clutching "desperately" at the bars of her nun's grille. Having chosen the epitome of spinsterhood, the convent, Sandy is heir to barrenness. "O, who can find a virtuous woman?" Miss Brodie tries to show her students a possible high road for the single girl; in so doing, she demonstrates both the allure of high-literary grandeur and its inevitable end.

THE SPINSTER'S NATURAL CLOTHING: *EXCELLENT WOMEN*

In striking contrast to Jean Brodie, Mildred of Pym's *Excellent Women* embodies the spinster's lacks, especially in her own humble opinion. The novel's very setting emphasizes lessening and loss: its postwar plot turns upon continued rationing, as well as bomb damage, displaced persons, and the difficulties of finding lodgings. Britons' generally shrinking expectations could make a spinster's limited life the epitome of minimized, late-modern literature. However, the spare nature of Pym's style also offers an unusual narrative freedom, as Judy Little has described:

> The validity, structurally and textually, in not having (not having a significant discourse) lies in the openness, looseness of structure, and the possibility of several alternatives. This is a Spartan or ascetic narrative ideology, and it evades the totalizing conventions of a "wonderful" great code or a quest for truth, fulfillment, and love. (83)

In avoiding totalizing conventions, Pym's quiet fictions proved nearly too radical for certain readers. While her spinsters may want love and marriage, they unaccountably refuse to call their single lives tragic. Mildred Lathbury, like Jean Brodie, longs for an exciting, unattainable man—her handsome neighbor Rocky—but must settle for less. Nevertheless, in the course of the novel, she quietly learns to affirm herself as an "excellent woman."

And of course postwar styles, like modest Mildred and like Pym herself, frequently were paradoxical. The New Look, which premiered about three months after *Excellent Women* ends,[3] was both conservative and rebellious. What we find bursting out in the New Look is an extravagance of stubborn self-expression, nevertheless demurely and even stringently controlled (that waist!). It is the same artistic paradox shown in Mildred's story, in Pym's fiction generally, and most broadly in postwar British literature. For Pym and for Mildred, the debates over retrogressive domesticity certainly apply.

That Pym's understated narrative style dovetails with her protagonist's modest dress style is hardly surprising, since the novel is told in Mildred's voice. But the marvel is that this plain prose, adorned only with postwar negation and qualifiers, is effective and funny. Negations appear on nearly every page: When told not to expect too much from a learned lecture, Mildred typically represses her actual thought: "I forebore to remark that women like me really expected very little—nothing, almost" (30). The qualifiers "really" and "almost" first insist on their subject's humility and then quietly recoup a tiny piece of ground: women like Mildred expect *almost* nothing. Her actual descriptions of clothing bespeak her desires that her personal style escape scrutiny, from the underclothes that "there is no need to describe" (75) to her unfortunate appearance when she encounters Everard on the streets of London: "I was not very well dressed that day—I had had a 'lapse' and was hatless and stockingless in an old cotton dress and a cardigan" (125). The negations ("not," "less") are softened by the qualifiers "very well." The overall effect is plain, even dowdy—but in a mild, undramatic mode, then made comic by Everard's lack of interest in her dress, and Mildred's subsequent consternation at his obliviousness.

In writing the novel, Pym herself gradually developed a more positive portrayal of Mildred and her single state: the original draft was headed "No Life of One's Own," and another working title was the ironic "A Full Life" (Pym Papers 14: np, 13: 1). Nor does "excellent women" seem an enviable label at first. The term is used for the virtuous middle-aged spinsters

---

3. *Excellent Women*, written in 1949–50 and published in 1952, is set in immediate postwar London: a note on a manuscript draft states that it begins in February 1946 (Pym Papers 14). It concludes with Mildred's dinner at Everard's apartment in November 1946, just before Advent (*Excellent Women* 227). All references to unpublished Pym notebooks, manuscripts, and letters are by manuscript number and page in the Bodleian Library's Pym Papers.

who faithfully support church activities, yet even here Mildred herself gently pushes against the stereotypes, arguing that although excellent women are by definition "unmarried... by that I mean a positive rather than a negative state" (170). She needs to insist on affirmation, because her understated style is so easily mistaken for self-immolation. "Dear Mildred," sighs the vicar, convinced despite her protests that she longs to marry him, "you are not the kind of person to expect things as your right" (120).

Excellent Women, one of Pym's few first-person narratives, focuses closely on Mildred's self-objectification. The action begins when a fascinating couple moves into the neighboring flat. Helena, the undomesticated wife, is far from Mildred's virtuous womanhood, as shown by her unusual attire of "gay trousers": she is pretty, unladylike, and more devoted to anthropology than to the charming aesthete she married. Her husband, Rocky, idly flirts with Mildred, and they introduce her to Helena's fellow scholar Everard Bone—handsome, stiff, and unresponsive to Helena's infatuated advances. Other characters include Mildred's girlhood friend Dora, also a spinster, and Dora's brother William, who takes Mildred to lunch annually, although—as she realizes—he is "not the kind of man to marry" (58). The local vicar Julian also plans to remain single, living with his spinster sister, although in the course of the novel a scheming widow temporarily entraps him. Mildred spends much of the novel observing, listening to others' troubles, and endeavoring to reconcile Rocky and Helena, who are the only significant married characters. Most of the others purport to be single by choice, but Mildred explains that defensiveness as "a kind of fiction that we always kept up, this not knowing anyone at the moment that we wanted to marry, as if there had been in the past and would be in the future" (90). Like Miss Brodie claiming that she could marry Mr. Lowther tomorrow, Pym's singles deny the narrowing both of their options and of their desires. Only Mildred is more frank, at least under the influence of wine, when she discloses to a shocked William that Rocky is "just the kind of person I should have liked for myself" (61). She is not destined to have Rocky, but by the novel's end the reserved Everard has shown a marked interest in her, even confiding that his ideal wife would be "a sensible sort of person"—in fact, an excellent woman (170).

In her self-objectification, Mildred casts a clear light upon her inner self, just as Spark's Sandy seeks to display Miss Brodie's sins. Mildred's revelations, however, are less grand: "The burden of keeping three people in toilet paper seemed to me rather a heavy one" (6). And unlike Spark,

Little observes, "Pym almost always refuses to transform the commonplace into the epiphanic" (84–85). As we have seen, in trivial details such as the amber necklace, Spark employed an elaborate, ironic symbolism. But Pym leaves promising metaphors unclaimed, while her protagonist both observes and seeks to validate her own subjectivity. To the condescending salesgirl behind a makeup counter, Mildred insists that she has a right to vividly colored lipstick: "'Thank you, but I think I will have Hawaiian Fire,' I said obstinately, savouring the ludicrous words and the full depths of my shame" (117). The incongruity, of casting a lipstick purchase as a milestone, again links the novel's plot to Mildred's own style, including an all-too-conscious sense of herself as potential object of ridicule.

Her gift for dédoublement, however, is not merely a matter of viewing herself objectively. Her apologetic irony deconstructs others too: "I couldn't help noticing . . . ," Mildred frequently murmurs, preparatory to another devastating deflation of human pretension. After her hard-won lipstick purchase, for instance, Mildred slips effortlessly from observing subject into a crowd of objects—that is, insecure females. She takes her Hawaiian Fire to the department store ladies' room:

> Inside it was a sobering sight indeed and one to put us all in mind of the futility of material things and of our own mortality. *All flesh is but as grass* . . . I thought, watching the women working at their faces with savage concentration, opening their mouths wide, biting and licking their lips, stabbing at their noses and chins with powder-puffs. (117)

Here grand language is employed only for parodic deflation. Most frequently, the disparities between Mildred's words and her thoughts show her clear-eyed understanding of others' motives: You see, the vicar comments sadly on his ex-fiancée, "'I thought her such a fine person.' She was certainly very pretty, I thought but I did not say it" (189).

Mildred is realistic about her own plain appearance. Decades earlier, Virginia Woolf had urged women writers to "say what your beauty means to you, or your plainness, and what is your relation to the everchanging and turning world of gloves and shoes and stuffs" (A Room 88). And Pym—through her protagonists—says these things over and over, especially in *Excellent Women*. The marvel of Pym's descriptions, especially of plain women and their hopeful relations to style, is that they are neither dull nor self-absorbed. There is always that humble, comical insight:

> I began taking off my apron and tidying my hair, apologizing as I did so, in what I felt was a stupid, fussy way, for my appearance. As if anyone would care how I looked or even notice me, I told myself scornfully.
>
> "You look very nice," said Rockingham, smiling in such a way that he could almost have meant it. (28)

Mildred's apologetic self-deprecation is vintage Pym, and so is the sly, gentle undercutting: Pym embeds "what [Mildred's] plainness means to her" in a deceptively plain narration that slides in the knife at the passage's end.

Yet the satire is gentle, like Mildred herself, perhaps because she refuses to romanticize her own story. Where *Miss Jean Brodie* offers sly allusions to Brontë's *Jane Eyre*, Mildred announces bluntly, "I . . . with my shapeless overall and old fawn skirt . . . am not at all like Jane Eyre, who must have given hope to so many plain women who tell their stories in the first person" (3). In both books, *Jane Eyre* serves as touchstone for unrealistic expectations of a final, blissful union with one's soul mate.[4] Miss Brodie reads *Jane Eyre* to her girls during their sewing class, leading Sandy to an elaborate fantasy about Mr. Rochester. In Pym's novel, Rocky is the Rochester figure: dark, handsome, and charming—but always undercut by his failures to fulfill his romantic promise. Their final meeting provides one last parody of romance:

> I could feel Rocky looking at me very intently. I raised my eyes to meet his.
> "Mildred?"
> "Yes?"
> "I was hoping . . ."
> "What were you hoping?"
> "That you might suggest making a cup of tea." (200)

The comic deflation of this tête-à-tête scarcely daunts Mildred. Likewise, the novel's tolerably happy ending is hardly like Jane's marriage with Mr. Rochester. Everard invites Mildred to his flat for dinner, plies her with wine—and then proposes that she help with his proofreading and index.

---

4. For allusions to Brontë's novel throughout Pym's fiction, see Rossen, "On Not Being Jane Eyre," 137ff.

She muses about Everard's curious family members, as well as the vicar needing her help, concluding, "So . . . it seemed as if I might be going to have what Helena called 'a full life' after all" (231).

That a woman's "full life" might be constituted by mild interests and tasks has seemed bitterly ironic to some readers: A. N. Wilson finds that in Pym's fiction the limited domestic routines suggest "a nihilistic sense . . . that life cannot hold out very exciting possibilities" (xi). But Pym herself defended the joys of small things: "What is wrong with being obsessed with trivia? . . . What are the minds of my critics filled with? What *nobler* and more worthwhile things?" (*Very* 260). Certainly Pym's piling up of trivial details (at one point, Mildred actually meditates on old laundry lists) may appear to be, as A. S. Byatt has claimed, not an effective postwar style but being "petty about pettiness" (862). It also could comprise a literary gulf between proponents of very different styles, or a gender gap between male and female perceptions of what counts in life—or both.

Even among postwar writers, women novelists tend to take trivia more seriously. For instance, the telling details of dress, so significant for Spark and Pym, are quarantined by Kingsley Amis into a corral for female bad taste. In *Lucky Jim*, Dixon's hysterical girlfriend Margaret is characterized repeatedly by her hideous "green Paisley frock in combination with the low-heeled, quasi-velvet shoes" (11, 19, 155), while the dream-girl Christine is notable only for blond beauty and large breasts. (The style of Dixon's ripped pants is never detailed.) If the details of dress are too petty even for postwar fiction by men, perhaps Woolf's truism still holds: women's values commonly are called trivial since women must deal with all the unrecorded details of everyday life (*A Room* 73). The small is writ large in women's lives for very practical reasons; therefore, to focus on the trivial is to focus on the real conditions of our lives and, perhaps, to acknowledge our own smallness. "After all, life was like that for most of us," Mildred remarks, "the small unpleasantnesses rather than the great tragedies, the little useless longings rather than the great renunciations and dramatic love affairs of history or fiction" (90).

A trivial style is, then, a humble style. It also is a style that signifies nonsignification: "The ideology of the trivial," Little writes, "is that it has no significant ideology, belongs to no master narrative, no great codes of quest or romance, and no *sermo patrius*" (76)—that is, no traditionally male genre of worthwhile literature, including high modernism. In *Miss Jean Brodie* Spark toys with signification, using small details to cue up those romantic "great codes" and then to mock them. In a very different vein, but with similar plays upon modernism, the trivia of *Excellent Women* offers imagery with all grandeur erased. When Mildred buys yet another brown hat, we are offered a serious trope for stagnation, despite Rocky's venture that the hat "brings out the colour of your eyes which look like a good dark sherry" (76). We know all too well what "brown" signifies, even in modernism: Eliot's *Waste Land* is a "brown land" of "brown fog" (ll. 175, 61), and Prufrock's potential love interest repels him by her arms, "downed with light brown hair!" (l. 63). In Pym's narrative, however, brown is neither grim nor repulsive. Mildred's brown dresses and coats exemplify merely an inconsequential dullness, summarized by Byatt as "brown frocks, knitted socks in clerical grey and cauliflower cheese" (862). Pym's details are not a complex of aesthetically stunning symbols.

Yet *brown* bore one important association for Pym, since she had foreseen her life as an "old brown spinster" (*Very* 69: 11 March 1938). And spinster style haunts and concludes Mildred's story, as it does Jean Brodie's. While traditionally suggesting lack and frustration, spinsterhood also offers the freedom to define oneself. If Jean Brodie cast back in time to do so, Mildred looks forward—and so perhaps succeeds in breaking out of the stereotypes. We are told that "it was not the excellent women who got married" (152), and William even argues that Mildred's gift for objectification requires her to remain single:

> But my dear Mildred, *you* mustn't marry. . . . I always think of you as being so very balanced and sensible, such an excellent woman. . . . Let Dora marry if she likes. She hasn't your talent for observation. (61)

Later Mildred responds in surprise to Everard: "You would consider marrying an excellent woman? But they are not for marrying" (170). Her possible escape from brown spinsterhood is signified when, at the novel's end, she buys a black dress and changes her hairstyle.

Does that black dress signify a transformed Mildred? Of course she is imitating Helena, and many other stylish women, who followed Chanel to make black the traditional glamorous color for women. Helena, Mildred recalls, "enliven[ed]" her black "with some brilliant touch of colour or 'important jewel.'" Mildred confesses that she herself has "no important jewels except for a good cameo brooch which had belonged to my grandmother, so I fastened this at the front of the little collar" (224).

Is it significant that Mildred has "no important jewels"—or that instead of brilliant color she employs a pale and decorous Victorian cameo? And what of that little white collar on her black dress? William describes Mildred's appearance as "*triste*," but it's hard not to suspect that, with her newly "scraped-back hair," she inadvertently has styled herself like a traditional maid (226). Yet we have no indication that Everard Bone even notices Mildred's new servant-style, and her dress enables her, both boldly and humbly, to enjoy her date with him while remaining clear-sighted about its implications. She anticipates a moderately "full life" which may include marriage with Everard but certainly will involve doing his indexing.

What is Pym doing with the marriage plot? Readers debate whether this novel's conclusion should be interpreted as covertly tragic (Everard, a modern-day St John Rivers, merely wants Mildred as a drudging helpmeet) or quietly romantic (surely he wouldn't marry her merely to gain a free indexer?). Barbara Everett comments judiciously that "*Excellent Women* looks from the outside like a love story and certainly gives the pleasure of romance," but the male characters are not that desirable: "Although Everard Bone may be the most marriageable, he is the book's hero rather in the sense that he is the shortest straw to be drawn" (73). Pym herself, Everett observes, fell in love with charming, verbose, egocentric men like Rocky or the Archdeacon in *Some Tame Gazelle* (73). In fact, Pym's conclusion both mocks conventional marriage plots, as she has done throughout the novel, and refuses despair. As Ellen Tsagaris has pointed out, a "happy ending" for Pym need not mean a blissful marriage (34).

Mildred's final state is neither desperate nor trapped. Rather, she realistically redefines the term "full life" as she has redefined her style—against Romantic stereotypes, against the modernist great narrative, perhaps against even the significance of small things as anything more than a comic marker for others' pretensions, including fallible male perceptions. Here is a typical compliment from Mildred's suitor: "'You seem to be very nicely dressed,' said Everard without looking" (131). And here is William, responding to Mildred's new style: "An improvement on the way you usually look? But how do you usually look? One scarcely remembers" (226). The jokes are on the men, who ignore the small details, but also on women, who place so much stock in trivial details. In fact, Mildred's style changes are as significant for her experience as Miss Brodie's poppy dress to hers, but the diminished style of the spinster appears to certain observers too painfully small to contemplate for long. Philip Larkin read the very funny *Excellent Women* as

> a study of the pain of being single, the unconscious hurt the world regards as this state's natural clothing ... time and again one senses not only that Mildred is suffering, but that nobody can see why she shouldn't suffer, like a Victorian cabhorse. (Larkin, *Selected Letters* 368)

Likewise, A. N. Wilson finds a "bleak Chekhovian question ... at the heart of Pym's comedy" (xvi)—against which we may set Pym's own query, "Why is it that men find my books so sad? Women don't particularly" (*Very* 223: 8 December 1963). This interpretive gulf between the sexes also may be regarded as a chasm between perceiving subject and comic object, categories breached by and through Pym's fictional spinsters. Still, the chasm gapes wider in Spark's *Girls of Slender Means*, which further explicates the single girl's dress in response to male-authored postwar fiction.

THE FIFTIES BLOKE VERSUS *THE GIRLS OF SLENDER MEANS*

That expectations are diminished is a given for postwar women, but a given that their male counterparts struggle to take in. These spinsters' lives are small, and their stories conclude in minor keys. Where, then, lies comedy, happiness, or laughter? The unexpectedness of Spark's destructive undercurrents "would be comic if we could laugh," John Updike mourned when he reviewed *The Girls of Slender Means* (1963). Yet anyone who has read portions of Spark's fiction aloud, or seen the stage or film interactions of Miss Brodie with her class, can attest that Spark often is hilarious. What should sober us, Updike explained, is the implication "that the farcical world of her portrayal is the *real* world"—in this case, the world of 1945 London, where a boarding house and an innocent young woman are about to be blown to shreds ("Between a Wedding" 311). Spark's shocking climax hinges upon choosing a fashionable dress over a human life, but *Girls* bears a typical disjunction between trivia and serious events. Spark and her protagonists demonstrate a detachment integral to the comedy of the object from the first. When Caroline of *The Comforters* (1957) is haunted by voices narrating her thoughts and life, she eventually uses them to reobjectify herself: "She possessed a large number of notes, transcribed from the voices, and these she studied carefully . . . [since] the narrative could never become coherent to her until she was at last outside it, and at the same time consummately inside it" (181). More discomfiting, Caroline finds her lover, Lawrence—and men in general—secondary, if not dispensable. "Where else," Updike uneasily asked, "in the fiction of the fifties, do we find a heroine whose heterosexuality is so calmly brought forward and assigned a secondary priority?" ("From the Forties" 148).

Certainly not in postwar novels by men; even those that entertain a woman's perspective assume sex and romance are female preoccupations, as in Amis's *Take a Girl Like You* (1960), or they find, as in Larkin's *A Girl in Winter* (1957), that the plight of the single woman is unutterably sad. In Larkin's novel, the lonely Katherine fields a nonmarriage proposal from the man of her dreams: "I mean," mutters her would-not-be boyfriend, "if I asked you, for instance, to marry me, you'd refuse, wouldn't you . . . wouldn't you?" (247). Katherine is impelled to accept a devastatingly lessened consolation. Unlike Pym's diminished happy endings, the conclusion of Larkin's novel is not comic: his emphasis is on irony and loss, far from Mildred's consoling hope for "a full life." If we seek humor, *Lucky Jim*'s Margaret, because always presented as an object, is never other than hilariously appalling. She remains the stereotypical man-obsessed but frigid spinster, and to sympathize too much with her, to share her perspective, Amis's protagonist concludes, would mean nothing but sharing her misery (238). Single women's lives are funnier, according to the male writers, when viewed from without.

Admittedly, as Pym discovered in portraying spinsters like herself, the comic object is a large risk when the mockery seems directed at oneself. In Baudelaire's description of comic dédoublement, laughter is linked with the individual observing his or her own fall. Therefore a willing self-division is necessary, in order to view oneself as a comic object—and also a willingness to fall. Pym's fiction does not fully acknowledge the harshness of these necessities: she makes us sympathize with her characters, and then claims no conflict between caring and amusement. It is Spark's gift, however, to ricochet mercilessly between sympathy and disinterested laughter.

The Girls of Slender Means employs this comic objectivity even in the trivial incidents that constitute most of the plot. The narrative begins as a fable: "Long ago in 1945 all the nice people in England were poor, allowing for exceptions" (7). And the climax turns, like "Cinderella," on a magically transformative dress. But Spark proceeds to puncture any fairy-tale expectations, observing that the bombed buildings look "like the ruins of ancient castles" only until one observes the lavatory chains dangling over ruined walls. Likewise, the May of Teck Club, where the girls of slender means dwell, will be leveled by a long-buried bomb. It is not the Golden Age microcosm that the self-obsessed writer Nicholas imagines—and yet its petty glamours and greeds propel him to a Catholic martyrdom. The catalyzing "action of savagery so extreme" (60) itself is wrapped up in female small-mindedness: Nicholas sees his lover, beautiful Selina, return as the fire looms, slipping through a bathroom window that only very slender girls can manage (as usual, Spark's title is a pun). Selina risks her life not to help the other girls but in order to steal a beautiful Schiaparelli dress. Meanwhile, Joanna, the saintly rector's daughter who is a Pym-ish excellent spinster, perishes along with her recitations of classic, idealistic poetry from the Bible, "the Book of Common Prayer, Shakespeare and Gerard Manley Hopkins" (11–12). Her neo-Romantic poetic tastes echo those of the young Spark; they may be limited but are broader than Selina's vapid Two Sentence mantra, emphasizing "Elegant dress" and "immaculate grooming" (50, 91). The novel's one significant garment—the Schiaparelli gown—capably figures Spark's narrative style here, pared-down yet dotted with brilliant flashes of detail, as in her description of various girls' means of slipping through the narrow bathroom window:

> Anne only managed it naked, having made her body slippery with margarine. . . . Anne said she would in future use her soap ration to facilitate the exit. Soap was as tightly rationed as margarine but more precious, for margarine was fattening, anyway. Face cream was too expensive. (33)

Anne, a minor character, serves to highlight the small details of wartime existence through the rationed substances and their telling relative values in the lives of the girls of slender means: appearance (face cream) matters most, while fattening substances such as margarine are lowest on the list of emollients. The trivia matters to the end, as does the slenderness (or not) of each girl.

As usual, Spark suggests a wittily allegorical interpretation for her tale, here centered upon the opposing recitations and the amazing Schiaparelli dress with its prewar avant-garde exoticism: "taffeta, with small side panniers stuck out with cleverly curved pads over the hips. It was coloured dark blue, green, orange and white in a floral pattern as from the Pacific Islands" (89). The girls borrow the dress in turn, and it transforms each one. It is a perfect image for the complete disconnect between their attractions and traditional ethics: "few people alive at the time," comments the narrator, "were more delightful, more ingenious, more movingly lovely, and, as it might happen, more savage, than the girls of slender means" (9). Just as Joanna's death reminds us that the era of elaborate Romantic poetry is over, so the retro-savage dress represents the coffin lid upon a modernist dream of infinite self-making. The Schiaparelli's disappearance is synchronized with the war's end, but already we knew that it was a masquerade costume, borrowed by each girl in turn in order to stage herself as stylish and desirable.

Each girl, that is, except for scheming, literary Jane, whom the dress does not fit. "Fat but intellectually glamorous" to her housemates (30), this observant spinster has some commonality with the "blokes" of male postwar fiction: Amis's Jim Dixon, John Wain's Charles Lumley in *Hurry on Down* (1953), Alan Sillitoe's Arthur Seaton in *Saturday Night and Sunday Morning* (1958), John Braine's Joe Lampton in *Room at the Top* (1957). All are sharp, tough-minded observers, ambitious and unscrupulous. Only the Spark and Amis protagonists, however, are outwardly unprepossessing (most Movement novelists chose big, handsome men as their fictional alter egos). On the other hand, only Jane and Jim triumph in the ends of their stories. But where Dixon's is a fairy-tale comic conclusion, in which he gets the princess and riches, Jane has sweated her way to her ideal job of gossip columnist but never to a happy love life. Spark's comic non–fairy tale, like Pym's fiction, includes faux-romantic scenes: at a bohemian party, Nicholas leads Jane "up to a bedroom where they sat on the edge of an unmade bed" and then says eagerly, "Tell me about Selina" (64). Jane wants a man, but she has only her father's old, made-over dark suit to wear, and she does not understand "that literary men, if they like women at all, do not want literary women but girls" (76): she never is an object of male desire. Nor are the Movement's handsome postwar heroes blissfully happy in the end, though they usually, like Dixon, get both the job and the desired girl. These protagonists dream in fairy-tale terms: "the fairy came down from the Christmas tree, the straw was spun into valuable gold," Charles exults (Wain 123), and even climber Joe Lampton sees the rich girl he courts as "the princess in the fairystories" (Braine 68). But they end disillusioned. For Lampton especially, a grisly tragedy reveals the price paid for his scramble, resulting in a concluding dédoublement far from comic: "I didn't like Joe Lampton," Lampton remarks. "He was a sensible young accountant.... Why, he even made a roll in the hay with a pretty little teen-ager pay dividends. I hated Joe Lampton, but he looked and sounded very sure of himself sitting at my desk in my skin" (280).

Why should an objective view of oneself be a grim discovery? Each of these male-authored postwar novels exemplifies a petty, desperate materialism: the protagonist counts his cigarettes, adds up the costs of drinks, announces his specific wages, and worries about their loss or delights in their increase. In fact, it is another version of "being petty about pettiness." (What is Jean Brodie's salary? Who has ever thought to ask?) The plots offer elaborate details of drunken and post-drunken states and sexual encounters, carefully segregated from the "princess" the hero hopes to win. In contrast to the feminine trivia of dress style, with its complex codes, nearly everything has a price in these novels, including fashionable clothing itself. Arthur Seaton of Sillitoe's *Saturday Night* is a "Teddy Boy," a quasi-dandy, yet we hear few details of his clothing; his suits are "the good hundred pounds' worth of property hanging from an iron-bar. These were his riches, and he told himself that money paid-out on clothes was a sensible investment because it made him feel good" (66). Joe Lampton, on the other hand, carefully details both male and female dress but always relates it to money and upward mobility. A coworker feels Joe's suit and comments, "Highgrade worsted.... My goodness, Mr. Lampton, however do you manage on your coupons?" (Braine 138). Even Joe's coveted rich girl Susan, wearing an expensive "black taffeta skirt and a white *broderie anglaise* blouse," prompts an economic reference: "If anyone ever needed a justification of the capitalist system, I thought, here it was" (160). Certainly Joe is an accountant whose ambitions are being satirized, but Braine's novel is only a more conscious version of each of these fifties narratives, in which (*Lucky Jim* aside) the conclusion finds a wealthier but sadder protagonist who cannot see where his detailed materialism went wrong.

Spark's girls, however, do not desperately struggle for pounds and shillings or against class barriers. Despite the penury indicated in the title, most girls have prospered through attention to the club's unwritten interests, "love and money.... Love came first, and subsidiary to it was money for the upkeep of looks and the purchase of clothing coupons at the official black-market price of eight coupons for a pound" (26). In the girls' formulations, clothing is not for the sake of making money, but money serves to get clothes: the comedy of the object teaches women to objectify their own desires as well as men's. In fact, Selina steals the dress, not to win Nicholas or any man, but because it is the most beautiful thing and she is the most beautiful girl. As Patricia Waugh notes, "Clothes are important commodities in the Sparkian world, for in a [modernist] culture where the aesthetic so often stands in for the ethical, the fetishization of items of clothing confers on them a kind of tantric or sacramental power" (85). This is why Nicholas is so shocked by Selina's devotion to the Schiaparelli dress at the novel's climax (P. Waugh 90–91); he had been "enamoured of the May of Teck club as an aesthetic and ethical conception . . . lovely frozen image that it was" (*Girls* 86). He had imposed an artificial, once-upon-a-time narrative upon reality, in which the aesthetic certifies the ethical, and assumed that Selina joined the two entities in her beautiful person. He errs not because he believes in her perfect virtue but because he sees her and her housemates as "lovely frozen" objects rather than humans with complex desires. But Selina refuses to play games in which female style only reflects male desires, erotic or monetary.

Not that the stylish single girl necessarily views the world in terms of traditional female desires, either: as Updike noted, eros is secondary for most of Spark's women, and this circumstance puzzles her men. Even Pym's women think independently, although they retain their fascination with (not, alas for them, a fascination *for*) the male sex. Her spinsters learn that "becoming minor," while living a life of trivial satisfactions, is no great tragedy. Nevertheless, Pym maintained that a gulf lies fixed between male perceptions of women and actual female existence. In 1970 she described helping a pair of elderly spinsters in her village: "Looking at one of them with her hairy chin and general air of greyness one couldn't help thinking that this was as much a woman as a glamorous perfumed model" (*Very* 306; 1 October 1977). Pym was all too aware that most men of her era would disagree. And however much comic insight Pym's women achieve into their selves, her men rarely move beyond seeing the women as objects.

Spark, however, refused to give up the fight. And finally, the question of her place among the male postwar novelists is figured metaphorically, as the author preferred. The unstylish Jane, like Sandy Stranger and like

Spark herself, shares with postwar male protagonists a desire for fame and success, but at the price of frequently being interpreted as bisexual or simply desexed. Only Jane is left a spinster at the book's end, on V-J Night—and yet she is no pathetic single woman to Nicholas, who provides the final and definitive perspective. Ultimately, it is neither the Schiaparelli-stealing Selina or the poetry-reciting Joanna but the unalluring Jane that he recalls, marveling at her stamina

> years later in the country of his death—how she stood, sturdy and barelegged on the dark grass, occupied with her hair—as if this was an image of all the May of Teck establishment in its meek, unselfconscious attitudes of poverty, long ago in 1945. (142)

In so concluding, Spark insists upon the persistence—beyond diminished postwar style, Romantic hopes, and gender stereotypes—of the self-styled spinster.

CHAPTER 7

Spark, Pym, and the Glamorous Ends of Style

PERHAPS NO BETTER IMAGE exists for modernism than Baudelaire's flâneur, strolling the city boulevards. He observes others and he displays himself, but his dandy dress covers the "latent fire" within; thus he demonstrates the ideal self-objectification of the modern artist. Modern women were less free to be detached observers: although Dorothy Sayers had endeavored to appropriate dandy style, Jean Rhys uncovered her culture's continuing assumptions that women always display themselves for men. And in a 1938 anecdote, the young Barbara Pym had mocked the unstated expectations for single girls:

> "Mrs Minshall seems to want us all to be either dead or married," said Mrs Pym to her daughter as they drove home in the car.
> "Well I do not see what else we can be," said Barbara in a thoughtful tone. "I suppose we all come to one state or the other eventually. I do not know which I would rather be in." (*Very Private* 80)

Prewar women, in literature and in life, were expected to end up "either dead or married."

But World War II seemingly changed the conditions for single girls: the death of nostalgic old-style modernism (that paradoxical construct described in chapter 5), and the creation of necessary homefront styles, heralded a slow landslide for women. The relations of modern women, literature, and fashion had been poignantly pictured through filmy tulle illusion that—like literary impressionism's haze of meaning—masked where the dress left off and the female body began. In understated postwar styles, the haze melted and women began to reveal themselves, to gaze back at men openly, to observe them as objects, and even to laugh occasionally at the ways men objectified them. Nevertheless, the war's overthrow of conventions and hierarchies had a price, as shown in Spark's wartime girls of slender means: "few people alive at the time were more delightful, more ingenious, more movingly lovely, and, as it might happen, more savage" (*Girls* 9). Late-modern glamour was beautiful, delightful, and totally separate from ethical traditions. As such, it partook of an emerging postmodern aesthetic that altered the image of the enticingly stylish woman.

If high modernism ended with World War II, modernism in general was passé by the sixties, as chronological modernity shaded into postmodernity. Likewise, Spark and Pym evolved in inevitably postmodern directions—although the "postmodern," like the "postmodernist," often includes, encompasses, and expands upon its precursor rather than directly rebelling against a previous aesthetic. In a famous definitional discussion of postmodernism, Ihab Hassan in 1982 pointed out that

> modernism and postmodernism are not separated by an Iron Curtain or Chinese Wall; for history is a palimpsest, and culture is permeable to time past, time present, and time future . . . an author may, in his or her own life time, easily write both a modernist and postmodernist work. (*The Dismemberment of Orpheus* 266)

Hassan nevertheless elaborately charted modernist and postmodernist characteristics, for instance associating modernism with "Form (conjunctive, closed)," "Purpose," "Design," "Hierarchy," "Mastery/Logos," "Art Object/Finished Work," and "Narrative/*Grande Histoire*." In contrast, he saw postmodernism as typified by "Antiform (disjunctive, open)," "Play," "Chance," "Anarchy," "Exhaustion/Silence," "Process/Performance/Happening," and "Anti-narrative/*Petite Histoire*" (267–68). As with previous descriptions of modernism, the many overlaps and contradictions do not obviate the usefulness of Hassan's observations—but they do limit most strict definitions, and warn us to beware of walling off postmodernism in the ways that practitioners and scholars of modernism attempted to guard their citadel.[1]

To the contrary, in this chapter the wildly elastic nature of postmodern fiction, which eschews formal literary schools and prescribed styles, is illustrated by the gulf between Pym's demure narration and Spark's flamboyance. When I describe Pym, as well as Spark, as "postmodern," I refer first of all to the historical period in which each woman was an inevitable if often reluctant participant. However, Spark's fiction also began to embody several signature postmodernist traits, including playful pastiche, antirationalism, and (most important for this study) an ethos in which style *is* the content. Furthermore, an important mode of early postmodern literature is elegy, a lament for lost innocence and the death of high seriousness—which appears repeatedly in Pym's final novels. It should be no surprise that in the sixties both Spark and Pym, albeit in very different modes, wrote about women whose styles lead them toward death.

STYLING THE SIXTIES

In 1967 novelist Angela Carter observed, "The inscrutable but imperative logic of change has forced fashion in the sixties through the barriers of space and time . . . the startling dandyism of the newly emancipated young reveals a kind of logic of whizzing entropy" (85). And indeed, Britain underwent incredibly swift technological change in the 1960s: birth-control pills, color TV, rockets to the moon. The decade's immense migration in cultural attitudes was shown through dramatic changes in both dress and literature. These new sixties styles stemmed from a populist modernism fueled, as Mark Donnelly points out, by the unprecedented rise of working-class youth with disposable incomes (35). Postwar efforts for a more equitable society, coupled with an economic boom beginning in the mid-fifties, fueled this rise, along with a new media fascination with youth music, clothes, and politics. Arguably a neo-Romantic backlash against fifties conventions, and indeed against most Western heritage,

---

    1. For an overview of many scholars' competing definitions, see Friedman, "Definitional Excursions," especially 495–98.

the protest movements in Britain included intense critiques of war, of traditional sexual constraints, and of life as a climb up the corporate ladder. More startlingly, after a staid decade, many legal barriers tumbled suddenly. The 1960 obscenity trial of Penguin Books, for reissuing the uncut *Lady Chatterley's Lover*, resulted in the publisher's vindication; other censorship laws were loosened in the next few years. Oral contraceptives became available in 1961, and laws restricting homosexual acts, abortion, and divorce were liberalized throughout that decade.

In this seemingly freer environment, many women continued to feel marginalized. The new protest movements were—still—led by men. While young women joined in public demonstrations and experienced loosened sexual constraints, the Women's Liberation Movement (WLM) did not become a major force in Britain until the later sixties. And while it is generally true that the WLM "reacted against the 'cult of domesticity' that enveloped women after the Second World War," the later feminisms aimed at much more than employment opportunities; in fact, late-sixties feminists wanted to see radical changes in gender expectations (Donnelly 161). But even job equity was slow to be legislated: although the Equal Pay Act passed in 1970, its implementation was delayed until 1975.

As young women, Spark and Pym had been trailblazers, but by 1960 they were successful writers approaching middle age. No matter how sympathetic to political critiques or complaints of sexism, they were part of the Establishment being picketed, members of the older generation who were shocked by the new morals and manners. For Pym especially, the swift decline in Anglican church-going was unsettling. Callum Brown has documented how, contrary to popular historical assumptions, the late forties and fifties "witnessed the greatest church growth that Britain had experienced since the mid-nineteenth century" (170). Perhaps because of the exigencies of war, or perhaps due to the ostensible return to domesticity, during the immediate postwar period, church attendance grew beyond 1930s levels; this resurgence appears in all of Pym's pre-sixties novels. But in the early sixties, church membership and involvement, including christenings, fell abruptly. Anglican church-goers over age fifteen amounted to 9.9 million in 1961; by 1966, that number had dropped to 5.4 million (Donnelly 53). Brown theorizes that changes in feminine consciousness drove religion's losses: since religious faith had become feminized in the early nineteenth century, women—Pym's "excellent women"—had been the mainstay of the Church of England. Consequently, as women sought freedom from sexual conventions and traditional gender roles, they deserted traditional religious groups en masse (C. Brown 58).[2] This correlation does not answer chicken-or-the-egg questions, but it does suggest a new radical feminism far beyond the satirical voices of Pym and Spark, who remained religious believers adhering to long-established churches.

The shock of rapid change also could be seen in literary styles. By the early sixties, the understated postwar novel had been joined by a colorful bouquet of disparate fictions. From the criminal dystopia of Anthony Burgess's *Clockwork Orange* (1962) to Angela Carter's magical realism, novels appeared that were both neo-Romantic and shocking in their uses of violence and sexuality. Carter, a war baby, paraded a discomfiting female perspective far from the previous generation's well-bred sly satire. But the older Doris Lessing also captured the radical new spirit in *The Golden Notebook* (1962) and her Children of Violence series: Marxist, multicultural, experimental, and seriously (not humorously) feminist. Meanwhile, the sixties' most significant traditional narratives came from a non-Briton who never settled in the United Kingdom: Chinua Achebe's *Things Fall Apart* (Heinemann, 1958) was followed by more Nigerian novels, epitomizing the coming globalization of Anglophone literature. In a more traditional setting, but still in contrast to the spare fictions of Spark and Pym, Anthony Powell wrote his twelve-part *Dance to the Music of Time* (four volumes already had appeared by 1960), and Paul Scott published *The Jewel in the Crown* (1966), initiating the Raj Quartet. These lush, expansive series gradually collected readers and weight. Meanwhile, Spark would successfully continue her short, stylish fictions (five, each under two hundred pages, during the decade), while experimenting with the longer *Mandelbaum Gate* (1965). But Pym found that sixties literary tastes left her understated works in the dust: after *No Fond Return of Love* (1961), she did not publish a novel for fifteen years.

The sixties' speed of change in mores and beliefs was temporary, as suggested in the decade's famous fashions that celebrated youth, colorful hyperbole, and a retro-modernist rejection of the past. Youth-culture dress included the clothes of the late-fifties Teddy Boys, privileged Mods, working-class skinheads, psychedelia-wearing hippies, and war protesters

---

2. The feminization of religion, starting around 1800 in America and in Britain, bears a fascinating chronological correlation with the feminization of fashion—a topic for another book.

in jeans and donkey jackets. All these styles were shocking, off-putting, and unwearable to Pym's and Spark's generation, as shown in the memories of Pym's Letty:

> The immediate post-war years were fixed in her memory by the clothes she had worn on particular dates—the New Look brought in by Dior in 1947, the comfortable elegance of the fifties, and in the early sixties the horror of the mini-skirt, such a cruel fashion for those no longer young. (*Quartet* 26)

Certainly the miniskirt's inventor, Mary Quant, deliberately intended to reject the past and oldster style by inculcating a postmodern playfulness: "I wanted everyone to retain the grace of a child," Quant recalled, "and not have to become stilted, ugly beings" (Lobenthal 11). The youth revolution was neo-Romantic, like much of sixties culture, and Romanticism always has revered childhood. But setting up youth as a stylistic goal for "everyone" is, like privileging the working class, an oxymoronic project. Miniskirts, hot pants, jeans, and hippie fashions were unsustainable because youth itself is unsustainable.

Certain elements of sixties style did linger, including the decade's egalitarian eschewal of couture. The drop in the purchase of exclusive designer clothing, unlike the dive in church adherence, began gradually. Dior had marketed his ideas and name to companies that sold expensive, off-the-peg clothing and accessories throughout the fifties (Thomas 29, 32). The late fifties also saw the beginnings of street fashion, which accelerated the waning of Parisian influence (Lobenthal 18; Hulanicki 53). And from the start in 1961, Quant mass-produced her fashions, advocating availability for all women (Quant 117). Exclusive high-fashion clothing was seen as old-fashioned: "Ça fait même," Brigette Bardot remarked, paraphrased by Valerie Steele as "That's for grannies" (*Paris Fashion* 278). Couture also was seen as classist: Barbara Hulanicki, founder of the style-setting boutique Biba, recalled traditional fashion shows as being "all about making you desire something you couldn't have." But her scorn extended this analysis to gender politics: "The couture was for kept women" (Lobenthal 20–21). The idea that women's fashionable dress proclaims their men's spending power, and therefore the dependent status of females, had been proposed by fashion critics from Thorstein Veblen to Germaine Greer, but never in such succinct terms—and in this case by an actual fashion designer. So couture was not only snobbish but sexist. Yet these young designers' stances seemed oxymoronic too, for what can it mean when the couturiers themselves reject couture?

It means, initially, that dress mavens recognized a dead-end quality in fashion, if it is tied to ceaseless innovation. Late modernity increased not only the speed of change but the challenge of finding something new. As Alex Cain reminds us, "a fashion comes but once; a fashion 'revival' is not the same thing repeated, one cannot step into the same fashion twice" (Furbank and Cain 214). Hence, revivals become briefer and ever more ironic over time. Where then can fashion designers and patrons of fashion go for freshness? Jeremy Gilbert-Rolfe has speculated that once fashion has no more barriers to overcome, like postmodern art it can only "[flirt] with transgression"—and, luckily for the clothing industry, fashion's role is playful rather than serious (91). The revivals and recapitulations of late-modern dress styles resemble literary revivals in the later twentieth century, except that the problem of meaning is no problem for recycled fashion, so long as it remains a game. Literature, however, despite its growing eclecticism, continued to feel a discursive onus.

For Spark and for Pym, the playful flux of styles created a conundrum: writing about dress styles, as opposed to merely wearing them, begs the question. If the body that fashion adorns ultimately is trivial, then a literature that depicts dress styles must spell that out. As Hollander pointed out, dress worries idealists:

> In their perpetual irksome worldliness, their common visibleness so inescapably attached to every body, ordinary clothes seem to drag at all the lofty aspirations of man.... The fiction that they are not important is thus generated out of an inability to deal easily with that intractable importance itself. Serious people, aspirers to unworldliness, devotees of the importance of things-not-seen, are particularly unhappy with the idea of clothes and especially with the phenomenon of fashion—the thing that makes clothes need to change their looks and thus stay persistently worldly. (*Seeing* 450)

In the postmodern age, when everything is permitted, the value and meaning of clothing becomes—ironically—an even more urgent issue. If the body matters, then clothing matters. And yet, if clothing must change and be changed with regularity, what does fashion's mutability say of the body?

Perhaps it says that we will die. In describing idealist philosophy's fear of fashion, Karen Hanson points out that not only is the Platonic philosopher distanced from physical desire and "other attentions . . . to our bodies" such as "smart clothes and shoes and other bodily ornaments," but Immanuel Kant's aesthetic categories are challenged by dress: "if, as Kant says, the satisfaction determined by the beautiful is unrelated to inclination, then one who would judge some fashionable dress beautiful will clearly have to cope with some difficult problems of desire" (65). Clothing testifies to our embodiment; fashionable clothing, "defined by *changing* desire, may cover the changing, always aging human body, but may also—in its very transitoriness—uncover, or underscore, that fact of mortality" (66). Stylish dress does not, of course, raise such serious thoughts for most people, most of the time—but eventually it did, for Spark and for Pym.

These middle-aged novelists became all too aware of mutability and mortality: traditional Britain as they knew it was at an end, for which the constant, playful fashion cycle provided a vivid image. Moreover, by the standards of their upbringings each woman had failed, since she had not achieved a permanent, happy marriage. Consequently, Pym's later novels seem to lose interest (as, perhaps, did her culture) in marriage-plot conclusions—an idea that Spark seemed to reject early on. Nevertheless, from the perspective of the new cultural protests, neither woman was sufficiently liberated from the chains of the past. The popular philosophy of the day was existentialism, celebrating individual choice and freedom. But Spark and Pym concentrated on older, Cartesian questions: do I exist if no one observes me? Accordingly, they began to write about single women whose dress captures a dilemma even more fundamental than longings for love and community. The very act of dressing acknowledges embodiment; if that act is attended by a desire to dress fashionably, it then is "somehow, somewhat, influenced by the dynamics of others' desires" (Hanson 68). But what if no one sees me, if my dress impinges on no one's desires? This was the quandary, of style and the single girl, now faced by Pym and Spark.

Two tropes dominate the novels examined in this chapter: first, an especially modern version of glamour; second, the ancient tradition of the femme fatale. *Glamour* was taken from Scots dialect by Sir Walter Scott, to signify an enticing bewitchment; however, by the early twentieth century, it indicated a slightly sinister feminine beauty: "Goodness, her glamour!" says Celia Ryder, of the noblewoman who will destroy her marriage (Waugh, *Brideshead* 240). The concept is ageless, but modern glamour incorporates peculiarly aestheticized elements. "Glamour is a coming to terms with loss," writes Judith Brown, "the loss of the ability to feel, among other things—and the reformulation of feeling within literature" (16). Brown associates glamour with "the impersonal style that modernism promoted": beyond aestheticism, beyond good and evil (7), like those lovely but savage girls of slender means. This objective separation of beauty from ethics has been described differently by Gilbert-Rolfe, who formulates the glamorous as "a secularized beauty . . . which in effect suspends the idealisms of power" (72). Loss, amorality (not immorality), and a powerful vulnerability: thus glamour naturally undergirds the postmodern femme fatale.

The deadly seductress is hardly a new image in literature. From Homer's many dangerous females to the biblical Delilah and Eve herself, a fear of dangerous female allure lies deep in human tradition. But modernist impersonality, leading into postmodern flux, made the glamorous single woman a key figure for Spark and for Pym. One might think, in the age of psychedelic flower-power and liberated women, that the femme fatale would be old-fashioned: "ça fait même." And in fact, the femme fatale's retro quality may be part of her menace in the postmodern world. Her glamour implies an ageless, classic fascination: Miss Jean Brodie approvingly quotes Walter Pater on the Mona Lisa, "She is older than the rocks on which she sits" (*Prime* 21). Miss Brodie does not repeat the Aesthetic master's next words, "like the vampire, she has been dead many times" (Pater, *Studies in the History of the Renaissance* 118), nor does she note the tragic implications for the woman herself, implications that inform this chapter's two novels.

Spark and Pym turn the deadly female inside-out. The seductress usually has been regarded as an object, but what happens when we enter her subjectivity? As film noir has shown repeatedly, the femme fatale's dangerous lures signal loss, not only for those who encounter her but also for herself. Moreover, of particular interest to these writers, the femme fatale hovers on the line of singleness: her power depends upon her possible availability. As a solitary woman, she is defined—even more than by beauty—by her enticing style, and rarely pitied because she is feared. Yet what does it mean, for one's identity to depend upon one's style? Clothing is self-staging, as Hollander reminds us (*Seeing* 315), and especially provident for a solitary person's self-image. If a woman is characterized by her style, what happens when her appearance has no impact? Or is a naïve, pre-Cartesian view of the self the single girl's only recourse? Both Spark's sociopathic Lise and Pym's aging Leonora confront these questions. These protagonists exhibit the two seemingly opposed aspects of glamour: shocking and dangerous or graceful and ageless. The traditionally glamorous woman had endeavored to make herself a thing of beauty, and Angela Carter claimed that the free-wheeling sixties updated that goal: "Style means the presentation of the self as a three-dimensional art object, to be wondered at and handled" (86). But it is a fatal goal, as Lise and Leonora show. Both the glamorous ends of style and the revolutionary promises of the sixties are undercut by the conditions of feminine singleness that persist in the postmodern world.

DRESSING FOR DEATH IN *THE DRIVER'S SEAT*

The Driver's Seat (1970) was born of a news story Spark read about a German tourist, garishly dressed, who was found in a park in Rome, tied up, raped, and stabbed to death. Oddly, the victim seemed deliberately to have provoked her own murder (Stannard 364). In Spark's re-visioning, the death-seeking Lise is not a seductive Delilah or sultry Mata Hari: her gaudy clothing startles everyone who sees her, Lise herself "is neither good-looking nor bad-looking," and she flatly tells men not to expect sex with her (18, 103, 106). Glamour resides in the unnamed southern European city she travels to, not in the woman herself. Nevertheless Lise is a femme fatale, both magnetic and frightening to men—and fatal to herself.

Spark herself, in later life, had turned from love affairs to a peaceful domestic existence with a female companion. Perhaps she did not reject marriage, but Stannard points out that she remained single despite opportunities to remarry (292–93). Even before entering the Roman Catholic church, Spark had publically written that "there is at present too little respect, and often a great deal of ignorant know-all contempt displayed towards celibacy" ("Does Celibacy Affect Judgment?" 10), and she showed an unusual predilection for writing about communities of women, not only in *The Prime of Miss Jean Brodie* and *The Girls of Slender Means* but in *The Abbess of Crewe* (1974). Still, as she moved from place to place, between publishers and between agents, the majority of her friends were men. Sometimes she maintained romantic or semiromantic relationships but, like Pym in later life, some of her closest friends were homosexual men.

Spark also grew more fashion-conscious as the years passed. She always had liked clothing, but her growing success was reflected in more stylish dress, to the point of a reinvented self. Stannard describes how, after reading a published interview where she was described as fortyish, plump, motherly, and buff-suited, the author remade herself as stylish and slender: from then on, her public persona was "dressed to kill" (215). Certainly various old friends and acquaintances recalled meeting and failing to recognize her after a space of years (282, 384); in 1971, the ever-tactless Philip Toynbee observed that Spark was very different "from the dumpy Bohemian girl" he used to know (Stannard 378). The many photographs of Spark in her fifties and sixties show a woman who appears unbelievably younger than her age, and also younger than her "fortyish," "motherly" self. She used clothing to present herself as her own work of art, as Angela Carter claimed typified sixties style; in fact, as Stannard reminds us, Spark followed in a long tradition of dandyism (241). Like Dorothy Sayers thirty years before, Spark may have closed herself off from emotional involvement as she learned to enjoy the performative power of the dandy's self-display. For Spark, however—unlike Sayers—dandy dress meant an ultra-expensive, high-fashion femininity, including dramatic jewelry and couture. In fact, Spark embraced glamour as a "reborn" single girl, styling herself cannily for the public.

Readers sensed glamour in Spark's writing style too. Her novels became ever more svelte and precisely executed: in *The Driver's Seat*, a limited-omniscient narrator coolly presents Lise's grim holiday. Lise dresses for, and plans, her own death—perhaps the ultimate version of a knowing dédoublement. There is something akin to fashion in the smooth, slippery surfaces of this fiction, and something akin to bright, shocking, plastic sixties styles in Lise's experiences as well as her outfits. Certainly Spark herself thought so: she gained publicity for *The Driver's Seat*, which she considered her best novel, through fashion-magazine interviews (Stannard 374, 365). If glamour inheres in Lise's unnamed holiday environment—probably an Italian city, perhaps Rome—she presumably chooses it as the necessary setting for her self-planned murder. Likewise, she needs certain clothes. The narrative opens with Lise dress shopping. She has donned a dress with "green and purple squares on a white background, with blue spots within the green squares, cyclamen spots within the purple." Lise terms the combination "lovely colors," but the narrator seems to concur with the bored salesgirl: it is "too-vivid" and therefore on the sale rack (8, 9). But it is the salesgirl's assurance that "the material doesn't

FIGURE 10. Muriel Spark, circa 1963: her own work of art. (Photo by Popperfoto/Getty Images).

stain" (7) that opens a wide gulf between Lise and the reader: Spark's protagonist reacts with outrage, pulling the dress off hastily and throwing it on the floor, accusing the shop girl of assuming she spills food on herself. In fact, she does not want "that new stain-proof" material for mysterious reasons of her own. She continues searching for "the necessary dress" (10). Eventually she buys one with a "lemon-yellow top with a skirt patterned in bright Vs of orange, mauve and blue"; despite the salesgirl's protest, she pairs it with a "summer coat w/narrow stripes, red and white, with a white collar" (11). Lise's purchases are not high-fashion couture, although from expensive shops. Class is no longer clearly marked by dress style, just as elegance is no longer a fashion option: Lise occupies a culture that eschews both. Her chosen outfits are shocking in being extreme, unsuccessful current styles, and because even for the times, the combinations she chooses seem to clash. Lise obstinately maintains that the colors "go together perfectly.... If only you knew! These colours are a natural blend for me. Absolutely natural" (12).

Why the garish styles? If Jean Brodie's red-poppy dress was "just right for [her] colouring," Lise's startling style is appropriate for her story. Bill, the macrobiotic disciple and the least perceptive of the men Lise encounters, calls her clothing "psychedelic" (31), a pop term for hallucinatory, patterned colors and one that often was applied to late-sixties and early-seventies styles. Lise does alarm people and get attention with her style; thus she affirms both her existence and her free will. More specifically, her clashing colors are a visual non sequitur, the imagistic equivalent of Jean Brodie's enchanting lessons—the sign of her unbalanced inner self and the enactment of a coming collision.

For why would she want a dress that stains? Usually astute readers assume that she wants the blood to show after she is killed. But this is a multiple non sequitur, since Lise will not be present to appreciate the aftermath—unless she can objectify herself so extremely as to enjoy the prospect of her murderer's prosecution, in advance. Certainly the new "stain-proof" material offers a problematic image for the polyester sixties. It is a world ruled by artifice under the guise of nature—like the Scandinavian furniture in Lise's modern apartment, which signifies that the "swaying tall pines" "have been subdued into . . . obedient bulks" (15). The natural is destroyed to make the natural look, like the garish colors that Lise insists are "absolutely natural" for her. But there is nothing more natural than blood, and nothing harder to subdue into art or, indeed, to bottle up again. In courting her own death, she chooses ironically, ridiculously, to embrace the trope of the *femme* who is fatal to herself.

The question of why Lise wants to be murdered, why she plots her own killing, lies just under the text's surface, never quite acknowledged. It is evident that she is odd and unbalanced: she frightens her coworkers and boss, and she has had a breakdown in the past (9–10). Her holiday trip is structured like a modern marriage-plot novel: a single girl's solo trip to an exotic destination might, in Mary Stewart's novels of the fifties and sixties, conclude with romance. Yet from the moment she steps on the airplane Lise is looking, not for her ideal lover, but for her ideal killer. The narrative is propelled by the parodic question, "Who's the lucky guy?" Lise tells Mrs. Fiedke, her newfound elderly friend, that she expects to meet her boyfriend: "He knows I've come all this way to see him. He knows it, all right" (69). Mrs. Fiedke, a kind, vague old lady, sees nothing strange about this young woman. They shop together, Lise buying scarves and neckties which she will provide to her murderer to tie her up with (66). They discuss the extremes of hippie and youth culture, and Lise complains about men: "Too much self-control, which arises from fear and timidity. . . . They're cowards, most of them" (71). To which the old lady concurs, in a remarkable misanthropic speech:

> They [men] are demanding equal rights with us . . . perfume, jewelry, hair down to their shoulders. . . . There was a time when they would stand up and open the door for you. They would take their hat off. But they want their equality today. All I say is that if God had intended them to be as good as us he wouldn't have made them different from us, to the naked eye. They don't want to be all dressed alike any more.

She observes a major style shift of the sixties: young men abjuring the traditional dark suit and competing with women to be stylish:

> fur coats and flowered poplin shirts on their backs . . . If we don't look lively . . . they will be taking over the homes and the children, and sitting about having chats while we go and fight to defend them and work to keep them. (71)

Mrs. Fiedke's upside-down rhetoric is broadly funny, almost Dickensian. But her monologue underlines Lise's upside-down feminism: she wants to sit in "the driver's seat," to rule her own life and death—and she does, twice, take the wheel and hijack a man's car. Yet despite her mod clothing, Lise despises the "timidity" of modern egalitarianism; she seeks a traditional man, which means one who will kill her. After fending off advances from various men who aren't "her type," the young man Lise fixes on is as traditional as Mrs. Fiedke could wish: in fact, he is Mrs. Fiedke's nephew and he wears a dark business suit (100). The shocking twist upon traditional gender expectations is echoed in Lise's startling psychedelic dress—and in her horrifying end, which satirically demonstrates the death of traditional single girls.

Do Lise's deliberate choices affirm her freedom? Certainly her careful plans slip at the end. Malcolm Bradbury saw the novel as a triumph, for her and for her creator:

> Lise's victory is that in the chaotic run of the present she has always known a future.... Miss Spark's victory ... lies in her art of narrative outwitting, her refusal of the humanistic novel, but also of the ostensible contingency of the *nouveau roman,* showing that even in a plotless world there is a plot. (277)

Like Jean Brodie, Lise is shown only from without; even the narrator remarks, "Who knows her thoughts? Who can tell?" (50). And her name, like her mysterious, impenetrable inner self, suggests that she is a postmodern version of the Mona Lisa, revered both by Walter Pater and by Jean Brodie as the ultimate example of a woman made into art, ancient and vampiric. Indeed a self-aestheticizer, Lise casually creates stories about herself for the delectation of various individuals (76, 77, 91). And for the general public she makes herself a psychedelic art-object, seemingly with perfect success.

But she slips from object to subject at the end, and back again, when her chosen murderer, the young man that she seems to prey upon, rapes her. In this upside-down world, Lise's insistence on her autonomy, on inventing and starring in her own story, has been chillingly convincing, though she is literally a victim. And in fact, she does not get her own way, which is why Gerard Carruthers has termed Lise's rape and killing the "darkest moment in all Spark's fiction" (83). Even the girl who "asks for it," who wants the most derogating, abject treatment offered by the other sex, cannot get what she wants, it seems. "She told me to kill her and I killed her," the culprit explains to the police—not mentioning the sexual assault (107).

The femme fatale brings death to her followers, but also to herself. Therefore *The Driver's Seat* concludes with the words "fear and pity, pity and fear," the proper response to a tragedy propelled by a flawed central figure. But it is also the proper response to a deadly self-aestheticization, reminding us that no woman is purely an object—until she is dead. Murder truly and finally objectifies a human being, and so Lise's quest for her own murder equates to a horrific postmodern self-objectification. Did Lise get what she wanted? Who can tell?

Why does Spark show an increasing grimness in her stylish-spinster fictions, and what is she saying about the project of self-aestheticization? It is a dangerous modern undertaking, and a deadly postmodern one. In *Miss Jean Brodie*, Sandy serves as successful objectifier and moral center—albeit an uneasy one, in retreat from the world. *The Girls of Slender Means* also have their outside observer, Nicholas the martyr, who like Sandy is fascinated by self-styling but also impelled by its amorality to retreat from the world of male-female relations. In *The Driver's Seat*, there is no one to convert, no one to serve as moral center, only blank tragedy. Spinsters, nuns, monks, like classic style, are becoming obsolete: we are left with an inevitable murder and a plausible end for one postmodern stylish single girl.

GLAMOUR IN PYM'S *THE SWEET DOVE DIED*

To move from Spark's mentally disturbed, psychedelic Lise to Pym's elegant Leonora is to oscillate between two spinsters, each a type of the femme fatale. Moderns would not have believed a spinster could be glamorous, but they feared her type because of her lacks, which presumably stimulated certain raging desires. Thus the late-modern spinster segues easily into the fearsome femme fatale: no longer a virtuous or dowdy single girl, she still alarms because she uses her attractions to enigmatic ends. The shocking Lise spells ruin for the men she meets, while courting her own death, but the graceful Leonora is fatal only to herself. Very different from Pym's previous protagonists, Leonora is a middle-aged woman who has constructed a perfect solitary life. She attracts and befriends the antique dealer Humphrey and his handsome nephew James, but Leonora avoids

Humphrey's romantic advances while drawing the malleable James into her polished existence. She easily vanquishes her ostensible competition for the young man's affections, his gauche literary girlfriend Phoebe. Eventually, however, she loses James to the predatory American Ned. In the end, Leonora refuses either to take James back or to contemplate a fuller relationship with Humphrey. With seeming complacency, she resumes her beautiful solitude. Yet her obsessive, objective self-regard—like her cool elegance—as surely as Lise's murder signifies the logical end of traditional gender expectations and therefore of the single girl.

A few earlier Pym protagonists had been attractive and well-dressed, but none so exquisite. And no other Pym spinster finally professes to have no desire for love or even companionship—an attitude that goes against the very grain of most Pym novels. Yet while she may appear to use her glamour on the vulnerable James, Leonora ultimately harms only herself. Attractive but sterile, in her black lace dresses and elegant chiffon scarves she dresses for death as surely as, if less deliberately than, Spark's Lise. Leonora's clothing, like that of Jean Brodie, repeatedly is associated with autumn; even the same Keats poem is invoked ("season of mists and mellow fruitfulness," 47, 107, 154), but with more heavy irony, since Leonora has no interest in erotic fruitfulness. This stylish spinster's autumnal state links her glamour with death.

As befits the femme fatale, however, she appears dangerous to others. The title alludes to a short Keats poem mischievously quoted by Ned:

> I had a dove and the sweet dove died;
> And I have thought it died of grieving:
> O, what could it grieve for? Its feet were tied,
> With a silken thread of my own hand's weaving.... (*Sweet* 146; Keats
>   ll. 1–4)

Leonora is obscurely troubled by the lines, but she does not recognize that the poem describes her relations with James: "Why, pretty thing! would you not live with me? / I kiss'd you oft and gave you white peas" (Keats ll. 8–9). Surrounded by references to death, she fails to recognize it as the natural end of her style. Thus *The Sweet Dove Died* differs markedly from Pym's earlier, sharply observed but genial novels. Her faithful fan Philip Larkin saw that "there's more potential *feeling* in this book than in any you have written" (*Selected Letters* 406). Indeed there was, since the novel was the complex product of three painful, multiyear evolutions in Pym's personal world: personal, professional, and cultural.

As she moved into her fifties, Pym seemed to accept that she would remain a spinster, like one of her own characters. She had no more full-fledged love affairs, though she continued to experience emotional attachments. Like Spark, she maintained close friendships with men who were homosexual or confirmed bachelors, sharing her interests in literature, food, and churches. Yet she also acknowledged the inadequacy of the "something to love" philosophy celebrated in her very first novel. Reciprocity was, she had learned, more important than it seemed in her youth. "Perhaps to be loved is the most cozy thing in life," she mused privately, "and yet many people, women I suppose I mean, know only the uncertainties of loving" (Very 192: 28 October 1955). She had missed marriage; she was not concerned with spinsterhood's societal stigma—which, after all, was lessening—but recognized that the very coziness she cherished might be hard to sustain in a single life. In odd ways, *The Sweet Dove Died* explores and explodes the possibilities, first of a happy one-way devotion, as proposed in *Some Tame Gazelle*, and then of a satisfied solitary existence.

The Sweet Dove fictionalizes Pym's painful emotional affair with Richard Roberts, a handsome young antique dealer that she met in the early sixties. Roberts was homosexual, as Pym knew, but she persisted in hoping that loving her "dearest Skipper" might be a sufficiently satisfying experience in itself. When inevitably it was not, Roberts proving less devoted than she, Pym was deeply unhappy. In her notebook jottings, she exhorted herself "not to take 'things' so much to heart ... don't stop loving (can't), just be there if and when needed," but she also admitted the hidden "fury and bitterness" evoked by their inconsistent relations (Very 235: 29 May 1965, 24 May 1965). Her humorous spinsters could put up with such lukewarm affairs, but Pym was not as meek and detached as her fictional characters. Nor was she the elegant, self-centered Leonora, and "Skipper" was not the naïve young James. Nevertheless, many elements of *The Sweet Dove* came directly from the real-life relationship, ranging from the world of antiques and auctions, introduced to Pym by Roberts, down to small incidents such as trying to cheer herself, "now Skipperless" and after a dental visit, with a "delicious creamy cake tasting of walnuts." Better, she comments drily, "to write the kind of novel that tells of one day in the life of such a woman" (Very 238: 26 September 1966). In fact she already had christened her protagonist, and nearly from the start, despite her emotional upheavals, was jotting notes: "If 'they' went to Covent Garden Leonora would like to feel the touch of his sleeve against her bare arm (but that would be as far as it would go)" (*Very* 227: 1 May 1964). A part of Pym always stood aside, objectifying her experiences as grist for fiction's mill.

Over a decade would pass, however, before *The Sweet Dove Died* appeared in print. Pym's biographer writes that by the sixties, "her books had replaced her love affairs as the chief preoccupation of her life" (Holt 193). If so, the substitution was cold comfort, for Pym's long professional hiatus began at this time. After six well-received novels (1950–61), she had been stunned when Jonathan Cape firmly rejected her newest manuscript on the grounds of its likely unprofitability. She sent it to other publishers, only to have it repeatedly turned down; she revised and resubmitted, to no effect. Rejection, in love or in literature, was equally painful, as she mused: "To receive a bitter blow on an early Spring evening (such as that Cape don't want to publish *An Unsuitable Attachment*—but it might be that someone doesn't love you any more)" (*Very* 215: 24 March 1963). Like Jean Rhys, Pym would disappear from the public eye so completely that some fans assumed she was dead (*Very* 307). Unlike Rhys, she persistently endeavored to publish throughout her approximately fifteen years of silence.

Soon Pym put aside the rejected manuscript and began the "Leonora" novel. From 1963 to 1969, she again wrote, rewrote, submitted and resubmitted—all without success. She considered numerous titles, including "A Younger Man," "Prisoners and Captives," "Grapes in the House," "The Triumph of Leonora," "Marble Men," and "The Pyrrhic Victory," some suggesting that she had not yet determined her narrative's conclusion. "An Object of Virtue" is the heading affixed to one manuscript; another title page presents "Leonora by Tom Crampton" (Pym Papers 29). Ironically, having realized that her comedies of manners were out of fashion, Pym tried, like Victorian women, submitting her novels under a male pseudonym. Even in 1969–70 she continued revising *The Sweet Dove*'s plot and themes rather drastically. Originally set partially in a village, and including a central confrontation between the excellent woman Rose Culver and the city-bred Leonora, the narrative eventually lost most of its village scenes and characters. Leonora was reshaped from a "formidable" woman with "handsome features" to the exquisite last gasp of Victoriana at the center of the published novel. A new sort of Pym woman, Leonora still seemed not sufficiently up-to-date for publishers.

Pym received several complimentary turn-downs, emphasizing the novel's perfect taste—"so you can see what is wrong," she commented ironically (Holt 221). Like Leonora herself, Pym's writing was too tasteful for the sixties, an era summed up by designer Mary Quant's exuberant motto, "Good taste is death, vulgarity is life" (Lobenthal 13).

And perhaps Pym's good taste might have been the death of her novel-writing career, had not Philip Larkin and Lord David Cecil simultaneously praised her fiction to the *Times Literary Supplement* in 1977. By that point, Pym had written yet two more unpublished novels. After she was puffed as the most neglected novelist of the twentieth century, the ensuing stampede of contrite publishing houses saw all of Pym's six earlier novels reprinted, plus two of her four additional manuscripts published before her death in 1980. *The Sweet Dove Died* appeared in 1978 to high praise from reviewers, although Pym observed that, unusually for her fiction, "more men reviewers than women seem to have liked it" (Pym Papers 162/2: folio 126). All sorts of things were unusual, however, about these final novels.

While her emotional and professional sufferings of the sixties are well documented, less emphasis has been put on the drastic cultural changes that affected Pym's final two decades, changes displayed prominently in her last books. Her loyal fans remain indignant over publishers' rejections of her work in the sixties and early seventies, but editors were right about the shifts in literary taste, though they mistakenly conflated style with content. When it came to content, Pym adjusted. In her last novels, as opposed to her late-modern fiction, she maintained her minimalist writing style, employing telling bits of trivia and comic understatement. But she recognized that the cozy worlds she was known for, the secure villages and insular London parishes, were passing away along with the traditional spinster. In these final novels, few people attend church or profess faith; in *The Sweet Dove*, church is replaced by antique auctions, and religion by Leonora's secular nostalgia for an aesthetically perfect existence. Likewise marriage is less venerated, or even considered as a goal, for a single woman. Yet Pym's lonely individuals—female and male—are more isolated than ever in a world of bell-bottomed androgynous youth, obscene language, and welfare bureaucracies.

Most poignantly, in Pym's last novels the excellent woman herself is passing away. "Beauty is seductive," writes Jeremy Gilbert-Rolfe in his monograph on postmodern aesthetics, "but goodness only productive, the production involved taking the form of a critique of the glamorous" (49).

The good, productive church spinster, by her very existence, critiqued the beautiful single woman—which is why Pym retained one quiet, significant meeting between Miss Culver and Leonora. It is staged as a contest and Leonora wins, at least by dominating the novel. Nevertheless they are ironically equated in a brief exchange between the excellent woman and her glamorous counterpart:

> "The odd thing about men is that one never really knows," said Miss Culver, "Just when you think they're close they suddenly go off."
> Leonora was startled and wondered if she had heard correctly. For a moment the two ageing unmarried women looked at each other in a way that seemed to ask, "What can *you* know of being close to a man?" (118)

Despite cultural shifts, the decorative Leonora and the virtuous Miss Culver share a state and an alienation from men that continued into the later twentieth century: "being close to a man" is unlikely, even for the postmodern single girl. Neither glamour nor goodness can guarantee a stable relationship with the other sex.

Thus Pym's late novel returns us to pivotal issues for style and the single girl: the gendering of fashion, which widens to query the gendering of beauty, and that foundational question, what is the spinster stylish *for*? Regarding the first, it might seem that the feminization of fashion was over, since sixties styles proffered dramatic shapes and bright colors not only to women but to the men young or bold enough to wear them. Certainly Leonora's retro-elegance constitutes a struggle to retain the field of beauty for women. Young James is both attractive, with unusual "golden-brown hair and dark eyes" (24), and bisexual: the opening pages mention a "tall man with a slightly raffish air" who eyes him at the auction, making him think that encountering Leonora may have "saved him from a fate worse than death" (8). The comically old-fashioned—and feminizing—phrase initiates the young man's malleable sexuality, emphasized further when Leonora treats him as her pet dove. While entering a cat show Leonora comments, "Just kittens and neuter cats . . . that sounds so cosy, doesn't it?" James protests, "Shall I be the only grown-up male thing there, then?" "Probably, darling," Leonora purrs, "though one doesn't think of you as male, exactly. Not all tweedy and pipe-smoking" (65). In fact, James's dress style is never detailed; Pym deliberately has assigned all glamour to Leonora. For instance, Leonora's L'Heure Bleue, a classic Edwardian scent that signaled sophistication in the twenties and thirties, was worn by Pym herself (*Sweet Dove* 46; Pym Papers 25: 30). But in a notebook jotting Pym identifies the perfume with Skipper, recalling "R. in full beauty on Tuesday night—in peacock blue shirt and smelling strongly of L'heure bleu [sic]—('because you like it').... If only I were the man and he the girl" (Pym Papers 62, Literary notebook XXIII [Aug. 1965–June 1966]). Two elements stand out here: first, the ostentatious reverse gendering of beauty in Pym's jotted memory, in which the young man makes himself an alluring object, brightly dressed and wearing woman's perfume; second, the ways in which, in her real-life uses—that is, her fictionalizing—of these elements, the author stages a competition. One party must be the desirer and the other the desired object; in Pym's notebook analogy, one must be "the man" and the other "the girl." Both cannot be glamorous. Therefore in the novel the young man's beauty is not emphasized, and the older woman wears the enticing perfume—suggesting that glamour is inherently feminine. Gilbert-Rolfe theorizes about why:

> Where the masculine seems unable to separate itself from the language of power, which obliges it to suspend sexuality in the service of an ideal—hardness and restraint as ideological imperatives—the feminine, fluid and unrestrained, could provide the possibility of a sexualized beauty which we know as the glamorous and which in effect suspends the idealisms of power ... by virtue of its implicit powerlessness. (71–72)

But if feminine sexual beauty is implicitly powerless, its seductions nonetheless may be adopted and employed by either sex, all the more effectively because of their ostensible lack of coercion. Certainly Leonora, like Pym herself, sees glamorous beauty as competitive. Although ostensibly first Phoebe, then Ned, are Leonora's rivals, in reality she competes with James himself—as becomes clear in the novel's conclusion. For if a woman's love for a homosexual man is, as Janice Rossen has observed, the most extreme Pym example of male indifference to women's sexual attractiveness (*World* 64–65),[3] those neglected attractions must be stressed.

---

3. Most obviously, in *A Glass of Blessings* (1958) the fashionable, bored young wife Wilmet becomes fascinated with good-looking, mysterious Piers and believes that Piers is attracted to her. But in that comic scenario, everyone but Wilmet, including the reader, sees Piers's sexual inclinations before she does—and only Wilmet's vanity is hurt.

What, then, are those attractions for? The question of why the spinster is stylish overshadows *Sweet Dove* more than any of the previously discussed texts. While self-aestheticization appears risky in several Spark novels, it constitutes an unlikely danger for most of Pym's humble, socialized excellent women. But Leonora consciously regards herself as a beautiful object not for everyday use. She covets James's fruitwood mirror with cupids because in its wavy old glass her face appears "fascinating and ageless" (87), a Mona Lisa. She competes with Phoebe to borrow the mirror and gets it. Phoebe, the opposite of a glamorous woman, always is characterized by being badly dressed, but James initiates meetings and even sex with her (41, 44, 60). He and Leonora, on the other hand, read sale catalogs together, and for Leonora the "seductive descriptions" of beautiful pieces equate to an aesthetic love-making: "the poetry of the phrases flowed over her in a delightful confusion so that she hardly knew what was being described, only that it was something exquisitely desirable, and that this was being another of their 'lovely evenings'" (52). In actuality, Leonora is herself an exquisite antique: when James observes "some new lines on her beautiful neck," he thinks of her as "some old fragile object that needed careful handling" (69). It is a perspective that James's uncle Humphrey misses. In a comic scene at Leonora's house, she wears green chiffon to match her crème de menthe aperitif. But as Humphrey makes a pass at her, his hand, "so accustomed to appraising objects of art and of vertu" (92), rips the shoulder seam of her dress—a doubly horrifying event for Leonora. No more than Spark's Lise does she enjoy "*that* kind of thing" (16). So it is thoroughly appropriate that the enterprising Ned, Leonora's highly sexual rival, eyes her in an "appraisal . . . completely lacking in sexuality or desire"—and that under Ned's influence, James reclaims his fruitwood mirror (144–45, 182).

Whereas most stylish spinsters and single girls discomfit their observers, who suspect that frustrated desires lie beneath the surface, the spinster's supposed fear of sexuality ironically is confirmed in the lovely Leonora. Her cold self-aestheticization crowns a sequence in which learning to dress for oneself, not for men, concludes in solipsism. As a woman who lived through the prewar years, Leonora's experiences evoke all our earlier single girls. Where Harriet Vane saw how the thirties' retrospective dress styles suggest a deliberate costume for catching men, Leonora recalls expecting to fall in love—but "something had invariably been not quite right" (195). Like Rhys's women, she values her furs, but not to impress men so much as because she likes the sensuous feel herself (22). And as she sees both James and her beauty slipping away, she—like the betrayed and dying Miss Brodie—"huddle[s] into her fur coat, feeling herself debased, diminished" (*Sweet Dove* 184). The encounter with Miss Culver had suggested that the femme fatale, no less than the excellent woman, is a spinster liable to disappointment from men. Certainly Leonora is not a standard Pym spinster. "No Bible, no book of devotion" mars "the worldly charm of her bedside table" (17), and she feels insulted when a well-meaning acquaintance suggests that she fill her days with good "voluntary works" (177). She gets rid of her saintly boarder Miss Foxe (50) and disdains the idea of being "like the people who fill the emptiness of their lives" with a pet (188). Even Keats's poetry does not truly interest Leonora.

Above all, Leonora represents the demise of a standard fictional trajectory: every other Pym novel concludes with a possibility, if not of love and marriage, at least of a companionable connection with another human being. But *Sweet Dove* embalms and buries the marriage plot: while Pym's earlier fictions ironize it, they leave the door open for a possible traditional happy ending in the future. We know Leonora will never marry. Her friend Meg advises, "You mustn't expect things to be perfect" (202), but Leonora does require perfection. And so, when James attempts to reconcile with her, she turns him away. If James proves no objet d'art to be bought and possessed, she nonetheless aims to maintain herself as a perfected object.

This novel's very narrative style ironically creates a serene, distanced text akin to Leonora's cool, exquisite clothing. Most strikingly, Leonora's thoughts of herself employ third-person pronouns throughout the novel. At first the reiterated "one" suggests her elegant old-fashioned persona, but eventually the habit creates a discomfiting objectified rhetoric. She uses "one" to distance herself from the thought of death: "Yet there was no reason why one's death should not, in its own way, be as elegant as one's life" (18). She uses it to distance herself from compassion, saying of elderly Miss Foxe, "One has to be tough with old people . . . otherwise they *encroach*" (50). But she also employs the pronoun to avoid self-knowledge. In the novel's conclusion, she coolly considers James's request for reconciliation: "One did forgive James, of course; one was, or saw oneself as being, that kind of person" (207). In the end, the crestfallen James departs and Leonora observes the ever-hopeful Humphrey arriving with a large bunch of flowers. In the novel's concluding lines, Pym builds her *ones* into a triumphant crescendo: The Chelsea Flower Show, Leonora thinks,

> was the kind of thing *one* liked to go to, and the sight of such large and faultless blooms, so exquisite in colour, so absolutely correct in all their finer points, was a comfort and satisfaction to *one* who loved perfection as she did. Yet, when *one* came to think of it, the only flowers that were really perfect were those, like the peonies that went so well with *one's* charming room, that possessed the added grace of having been presented to *one*self. (208; my emphases)

Perfect beauty in itself is insufficient; it must belong to Leonora, but she only can acknowledge her possessive fervor through objectifying herself, as the "one" who owns the "faultless," the "exquisite," the "correct," "perfect," and "charming" attributes of a beautiful object.

Leonora is not a deathless perfect object, of course, which is why several of Pym's perceptive readers, such as David Cecil and Philip Larkin, found themselves sympathizing with this seemingly cold protagonist (Holt 265–66). Leonora feels hurt, and she even weeps near the end, but she retreats into self-aestheticization, presaging her eventual future as a beautiful dead object. This femme is fatal to herself through her desire to remain "one," for early in the narrative, her sterile bed "with its neo-Victorian" headboard segued into thoughts of death and a private resolution that "one's death" should be elegant too (17–18). She is the ideal impersonal modern single girl in that she dresses for no end and for no one but herself. Yet if glamour means "coming to terms with loss" (J. Brown 16), Leonora suppresses her losses, even to herself. In fact, she combines the scraps of fashion tradition with fading modernist conventions to show the anxieties that persist in women's styles in the postmodern world.

GLAMOROUS ENDS

Leonora's deadly good taste and Lise's dressing for death suggest a grim postmodern prognosis for style and the single girl. After the blithe stylistic independence demonstrated by some of Sayers's and Spark's women, combined with Rhys's admonitory illustrations of what happens to women who dress for men, we might expect better. But the chief question of the stylish spinster was, Why dress at all? Lise's reply is, So that you will track my progress into death; Leonora answers, In order to be a perfectly beautiful object. In both cases we are reminded that, even in postmodern glamour, the femme fatale intends to attract the gaze of others, particularly men, even if she has no interest in more intimate relations with them. And the very project of dressing with style cannot escape that inevitable end, a link with others.

Yet, while these highly stylized novels are not optimistic about prospects for their single girls, their very creation provided an aesthetic answer, beyond the self, for their writers—who were not confined to the pages of a book. Spark herself learned to self-aestheticize, rather surprisingly, around the time that she shut herself off from marriage, in the non-elegant postmodern era of Lise's psychedelic dress. Like Miss Brodie she was past her prime, in a time that worshiped youth—like the speaker in W. B. Yeats's "Sailing to Byzantium," which is about making oneself into art, in lieu of authentic human relations and in response to aging. Spark's later books grew more stylish and more bland, because the substance (as she saw it) had gone out of society. Yet she also seems to have been aware of the personal cost of the project, and now that she is gathered "into the artifice of eternity" (Yeats l. 24) we might term Spark herself the most stylish of her spinsters.

Pym had further resources. She was less Leonora than Miss Foxe, who puzzles her elegant neighbor by cheerfully retiring to an Anglican priory. Pym also bore a relation to the awkward but literary Phoebe, using writing to analyze, distance, and laugh at her own inclinations. When Larkin published "Aubade," his famous poem about lying alone at night fearing death, Pym wrote to him with admiration, seasoned with her own brand of pragmatic cheerful sense. "But when I wake in the small hours I don't think of death," she remarked. "I always try to switch my thoughts to something frivolous like clothes or planning a scene in a novel" (*Very* 314: 5 March 1978). To say that clothes and fiction writing are "frivolous" is mere self-deprecating, for Pym; in fact, both provided her with opportunity for self-presentation and self-reflection, along with a creative way to express hope beyond death. In *A Few Green Leaves*, completed as she was dying of cancer, Pym depicted an English village passing away: the local gentry have left their manor, and the lonely parish rector Tom presides over a near-empty church while most villagers sit inside watching telly. Emma, dowdy and thirtyish, has moved to the village in order to study it objectively, yet she finds herself drawn into its life and distanced from her anthropological colleagues. In the end, the long-sought traces of a deserted medieval village are uncovered and Emma, attracted to the village and to Tom, has decided to stay: "*She* could write a novel and even, as she was beginning to realize, embark on a love affair which need not necessarily be an unhappy one" (249–50). These concluding words capture Pym's twin interests of writing and love; appearing as they do at the very end of her life, the hesitant negations and qualifiers suggest not doubt but a persistent hope, that love and writing will survive.

CODA

Lasting Modes

THE RICH VARIETY of styles in these women's novels should warn us not to impose a one-size-fits-all theory on either fictions or fashions. As Carolyn Steedman advises, clothes are "ways of dreaming, or imagining *yourself, not others*, in new ways," and therefore the historical meanings of clothes "were those people's—their wearers'—meaning, not ours" (36, 37; emphasis in original). Those meanings may be obscure to us, even ultimately unreadable. After making her persuasive case for the relation of sex to suits, Anne Hollander adds a caveat: "The famous message of dress, the well-known language of clothes, is very often not doing any communicating at all; a good deal of it is a form of private muttering" (*Sex and Suits* 189). There is no one mode for modern fiction, for fashion, or for females; there is no one code that, once broken, yields an absolute answer regarding women's dresses and desires. We should keep in mind Sigmund Freud's fabled remark about his smoking habits: perhaps our styles do betray us, but—just as sometimes a cigar is just a cigar—sometimes a dress is just a dress.

Yet often clothing speaks. As I have argued, these writers re-dressed the modern novel by questioning assumptions about single women, about why women dress the ways they do, and about what women really ask from clothing, of men, and in life. Sayers and Rhys demonstrated the depths beneath the clichés, of dandy dress, of spinster style, and—most poignantly—of the single girl who does dress for men. The exigencies of World War II, which ended high modernism and halted haute couture, leveled styles but did not simplify the language of dress; nor did the war permanently clarify relations between the sexes. Pym and Spark found gendered assumptions still at work in the postwar world; dress, because it is both rhetorical and relational, speaks of their quandaries. Women may laugh at the ways they are objectified and in turn regard men as objects of amusement. More grimly, a single girl may flatly undercut the marriage plot through death, or she may simply adorn herself for herself alone, which constitutes a subtler form of death.

Even *Wide Sargasso Sea* (1966), where Antoinette (Bertha) Rochester enacts Jean Rhys's attack on the traditional marriage plot of *Jane Eyre*, suggests troubling limits to re-dressing the modern novel. *Wide Sargasso*'s conclusion is permeated with references to Antoinette's red dress, "the colour of fire and sunset. The colour of flamboyant flowers" (185). Through her protagonist's wandering thoughts, Rhys evokes the sexualized beauty associated with red but also the denigrating stereotypes of scarlet women as "intemperate and unchaste" (186). Above all, the dress links Antoinette's passionate inner self to the uncontrollable rage that becomes a fiery destruction: "I looked at the dress on the floor and it was as if the fire had spread across the room. It was beautiful and it reminded me of something I must do" (187). But the destruction she brings about is self-destruction: all of Antoinette's attempts to revenge herself upon her husband ironically further *his* marriage plot, his final happy union with Jane Eyre.

In more recent fiction by women, dress still speaks, though in increasingly casual tones. Anita Brookner's *Hotel du Lac* (1984) uses clothing in elaborate ways, as Clair Hughes has delineated.[1] Margaret Atwood's *Robber Bride* (1993) updates the power inequities of Elizabeth Bowen's demon lover but also continues the complexities of women's dress in yet another postmodern femme fatale. Most recently Jane Gardam, in *The Man in the Wooden Hat* (2009), employs a Chinese green-silk dress to capture both

---

1. See *Dressed in Fiction* (Berg, 2006).

her protagonist's sensual rebellion and its neat placement in the past—after her marriage. In fact, whether connected to marriage or not, dress always will be linked to relations with others. Otherwise it is, as Spark and Pym show, deadly.

Finally, as we have seen, writing style and dress style bear more than passing similarities, not least in their statuses as rhetorics. We know all about the marvelous possibilities of literature, and we should acknowledge that clothing too, like the human beings it adorns, and like single girls and spinsters, may contain untold depths. "The English language has a deceptive air of simplicity," remarked Dorothy Sayers. "So have some little frocks; but they are not the kind that any fool can run up in half an hour with a machine" ("The English Language" 89). The potential of dress is that it can say many complicated things, beautifully. The potential of the single girl lies in just that—her continuing potential. Thus Spark's established spinster Greggie remarks that VE Day is "something between a wedding and a funeral" (*Girls of Slender Means* 17), like the lives of all these single women, which afford spaces not of lack but of extraordinarily free choice.

WORKS CITED

References to British *Vogue* and Cyril Connolly's 1939–1949 journal *Horizon* are cited by date and page number within the text.

Allingham, Margery. *The Oaken Heart*. London: Michael Joseph, 1941.

Amis, Kingsley. *Lucky Jim*. 1954. London and New York: Penguin Books, 1992.

Andrade, Susan Z. "Representing Slums and Home: Chris Abari's *Graceland*." *The Legacies of Modernism: Historicising Postwar and Contemporary Fiction*. Ed. David Jones. Cambridge and New York: Cambridge UP, 2012. 225–42.

Angeletti, Norberto, and Alberto Oliva. *In Vogue: The Illustrated History of the World's Most Famous Fashion Magazine*. New York: Rizzolli, 2006.

Angier, Carole. *Jean Rhys: Life and Work*. Boston: Little, Brown, 1990.

Anonymous. "The Wit and Wisdom of George Eliot." *The Spectator* 45.2272 (13 Jan. 1872): 43–44.

Aristophanes. *Aristophanes*. Vol. 1. Loeb Classical Library. Trans. Benjamin Bickley Rogers. Cambridge, MA: Harvard UP, and London: W. Heinemann, 1924.

Arnold, Matthew. "The Study of Poetry." *The Complete Prose Works of Matthew Arnold*. Vol. 9. Ed. R. H. Super. Ann Arbor: The U of Michigan P, 1973. 161–88.

Auden, W. H. "The Guilty Vicarage: Notes on the Detective Story, By an Addict." *Harper's Magazine* (May 1948): 406–12.

———. "September 1, 1939." *Selected Poems*. New ed. Ed. Edward Mendelson. New York: Random House, 1979. 86–89.

Auerbach, Erich. *Mimesis: The Representation of Reality in Western Literature*. 1946. Garden City, NY: Doubleday [Princeton UP], 1953.

Auerbach, Nina. "Dorothy L. Sayers and the Amazons." *Romantic Imprisonment: Women and Other Glorified Outcasts*. New York: Columbia UP, 1985. 184–94.

Austen, Jane. *Mansfield Park*. 1814. New York: Barnes & Noble Classics, 2004.

———. *Northanger Abbey*. 1817. Ed. Barbara M. Benedict and Deirdre LeFaye. Cambridge: Cambridge UP, 2006.

Baker, Niamh. *Happily Ever After: Women's Fiction in Postwar Britain, 1945–60*. New York: St. Martin's Press, 1989.

Barnard, Malcolm. *Fashion as Communication*. London and New York: Routledge, 1996.

———. *Fashion Theory: A Reader*. London and New York: Routledge, 2007.

Barthes, Roland. *The Fashion System*. Trans. Matthew Ward and Richard Howard. New York: Hill & Wang, 1983.

Barzun, Jacques. *From Dawn to Decadence: 500 Years of Western Cultural Life*. New York: Harper Collins, 2000.

Baudelaire, Charles. "De l'essence du rire." *Curiosités Esthéthiques*. Paris: Louis Conard, 1923. 369–96.

———. "La Beauté." *Les fleurs du mal*. Paris: Calmann-Lévy, 1925. 29.

———. "Le peintre de la vie moderne." *L'Art romantique. Oeuvres Complètes*. Vol. III. Paris: Calmann-Lévy, 1925. 51–114.

———. "Le Voyage." *Les fleurs du mal*. Paris: Calmann-Lévy, 1925. 262–69.

Beaton, Cecil. *The Glass of Fashion*. Garden City, NY: Doubleday, 1954.

Beauvoir, Simone de. *Le deuxième sexe*. 1949. Vol. 1. Paris: Gallimard, 1976.

Bell, Josephine. "A Face-to-Face Encounter with Sayers." *Murderess Ink: The Better Half of the Mystery*. Ed. Dilys Winn. New York: Workman, 1979. 55–57.

Bender, Todd K. "Jean Rhys and the Genius of Impressionism." *Studies in the Literary Imagination* 11.2 (Fall 1978): 43–53.

Benjamin, Walter. "The Paris of the Second Empire in Baudelaire." 1938. Trans. Harry Zohn. *The Writer of Modern Life: Essays on Charles Baudelaire*. Ed. Michael W. Jennings. Cambridge, MA, and London: Harvard UP, 2006. 46–133.

Bentley, E. C. *Trent's Last Case*. 1934. New York: Harper & Row, 1978.

Berger, John. *Ways of Seeing*. New York: Viking, 1973.

Bergonzi, Bernard. *Wartime and Aftermath: English Literature and Its Background, 1939–60*. New York: OUP, 1993.

Berrong, Richard M. "Modes of Literary Impressionism." *Genre* 39 (Summer 2006): 203–28.

Blumer, Herbert. "Fashion: From Class Differentiation to Collective Selection." *Sociological Quarterly* 10.2 (Summer 1969): 275–91.

Boone, Joseph Allen. *Tradition Counter Tradition: Love and the Form of Fiction*. Chicago and London: U of Chicago P, 1987.

Booth, Michael R., and Joel H. Kaplan. *The Edwardian Theatre: Essays on Performance and the Stage*. Cambridge and New York: Cambridge UP, 1996.

Boswell, James. *Life of Johnson*. Vol. II. New York: OUP, 1933.

Bowen, Elizabeth. *The Collected Stories of Elizabeth Bowen*. New York: Knopf, 1981.

———. "Contemporary." *The New Statesman and Nation* 23 (23 May 1942): 340.

———. "The Demon Lover." *The Collected Stories*. 661–66.

———. "Dress." *Collected Impressions*. 1937. New York: Alfred A. Knopf, 1950. 111–15.

———. "Green Holly." *The Collected Stories*. 719–27.

———. "Ivy Gripped the Steps." *The Collected Stories*. 686–711.

———. Preface. *Ivy Gripped the Steps and Other Stories*. New York: Knopf, 1946. vii–xiv.

———. "Songs My Father Sang Me." *The Collected Stories*. 650–60.

Bowen, Stella. *Drawn from Life: A Memoir.* London: Collins, 1941.
Bradbury, Malcolm. "Muriel Spark's Fingernails." *No, Not Bloomsbury.* New York: Columbia UP, 1988. 268–78.
Braine, John. *Room at the Top.* Boston: Houghton Mifflin, 1957.
Braybon, Gail, and Penny Summerfield. *Out of the Cage: Women's Experiences in Two World Wars.* London and New York: Pandora, 1987.
Breward, Christopher. *The Hidden Consumer: Masculinities, Fashion and City Life 1860–1914.* Manchester and New York: Manchester UP, 1999.
Brittain, Vera. *Testament of Youth: An Autobiographical Study of the Years 1900–1925.* New York: Macmillan, 1934.
Brown, Callum G. *The Death of Christian Britain: Understanding Secularisation, 1800–2000.* 2nd ed. London and New York: Routledge, 2009.
Brown, Judith. *Glamour in Six Dimensions: Modernism and the Radiance of Form.* Ithaca and London: Cornell UP, 2009.
Buckley, Cheryl, and Hilary Fawcett. *Fashioning the Feminine: Representation and Women's Fashion from the Fin de Siècle to the Present.* London and New York: I. B. Tauris, 2002.
Burstein, Jessica. *Cold Modernism: Literature, Fashion, Art.* University Park: The Pennsylvania State UP, 2012.
Byatt, A. S. "Marginal Lives." *Times Literary Supplement* (8 August 1986): 862.
Calder, Angus. *The People's War: Britain—1939–1945.* New York: Random House, 1969.
Carlyle, Thomas. *Sartor Resartus: The Life and Opinions of Herr Teufelsdröckh in Three Books.* 1833–34. Berkeley and Los Angeles: University of California Press, 2000.
Carruthers, Gerard. "Muriel Spark as Catholic Novelist." *The Edinburgh Companion to Muriel Spark.* Ed. Michael Gardiner and Willy Maley. Edinburgh: Edinburgh UP, 2010. 74–84.
Carter, Angela. "Notes for a Theory of Sixties Style." 1967. *Nothing Sacred: Selected Writings.* London: Virago, 2000. 85–90.
Carter, Michael. *Fashion Classics from Carlyle to Barthes.* Oxford and New York: Berg, 2003.
Caryll, Ivan, and Lionel Monckton. *Our Miss Gibbs: A Musical Play in Two Acts by "Cryptos"* [Adrian Ross and Percy Greenbank]. London: Chappell and Co., 1909.
Cendrars, Blaise. "Sur la robe elle a un corps." 1914. *Poésies Complètes de Blaise Cendrars.* Paris: Les Editions de Noël, 1944. 113.
Chase, Edna Woolman, and Ilka Chase. *Always in Vogue.* Garden City, NY: Doubleday, 1954.
Chesterfield, Philip Dormer Stanhope, Earl of. "Letter CVIII." *The Elements of a Polite Education, Carefully Selected from the Letters of the Late Right Honble Philip Dormer Stanhope, Earl of Chesterfield, to His Son.* London: R. Phillips, 1800. 283–87.
Christie, Agatha. "A Christmas Tragedy." 1928. *Thirteen Problems.* New York: Dodd, Mead, 1973. 146–65.
Cohen, Lisa. "'Frock Consciousness': Virginia Woolf, the Open Secret, and the Language of Fashion." *Fashion Theory* 3.2 (June 1999): 149–74.
Connolly, Cyril. *The Unquiet Grave: A Word Cycle by Palinurus.* New York and London: Harper & Brothers, 1945.

Connolly, Thomas E., ed. *Scribbledehobble: The Ur-Workbook to Finnegans Wake*. Evanston, IL: Northwestern UP, 1961.

Conrad, Joseph. *Heart of Darkness*. 1899. Ed. Ross C. Murfin. 2nd ed. Boston and New York: Bedford/St. Martin's, 1996.

Cotsell, Michael. *Barbara Pym*. New York: St. Martin's P, 1989.

Dale, Alzina Stone, ed. *Dorothy L. Sayers: The Centenary Celebration*. New York: Walker, 1993.

Davis, Fred. "Antifashion." In Barnard, ed. *Fashion Theory*. 89–102.

———. *Fashion, Culture, and Identity*. Chicago and London: The U of Chicago P, 1992.

Delafield, E. M. *The Provincial Lady in Wartime*. New York and London: Harper, 1940.

Dell'Amico, Carol. *Colonialism and the Modernist Moment in the Early Novels of Jean Rhys*. New York and London: Routledge, 2005.

Detmold, Rita. "Frocks and Frills." *The Play Pictorial* 108 (1911): n. pag.

Doan, Laura, ed. *Old Maids to Radical Spinsters: Unmarried Women in the Twentieth Century Novel*. Urbana: University of Illinois Press, 1991.

Donnelly, Mark. *Sixties Britain: Culture, Society and Politics*. Harlow and London: Pearson Education, 2005.

Downing, Crystal. *Writing Performances: The Stages of Dorothy L. Sayers*. New York and Houndsmills, Basingstoke, Hampshire: Palgrave Macmillan, 2004.

Edson, Laura Gwyn. "Kicking Off Her Knickers: Virginia Woolf's Rejection of Clothing as Realistic Detail." *Virginia Woolf and the Arts: Selected Papers from the Sixth Annual Conference on Virginia Woolf*. Ed. Diane F. Gillespie and Leslie K. Hankins. New York: Pace UP, 1997. 119–24.

Edwards, Tim. *Fashion in Focus: Concepts, Practices and Politics*. London and New York: Routledge, 2011.

Eliot, George. "Silly Novels by Lady Novelists." 1856. *The Essays of "George" Eliot*. Ed. Nathan Sheppard. New York: Funk & Wagnalls, 1883. 178–204.

Eliot, T. S. "Little Gidding." *The Complete Poems and Plays: 1909–1950*. New York: Harcourt, Brace & World, 1971. 138–45.

———. "The Love Song of J. Alfred Prufrock." *The Complete Poems and Plays*. 3–7.

———. "The Waste Land." *The Complete Poems and Plays*. 37–55.

Ellmann, Maud. *Elizabeth Bowen: The Shadow Across the Page*. Edinburgh: Edinburgh UP, 2003.

Ellmann, Richard. *Oscar Wilde*. Toronto: Viking Press, 1987.

Emery, Mary Lou. *Jean Rhys at "World's End": Novels of Colonial and Sexual Exile*. Austin: U of Texas P, 1990.

Esty, Jed. *A Shrinking Island: Modernism and National Culture in England*. Princeton and Oxford: Princeton UP, 2004.

Etherington-Smith, Meredith. *Patou*. New York: St. Martin's/Marek, 1983.

Evans, Caroline. "Multiple, Movement, Model, Mode: The Mannequin Parade 1900–1929." *Fashion and Modernity*. Ed. Christopher Breward and Caroline Evans. Oxford and New York: Berg, 2005. 125–45.

Everett, Barbara. "*Excellent Women* and After: The Art of Popularity." *"All This Reading": The Literary World of Barbara Pym*. Ed. Frauke Elisabeth Fenkos and Ellen J. Miller. Cranbury, NJ, and London: Associated UP, 2003. 64–75.

Eysteinsson, Astradur. *The Concept of Modernism*. Ithaca and London: Cornell UP, 1990.

Feldman, Jessica R. *Gender on the Divide: The Dandy in Modernist Literature*. Ithaca and London: Cornell UP, 1993.

Felski, Rita. *The Gender of Modernity*. Cambridge, MA, and London: Harvard UP, 1995.

Finkelstein, Joanne. *Fashion: An Introduction*. New York: New York UP, 1998.

Flaubert, Gustave. *Correspondance*. Vol. II (1847–1852). Paris: Louis Conard, 1926.

Flügel, J. C. *The Psychology of Clothes*. 1930. London: The Hogarth Press and The Institute of Psycho-Analysis, 1950.

Ford [Hueffer], Ford Madox. *Joseph Conrad: A Personal Remembrance*. Boston: Little, Brown, 1924.

———. "On Impressionism." *Poetry and Drama* 6 (June 1914): 167–75.

———. "On Impressionism: Second Article." *Poetry and Drama* 8 (December 1914): 323–34.

———. "Preface: Left Bank." *The Left Bank and Other Stories*. By Jean Rhys. 1927. Freeport, NY: Books for Libraries Press, 1970. 7–27.

Freedman, Ariela. "Dorothy Sayers and the Case of the Shell-Shocked Detective." *Partial Answers* 8.2 (2010): 365–87.

Friedman, Susan Stanford. "Definitional Excursions: The Meanings of *Modern/Modernity/Modernism*." *Modernism/modernity* 8.3 (September 2001): 493–513.

———. "Periodizing Modernism: Postcolonial Modernities and the Space/Time Borders of Modernist Studies." *Modernism/modernity* 13.3 (September 2006): 425–43.

Furbank, P. N., and Alex Cain. *Mallarmé on Fashion: A Translation of the Fashion Magazine La Dernière Mode, with Commentary*. Oxford and New York: Berg, 2004.

Fussell, Paul. *Wartime: Understanding and Behavior in the Second World War*. New York and Oxford: OUP, 1990.

Gardiner, Michael, and Willy Maley, eds. *The Edinburgh Companion to Muriel Spark*. Edinburgh: Edinburgh UP, 2010.

Garrity, Jane. "Virginia Woolf and Fashion." *The Edinburgh Companion to Virginia Woolf and the Arts*. Ed. Maggie Humm. Edinburgh UP, 2010. 195–211.

———. "Virginia Woolf, Intellectual Harlotry, and 1920s British *Vogue*." *Virginia Woolf in the Age of Mechanical Reproduction*. Ed. Pamela L. Caughie. New York and London: Garland, 2000. 185–218.

Gautier, Théophile. "Charles Baudelaire." *Art and Criticism: The Works of Theophile Gautier*. Vol 23. Trans. and ed. F. C. de Sumichrast. New York: George D. Sproul, 1908. 17–126.

Gilbert, Michael. "A Personal Memoir." *Dorothy L. Sayers: The Centenary Celebration*. Ed. Alzina Stone Dale. New York: Walker, 1993. 15–21.

Gilbert-Rolfe, Jeremy. *Beauty and the Contemporary Sublime*. New York: Allworth Press, 1999.

Goldie, David. "Muriel Spark and the Problems of Biography." *The Edinburgh Companion to Muriel Spark*. Ed. Michael Gardiner and Willy Maley. Edinburgh: Edinburgh UP, 2010. 4–15.

Goldman, Jane. *Modernism, 1910–1945, Image to Apocalypse*. Houndmills, Basingstoke, Hampshire, and New York: Palgrave Macmillan, 2004.

Greene, Graham. *A Sort of Life*. New York: Simon, 1971.

Greer, Germaine. *The Female Eunuch*. New York: McGraw-Hill, 1971.

Gregson, Ian. "Muriel Spark's Caricatural Effects." *Essays in Criticism* 55.1 (January 2005): 1–16.

Gubar, Susan. "'This Is My Rifle, This Is My Gun': World War II and the Blitz on Women." *Behind the Lines: Gender and the Two World Wars*. Ed. Margaret Randolph Higonnet et al. New Haven and London: Yale UP, 1987. 227–59.

Hall, Carolyn. *The Forties in Vogue*. New York: Harmony Books, 1985.

Hanson, Karen. "Dressing Down Dressing Up: The Philosophic Fear of Fashion." *Aesthetics: The Big Questions*. Ed. Carolyn Korsmeyer. Malden, MA: Blackwell, 1998. 59–71.

Hartley, Jenny. *Hearts Undefeated: Women's Writing of the Second World War*. London: Virago, 1995.

Harvey, David. "Modernity and Modernism." *Modernism: Critical Concepts in Literary and Cultural Studies. Volume V. 1992–2001*. Ed. Tim Middleton. London and New York: Routledge, 2003. 268–93.

Hassan, Ihab Habib. *The Dismemberment of Orpheus: Toward a Postmodern Literature*. 2nd ed. Madison: U of Wisconsin P, 1982.

Hazlitt, William. "Brummelliana." *The Complete Works of William Hazlitt in Twenty-One Volumes*. Vol. 20. Ed. P. P. Howe. London and Toronto: J. M. Dent & Sons, 1930. 152–54.

———. "On Fashion." *The Complete Works*. Vol. 17. 51–56.

Heilbrun, Carolyn. "Biography between the Lines." *Dorothy L. Sayers: The Centenary Celebration*. Ed. Alzine Stone Dale. New York: Walker, 1993. 1–13.

———. *Hamlet's Mother and Other Women*. New York: Columbia UP, 1990.

Higonnet, Margaret Randolph, Jane Jenson, Sonya Michel, and Margaret Collins Weitz, eds. *Behind the Lines: Gender and the Two World Wars*. New Haven and London: Yale UP, 1987.

Hollander, Anne. *Seeing through Clothes*. New York: Viking, 1978.

———. *Sex and Suits*. New York: Alfred A. Knopf, 1995.

———. "Women and Fashion." *Women, the Arts, and the 1920s in Paris and New York*. Ed. Kenneth W. Wheeler and Virginia Lee Lussier. New Brunswick, NJ, and London: Transaction, 1982. 109–25.

Holt, Hazel. *A Lot to Ask: A Life of Barbara Pym*. New York and London: Dutton/Penguin, 1991.

Holtby, Winifred. "Are Spinsters Frustrated?" *Women and a Changing Civilisation*. New York: Longmans, Green, 1935. 125–33.

Hopkins, Harry. *The New Look: A Social History of the Forties and Fifties in Britain*. Boston: Houghton Mifflin, 1963.

Horizon. London, 1939–46.

Horwood, Catherine. *Keeping Up Appearances: Fashion and Class between the Wars*. Phoenix Mill, Gloucestershire: Sutton, 2005.

Howard, Sidney. *Gone with the Wind: The Screenplay*. New York: Dell Publishing, 1989.

Hulanicki, Barbara. *From A to BIBA: The Autobiography of Barbara Hulanicki*. London: V&A Publications, 2007.

Humble, Nicola. *The Feminine Middlebrow Novel, 1920s to 1950s: Class, Domesticity, and Bohemianism.* Oxford and New York: OUP, 2001.

Jackson, Winefride. "200-Year Vista of Fashion—The Queen Visits Historical Show." *Daily Telegraph* (6 Dec. 1950): n. pag.

Jameson, Frederic. *Postmodernism, or, the Cultural Logic of Late Capitalism.* Durham, NC: Duke UP, 1991.

Jeffreys, Sheila. *The Spinster and Her Enemies: Feminism and Sexuality 1880–1930.* London, Boston & Henley: Pandora, 1985.

Johnson, Samuel. "Preface to a Dictionary of the English Language." *Samuel Johnson: Rasselas, Poems, and Selected Prose.* 3rd ed., enlarged with *The Life of Savage.* Ed. Bertrand H. Bronson. New York and Chicago: Holt, Rinehart and Winston, 1971. 234–60.

Jones, Jennifer M. *Sexing La Mode: Gender, Fashion and Commercial Culture in Old Regime France.* Oxford and New York: Berg, 2004.

Joyce, James. *A Portrait of the Artist as a Young Man.* 1916. Ed. Seamus Deane. New York: Penguin Books, 1993.

———. *Ulysses: The Corrected Text.* Ed. Hans Walter Gabler. New York: Random House, 1993.

Kaplan, Joel H., and Sheila Stowell. *Theatre and Fashion: Oscar Wilde to the Suffragettes.* Cambridge and New York: Cambridge UP, 1994.

Keats, John. "I Had a Dove." *Complete Poetry and Selected Prose of John Keats.* Ed. Harold E. Briggs. New York: Random House, 1951. 253–54.

Kenney, Catherine. *The Remarkable Case of Dorothy L. Sayers.* Kent, OH, and London: The Kent State UP, 1990.

Kineke, Sheila. "'Like a Hook Fits an Eye': Jean Rhys, Ford Madox Ford, and the Imperial Operations of Modernist Mentoring." *Tulsa Studies in Women's Literature* 16.2 (Autumn 1997): 281–301.

Knowles, Sebastian D. G. *A Purgatorial Flame: Seven British Writers in the Second World War.* Philadelphia: U of Pennsylvania P, 1990.

Koestler, Arthur. *Darkness at Noon.* 1940. Trans. Daphne Hardy. New York: Macmillan, 1958.

Koppen, R. S. *Virginia Woolf, Fashion and Literary Modernity.* Edinburgh: Edinburgh UP, 2009.

Kronegger, Maria Elisabeth. *Literary Impressionism.* New Haven, CT: College and University Press, 1973.

Ksinan, Catherine. "Wilde as Editor of *Woman's World*: Fighting a Dull Slumber in Stale Certitudes." *English Literature in Transition, 1880–1920* 41.4 (1998): 408–27.

Kungl, Carla T. *Creating the Fictional Female Detective: The Sleuth Heroines of British Women Writers, 1890–1940.* Jefferson, NC, and London: McFarland, 2006.

Larkin, Philip. "Church Going." *Collected Poems.* Ed. Anthony Thwaite. New York: Farrar, Straus, & Giroux, 2004. 58–59.

———. *A Girl in Winter.* 1957. New York: St. Martin's Press, 1963.

———. *Jill: A Novel.* 1946. New York: St. Martin's Press, 1964.

———. *Selected Letters of Philip Larkin.* Ed. Anthony Thwaite. New York: Farrar, Straus, Giroux, 1993.

---. "Talking in Bed." *Collected Poems*. Ed. Anthony Thwaite. New York: Farrar, Straus, & Giroux, 2004. 100.

Latham, Sean. *"Am I a Snob?": Modernism and the Novel*. Ithaca and London: Cornell UP, 2003.

---. *The Art of Scandal: Modernism, Libel Law, and the Roman à Clef*. Oxford and New York: OUP, 2009.

Lauer, James. *The Concise History of Costume and Fashion*. New York: Harry N. Abrams, 1969.

Lawrence, D. H. *Women in Love*. 1920. New York: Viking, 1950.

Leavis, Q. D. "The Case of Miss Dorothy Sayers." *Scrutiny* 6.3 (December 1937): 334–40.

---. *Fiction and the Reading Public*. London: Chatto & Windus, 1932.

Ledger, Sally. "The New Woman, Modernism and Mass Culture." *Modernism: Critical Concepts in Literary and Cultural Studies. Volume V. 1992–2001*. Ed. Tim Middleton. London and New York: Routledge, 2003. 269–88.

Lehmann, Ulrich. *Tigersprung: Fashion in Modernity*. Cambridge, MA, and London: MIT P, 2000.

Leonardi, Susan J. *Dangerous by Degrees: Women at Oxford and the Somerville College Novelists*. New Brunswick and London: Rutgers UP, 1989.

Lewis, C. S. "Learning in War-time." *Fern-seed and Elephants, and Other Essays on Christianity*. Ed. Walter Hooper. Glasgow: William Collins, 1978. 26–38.

---. "A Panegyric for Dorothy L. Sayers." *Of This and Other Worlds*. Hammersmith, London: HarperCollins, 1982. 104–8.

Little, Judy. *The Experimental Self: Dialogic Subjectivity in Woolf, Pym, and Brooke-Rose*. Carbondale and Edwardsville: Southern Illinois UP, 1996.

Lobenthal, Joel. *Radical Rags: Fashions of the Sixties*. New York: Abbeville Press, 1990.

Longmate, Norman. *The G. I.'s: The Americans in Britain, 1942–1945*. New York: Charles Scribner's Sons, 1975.

---. *How We Lived Then: A History of Everyday Life During the Second World War*. London: Hutchinson, 1971.

Lurie, Alison. *The Language of Clothes*. New York: Random House, 1981.

MacKay, Marina. *Modernism and World War II*. Cambridge: Cambridge UP, 2007.

MacLeish, Archibald. "Ars Poetica." *Collected Poems, 1917–1982*. Boston: Houghton Mifflin, 1985. 106–7.

Macqueen-Pope, W. *Gaiety: Theatre of Enchantment*. London: W. H. Allen, 1949.

Marly, Diana de. *Worth: Father of Haute Couture*. London: Elm Tree Books, 1980.

Marshik, Celia. *British Modernism and Censorship*. Cambridge: Cambridge UP, 2006.

Martin, Ann. *Red Riding Hood and the Wolf in Bed: Modernism's Fairy Tales*. Toronto and Buffalo: U of Toronto P, 2006.

McLaughlin, Patrick, Norah Lambourne, and Barbara Reynolds. "Dorothy L. Sayers As We Knew Her." *Publications of the Dorothy L. Sayers Society* (March 1989): 1–25.

McNeil, Peter. "'Put Your Best Face Forward': The Impact of the Second World War on British Dress." *Journal of Design History* 6.4 (1993): 283–99.

---. "'That Doubtful Gender': Macaroni Dress and Male Sexualities." *Fashion Theory* 3.4 (December 1999): 411–47.

Mengham, Rod. "Broken Glass." *The Fiction of the 1940s: Stories of Survival.* Ed. Rod Mengham and N. H. Reeve. Houndmills, Basingstoke, Hampshire, and New York: Palgrave, 2001. 124–33.

Mephim, John. "Varieties of Modernism, Varieties of Incomprehension: Patrick Hamilton and Elizabeth Bowen." *British Fiction After Modernism: The Novel at Mid-Century.* Ed. Marina MacKay and Lyndsey Stonebridge. Houndmills, Basingstoke, Hampshire, and New York: Palgrave Macmillan, 2007. 59–76.

Middleton, Tim, ed. *Modernism: Critical Concepts in Literary and Cultural Studies. Volume V. 1992–2001.* London and New York: Routledge, 2003.

Miller, Jane Eldridge. "The Crisis of 1895: Realism and the Feminization of Fiction." *Modernism: Critical Concepts in Literary and Cultural Studies. Volume V. 1992–2001.* Ed. Tim Middleton. London and New York: Routledge, 2003. 38–69.

Miller, Lee. *Lee Miller's War: Photographer and Correspondent with the Allies in Europe 1944–45.* Ed. Antony Penrose. Boston: Little, Brown, 1992.

Miller, Tyrus. *Late Modernism: Politics, Fiction, and the Arts Between the World Wars.* Berkeley: U of California P, 1999.

Moers, Ellen. *The Dandy: Brummell to Beerbohm.* Lincoln and London: U of Nebraska P, 1978.

Morris, Virginia B. "Arsenic and Blue Lace: Sayers' Criminal Women." *Modern Fiction Studies* 29.3 (Autumn 1983): 485–95.

Morrison, Blake. *The Movement: English Poetry and Fiction of the 1950s.* Oxford and New York: OUP, 1980.

Nicholson, Virginia. *Singled Out: How Two Million British Women Survived without Men after the First World War.* Oxford and New York: OUP, 2008.

Orwell, George. "Inside the Whale." 1940. *Such, Such Were the Joys.* New York: Harcourt, Brace & Company, 1953. 154–99.

———. "The Lion and the Unicorn." 1941. *The Collected Essays, Journalism and Letters of George Orwell.* Vol. 2. Ed. Sonia Orwell and Ian Angus. Harmondsworth: Penguin, 1970. 74–134.

———. "Raffles and Miss Blandish." *Horizon* 10.58 (Oct. 1944): 232–44.

Parsons, Deborah L. *Streetwalking the Metropolis: Women, the City, and Modernity.* Oxford and New York: OUP, 2000.

Pater, Walter. *Studies in the History of the Renaissance.* London: Macmillan, 1873.

———. "Style." 1889. *Appreciations; With an Essay on Style.* London and New York: Macmillan, 1910. 5–38.

Paulicelli, Eugenia. *Fashion under Fascism: Beyond the Black Shirt.* Oxford and New York: Berg, 2004.

Paxton, Nancy L. "Eclipsed by Modernism." *Outside Modernism: In Pursuit of the English Novel, 1900–30.* Ed. Lynne Hapgood and Nancy L. Paxton. London and New York: Macmillan & St. Martin's, 2000. 3–21.

Pizzichini, Lillian. *The Blue Hour: A Life of Jean Rhys.* New York and London: W. W. Norton, 2009.

Plain, Gill. *Women's Fiction of the Second World War: Gender, Power, and Resistance.* Edinburgh: Edinburgh UP: 1996.

Plock, Vike Martina. "Sartorial Connections: Fashion, Clothes, and Character in Elizabeth Bowen's *To the North*." *Modernism/Modernity* 19.2 (April 2012): 287–302.

Plutarchus, Lucius Mestrius. *Plutarch's Lives*. Vol. 4. Trans. A. H. Clough. New York and Pittsburg: The Colonial Company, 1905.

Pound, Ezra. "A Retrospect." 1918. *Early Writings: Poems and Prose*. Ed. Ira B. Nadel. New York: Penguin Books, 2005. 253–56.

Pym, Barbara. *Crampton Hodnet*. 1985. New York: Penguin, 2005.

———. *Excellent Women*. 1952. New York and London: Penguin, 2006.

———. *A Few Green Leaves*. 1980. London: Moyer Bell, 1999.

———. *Jane and Prudence*. 1953. London: Moyer Bell, 1999.

———. Pym Papers, 1929–1996. Bodleian Library, University of Oxford.

———. *Quartet in Autumn*. 1977. New York: Penguin, 1992.

———. *Some Tame Gazelle*. 1950. New York: Harper & Row, 1986.

———. *The Sweet Dove Died*. 1978. New York: Harper & Row, 1980.

———. *A Very Private Eye: An Autobiography in Diaries and Letters*. Ed. Hazel Holt and Hilary Pym. New York: Random House, 1985.

Quant, Mary. *Quant by Quant*. New York: G. P. Putnam's Sons, 1966.

Rabine, Leslie W. "A Woman's Two Bodies: Fashion Magazines, Consumerism, and Feminism." *On Fashion*. Ed. Shari Benstock and Suzanne Ferriss. New Brunswick, NJ: Rutgers UP, 1994. 59–75.

Rabinovitz, Rubin. "The Reaction against Modernism: Amis, Snow, Wilson." *Columbia History of the British Novel*. Ed. John J. Richetti. New York: Columbia UP, 1994. 895–917.

Rappaport, Erika Diane. *Shopping for Pleasure: Women in the Making of London's West End*. Princeton, NJ: Princeton UP, 2000.

Rawlinson, Mark. *British Writing of the Second World War*. Oxford: Clarendon Press, 2000.

Reynolds, Barbara. *Dorothy L. Sayers: Her Life and Soul*. New York: St. Martin's Press, 1993.

Rhys, Jean. *After Leaving Mr Mackenzie*. 1931. New York: Random House, 1974.

———. *Good Morning, Midnight*. 1939. New York and London: W. W. Norton, 2000.

———. *The Left Bank and Other Stories*. 1927. Freeport, NY: Books for Libraries Press, 1970.

———. *The Letters of Jean Rhys*. Ed. Francis Wyndham and Diana Melly. New York: Viking, 1984.

———. *Quartet*. 1928. New York and London: W. W. Norton, 1997.

———. *Smile Please: An Unfinished Autobiography*. New York: Harper & Row, 1979.

———. *Voyage in the Dark*. 1934. London and New York: Penguin, 2000.

———. *Wide Sargasso Sea*. 1966. New York and London: Norton, 1992.

Richards, I. A. *Science and Poetry*. 2nd ed., rev. and enlarged. London: Kegan Paul, Trench, Trubner, 1935.

Riley, Denise. "Some Peculiarities of Social Policy Concerning Women in Wartime and Postwar Britain." *Behind the Lines: Gender and the Two World Wars*. Ed. Margaret Randolph Higonnet et al. New Haven and London: Yale UP, 1987. 260–71.

Robinson, Lillian S. "The Mysterious Politics of Dorothy Sayers." *At Home and Abroad: British Women Write the 1930s*. Ed. Robin Hackett, Freda Hauser, and Gay Wachman. Newark, NJ: U of Delaware P, 2009. 222–33.

Rossen, Janice. "On Not Being Jane Eyre." *Independent Women: The Function of Gender in the Novels of Barbara Pym*. Ed. Janice Rossen. New York: St. Martin's Press, 1988. 137–56.

———. *Women Writing Modern Fiction: A Passion for Ideas*. Houndmills, Basingstoke, Hampshire: Palgrave Macmillan, 2003.

———. *The World of Barbara Pym*. New York: St. Martin's P, 1987.

Rowbotham, Sheila. *Hidden from History: Rediscovering Women in History from the 17th Century to the Present*. New York: Random House, 1975.

Rubens, Paul. "No. 11 Song—Delia and Chorus—A Tiny Touch." From *The Sunshine Girl. Victorian and Edwardian Musical Shows*. Ed. Colin M. Johnson. N. pag., n.d. 1 Oct. 2011. <http://www.halhkmusic.com.>

Sayers, Dorothy L. "Are Women Human?" 1938. *Unpopular Opinions*. London: Victor Gollancz, 1946. 106–16.

———. *Begin Here: A War-Time Essay*. London: Victor Gollancz, 1940, 1942.

———. *Busman's Honeymoon*. 1937. New York: Harper Collins, 2006.

———. *Clouds of Witness*. 1927. New York: Harper & Row, 1987.

———. "The English Language." 1936. *Unpopular Opinions*. London: Victor Gollancz, 1946. 89–97.

———. "The Entertaining Episode of the Article in Question." *Lord Peter: A Collection of All the Lord Peter Wimsey Stories*. New York: Harper & Row, 1971. 21–32.

———. *Five Red Herrings*. New York: Avon, 1931.

———. *Gaudy Night*. New York: Harper & Row, 1936.

———. "Gaudy Night." *Titles to Fame*. Ed. Denys Kilham Roberts. London: Thomas Nelson, 1937. 75–95.

———. *Have His Carcase*. New York: Harper & Brothers, 1932.

———. "The Human-Not-Quite-Human." 1941. *Unpopular Opinions*. London: Victor Gollancz, 1946. 116–22.

———. "The Importance of Being Vulgar." Unpublished ms for speech (12 Feb. 1936). MS-118, Wade Collection, Wheaton College, Wheaton, IL.

———. Introduction. *The Omnibus of Crime*. New York: Payson & Clarke, 1929. 9–47.

———. *The Letters of Dorothy L. Sayers*. Vols. 1 & 2. Ed. Barbara Reynolds. New York: St. Martin's Press, 1995, 1997.

———. *The Letters of Dorothy L. Sayers*. Vols. 3 & 4. Ed. Barbara Reynolds. Swavesey, Cambridge: The Dorothy L. Sayers Society, 1998, 2000.

———. *The Mind of the Maker*. 1941. Cleveland and New York: The World Publishing, 1964.

———. *The Song of Roland*. 1937. Trans. Dorothy L. Sayers. Harmondsworth, Middlesex, England: Penguin, 1975.

———. *Strong Poison*. 1930. New York: Harper & Brothers, 1958.

———. "Style in Crime Stories: Why Good Writing Pays." *The Sunday Times*. No. 5789 (25 March 1934): 9.

———. *Unnatural Death*. 1927. New York: Harper Collins, 1995.

———. *The Unpleasantness at the Bellona Club*. New York: Harper & Brothers, 1928.

———. *Whose Body?* New York: Harper & Brothers, 1923.

Sayers, Dorothy L., and Robert Eustace. *The Documents in the Case*. New York: Harper & Row, 1930.

Schaeffer, Talia. "Fashioning Aestheticism by Aestheticizing Fashion: Wilde, Beerbohm, and the Male Aesthetes' Sartorial Codes." *Victorian Literature and Culture* (2000): 39–54.

Scherman, David E. Foreword. *Lee Miller's War: Photographer and Correspondent with the Allies in Europe 1944–45*. By Lee Miller. Ed. Antony Penrose. Boston: Little, Brown, 1992. 7–13.

Schneider, Karen. *Loving Arms: British Women Writing the Second World War*. Lexington, KY: The UP of Kentucky, 1997.

Schneider, Mary W. "The Double Life in Muriel Spark's *The Prime of Miss Jean Brodie*." *Midwest Quarterly* 18.4 (July 1977): 418–31.

Schomberg, Ralph. *Fashion. A Poem. Addressed to the ladies of Great-Britain*. Printed by R. Cruttwell and sold by F. Newberry, 1775.

Scowcroft, Philip L. "Clothes and Lord Peter." *Sidelights on Sayers* 11 (1985): 19–24.

Shaw, Marion, and Sabine Vanacker. *Reflecting on Miss Marple*. London and New York: Routledge, 1991.

Showalter, Elaine. *The Female Malady: Women, Madness, and English Culture, 1830–1980*. New York: Pantheon, 1985.

Sillitoe, Alan. *Saturday Night and Sunday Morning*. 1958. New York: Alfred A. Knopf, 1959.

Simmel, Georg. "Female Culture." *Simmel on Culture*. 46–54.

———. "The Philosophy of Fashion." *Simmel on Culture*. 187–206.

———. "The Problem of Style." *Simmel on Culture*. 211–17.

———. *Simmel on Culture: Selected Writings*. Ed. David Frisby and Mike Featherstone. London: Sage Publications, 1997.

Simpson, Christine R. "Women's Fashions." *Sidelights on Sayers* 24 (1988): 3–15.

Simpson, Mark. "Meet the Metrosexual." *Salon.com*. 22 July 2002.

Sitwell, Sir Osbert. *Left Hand, Right Hand*. Boston: Little, Brown, 1944.

Spark, Muriel. *The Comforters*. New York: New Directions, 1957.

———. *Curriculum Vitae: Autobiography*. Boston and New York: Houghton Mifflin, 1993.

———. "Does Celibacy Affect Judgment?" *The Church of England Newsletter* 70.3021 (16 Nov. 1951): 10.

———. *The Driver's Seat*. 1970. London and New York: Penguin, 2006.

———. *The Girls of Slender Means*. 1963. New York: New Directions, 1998.

———. *Loitering with Intent*. New York: Coward, McCann & Geoghegan, 1981.

———. *The Prime of Miss Jean Brodie*. 1962. New York: HarperCollins, 1999.

Spencer, Herbert. "Manners and Fashion." *The Works of Herbert Spencer*. Vol. 15. Osnabrück: Otto Zeller, 1966. 1–51.

———. *The Principles of Sociology*. 1870–96. 3 vols. Westport, CT: Greenwood, 1975.

Stannard, Martin. *Muriel Spark: The Biography*. London: Weidenfeld & Nicolson, 2009.
Steedman, Carolyn. "Englishness, Clothes and Little Things." *The Englishness of English Dress*. Ed. Christopher Breward et al. Oxford and New York: Berg, 2002. 29–44.
Steele, Valerie. *Paris Fashion: A Cultural History*. New York and Oxford: OUP, 1988.
——. *Women of Fashion: Twentieth-Century Designers*. New York: Rizzoli, 1991.
Stein, Gertrude. *The Autobiography of Alice B. Toklas*. New York: Harcourt, Brace, 1933.
Strachey, Lytton. *Eminent Victorians*. 1918. New York: Weidenfeld & Nicolson, 1988.
Stuart, Ian. "An Unsteady Throne." *Dorothy L. Sayers: The Centenary Celebration*. Ed. Alzina Stone Dale. New York: Walker, 1993. 23–30.
Stubbes, Phillip. *The Anatomie of Abuses containing, a discouerie, or briefe summarie of such notable vices and imperfections. . . .* London: by John Kinston for Richard Jones, 1583.
Symons, Arthur. *The Symbolist Movement in Literature*. New York: E. P. Dutton, 1919.
Symons, Julian. *Bloody Murder from the Detective Story to the Crime Novel: A History*. London: Faber & Faber, 1972.
Taylor, Lou, "Paris Couture: 1940–1944." *Chic Thrills: A Fashion Reader*. Ed. Juliet Ash and Elizabeth Wilson. Berkeley and LA: U of California P, 1992. 127–44.
Thirkell, Angela. *Cheerfulness Breaks In: A Barsetshire War Story*. 1940. New York: Alfred A. Knopf, 1941.
Thomas, Dana. *Deluxe: How Luxury Lost Its Luster*. New York: Penguin, 2007.
Tinkler, Penny, and Cheryl Krasnick Marsh. "Feminine Modernity in Interwar Britain and North America: Corsets, Cars, and Cigarettes." *Journal of Women's History* 20.3 (Fall 2008): 113–43.
Toffler, Alvin. *Future Shock*. New York: Random House, 1970.
Tsagaris, Ellen M. *The Subversion of Romance in the Novels of Barbara Pym*. Bowling Green, OH: Bowling Green State University Popular Press, 1998.
Updike, John. "Between a Wedding and a Funeral." *Assorted Prose*. New York: Alfred A. Knopf, 1965. 310–14.
——. "From the Forties." *New Yorker* 57 (8 June 1981): 148–58.
Veblen, Thorstein. *The Theory of the Leisure Class: An Economic Study of Institutions*. 1899. New York: The Modern Library, 1934.
Veillon, Dominique. *Fashion under the Occupation*. Oxford and New York: Berg, 2002.
Vogue. London: Condé Nast, 1939–47.
Wain, John. *Hurry on Down*. 1953. New York: The Viking Press, 1965.
Walford, Jonathan. *Forties Fashion: From Siren Suits to the New Look*. New York: Thames & Hudson, 2008.
Warner, Rex. *The Aerodrome: A Love Story*. 1941. Oxford and New York: OUP, 1982.
Warton, Joseph. *Fashion: An Epistolary Satire to a Friend*. London: For R. Dodsley, 1742.
Waugh, Evelyn. "The Books You Read." *The Essays, Articles, and Reviews of Evelyn Waugh*. Ed. Donat Gallagher. Boston: Little, Brown, 1983.
——. *Brideshead Revisited: The Sacred and Profane Memories of Captain Charles Ryder*. Boston: Little, Brown, 1945.
——. *The Diaries of Evelyn Waugh*. Ed. Michael Davie. Boston and Toronto: Little, Brown, 1976.

———. *The Letters of Evelyn Waugh*. Ed. Mark Armory. New York: Penguin, 1982.

———. Preface. *Brideshead Revisited*. Rev. ed. New York: Penguin, 1962.

———. *Put Out More Flags*. Boston: Little, Brown: 1942.

———. "Work Suspended." 1941. *Tactical Exercise*. New York: Books for Libraries, 1971. 129–234.

Waugh, Patricia. "Muriel Spark and the Metaphysics of Modernity: Art, Secularization, and Psychosis." *Muriel Spark: Twenty-First-Century Perspectives*. Ed. David Herman. Baltimore: The Johns Hopkins UP, 2010. 63–93.

Weaver, Richard. *Language Is Sermonic*. Baton Rouge: Louisiana State UP, 1970.

Wesley, Samuel. *Samuel Wesley's Epistle to a Friend Concerning Poetry (1700) and the Essay on Heroic Poetry*. The Augustan Reprint Society, No. 5 (January 1947).

Wicke, Jennifer. "Lingerie and (literary) history: Joyce's *Ulysses* and fashionability." *Critical Quarterly* 36.2 (Summer 1994): 25–41.

Wilde, Oscar. *The Complete Plays*. London: Methuen, 1988.

———. "De Profundis." 1905. *De Profundis and Other Writings*. London and New York: Penguin Books, 1986. 97–211.

———. "The Decay of Lying." 1889, 1891. *De Profundis and Other Writings*. London and New York: Penguin Books, 1986. 55–87.

———. *The Letters of Oscar Wilde*. Ed. Rupert Hart-Davis. New York: Harcourt, Brace & World, 1962.

———. *The Picture of Dorian Gray*. 1890. Ed. Norman Page. Ontario: Broadview, 1998.

Williams, Raymond. "The Metropolis and the Emergence of Modernism." *Modernism: Critical Concepts in Literary and Cultural Studies, Vol. IV, 1985–1991*. Ed. Tim Middleton. London and New York: Routledge, 2004. 1–43.

Wilson, A. N. Introduction. *Excellent Women*. By Barbara Pym. 1952. New York and London: Penguin, 2006. ix–xvi.

Wilson, Elizabeth. *Adorned in Dreams: Fashion and Modernity*. Rev. and upd. New Brunswick, NJ: Rutgers UP, 2003.

———. *Only Halfway to Paradise: Women in Postwar Britain, 1945–1968*. London and New York: Tavistock, 1980.

Winter, Jay. *Sites of Memory, Sites of Mourning: The Great War in European Cultural History*. Cambridge and New York: Cambridge UP, 1995.

Wollstonecraft, Mary. *A Vindication of the Rights of Men and A Vindication of the Rights of Woman*. Ed. Sylvana Tomaselli. Cambridge Texts in the History of Political Thought. Cambridge: Cambridge UP, 1995.

Woolf, Virginia. *The Diary of Virginia Woolf*. 5 vols. Ed. Anne Olivier Bell. New York: Harcourt Brace Jovanovich, 1977–82.

———. "Modern Novels." 1919. *The Essays of Virginia Woolf*. Vol. 3. 1919–24. Ed. Andrew McNeillie. San Diego: Harcourt Brace Jovanovich, 1986. 30–36.

———. *Mrs. Dalloway*. 1925. San Diego and New York: Harcourt Brace Jovanovich, 1985.

———. "The New Dress." 1927. *The Complete Shorter Fiction of Virginia Woolf*. 2nd ed. San Diego: Harcourt Brace Jovanovich, 1989. 170–77.

———. *A Room of One's Own*. 1929. Orlando and Austin: Harcourt, 2005.

———. "A Sketch of the Past." 1939. *Moments of Being*. Ed. Jeanne Shulkind. San Diego: Harcourt, 1985. 64–137.
———. *To the Lighthouse*. 1927. San Diego and New York: Harcourt, 1981.
———. *The Voyage Out*. 1915. New York: Modern Library, 2001.
———. *The Waves*. New York: Harcourt, Brace, 1931.
Yeats, William Butler. *The Collected Poems of W. B. Yeats*. New York: Macmillan, 1956.

INDEX

Abbott, Reginald: "What Miss Kilman's Petticoat Means," 38n13
Achebe, Chinua: *Things Fall Apart*, 235
Adam, H. Pearl, 102–103, 105
Aesthetic movement, xx, 5–7, 8, 28, 29, 32–33, 57, 78, 159–60, 162–63, 169, 171, 173, 174, 175, 213, 239
After Leaving Mr Mackenzie (Rhys), 92, 99, 109–113, 115–116, 117–118
Alfie (film), 176n12
Allingham, Margery, 159
Amis, Kingsley, 194, 195, 211; *Lucky Jim*, 197, 221, 225, 227; *Take a Girl Like You*, 225
Andrade, Susan, 33
Angeletti, Norberto, 148–49
Angier, Carole, 94, 98, 99, 100, 103
"Angry Young Men," 194, 211
Anthony, Susan B., xivn1
Apollinaire, Guillaume, 2
Ardis, Ann L.: *Women's Experience of Modernity*, 49n3
Aristophanes: *The Clouds*, 17
Arnold, Matthew, 11, 49
Atlee, Clement, 144, 155
Atwood, Margaret: *The Robber Bride*, 259
Auden, W. H., 160–61; "The Guilty Vicarage," 86; "September 1, 1939," 158
Auerbach, Erich, 33n9
Auerbach, Nina, 82, 83
Austen, Jane, 36, 48, 49, 164, 186; *Emma*, 54; *Mansfield Park*, 3; *Northanger Abbey*, 8; *Pride and Prejudice*, 50n4

Baker, Niamh, 192
Bardot, Brigette, 236
Barnard, Malcolm: *Fashion as Communication*, xv
Barnes, Djuna, 161n1
Barnes, F. J.: "In These Hard Times," 120n8
Barthes, Roland: *The Fashion System*, xvii
Barzun, Jacques, 86
Bath Costume Institute, 64
Baudelaire, Charles, xviii, xx, 3, 4, 8, 15, 16, 18, 29–30, 31, 36, 39, 58, 93, 111, 183, 231; "La Beauté," 13; "De l'essence du rire," 200, 209, 225; *Les fleurs du mal*, 13–14, 210; "The Painter of Modern Life," 12–14, 28–29; "Le Voyage," 14. *See also* dandyism
BBC (British Broadcasting Corporation), 51, 88, 169, 204
Beaton, Cecil, 141, 144, 155, 166
Beauvoir, Simone de, 36
Beckett, Samuel, 161
Bell, Josephine, 62n2
Bender, Todd, 102
Benito, Carmel, 148
Benjamin, Walter, 58; *The Arcades Project*, 111n5
Bentley, E. C.: *Trent's Last Case*, 86–87
Berger, John, 210
Bergonzi, Bernard, 163, 164, 195
Berlei (corset), 137
Bernhardt, Sarah, 24

Berrong, Richard M., 41n15, 102
Bertin, Rose, 24
Betjeman, John, 172n10
Bible, 226, 254; Isaiah, 17–18; Proverbs, 213; I Timothy, 17–18
Blanch, Leslie, 130, 152, 179
Bloomer, Amelia, xivn1, 45
Blumer, Herbert, 18
Book of Common Prayer, 226
Boone, Joseph Allen: *Tradition Counter Tradition*, xix
Boote, Rosie, 94–95. See also Gaiety Theatre
Booth, Michael R.: *The Edwardian Theatre*, 96
Booth, Wayne C.: *The Rhetoric of Fiction*, xvii
Borges, J. L., 86
Boswell, James, 21
Bowen, Elizabeth, 161, 161n2; on dress, xiii; wartime stories, xxii, 160, 169n8, 191, 193; "Contemporary," 159, 164; "The Demon Lover," 180–81, 184, 185, 212, 259; "Green Holly," 184–87; *The Heat of the Day*, 159, 183; "Ivy Gripped the Steps," 182–83; "Preface," *Ivy Gripped the Steps*, 179; "Songs My Father Sang Me," 183–84
Bowen, Stella, 108n4; *Drawn from Life*, 102, 104, 109
Bradbury, Malcolm, 245
Braddock, Bessie, 153
Braemar (knitwear), 137
Braine, John: *Room at the Top*, 176n12, 227–28
Braun, Eva, 138n4, 138n5
Braybon, Gail, 46, 47–48, 191, 192
Breward, Christopher, 27
Brideshead Revisited (Waugh), 129, 163, 171–72, 172n9, 173–74, 177, 178, 238
Brittain, Vera, 59
Brodie, Deacon, 212
Brontës (Anne, Emily, Charlotte), 36, 48, 49, 50n4, 51 ("Currier Bell"). See also *Jane Eyre*
Brookner, Anita: *Hotel du Lac*, 259
Brown, Callum, 234, 235

Browning, Elizabeth Barrett, 51
Brown, Judith, 239, 255
Brummell, George ("Beau"), 20, 24–27, 28, 29, 60, 67, 141, 142; as dandy, 28, 58, 60, 66. See also dandyism. See under dress styles: the male dark suit
Buchenwald (concentration camp), 144
Buckley, Cheryl, 77, 128n1, 134n2
Burgess, Anthony: *Clockwork Orange*, 235
Burney, Frances, 36, 48
Burstein, Jessica, 4, 41n15
Burton, Robert, 1
Byatt, A. S., 221, 222
Byron, Lord (George Gordon), 65, 141

Caesar, Julius, 3n2, 214, 215
Cain, Alex: *Mallarmé on Fashion*, 14–16, 237
Calder, Angus, 130, 132, 135, 136, 139, 141, 148, 164–65, 191–92
Campbell, Robin (Captain): "Prisoner of War," 166
Cape, Jonathan (publisher), 249
Carlyle, Thomas, 8–10; *Sartor Resartus*, 9
Caron, Leslie, 196
Carruthers, Gerard, 245
Carter, Angela, 233, 235, 240, 241
Carter, Michael, 11
Caryll, Ivan: *Our Miss Gibbs*, 94–97. See also Gaiety Theatre
Cecil, David, 196, 250, 255
Cendrars, Blaise, 91
Chambre Syndicale de la Haute Couture, 150
Chanel, Gabrielle ("Coco"), xivn1, 18, 21, 47, 113, 149, 150, 196, 222
Chanteclair, 94
Chase, Edna Woolman, 129, 131
Chase, Ilka, 129, 131
Chase, James Hadley: *No Orchids for Miss Blandish*, 164n5
Chase, Mary Ellen, 62n2
Chesterfield, Lord (Philip Dormer Stanhope), 5, 7
Christie, Agatha, 53n7, 69n5, 71, 161n2; "The Tuesday Night Club," 72n7. See also detective fiction; Marple; Poirot

Churchill, Winston, 132, 144
clothing. *See* dress; dress styles; fashion
Cohen, Lisa, 40, 41
Colette: *Gigi*, 93
Collins, Wilkie, 51
comedy of the object, xxii, 199–201, 209–210, 211–24, 229
Connolly, Cyril, xxi, 51, 124, 159–60, 162, 164–71, 172, 193; *Enemies of Promise*, 162; *The Rock Pool*, 162; *The Unquiet Grave*, 162, 169–71. See also *Horizon*
Connolly, Thomas E.: *Scribbledehobble*, 157
Conrad, Joseph, 33, 102; *Heart of Darkness*, 5, 6
Cooper, Gladys, 95. *See also* Gaiety Theatre
Corelli, Marie, 48, 50
cosmetics, 62, 141; Arden, Elizabeth, 138n4; Cyclax of London, 138; Tattoo, 137–38; Yardley, 137
costume. *See* dress; dress styles; fashion
Cotsell, Michael, 195, 213
Count of Luxembourg, The, 94, 95, 96. *See also* Gaiety Theatre
Cournos, John, 60–61
Coventry Cathedral, 166
Cunard, Nancy: "Letter from Paris," 169
Curie, Eve, 143

Dachau (prison camp), 145
Daily Express, 155
Dalton, Hugh, 139
dandyism, xvi, xvii, xx, xxi, 4, 8, 9, 20–30, 31, 32–33, 35n11, 58, 64–67, 68, 70, 228, 231, 233, 241, 259; and the metrosexual, 30n7; and the spinster, 71. *See also under* Baudelaire; Brummell; Sayers; Spark; Wilde, Oscar. *See also* flânerie; Sayers: Lord Peter Wimsey
Dante (Dante Alighieri), 58, 88, 160
Davis, Fred: "Antifashion," xivn1; *Fashion, Culture, and Identity*, xv, 19n4, 42
Davis, Laura: *Virginia Woolf and Communities*, 38n13

Delafield, E. M.: *A Provincial Lady in Wartime*, 140, 179
Delaunay, Sonia, 91
Delilah, 239, 240
Dell'Amico, Carol, 118
demimonde, 55, 92–94, 96–99, 103
detective fiction, xx, 50–51, 57, 68–69, 77, 85–87, 159, 172, 194. *See also* Christie; Doyle; Holmes; Marple. *See also under* Sayers
Detmold, Rita, 96
Dickens, Charles, 27, 28, 49, 51, 164, 185, 244; *Great Expectations*, 54
Dior, Christian, xxi, 152–55, 157, 187, 189, 192, 193, 196, 236. *See also* New Look
Disraeli, Benjamin, 27, 28
Doan, Laura, 53
Donnelly, Mark, 233, 234
D'Orsay, Albert, 28, 30
Downing, Crystal, 67
Dowson, Ernest, 93
Doyle, Arthur Conan, 51. *See also* Holmes, Sherlock; detective fiction
dress: as gendered, ii, xxii, 7, 20–24, 30n7, 42, 91, 109, 138–43; definitions of, 7; and democracy, 19, 23, 28, 66, 128, 130, 155, 196; and Industrial Revolution, 19, 46; in modernity, 18, 21, 32, 44–48, 237; and religion, 17–18, 27, 27n6. *See also* dress styles. *See also under* Pym; Rhys; Sayers; Spark
dress styles: Edwardian through Depression era, 44–48, 77–78, 153; hats, 20, 36, 39, 44, 47, 61–62, 64n3, 67, 79, 81, 92, 96, 97, 99, 100, 104, 112, 135, 136, 147; infantilized, 100, 184; lingerie, 23, 34–35, 36, 38n12, 45–46, 72, 96, 131–32, 134, 202, 206; the male dark suit, 23, 24, 26–27, 47, 66, 139, 141–42; mourning, xvi, 1–2, 31; in Occupied France, xxi, 127, 147–52; punk, xvii; and sexual availability, 44–45, 47; trousers for women, 124, 139–42, 155, 179, 218; wartime, 127, 131–136, 147–52. *See also* dandyism; New Look; haute couture

Driver's Seat, The (Spark), xxii, 209, 240–41, 243–46, 253, 255–56
Dumas, Alexander (*fils*), 93
DuPlessis, Rachel Blau: *Writing beyond the Ending*, xix

Edson, Laura Gwyn: "Kicking Off Her Knickers," 38n13, 41
Edwardes, George, 95, 96. *See also* Gaiety Theatre
Edwards, Tim: *Fashion in Focus*, 23n5
Eliot, George, 48, 49, 49n1, 51; "Silly Novels by Lady Novelists," 36
Eliot, T. S., 34, 143, 170; *Four Quartets*, 160; "Little Gidding," 160; *The Love-Song of J. Alfred Prufrock*, 34n10, 175, 222; *The Waste Land*, 161, 174, 222
Ellington, Duke, 51
Ellis, Havelock, 52, 53n7
Ellmann, Maud, 183, 184
Ellmann, Richard: *Oscar Wilde*, 32
Elsie, Lily, 95, 96. *See also* Gaiety Theatre
Emery, Mary Lou, 122
Enright, D. J.: "Saying No," 194
Erwin, Nancy, 95, 98. *See also* Gaiety Theatre
Esty, Jed, 161n1
Etherington-Smith, Meredith, 91
Eugénie (Empress), 24
Eustace, Robert: *The Documents in the Case* (Sayers and Eustace), 64, 76
Evans, Caroline, 96
Eve, 106, 239
Everett, Barbara, 223
Excellent Women (Pym), xvi–xvii, 199, 201, 203, 206, 210, 216–224; date of writing, 217n3
Eysteinsson, Astradur, 33

Faber, Geoffrey, 161
fashion: birth of, 17, 19n4; definitions of, 7–8; as female, 12, 18–19, 42, 141; and feminism, xiv, xivn1, 36–37, 45–48, 59; feminization of, 4, 8–10, 20–24, 30n7; as French, 21, 26, 27n6, 91, 130, 148–50; theory, xvii, xviii, 3, 18, 91, 127. *See also* haute couture; dress: in modernity. *See also under* modernism

Fawcett, Hilary, 77, 128n1, 134n2
Feldman, Jessica, 65
Felski, Rita: *The Gender of Modernity*, 37, 49n3, 78
femme fatale, xxii, 106, 187, 238–40, 244, 246, 247, 254, 256, 259. *See also* Bowen: "Green Holly"; *The Driver's Seat*; glamour; *The Sweet Dove Died*
Finkelstein, Joanne, 18–19, 211
Fitzgerald, Zelda, 91
flânerie, 32, 58, 111–112, 111n5, 118, 231
Flaubert, Gustave, 6, 8, 12, 87, 105, 170
Fleming, Atherton ("Mac"), 51n6, 61, 70n6
Fleming, John Anthony, 61
Flügel, J. C., 23. *See also* fashion: feminization of
Flynn, Deirdre: "Virginia's Women," 38n13
Ford, Ford Madox, 33, 50, 91, 100, 108n4, 113, 161; affair with Rhys, 91, 102–104, 109; *Joseph Conrad*, 102; "On Impressionism," 103; "On Impressionism: Second," 103; "Preface" to *The Left Bank*, 92, 105; *When the Wicked Man*, 102. *See also* impressionism (literary)
Forster, E. M.: *A Passage to India*, 54; *A Room with a View*, 54
Freedman, Ariela, 70n6
French, Kilgour, and Stanburg (fashion house), 147
Freud, Sigmund, 42, 53n7, 258; *Civilization and Its Discontents*, 119n7
Friedman, Susan Stanford: "Definitional Excursions," 233n1; "Periodizing Modernism," 2n1
Furbank, P. N.: *Mallarmé on Fashion*, 14–16
Fussell, Paul, 165

Gaiety Theatre, 92, 94–98
Gardam, Jane: *The Man in the Wooden Hat*, 259–60
Garrity, Jane: "Virginia Woolf and Fashion," 37, 41n15; "Virginia Woolf, Intellectual Harlotry, and 1920s British *Vogue*," 143

Gaskell, Elizabeth, 48, 51
Gaudy Night (Sayers), 59, 60, 64, 77, 82–85, 86, 87
Gautier, Théophile, 209–210
Gilbert, Michael, 61–62
Gilbert-Rolfe, Jeremy, 237, 239, 250, 252
Girls of Slender Means, The (Spark), 201, 208, 209, 210, 224–30, 232, 240, 246, 260
glamour, xxii, 232, 238–40, 241, 246, 247, 251–52, 255, 256. See also femme fatale
Goldie, David, 208
Goldman, Jane, 161n1
Gone with the Wind: film, xv–xvi, xvin2; novel (Mitchell), xvin2
Good Morning, Midnight (Rhys), xxi, 113, 115–122
Göring, Emma, 149n7
GOR-RAY skirt, 143
Green, Henry, 171
Greene, Graham, 124, 161, 210
Greer, Germaine: *The Female Eunuch*, xivn1, 36, 236
Gregson, Ian, 214
Gubar, Susan, 191, 193
Guys, Constantin, 12

Hall, Carolyn, 139
Hamer, Max, 117
Hanson, Karen, 200, 238
Hari, Mata, 240
Hartley, Jenny, 169n8
Harvey, David, 118n6
Harvey, Henry ("Lorenzo"), 202–203, 204, 205, 206
Hassan, Ihab: *The Dismemberment of Orpheus*, 232–33
haute couture, xx, 91, 105, 106, 107, 117, 119, 128n1, 148–53, 155, 196, 259. See also Worth; Rhys; Dior
Have His Carcase (Sayers), 77–78, 80–82
Hazlitt, William: "Brummelliana," 26; "On Fashion," 9
H. D. (Hilda Doolittle), 91
Heilbrun, Carolyn: "Biography between the Lines," 62, 78n9; *Hamlet's Mother*, 67, 82, 83n10, 84

Heine, Heinrich: "Lyrical Intermezzo," 119n7
Hemingway, Ernest, 33
Hitler, Adolf, 130, 138n5, 145–47, 155, 158, 191, 215
Hollander, Anne: *Sex and Suits*, 24, 27, 196, 258; *Seeing through Clothes*, xiv, 47, 122, 237, 239; "Women and Fashion," 100
Holmes, Sherlock, 66, 67, 68, 69. See also detective fiction; Doyle
Holt, Hazel, 196, 202, 204–205, 249, 250, 255
Holtby, Winifred, 52; "Are Spinsters Frustrated?," 71
Homer, 239
Hopkins, Gerard Manley, 226
Hopkins, Harry, 155, 191, 192
Horizon, xxi, 51, 124, 159, 160, 162, 164–69, 170, 172, 193–94. See also Connolly, C.
Horwood, Catherine, 48, 137
Hughes, Clair: *Dressed in Fiction*, 259
Hulanicki, Barbara, 236
Humble, Nicola, 50, 70n6, 161n2
Hutchison, Sir William, 62, 63, 89
Huxley, Aldous: *Chrome Yellow*, 206

Imagism, 215
impressionism, literary, xx, xxi, 3, 4, 5, 41n15, 90, 91, 100, 102–103, 113, 122, 232. See also Conrad; Ford; Woolf. See also under Rhys
Incorporated Society of London Fashion Designers, 135

Jackson, Winefride, 64n3
James, Henry, 170
Jameson, Frederic, 33n9
Jane Eyre (Brontë), 50n4, 54, 213, 220, 220n4, 223, 259. See also Rossen: "On Not Being Jane Eyre"
Jeffreys, Sheila, 52, 53n7
Johnson, Samuel, 5–7, 21
Jones, Jennifer M., 15
Joyce, James, 33, 38n12, 93n1, 143, 157, 160, 161, 170, 207; *A Portrait of the Artist*, 195; *Ulysses*, xvi, xx, 1, 34–36, 116, 161n3

Kaplan, Joel H.: *The Edwardian Theatre*, 96; *Theatre and Fashion*, 31, 96
Kay, Christina, 211–212
Keats, John, 254; "To Autumn," 215, 247; "I had a dove," 247
Kennedy, Jacqueline (Jacqueline Kennedy Onassis), xvi
Kenney, Catherine, 74n8, 75, 84
Kineke, Sheila, 103n3
Knowles, Sebastian: *A Purgatorial Flame*, 160, 194n2
Koestler, Arthur, 124, 160, 171; *Arrival and Departure*, 166; *Darkness at Noon*, 175, 178
Koppen, R. S.: *Virginia Woolf, Fashion, and Literary Modernity*, xviii, 39n14
Kronegger, Maria Elisabeth, 103
Ksinan, Catherine, 30–31
Kungl, Carla T., 72

Lady Chatterley's Lover (Lawrence), 234
Lake, Veronica, 136
Lambourne, Norah, 62, 62n2, 64, 65
Land Girls, 46, 141
Larkin, Philip, 160, 171, 194, 196, 202, 224, 247, 250, 255; "Aubade," 256; "Church Going," 195; *A Girl in Winter*, 225; *Jill*, 175, 176–78; "Talking in Bed," 195
Latham, Sean: "Am I a Snob?," xiii; *The Art of Scandal*, 108n4
Lauer, James, 19, 136, 252
Lawrence, D. H., xx, 33, 160, 161; *Women in Love*, 35–36. See also *Lady Chatterley's Lover*
Leavis, Q. D.: "The Case of Miss Dorothy Sayers," 86; *Fiction and the Reading Public*, 49
Ledger, Sally, 49n3
Lehmann, John, 167
Lehmann, Rosamond, 171
Lehmann, Ulrich: *Tigersprung*, xviii, 4, 12, 14, 15
Leigh, Vivian, 51
Lelong, Lucien, 150, 151–52, 153
Lenglet, Jean, 99–100, 105, 117; *Sous les Verrous*, 102

Leonardi, Susan, 46–47, 58, 59, 74n8
Lessing, Doris: *The Golden Notebook*, 235
Lewis, Alun, 165
Lewis, C. S., 61n1, 62; "Learning in Wartime," 157–58, 159
Lewis, Leslie W.: *Women's Experience of Modernity*, 49n3
Lewis, Wyndham, 161
Liddell, Robert ("Jock"), 204, 205
Little, Judy, 195, 216, 219, 221
Lobenthal, Joel, 236, 250
London Times, 138, 161
Longmate, Norman: *The G. I.'s*, 136, 136n3; *How We Lived Then*, 139
Loy, Mina,, 161n1
Lucile (Lucy Duff-Gordon), 45, 96
Lurie, Alison: *The Language of Clothes*, xv

MacArthur, Douglas, 143
MacKay, Marina, 157, 161, 171, 172n9
Maclaren-Ross, J., 165
MacLeish, Archibald: "Ars Poetica," 215
Macqueen-Pope, W. J., 95, 96
Mallarmé, Stéphane, xviii, 4, 8, 12, 17, 31; *La Dernière Mode*, 14–16, 23
Man Ray, 131
Manning, Olivia, 190
Mansfield, Katherine, 50
Marie Antoinette, 24
Marple, Miss, 68, 69, 69n5, 71–72, 72n7, 76. See also Christie; detective fiction
marriage plot, xix, xxii, 78, 85, 94–95, 113, 116, 117, 160, 184–85, 201, 208–209, 223, 238, 254, 259
Marsh, Cheryl Krasnick, 46
Marshik, Celia: *British Modernism and Censorship*, 93n1, 113
Martin, Ann, 35n11
Mass Observation, 132, 165
Matthews, Geoffrey: "Poem for a Friend Joining the RAF," 166
McLaughlin, Patrick, 62, 64, 65
McNeil, Peter: "That Doubtful Gender," 30; "'Put Your Best Face Forward,'" 128, 135
McVicker, Jeannette: *Virginia Woolf and Communities*, 38n13

Mengham, Rod, 187
Mephim, John, 183
Millar, Gertie, 95, 97
Miller, Jane Eldridge, 49n3
Miller, Lee, 131, 138n4, 144–48, 151;
   in Hitler's bathtub, 145–46
Miller, Tyrus: *Late Modernism*, 117, 118,
   122, 161, 200
Miss Modern, 48
Mitford, Nancy, 174
modernism, xviii, xix, 30, 48–49, 92, 103,
   110–111, 171, 222, 231–32; definitions of, 2, 2n1, 12, 33–34, 43; and
   fashion, 10–13, 17–20, 105–107, 117,
   180; high, 34–36, 37, 49–50, 105–107,
   122, 124, 157, 159–62, 170, 175, 179,
   215, 221; late, xxi, 116, 117, 122,
   160–62, 161n1, 189–90, 193–97, 200;
   and realism, 33; versus modernity, 1–3,
   4, 12, 13, 32, 44, 232; and women,
   xx, xxii, 1, 2–3, 33–34, 43, 48–51,
   90–91, 157. *See also* Connolly, C.;
   Ford; Joyce; impressionism (literary);
   postmodernism; Rhys; Woolf
modernity: definitions of, 1–2, 4–5, 12;
   and women, 37, 44–48, 51–55, 74,
   111, 116. *See also* modernism. *See also
   under* dress
Moers, Ellen, 26, 28
Molyneux (fashion house), 149
Monckton, Lionel: *Our Miss Gibbs*, 95,
   96. *See also* Gaiety Theatre
Monet, Claude, 102
Moore, Doris Langley, 64, 64n3
Morris, Virginia B., 74n8
Morrison, Blake, 194–95, 197
Moss Brothers, 149–50
Movement, The (literary), 176, 190,
   194–95, 197, 200, 211, 227. *See also*
   Amis; "Angry Young Men"; Larkin
Mussolini, Benito, 130, 138n5, 149n7,
   211, 214, 215

Nabokov, Vladimir: *Lolita*, 100
Nash, Paul, 143
Nast, Condé, 144
Nelson, Admiral (Horatio), 138

Neruda, Pablo, 86
New Criticism, 215
New Look: dress style, xxi, 44, 127, 152–55, 187, 189, 192, 193, 196, 201, 217, 236; literary postwar, 160, 174–75
New Woman, 35, 43, 45, 49n3, 61, 65, 112, 208
Nicholson, Harold, 144
Nicholson, Virginia, 53–54
Nightingale, Florence, 52–53

Observer, 207
Oliva, Alberto, 148–49
Orczy, Baroness (Emmuska Orczy), 66
Orwell, George, 124, 159, 161, 172; *Animal Farm*, 158; "Inside the Whale," 158; "The Lion and the Unicorn," 189; *1984*, 158, 175; "Raffles and Miss Blandish," 164n5
Our Miss Gibbs (Caryll and Monckton), 94–95, 96–98. *See also* Gaiety Theatre
Oxford (University of), 44, 46–47, 55, 58, 59, 60, 82–86, 157–58, 163, 177, 201–202, 204

Paquin (fashion house), 149, 149n7
Parker, Dorothy, 190
Parsons, Deborah, 111–112
Pater, Walter: *Studies in the History of the Renaissance* (Mona Lisa), 213, 239, 245; "Style," 6–7, 174
Patience (Gilbert and Sullivan), 29
Patou, Jean, 91
Paulicelli, Eugenia, 149n7.
Paxton, Nancy, 33–34
Penguin New Writing, 164–165
Penguin (publishers), 58, 164, 234
Pepys, Samuel, 21
Peter Scott Sportswear, 136–37
Picasso, Pablo, 131
Pickford, Mary, 100
Pizzichini, Lillian: *The Blue Hour*, 93
Plain, Gill, 69, 169n8, 191, 193
Plautus, Titus Maccius, 119n7
Plock, Vike Martina, 161n2, 180
Plutarchus, Lucius Mestrius, 3
Poe, Edgar Allan, 51

Poetry London, 195
Poiret, Paul, 96
Poirot, Hercule, 69. *See also* Christie; detective fiction
Postmodernism, xx, xxi, 190, 232–33, 236–37, 239, 240, 246, 250, 255–56
Postwar era, 191–93; dress styles, xxi, 152–56, 196; literature and new style, xx, xxii, 125, 160, 170, 178, 189–90. *See also* New Look
Pound, Ezra, 34, 43, 143, 160, 215
Powell, Anthony: *A Dance to the Music of Time*, 235
Prime of Miss Jean Brodie, The (Spark), 197, 199, 201, 207, 208, 210–216, 218, 220, 221, 239, 240, 246
Prince Regent (George IV), 24
Proust, Marcel, 12, 93, 170
Punch, 29
Pym, Barbara, xvi–xvii; xviii–xix, xx, xxii, 30, 55, 190, 193–96, 200, 208–210, 225, 226, 227, 229, 231, 232–33, 259–60; early career, 201–203, 206; at Oxford, 201–202; and dress, 201–202, 217, 222–23; and marriage, 203–206; in 1960s, 233, 234–35, 236, 237–38, 239–40; and singleness, 55, 189, 208–209, 210, 218; literary comeback, 196, 250; death, 256–57; *Crampton Hodnet*, 205; *A Few Green Leaves*, 256–57; *A Glass of Blessings*, 252n3; *Jane and Prudence*, 205; *No Fond Return of Love*, 235; *Quartet in Autumn*, 189n1, 195, 236; *Some Tame Gazelle*, 204, 206, 223, 248; *A Very Private Eye*, 189, 202, 204–206, 221, 222, 224, 229, 231, 248, 249, 256; *Young Men in Fancy Dress*, 206. *See also Excellent Women*; spinster; *The Sweet Dove Died*
Pym, Hilary, 203–204

Quant, Mary, 236, 250
Quartet (Rhys), 99, 102, 104, 107–109, 115

Rabine, Leslie W., 18–19, 36
Rabinovitz, Rubin, 195, 211

Radcliffe, Ann, 48
RAF (Royal Air Force), 144, 166
Rappaport, Erika Diane, 96
Rational Dress Society, xivn1, 31, 45
Rawlinson, Mark, 165n6
Reynolds, Barbara, 59, 62, 64, 65
Rhys, Jean, xviii–xix, xx–xxi, xxii, 43, 48, 51, 55, 90–91, 124, 178, 194, 200, 208, 231, 249, 253, 255, 259; early life, 44, 55, 92–99; as chorus girl, xxi, 90–98, 113, 194; and singleness, 50, 55, 106–107, 109, 120; marriages, 99–100, 102, 105, 108–109, 116–117; and Ford, 50, 91, 92, 100, 102–105, 107, 108, 109, 113; and literary impressionism, 92, 102–105, 110–111, 113; and dress, 44, 91–92, 100, 105, 106, 113; "Illusion," 106–107; *The Left Bank*, 99, 100, 105; "Mannequin," 106–107; *Smile Please*, 94, 98–99, 100, 122; "Vienne," 100; *Wide Sargasso Sea*, 90, 93n2, 117, 194, 259. *See also After Leaving Mr Mackenzie*; *Gaiety Theatre*; *Good Morning, Midnight*; haute couture; *Quartet*; *Voyage in the Dark*
Richards, I. A.: *Science and Poetry*, 49n2
Riley, Denise, 191
Roberts, Richard ("Skipper"), 248, 252
Robinson, Lillian, 86
Rossen, Janice: *Women Writing Modern Fiction*, 50n5; "On Not Being Jane Eyre," 220n4; *The World of Barbara Pym*, 252
Rossetti, Christina, 55
Roussel, J. (corset), 137
Rowbotham, Sheila, 77
Rowse, A. L., 144
Royal Magazine, 72n7
Rubens, Paul: *The Sunshine Girl*, 95–96. *See also* Gaiety Theatre
Russell, Bertrand, 86

Sackville-West, Vita, 141
Sacre du Printemps (Igor Stravinsky), 2
Sanforized woolens, 137
Sansom, William: "The Wall," 165

Sarfatti, Margherita, 149n7
Sartre, Jean-Paul, 169
Sayers, Dorothy L., xvi, xviii–xix, xx–xxi, xxii, 43, 55, 57–89, 90, 106, 109, 124, 170, 179, 194, 201–202, 208, 241, 255, 259; early life, 44–45, 58–61; at Oxford, 44, 45, 46, 55, 58–59, 202; son, 61, 208; marriage, 51n6, 61, 64, 70n6, 76; portrait, 63, 89; death, 89; and dandyism, xxi, 57–58, 59–60, 64–67, 77, 78, 79, 81, 84, 89, 208, 231, 241; and detective fiction, 50–51, 57–58, 60–65, 69, 70n6, 71–75, 77, 84, 85–87, 88, 124, 194; and dress, 44, 45, 48, 59, 60, 61–65, 106; and singleness, 51–53, 54, 55, 60–61, 71–76, 77–79, 80–81, 82, 83n10, 109; Harriet Vane (fictional character), 53, 58, 59, 64, 66, 77–85, 86, 253; Lord Peter Wimsey (fictional character), xvi, xxi, xxii, 58, 65–85, 88, 89, 90, 173n11; "Are Women Human?," 62–63, 88; Begin Here, 88; Busman's Honeymoon, 64, 69; Clouds of Witness, 76, 81; The Documents in the Case (Sayers and Eustace), 64, 76; "The English Language," 260; "The Entertaining Episode," 65; Five Red Herrings, 64; "Gaudy Night," 78, 82, 85; "The Importance of Being Vulgar," 87; "The Human-Not-Quite-Human," 88; The Man Born to Be King, 88; The Mind of the Maker, 86, 88; Song of Roland (Chanson de Roland), 58, 69; "Style in Crime Stories," 87; The Unpleasantness at the Bellona Club, 70, 76, 81. See also Gaudy Night; Have His Carcase; Strong Poison; Unnatural Death; Whose Body?
Scarlet Pimpernel, 66
Schaeffer, Talia, 64
Scherman, David, 145–46, 147
Schiaparelli, Elsa, 117, 131, 149n7, 209, 226–27, 229, 230
Schneider, Karen, 193
Schneider, Mary, 215
Schomberg, Ralph: Fashion: A Poem, 21

Scott, Paul: The Jewel in the Crown (Raj Quartet), 235
Scott, Sir Walter, 238
Scowcroft, Philip L., 81
Shakespeare, William, 87, 185, 226
Shaw, George Bernard, 93n1
Shaw, Marion, 75–76
shell shock, 66, 68–70, 181
Showalter, Elaine, 69–70.
Sillitoe, Alan: Saturday Night and Sunday Morning, 195, 227, 228
Simmel, Georg, 10–11, 12, 18, 40; "Female Culture," 11; "The Metropolis and Mental Life," 118n6; "The Philosophy of Fashion," 8, 10; "The Problem of Style," 10, 11
Simpson, Christine, 58
Simpson, Mark, 30n7
Sitwell, Edith, 171
Sitwell, Osbert, 149, 162–63, 171, 174
Smith, Lancelot Grey Hugh, 98, 99, 100, 104, 112, 114
Smith, Leslie Tilden, 116–117
Spark, Muriel, xviii–xx, xxii, 190, 193, 194, 196–97, 199–201, 210–211, 218, 219, 221, 224–25, 229, 231–33, 247–48, 253, 255–56, 259–60; early life, 207–208; marriage, 207, 208–209, 240, 256; Roman Catholicism, 207–208, 235, 240; breakdown, 208; honors, 208; in 1960s, 234–40; and dandyism, 241; and dress, 197, 209, 226–27, 241; and singleness, 55, 190, 208–209, 239, 240; Miss Jean Brodie (fictional character), 197, 199, 211–216, 218, 220, 222, 223, 224, 228, 239, 243, 245, 247, 254, 256; The Abbess of Crewe, 240; The Comforters, 208, 224–25; Curriculum Vitae, 207, 209, 211–212; Loitering with Intent, 208; The Mandelbaum Gate, 235. See also The Driver's Seat; The Girls of Slender Means; The Prime of Miss Jean Brodie
Spark, Sydney Oswald, 207
Spectator, 49n1
Spencer, Herbert, 8–10; "Manners and Fashion," 10

Spender, Stephen, 160–61; "Air Raid," 166
spinster, xx, 43, 51–55, 56–58, 65, 71–76, 80, 82, 83, 106–107, 186, 189–90, 191, 195, 199–201, 204–206, 211–212, 215–16, 217–224, 225, 226, 227, 246, 247–50; sexuality of, 52–53, 53n7, 71, 73–75, 140, 192–93, 213, 229–30. See also *Excellent Women*; *The Prime of Miss Jean Brodie*; Rhys, "Illusion"; *Unnatural Death*
Stanford, Derek, 208, 209n2
Stanley, Louis, 153
Stannard, Martin, 209n2, 211, 214, 240, 241
Steedman, Carolyn, 258
Steele, Valerie: *Paris Fashion*, 196, 236; *Women of Fashion*, 196
Stein, Gertrude, 2, 37, 50, 62
Steinbeck, John, 212
Steinem, Gloria, xivn1
Stevenson, Robert Louis, 214
Stewart, Alan, 128
Stewart, Lt. John G., 143
Stewart, Mary, 244
Stowell, Sheila: *Theatre and Fashion*, 31, 96
Strachey, Lytton: *Eminent Victorians*, 52–53
Strong Poison (Sayers), 53, 66, 77–80, 82
Stuart, Ian, 66n4
Stubbes, Phillip: *Anatomie of Abuses*, 20–21
style, etymology of, 3, 7
Suetonius (C. Suetonius Tranquillus), 3n2
Summerfield, Penny, 46, 47–48, 191, 192
Sunshine Girl, The (Rubens), 95–96. See also Gaiety Theatre
Sweet Dove Died, The (Pym), xxii, 30, 246–56
Symbolism, 11, 12
Symons, Arthur, 11
Symons, Julian, 66n4, 194n2

Taylor, Elizabeth, 190
Taylor, Lou, 150
Tennyson, Lord Alfred: "The Lady of Shalott," 213

Thackeray, Henry Esmond, 49
Thirkell, Angela: *Cheerfulness Breaks In*, 140, 179
Thomas, Dana, 196, 236
Thomas, Dylan, 171
Thorndike, Sybil, 211
Times Literary Supplement, 196, 250
Tinkler, Penny, 46
Toffler, Alvin, 2
Toklas, Alice B., 2
Toynbee, Philip, 167, 207, 241
Trollope, Anthony, 164
Tsagaris, Ellen, 223

Universal Exposition of Paris, 148–49
Unnatural Death (Sayers), 71–76
Updike, John, 229; "Between a Wedding and a Funeral," 224; "From the Forties," 225
Ustinov, Peter, 139
Utility Clothing Scheme, 135, 142–143, 147, 153, 196

Valéry, Paul, 169
Van Vechten, Carl, 2
Vanacker, Sabine, 75–76
Veblen, Thorstein, 9–10, 14, 23, 236
Veillon, Dominique: *La mode sous l'Occupation (Fashion Under the Occupation)*, 150
Victoria (queen), xvi, 46, 53n7
Vionnet, Madeleine, 149
Vogue (British), xiv, xxi, 39–40; adaption to shortages, 131–138, 142–143; concentration camp photos, 124, 144–45; different from American *Vogue*, 123n1, 128n1; dress patterns, 134, 134n2, 135; during World War II, 123–125, 147–48, 149–50, 151–53, 159, 165, 167–68, 179, 190; early-war, 127–131; nonfashion articles, 143–44; wartime advertisements in, 131, 134, 136–38, 141–143
Vogue Pattern Book, 134
Volpone (Ben Jonson), 65
Voyage in the Dark (Rhys), 92, 93, 93n1, 98, 100, 109, 113–15

Wain, John: *Hurry on Down*, 227
Walford, Jonathan, 132, 133, 134–135, 138, 138n5, 141, 147n6, 149n7, 151, 153
Warhol, Andy, xvi
Warner, Rex, 160, 171; *The Aerodrome: A Love Story*, 175–76, 177, 178
Warton, Joseph: *Fashion: An Epistolary Satire*, 21, 23
Waugh, Evelyn, xxi, 124, 139, 140, 158, 160, 161–64, 169, 171; *Basil Seal Rides Again*, 173n11; "The Books You Read," 161n3; *Put Out More Flags*, 162, 171, 172n9, 173, 174; *Sword of Honour*, 159; "Work Suspended," 172–73, 172n10, 176. See also *Brideshead Revisited*
Waugh, Patricia, 213, 229
Weaver, Richard, xvii
Wesley, Samuel, 5, 6, 7
Weston, R. P.: "In These Hard Times," 120
Whose Body? (Sayers), 58, 65, 67–69, 70, 79, 84
Wicke, Jennifer, 34, 45
Wilde, Constance, 31
Wilde, Oscar, 20, 29–33; as dandy, 29–30, 64, 65, 66, 89; editing *Woman's World*, 24, 30–31, 45; "The Decay of Lying," 6; *De Profundis*, 32; *An Ideal Husband*, 31, 32; *Lady Windermere's Fan*, 31, 32; *The Picture of Dorian Gray*, 31; *A Woman of No Importance*, 31. See also Aestheticism; dandyism
Williams, Raymond, 2, 118n6, 157
Wilson, A. N., 221, 224
Wilson, Elizabeth: *Adorned in Dreams*, xviii, 18; *Only Halfway to Paradise*, 192
Winter, Jay, 180
Withers, Audrey, 146
WLM (Women's Liberation Movement), 234
Wodehouse, P. G., 51, 68. See also Wooster, Bertie
Wolff, Janet: "The Invisible Flâneuse," 111n5

Wollstonecraft, Mary, 7, 36
Wood, Sir Kingsley, 133
Woolf, Virginia, xx, 4, 11, 33, 34, 36–37, 43, 49, 50, 51, 93n1, 102, 143, 160–61, 161n2, 170, 183; personal dress interests, 39–40, 42; in *Vogue*, 39–40, 143; *Between the Acts*, 55; "Modern Novels," 5–6, 16; *Mrs. Dalloway*, 38–39, 54, 70; "The New Dress," 40–42; *A Room of One's Own*, 42, 50n4, 219, 221; "A Sketch of the Past," 42; *To the Lighthouse*, 39, 54–55; *The Voyage Out*, 37, 129; *The Waves*, 37–38. See also impressionism (literary)
Wooster, Bertie, 66. See also Wodehouse
World War I (Great War), 45, 46, 53–54, 55, 69, 70n6, 120, 128n1, 180, 181, 182, 184, 185, 191, 211, 212; Flanders Field, 214; resulting in spinsters, 53–55. See also shell shock
World War II, xviii, xix, xx, xxi, 44, 51, 55, 116, 121, 123–125, 182, 190–93, 202–203, 206, 212–213, 232; Austerity restrictions, 134–135, 145, 147, 151, 153, 189, 201, 259; black market, 132, 150; clothes rationing, 131–135; French dress during, 147–52; literature during, 157–97; restrictions on men's styles, 138–39; V-J day, 230. See also dress styles: wartime; Utility Clothing Scheme
Worth, Charles Frederick, 14, 24, 30, 64, 96, 148, 149
Wrens (WRNS, Women's Royal Naval Service), 143, 202–203
WVS (Women's Voluntary Service), 130, 132

Yeats, W. B., 160; "Sailing to Byzantium," 256
Young, Filson: *Sands of Pleasure*, 93

Zola, Émile: *Nana*, 93

www.ingramcontent.com/pod-product-compliance
Lightning Source LLC
Chambersburg PA
CBHW020639230426

43665CB00008B/234